ιe story of the British political syste[r]
ction to the Irish unrest is told, and
ιrtant episode in Mr Gladstone's ι
eveale

ιgrƨ   wƨ

IRISH LAND AND
BRITISH POLITICS

IRISH LAND
AND
BRITISH POLITICS

Tenant-Right and Nationality
1865–1870

E. D. STEELE

CAMBRIDGE UNIVERSITY PRESS

Published by the Syndics of the Cambridge University Press
Bentley House, 200 Euston Road, London NW1 2DB
American Branch: 32 East 57th Street, New York, N.Y.10022

© Cambridge University Press 1974

Library of Congress Catalogue Card Number: 73–91618

ISBN 0 521 20421 6

First published 1974

Printed in Great Britain
at the University Printing House, Cambridge
(Brooke Crutchley, University Printer)

'I think if a man writes history, it is necessary to detail the truth...There is some good or other that will always come 'out of the truth.'

(PAUL CULLEN, Cardinal Archbishop of Dublin, giving evidence before the Royal Commission on Irish Education, 25 February 1869)

The author wishes to acknowledge financial assistance with publication from the University of Leeds.

CONTENTS

Preface   *page* ix

Map of Ireland   x

Introduction   1

1   Tenant-right and nationality in nineteenth-century
    Ireland   3

2   Irish land and British politics in the 1860s   43

3   The approach to legislating, January to August 1869   74

4   First thoughts and reactions in the cabinet, September
    and October   117

5   The adoption of a plan   156

6   The cabinet debate, October to December   200

7   Outside the cabinet, October to December   255

8   The last stages in the cabinet and the mood of two
    countries   277

9   The passing of the Bill   298

Notes   316

Bibliography   351

Index   357

PREFACE

I have to acknowledge the gracious permission of Her Majesty the Queen to make use of material in the Royal Archives, and I am deeply grateful to the owners, custodians and archivists of other MSS. listed in the bibliography. Miss Felicity Ranger, Registrar of the National Register of Archives, and Mr Brian Trainor of the Public Record Office of Northern Ireland could not have been more helpful.

My principal debts of gratitude incurred during the making of this book and its submission to a publisher are to those whom I now thank. First among them is Father F. X. Martin, O.S.A., professor of medieval history in University College, Dublin, in whose charity and intelligence the priest, the historian and the patriot are reconciled. The Quaker doyen of Irish historians, Professor T. W. Moody of Trinity College, Dublin, bestowed his imprimatur upon the book, with typical generosity, despite our differences of outlook. I learnt more than she realized from the late Maureen Wall of University College, Dublin, whose premature death deprived historical studies in Ireland of a fine mind. Joseph Lee of University College, Dublin, and Peterhouse, Cambridge, found time to read and reassure me about the first chapter when he was extremely busy. My sense of obligation to Professor G. R. Elton and Dr Christine Challis is profound. Over many years, Dr R. C. Smail of Sidney Sussex College and Professor P. N. S. Mansergh of St John's College, Cambridge, have been very kind and unfailingly courteous. Then there are those in an English provincial university whose friendship has sustained me. Only my wife knows what I owe to her.

E. D. STEELE

29 July 1973

ix

IRELAND IN 1870

King's and Queen's Counties are known as Offaly
and Leix, respectively.

INTRODUCTION

The subject is the legislation which in the 1890s Lecky called 'one of the most important measures of the present century'.[1] The purpose of this book is to explain why the Irish land bill of 1870 was momentous in its implications for Anglo-Irish relations and for the domestic policy of Britain. Chapter 1 re-examines the character of agrarian discontent and violence in Ireland. Irish historians have naturally written a good deal about some aspects of the land question, but have strangely neglected to ask what exactly was 'tenant-right'. The bill that emerged from the cabinet at the start of the Parliamentary session of 1870 was *not* what Gladstone had hoped for. Chapters 3 to 8 describe the evolution of his ideas; why they were unacceptable; and how the eventual compromise was reached. John Morley in his *Life of Gladstone* and J. L. Hammond in *Gladstone and the Irish Nation*, whom later writers[2] have followed, used little of his extensive correspondence. The letters they picked out need to be collated with the rest, and with his numerous and full memoranda as well as with the correspondence and memoranda of ministers and others. The nature and scale of the cabinet's internal 'negotiation' – the expression is Granville's – have not been realized. But it is quite wrong to say, as a modern authority on the British cabinet does, that Gladstone failed to consult outside the government with the different interests involved.[3]

These chapters look closely at what Mr Maurice Cowling terms 'high politics'. This kind of politics is not necessarily an elaborate game with power and place as rewards.[4] It depends on what is really at stake. The status of property-rights and the future of landed property in Ireland and Britain were of fundamental concern to Gladstone and his cabinet. Incidentally, the behaviour of the aristocratic Liberals who comprised half their number does not support the cynical generalization recently made about them: 'Whigs ...at ministerial level...knew each other too well to like or respect each other.'[5] The atmosphere in Gladstone's cabinets, at its worst, was not comparable to that in Disraeli's, or Lloyd George's. It is one of the book's aims to try and elucidate the movement of British public opinion that astonished contemporaries. Gladstone exploited this development with the skill for which he is celebrated. His success reflected the sensitivity of colleagues to the political climate existing after the 1867 Reform Act and his personal triumph in the general election of 1868. In such a climate, the cabinet went much further than had seemed possible only shortly beforehand. Neither the Liberals in Parliament nor the Opposition cared, for reasons set out at length in this study, to put up an obstinate resistance when the representatives of the landed interest in the cabinet had conceded so much.

The 1870 land bill was, to quote a strongly nationalist history of modern Ireland, 'the beginning of the undoing of the conquest'[6] – the conquest and dispossession of the native Irish that stretched from the arrival of Strongbow in the twelfth century to the victories of Cromwell and William III in the seventeenth. There were owners of Irish land who saw the bill in this light. On the whole, British politicians and the press saw it otherwise – as an act of conciliation, if not of supererogation, that had been extorted as much by Gladstone's extraordinary influence in Britain at the time as by Irish unrest. His second Irish land bill of 1881 flowed from the first. Did his conversion to Home Rule and its corollary, the transfer of tenanted land to the occupiers, also derive from the legislation of 1870? It is clear that as the result of his education in Irish feeling and history when at work on the first land bill, Gladstone's understanding of Ireland became far more perceptive and generous than biographers and historians have allowed that it was at this date. The connexion between the land and nationalism was not difficult to perceive, especially for a statesman who had told the Commons as early as 1866, 'we are an united Kingdom made up of three nations...we ought of course...to act...not making the opinion of the one country overrule the...others, but dealing with the...interests of each as nearly as we can in accordance with the...sentiments of the natives...whether the questions...refer to political...or social arrangements.'[7] It is hard to agree with a distinguished Anglo-Irish historian that until after the end of his administration of 1868–74 'there is no evidence... Gladstone was aware...the problem might go deeper [than agrarian and religious grievances special to Ireland]...might lie in the existence of an Irish nationality, confronting an English nationality and challenging some of its most deeply cherished convictions.'[8]

1

TENANT-RIGHT AND NATIONALITY
IN NINETEENTH-CENTURY IRELAND

THE NATURE OF THE AGRARIAN STRUGGLE

Agrarian outrage and combinations against the landlords were
endemic in nineteenth-century Ireland. According to a survey of
landownership made in the 1870s fewer than 6,500 proprietors,
with at least 500 acres each and averaging over 2,700 acres, had
nearly ninety per cent of Irish land.[1] The deficiencies of the
survey were considerable. In fact, half the country belonged to
a thousand people with an average of around 10,000 acres each.[2]
Great and small, the landlords were, as a body, British, or Anglo-
Irish, and Protestant. Their tenantry – numbering over half a
million then – and the general population of Ireland were overwhelmingly Celtic and Catholic outside those districts which are
now mostly within Northern Ireland. About a quarter of the
whole area of the country belonged to absentees resident in
Britain.[3] The isolation of the landlords was immensely enhanced
by the circumstances in which their forbears had got possession
of the land. They had been planted by the final English conquest
of the sixteenth and seventeenth centuries, when the confiscations
of Irish land had been accompanied by harsh, and otherwise
ineffective, religious persecution of the native Irish. The enduring
animosity that resulted was the root cause of what nineteenth-
century Britain knew as 'the Irish land question'.

For several decades the combinations among the peasantry
went under a bewildering variety of names, of which 'Whiteboys'
and 'Rockites' were the best known.[4] Before the mid-century
these names were generally replaced by the appellation of 'Ribbonism'. It was derived from the Ribbonmen of the Northern
and midland counties, a particularly formidable example of the
tradition of peasant conspiracy. It seems there never was any
nationwide organization of 'Ribbonism', despite allegations to
the contrary. The Ribbon lodges existed on a local, or regional

basis. They did, however, conform to a rough pattern. The Ribbon oath, originally Northern, was widely copied and couched in much the same language wherever found. These localized secret societies were symptomatic of deep-seated popular disaffection.[5] A great deal of outrage was the work of individuals who counted on being protected by the collective unwillingness to help lawful authority in such cases. The continuing resistance to the landlords and their law was the stronger for its amorphous character, for its spontaneity and lack of central direction. It could be contained but not eradicated, its influence was felt at the quietest of times, and was always liable to expand when the circumstances, economic or political, or both, were propitious. It was an expression of nationalism, as much as of economic discontent, and certainly not of socialist ideas, which held no appeal for the peasantry.

THE VIEWS OF RECENT HISTORIANS

In an essay entitled 'Some Political and Economic Interactions in later Victorian England', the late R. C. K. Ensor dealt with the effects of agrarian outrage in Ireland on British domestic politics at a critical period. He argued that the revulsion in Britain against atrocities committed by the peasantry during the Land War of the 1880s was fatal to the attempted grant of Home Rule in 1886.[6] That is certainly true. At the same time it is arguable that the persistent strength of peasant violence, more than anything else, wore away the belief of British statesmen in the possibility of assimilating Ireland to the United Kingdom of which she had been constitutionally a part since 1800. This raises the question of the relationship between the violence and political nationalism, both constitutional and revolutionary. In the opinion of another British historian, the Rev. Dr E. R. Norman, agrarian outrage was 'politically illiterate'.[7] According to Professor J. C. Beckett, in a standard work, the Fenians of the 1850s and 1860s pursued national independence to the exclusion of social objectives.[8] It is hard to make out from Professor F. S. L. Lyons' massive survey of *Ireland since the Famine* (1970) what he thinks the constitutional nationalists owed to agrarian outrage, which they deplored at intervals. Dr R. B. McDowell has written that one of the features of Irish politics under the Union was 'the predominance of moderate men'.[9] Perhaps – but how far were

they indebted to peasant violence for the success they had?
P. S. O'Hegarty, a veteran of the Irish Republican Brotherhood,
was sure of the answer in his *History of Ireland under the Union*.[10]

THE MEANING OF TENANT-RIGHT

In the index to O'Hegarty's book, the entry under landlords
reads simply: 'Landlords, iniquity of...increased inquity of...'[11]
It is not a view now held by many Irish historians, whether or
not they are nationalists. On the other hand they have strangely
failed to explore the land question in depth, and especially the
significance, emotional and economic, of 'tenant-right'.

The landlords stand acquitted, as a class, of deliberate oppression.
One source of trouble with their tenantry was the inability of
many occupiers, because their holdings were too small, to pay
any rent without hardship, unless their incomes were supplemented
by labouring on the larger holdings and landlords' demesnes, or
by joining the harvest migration to British farms. Wherever their
sympathies lay, very few witnesses appearing before the Devon
Commission of 1843–5 thought that less than 5 acres would
enable a family to live adequately by the unexacting standards
of the peasantry, after paying an average rent. Eight acres was
taken to be a realistic minimum by the Commission's secretary,
J. P. Kennedy, a recognized authority on Irish agriculture.[12] In
this study, the terms 'large', 'medium' and 'small' applied to
farm size will be defined as in T. W. Freeman's invaluable *Pre-
Famine Ireland*.[13] That is, 'large' refers to holdings over 100
acres, 'medium' to those between 30 and 100, and 'small' to
those under 30. 'Very small' will be added to this classification to
describe holdings between 1 and 15 acres, which accounted for
two-thirds of some 750,000 holdings above 1 acre on the eve of the
Great Famine.[14] In addition, there were 135,000 holdings of up to
1 acre. It has been said of the occupiers of such minuscule plots,
and of many of those towards the bottom of the category of 'very
small' tenants, that before the Great Famine of 1845–50 they, like
the landless labourers, were 'only vestigially in contact with a money
economy'.[15] The problem of uneconomic holdings was complicated
by the extent to which their tenants lived outside a system of cash
payments. Agricultural labour was paid partly in kind – by leave
to raise a crop (the practice known as conacre), or to pasture stock,

5

on a piece of the employer's land. The scarcity of money was indicative of the backwardness then of a vast area, containing over three-quarters of the population. The occupiers of many small holdings and of plots' below one acre were among the principal victims of the Great Famine: but they survived it in strength.

At no time, however, were the sympathy and collusion indispensable to persistent and successful outrage confined to the poorer tenants and landless labourers. Nor were the regions of lowest farm size and productivity specially affected, where rents bore most heavily on the tenants and the landless were worst off. The rôle of substantial tenants, of 50 or 100 acres, in the agrarian unrest was clarified when the Irish land bill of 1870 was being drafted, and again on its way through Parliament. Gladstone heeded the advice of a good authority, the Earl of Bessborough, not to change his mind and yield to persuasion from colleagues to deny the largest tenants the major concession envisaged for smaller occupiers.[16] An extensive Irish landowner, a model one, and a practical politician, Bessborough repeated in the Lords, where he was the chief government whip, the arguments he had used to the prime minister. Speaking against an Opposition amendment he was emphatic that 'nothing could be more mischievous to the success of the bill or the peace of Ireland' than the proposed exclusion of the top five per cent of tenants from the operation of a vital clause. Everyone who knew the country was aware that the tenants concerned 'exercised a great influence on those below them, and if they were dissatisfied with the provisions...as they certainly would be if the amendment were adopted – there was little hope of the measure pacifying Ireland.'[17] Supporting him, another politically experienced Irish landlord called the substantial tenants 'the leaders of public opinion' in the countryside.[18] Their influence grew after the Irish Franchise Act of 1850 replaced the £10 freehold qualification in the counties, fixed in 1829, with a £12 rating occupation franchise. The county electorate was multiplied by five in 1850, while still excluding the great bulk of the tenantry. The ability of the landlords before the 1880s to control a majority of Irish seats through the small and unrepresentative electorates, though not without some concessions to the genuine public opinion of the country, was one reason why the rural discontent was not properly appreciated in Britain until Gladstone gave it the attention it merited.

THE MEANING OF TENANT-RIGHT

The conflict between the owner and the occupier of the soil is only partly susceptible of a straightforward economic explanation. Opposing notions of a tenant's status were crucial. Under English law, which was in all essentials the same as Irish, the tenant had no proprietary rights in the land. Whatever the law and the courts said, Irish tenants assumed they possessed rights of that kind, as indeed they did under the native customary tenures which had had no legal existence since the courts ruled against them in the seventeenth century. Broadly speaking, Celtic society vested the land in the people, in the members of the sept, among whom it was variously partible, although it was charged with the support of the aristocracy and there were landless men. The peasantry, and not only the native aristocracy, were thus losers by the English conquest.[19] In practice, for the peasantry, the old ways largely survived. At the start of the nineteenth century much land was still occupied in joint tenancies under which the tenants frequently enjoyed complete freedom to add to their numbers. That was what J. L. Foster, the politician and judge, found on an estate that he acquired in Kerry in 1811. The occupiers were not the poorest of the poor, scraping a subsistence from inhospitable ground, but dairy farmers on good land. The fifty-three families on the property comprised several joint tenancies, each consisting of eight or ten families. As Foster explained, when Ireland was effectively conquered in the sixteenth and seventeenth centuries tenure in common, and the admission of a man's sons to share in it, was widespread. The new landlords brought in by the confiscations were often content to leave this state of things untouched, and limited themselves to drawing rent. Subsequently, the landlords were driven to intervene by a spreading awareness of better methods of estate management, by overcrowding on the land with the rapid growth of population for several generations before the Famine, and by the difficulty of collecting rent under such conditions. Individual tenancies, to which the landlords had increasingly converted joint holdings, also perpetuated 'the ancient habits of the Irish'.

Foster told a Parliamentary committee how he had rearranged his Kerry estate into fifty-three holdings of between 10 and 50 acres: but he described as almost irresistible the tendency to alienate the occupancy of holdings, to sublet, or subdivide among children.[20] For the tenant did not merely assume that the holding, subdivided or entire, should stay in his family. The occupancy-right of tenants-at-will was treated as being fully their disposable property, which might be sold to strangers. The claim to bestow or sell the right of occupancy was what tenant-right meant in Irish, but not English, parlance. Tenant-right in Ireland did not have its restricted English meaning of compensation for improvements. Their value only added to the price of tenant-right and was not its principal determinant. The price was naturally affected by the rent: a low rent pushed it up, and vice versa. A customary claim on the part of the tenant to sell the occupancy was unknown in England. Tenant-right there was purely compensation for certain limited outlays or improvements – way-going crops and other unexhausted processes of cultivation – payable by the incoming tenant or landlord to the outgoing tenant. These English customs did not apply to more substantial improvements because they were usually provided by the landlords.[21] In 1826 Irish landlords obtained the Sub-Letting Act to strengthen the law against subdivision without their consent. The Catholic Association opposed the Act, and O'Connell attacked it as a measure that hit the tenant hard.[22] It would, he said, take away 'the freedom of the only trade they had in Ireland – namely, the trade in land'.[23] In other words, the liberty of the occupier to do what he would with his tenant-right.

Englishmen found it hard to appreciate the undiminished vigour of the usage after the Act. One who achieved a sympathetic insight into the value of the peasantry's sentiment for the land, and the consequences for tenure, was J. E. Bicheno.[24] An economist and a member of the official inquiry into the state of the Irish poor that reported in 1836, he was moved to write an extended comment on the evidence collected from over thirty baronies among the four provinces of Ireland. The evidence, he observed, was 'a rich storehouse of facts, disclosing the secret agencies which operate upon the institutions of the people, and particularly upon that of landlord and tenant'. He defined tenant-right or goodwill – another term for the same thing – as 'the right of quiet possession', enforced, if need be, by unquiet means. This claim of the tenant's appeared all over Ireland. In the half-Protestant province of Ulster it was openly recognized. Elsewhere the landlords tolerated it with more or less reluctance. When a landlord dispossessed tenants, he sometimes gave them a sum

of money, and was said to have bought them out. Bicheno underlined the implications of that language. Much more frequently,
the departing tenant disposed of his tenant-right to a purchaser,
and any arrears of rent were paid to the landlord out of the money.
Tenant-right was property. Occupiers who held at will, whose
maximum security of tenure was six months, drew up testaments
bequeathing farms as if they owned them, and charged this
legally non-existent property with the payment of widows'
portions and dowries. The Poor Law Inspectorate was specially
directed to check on these and other manifestations of tenant-
right when investigating landlord–tenant relations a generation
later, in 1869. Their findings confirmed Bicheno's conclusions, as
had the information amassed by the Devon Commission. The price
of tenant-right varied a good deal but was very seldom cheap
and could exceed the freehold value of the holding. The average
seems to have been nearer ten than five years' rent of the holding.[25]

It must be asked how the tenants afforded such sums when,
according to a belief that dies hard, high rents prevented the
accumulation of substantial savings. In the first place, rents did
reflect the fact that in Ireland agricultural 'improvements' – often
a singularly inappropriate description – were largely left to
tenants, who drained, fenced and erected farm buildings for
themselves – to name some major items of expenditure which in
Britain were generally borne by the landlords. The low average
size of Irish holdings was in itself a deterrent to landlord investment
in improving tenanted farms: financial responsibility for the
buildings on every one of the farms on a typical Irish estate was
too heavy to contemplate. Thus the structure of landholding
inclined landlords to a more passive economic rôle than they –
sometimes the same men – undertook on British estates. The
greater part, if not most, of the land won from the bog and waste
in the eighteenth and nineteenth centuries was reclaimed by the
peasantry with little or no help from its owners. Secondly, and
more especially on the big estates which took up one half of
the whole country, the landlords, in Ireland as in Britain, did
not set rents simply by reference to financial criteria. Such an
approach to landowning was contrary to the prejudices of their
class, and to its political and social interests. Exorbitant rents
were the exception, not the rule, and they occurred mainly on
the properties of lesser landlords, owned by financially embarrassed

heirs of the free-spending Anglo-Irish gentry of the eighteenth century, or by speculators who acquired their encumbered lands under special legislation after the Great Famine, which ruined landlords as well as tenants.[26]

For tenants below a level far higher than 8 acres, the purchase of tenant-right or the family obligations secured upon its possession, could be a crippling burden on top of the rent. They ran into debt with their more prosperous fellows, or with the village usurer, and into arrears with the rent. These difficulties of the tenants were one reason given by landlords for refusing to countenance tenant-right or for restricting the amounts paid for it – to about four years' rent, for instance, on Earl Fitzwilliam's Wicklow estate in the 1840s. The Hon. William Le Poer Trench, agent to his nephew, the Earl of Clancarty, in County Galway, told the Devon Commission that the Earl allowed the sale of tenant-right exceptionally, because 'the effect would obviously be to convert a moderately set estate into a severe rack-rent setting.'[27] After the Famine had exposed the vulnerability of small tenants to misfortune, some landlords and agents redoubled their efforts to curb tenant-right. They met with little success. Transactions to which they objected were concealed from them. If a new tenant was put in without reference to the old, the latter looked to receive an acceptable sum, regardless of the landlord's attitude to tenant-right payments. It did not do to inquire too closely into what went on. The compromise that represented normality was described by one of the Poor Law Inspectors in 1869, whose district stretched from the Ulster border through the West of Ireland to King's County and Tipperary: 'As a rule, landlords have no intention to recognize a saleable occupation-right by their tenants, but the force of public opinion, and the necessity of yielding something for peace' sake, lead to concession.'[28]

Peasant aspirations did not stop at the acknowledgment of tenant-right, although that was the practical limit – an extreme one in British eyes – until the 1880s. Throughout the century landlords encountered an unwillingness to pay rent, which was by no means always related to the inability to pay. The practice, penalized by Gladstone's first Irish Land Act in 1870, of issuing notices to quit with, or even printed on the reverse of, the regular demands for rent, was not the positive proof of tyranny that it seemed to shocked Englishmen with little knowledge of the country. They could not understand why a few landlords thought it necessary to serve the notices, which were withdrawn on receipt of the rent. British opinion tended to condemn the actions of both landlords and tenants as if the tenure of land in Ireland was governed by the same conventions, and not only by the same law, that applied in Britain. Before 1870 government and Parliament, select committees and Royal Commissions, like Lord Devon's, proceeded on the assumption that the spirit of the landlord–tenant relationship in Ireland was being anglicized, however slowly, as the letter had been two hundred years earlier. All the evidence that pointed the other way did not shake this confidence until the upper and middle classes began to have doubts about the future of the land system in Britain herself. Irish landlords were expected to consolidate holdings below variously specified levels up to 50 acres, and move towards the creation of a well-affected rural middle class such as Britain had – and to do so without inhumanity and without stirring up strife. These expectations rested on an underestimate of the Irish will to resist assimilation which is scarcely credible, even when every allowance is made for the contemporary belief in British institutions.

Irish landlords felt strongly that the problems and hazards they faced were not realized. In 1840 the magistrates of King's County submitted an eloquent plea to government, seeking to explain that in Ireland they had to reckon with difficulties arising from 'the feeble Exercise of the Rights of Property', compared with England.[29] They complained of tenants-at-will and tenants with expired leases who transferred their farms 'perhaps to a Man the landlord has never seen or heard of; who thus acquires Possession trusting for a title to the Efficacy of Intimidation'. They complained of subdividing in breach of the landlord's express prohibition; and of tenants who would pay no rent and withstood efforts to turn them out. 'All,' they said, 'Cases of Common Occurrence.' They had experienced two successful and six attempted assassinations. The reply from Dublin Castle, where the situation was better understood than at Westminster, was balanced and sensible.[30] It told them their case had been fairly stated, but asked them to remember that the attitude of the tenantry was conditioned by economic necessity, and by history, and needed time to change. In the absence until 1838 of a system of poor relief the tenant who gave up possession, or did so without selling the occupancy, was too often destitute. As for history, there were 'the Traditions handed down, and fondly cherished, of Properties transferred by Right of Conquest'. It was tactfully suggested that not long enough had elapsed since Irish landlords began to tackle estate management in an improving spirit. This last point emerged clearly from the report of the Devon Commission five years later.

Yet the surest way of causing trouble on an Irish estate was just such an improving spirit as government and British opinion generally desired to see and Irish landlords displayed, increasingly if unevenly, until the Land War of the 1880s broke their power for good or evil. There could be no transformation of most estates on English lines without getting rid, somehow, of a high proportion of the tenants with their vested interests. They might be bought out: but the cost on a large scale was enormous and quite prohibitive. Shortly after the Famine, an immensely wealthy Scot, Allan Pollok, acquired 32,000 acres – 25,000 being arable land – in County Galway for half a million pounds. Over the next few years, he removed the great majority of the tenants, small farmers typical of the county, and introduced high farming, letting the land in large units. The cost of compensation to those tenants, before spending anything on agricultural improvement, was nearly half a million pounds. Pollok stated in 1869 that he had never dispossessed a single person except by buying him out by voluntary agreement. He said it would be impossible to do again what he had done, for two reasons. Firstly, the freehold of the estate had been going relatively cheap at the time of acquisition, when land prices were depressed. Secondly, he was sure that small tenants would not again consent to be bought out: they had been unnaturally ready to depart in the years of uncertainty and despondency after the Famine.[31]

The alternative to Pollok's method was too costly, or too risky, in other than monetary terms. If tenants were put out with no compensation, or inadequate compensation, if their goodwill, in both senses of the word, was not purchased, the price might be terrible. In 1835 Lord Lorton decided to clear lands, inherited through his wife, at Ballinamuck, County Longford, of unsatisfactory tenants whose leases had expired and of all the subtenants brought in by them and by other former leaseholders who were retained on the estate. All the evicted were given sums

12

of money ranging from five to twenty guineas. Not insignificant amounts to Irish peasants at that period; enough to pay, as they were informed, their passage abroad: but not adequate compensation for everything that the loss of occupancy implied. It must be added that heavy arrears of rent were forgiven besides. The holdings of the dispossessed were used to enlarge those of the remaining tenantry and to create a number of sizeable farms let to men from outside the estate. There were nine of these outsiders, all Protestants. In the course of three and a half years four were killed, two badly wounded, and three had their livestock maimed or slaughtered. The village of Ballinamuck itself with some surrounding land was held by a middleman on an unexpired lease. His subtenants were suspected of being principally involved in the series of attacks. In February 1838, when the lease fell in, Lord Lorton cleared this area of inhabitants and buildings. A year earlier he had issued a public warning of his intention to take such action in the event of further attacks carried out, like preceding ones, with impunity.[32] J. G. Adair acted similarly on his Donegal property under like circumstances in 1861. The prime minister of the day, Lord Palmerston, opposed a call from Irish members for an inquiry. He was careful to say, repeatedly, that he did not mean to justify Adair, although, as an Irish landlord himself, he added that a possible justification was 'the interest of society' in making Ribbonism hesitate to strike for fear of hurting its friends.[33]

Irish popular resistance to large-scale clearances was too great for them to be contemplated without apprehension, and they disturbed the British public. They were not general except during the Famine years when the peasantry was demoralized by starvation and disease. Then the official figure for outrages was very high: but the proportion of outrages to evictions was lower than it ever had been or was to be.[34] In Britain the landlords were indignantly reproached with inhumanity. Some were impelled to evict by their own desperate financial position, as one crop failure succeeded another for several years. Evicting landlords in this crisis were stiffened by the conviction they that were only doing their social duty, taking what so many influential voices in Britain advised was the painful and unavoidable course ultimately beneficial to everybody.[35] For all its horror, the Famine appeared in Britain to present the opportunity of reconstructing Irish landholding with unhoped-for speed and thoroughness. The Whig prime minister, Russell, the Tory Peel, the radical Bright, looked to an influx of English and Scottish capital, knowledge and determination for the regeneration of Ireland.[36] The Encumbered Estates Act, to compel the sale of settled estates on the petition of creditors, was designed to provide a land market to attract the British investors who, it was hoped, would reorganize land-holding and develop agriculture. The great change did not material-ize. The casualties of the Famine, the peasants who died or fled, were landless labourers and the kind of tenants scarcely distinguishable from them. There was a slow trend towards bigger holdings. Over the twenty years from 1851 to 1871 all those above 1 acre declined from 570,000 to 544,000. Those between 1 and 15 acres accounted for 23,000 of the loss, but still made up forty-five per cent of the total as against forty-nine per cent in 1851.[37] The number of plots of up to 1 acre fell from 135,000 in 1845 to 38,000 in 1851. Over those six years, the category of 'very small' holdings (1–15 acres) shrank from 493,000 to 280,000, while 'small' holdings (15–30 acres) declined much less spectacularly. 'Medium' and 'large' farms, taken together, increased.[38] In Great Britain the average size of a farm was 102 acres at the mid-century,[39] while in Ireland in 1861 when the Encumbered Estates Act had been operative for a dozen years, farms exceeding 100 acres comprised about five per cent of all holdings above 1 acre, less than one-sixth of that total being over 50 acres, Peasant society was strengthened by the relative increase since 1845 in holdings capable of yielding more than a bare living. The occupiers had more to fight for, and, on the whole, they fought successfully.

The magistrates of King's County had said in 1840, uttering a truism, that capital was deflected by agrarian outrage. Mid-Victorian Britain exported capital across the world. Very little of it went into Irish land. Within a few months of the Encumbered Estates Act, Russell was writing: 'How should men of small capital, or of large, lay it out in Ireland...when rents are only to be collected at the risk of assassination?'[40] The buyers of encumbered estates were chiefly Irishmen who knew what they could and could not do with the land. They were not frightened off, like British investors, by the prospect of violence when rents had to be collected in those years of distress. Many had relatively modest commercial or professional backgrounds, and some lacked the hereditary landowner's scruples about raising rents to get a better and quicker return on an investment. On the other hand, they could not afford to buy out tenants wholesale, and they were not at all eager to incur the odium and danger of clearances.[41]

Putting up rents beyond the prevailing levels of the district for the different types and qualities of land was highly unpopular. It ate into the tenant's share of farm profits and their capital value expressed as the price of tenant-right. The consolidation of holdings, a disregard for rights of occupancy, were positively dangerous. This was part of the conventional wisdom of landlords and agents. The removal, even with compensation, of obviously bad and broken-down farmers was risky, when forcible. It had been confidently anticipated that the establishment of a system of poor relief would diminish the tenantry's objection to being compelled to leave their holdings. It did not, and it is very unlikely that they would have thought differently had the poor law been conceived and administered with much greater generosity, and had it not collapsed over wide areas in the Famine. Violence and agitation were liable to flare up in periods of prosperity as well as of recession. During twenty-five years after the Famine rents rose slowly from the levels to which they had been reduced by the disaster. The tenants were able to pay; to meet the obligations secured upon tenant-right; to finance its purchase, in many cases; and to accumulate the savings which covered Ireland with a network of branch banks in that quarter of a century. Nevertheless, 1868–70 saw the upsurge of agrarian discontent and outrage which the 1870 Land Act was passed to appease.

THE EFFECTIVENESS OF AGRARIAN 'OUTRAGE'

The effectiveness of outrage, or the threat of it, was the basic argument when in 1845 Lord Stanley, later the 14th Earl of Derby, brought in the first of a series of government bills offering the tenants something far short of what they wanted. Referring to the provinces beyond Ulster where it was not usual to accept tenant-right openly and as a binding custom, he said: 'There the tenant holds by a more dangerous tenure; not by the character of his tenancy on the payment of rent but by the security he draws from the fears of his landlord...throughout the South of

Ireland, if a tenant continues to pay his rent, however ill he may farm the land, and however little hold he may have by law upon the land, the bulk of landlords dare not, and therefore do not, attempt to remove even the most disorderly, idle and objectionable tenant, though for the purpose of substituting the most industrious man...possessing capital, and willing to expend it.' He spoke with first-hand knowledge from his Tipperary and Limerick estates, in the running of which he took a close interest. Since it was not feasible to consolidate holdings or to introduce outsiders keen to improve, he argued, the existing tenants must be provided with an incentive to spend the money they undoubtedly had on making their holdings more productive. The bill let the tenant apply for permission to make certain classified improvements calculated to add to the letting value of the holding. If these were sanctioned, the landlord's objection would be overruled. No check was to be placed on his legal power of eviction: which, it followed from Stanley's remarks, could not safely be used in such a case.[42] This bill, like all its successors until the Act of 1870, did not reach the statute book. Derby's subsequent experience with his Irish estates showed the strength of the tenants' proprietary attitude towards the land. In 1859 his under-agent was killed in broad daylight before witnesses. Derby was, as leader of the Conservative party, peculiarly exposed to public opinion in Britain and Ireland. It forced him to withdraw the evictions that had been ordered of those suspected of being implicated in, and withholding information about, his employee's death.[43] A decade later, he told the House of Lords that relations with his Irish tenantry were good: he did not draw more rent than he had forty-five years ago, reinvested a considerable amount annually, and had seen a marked change for the better in their condition. He also described the limits within which he had to work. There were farms of 3, 4 or 5 acres on the estates: 'I have...the right by law to consolidate the holdings...but a compulsion is put on me to prevent it.' Irish landlords found it extremely awkward to alter even the line of a ditch on a give-and-take basis when the tenants concerned saw in the proceeding 'a violation of their rights of occupation'.[44]

The resolution and pugnacity that guarded tenant-right made the occupancy of a farm under tenure-at-will as marketable as one under an excellent lease. To illustrate the point, a Tipperary newspaper in the 1860s cited ten years' purchase given for the interest in 40 acres under such a lease, and nine years' for the interest in 14 acres under tenure-at-will. [45] Before and after the Famine the Irish tenant enjoyed far greater security and far more of the status of a proprietor than is usually supposed. The Famine years were wholly exceptional. At their close evictions dropped from the historic peak of 20,000 families, of whom 5,400 were afterwards readmitted to the holdings, to 636 in 1860, of whom 65 were readmitted. Agrarian outrages fell from 1,362 in 1850 to 232 in 1860. The ratio of outrages to evictions rose steadily over ten years.[46] What it was before the Famine is not discoverable with the precision attempted by official records from 1849. There seem to have been more evictions in any year up to 1845 than was normal after the mid-fifties, because very small tenants, subsistence farmers, were so numerous in the former period, when outrages were usually higher too, 1,001 in 1844. As one Englishman summed it up: 'In Ireland there are two sets of laws – the English...and the laws and customs of the country, which, enforced in a different way, are as active and effective.'[47] The enforcement of native justice was the business of the Ribbon lodges, although a great deal of agrarian violence was perpetrated by individuals who escaped detection, as they did much more often than not, by relying on the collective aversion to helping magistrates and police in the pursuit of such offenders.

The victim of agrarian outrage was very often a peasant who transgressed the popular code by taking land in respect of which someone had unsatisfied claims. He might be attacked because his predecessor, with the approval of the countryside, had imposed an absolute prohibition on any new occupier. There were instances of farms which no one would, or dared, take and lay vacant for years. Family quarrels among the peasantry over the inheritance of land were a common cause of violence, which might involve the landlord when he had to prefer one member of a family to another. The power of the peasantry was apparent in the consolidation that did take place outside the Famine period. Before 1845 they were beginning to realize for themselves the disadvantages of minuscule holdings. Mr John Wiggins, surveyor and agent, described to the Devon Commission how he had effected consolidation on Lady Headley's Rossbegh estate in County Kerry. He had called the tenantry together, got them to elect a committee and discussed with it for five days, 'taking down the proper situation of each family...so as to bring him [sic]...within reach of what he was able to cultivate or pay rent for, and considering all his circumstances'. He thus reapportioned 15,000 acres and won the committee's consent to banishing up to a score of bad characters from the estate.[48]

Following the experience of the Famine, the Irish peasantry were much less prone to subdivide. They had had a terrible lesson in the dangers of excessive fragmentation, and they were quick to perceive the rewards of keeping farms intact in the economic conditions prevailing from the 1850s. Good prices for pastoral products obtained in most years for nearly a generation, and the spread of railways furnished easier access to the great British market. There was a dramatic expansion in the numbers of livestock – those of cattle doubled between 1841 and 1866. The smaller the holding the less its occupier was able to profit from this type of farming. Official statistics show that farms over 15 acres did better. For these good reasons, tenants were readier to meet the landlords' desire to prevent subdivision, a desire immensely reinforced by the severe and rather unfair criticism of them for having permitted the multiplication of tiny holdings in previous generations. The post-Famine tenant was inclined to pass his farm undivided to the eldest son, subject to the payment of portions to younger sons. They had to choose between staying at home as landless men, or emigrating.[49] Without this degree of co-operation from the peasantry, it is very doubtful whether the landlords would have achieved the consolidation that they did following the Famine.

In a way that was deeply felt, landless men were then actually worse off than before, in spite of the tremendous decline in their numbers, which helped to push up wages. The disfavour with which subdivision was regarded by both landlords and tenants diminished the practice of paying the agricultural labourer at least partly in land, and tended to substitute simple wage labour. Among the peasantry the occupier of a single acre or less enjoyed a standing denied to mere labourers, who bitterly resented their exclusion, for which they blamed the landlords.[50] The feeling of the labourers was important because the perpetrators of outrage were mainly drawn from this class, which had little to lose. Its interests were not identical with those of the peasants who gave them largely seasonal employment. There was friction, leading to violence, between the two classes but no generalized conflict such as united them against the landlords. When an attack was planned by a Ribbon lodge or an *ad hoc* conspiracy, the individual or individuals chosen to carry it out would sometimes be brought in from another district. These men were paid for their services, but it would be wrong to think of them as mercenaries. They served the popular cause.

THE MORAL STRENGTH OF TENANT-RIGHT

Replying to the King's County magistrates, Dublin Castle mentioned the enduring effect of the sixteenth and seventeenth century confiscations on the peasant outlook. Out of ignorance, out of wishful thinking, this was persistently ignored or underestimated in Britain. John Blake Dillon, the Young Ireland revolutionary who had become a noted and moderate spokesman for agrarian agitation, tried to explain to a committee of the Commons in 1865 the immediacy with which the Irish people continued to feel their historic dispossession. Dillon told the committee that 'very recent...and very extensive confiscations' exercised 'a most important influence' on relations between landlord and tenant. He was referring, he made it clear, to the seventeenth century, at the latest. Asked if that was what he understood by 'very recent', he answered: 'Any act that has an important bearing upon the present condition of the country is sufficiently recent to justify me in describing it as very recent.'[51]

He was quite right. Behind agrarian outrage and agitation, behind tenant-right, except in the Protestant North, lay an unchanging attitude. To Charles Gavan Duffy, a founder of the Tenant League in 1850 and its historian, the peasantry had a living claim as the descendants of those who had owned the land in common with the Celtic chiefs and had been wrongfully deprived of their property.[52] When Duffy's old associate, Sir John Gray, launched a critical phase of agitation with his speech at Kilkenny in January 1868, he declared in front of an enthusiastic audience that the title-deeds of nearly all the landlords who opposed the tenants' demands were traceable to confiscation. He recalled how in their preambles the statutes stripping the Catholic Irish of their lands gave 'the settling of Ireland' as a reason. Surely, he

19

said, the justification applied in reverse to a statutory tenant-right of occupancy, at a fixed rent and freely saleable.[53] It was the language of a prominent moderate in Irish politics. Another such, The O'Donoghue, asserted in the Commons that 'in almost every instance in Ireland the occupiers had ancient prescriptive titles to their farms, and although this might count for little in the arithmetic of the political economist, it should be considered by those who wished to approach the difficulty in a true spirit.'[54] Some tenants certainly did consider themselves entitled to the ownership of particular lands by descent from a Celtic chieftain or sept. Far more powerful was the sentiment of being dispossessed as a race.

Tenant-right was a manifestation of that sentiment. In the poor law inspectors' reports of 1869–70 on landlord–tenant relations, one official wrote of a district that reached from King's County to Kerry and Limerick: 'There can be no doubt that, from a remote period, a certain limited right of property, and a distinct value, have been attached by tenants...to the occupancy of a farm...It accounts for the impatience with which they view such rules in the management of an estate as seem to interfere with their complete independence...And it is this right which they are disposing of when selling the "goodwill".'[55] A second inspector, whose district ran from Carlow to Cork and included the whole of Waterford, found the sale of goodwill practised 'frequently if not invariably' – in general with the landlords' consent but sometimes without it.[56] A third, covering Wicklow and parts of seven more counties in Leinster, stated that the practice existed in all of them, and was openly sanctioned on about one-third of the estates replying to his inquiries.[57] A fourth official, responsible for an area from Cavan and Roscommon across to Dublin, Kildare and Queen's County, distinguished between Cavan, an Ulster county, and the others, where, by contrast, the disposal of goodwill was permitted 'as a favour or privilege', although there too the outgoing tenant expected payment by his successor or the landlord.[58] Landlords would not openly recognize 'a saleable occupation-right' but popular pressures ensured a compromise by which the tenant got something. That was how another inspector put the position in a district running from Tipperary and King's County up through Connaught to the edge of Ulster.[59]

THE MORAL STRENGTH OF TENANT-RIGHT

The landlords did not like tenant-right because, to quote the report first cited, they were governed by 'jealousy of this claim to a species of property in land'.[60] Many were, however, quite prepared to tolerate it while rejecting the suggestion that it should be established by law, as it was by convention in Ulster. The first Marquess of Clanricarde, the Whig magnate and cabinet minister, allowed the custom on his 56,000 acres in Galway, subject to the right of veto on any arrangements the tenant might make, but remained a persistent critic of legislative interference between owners and occupiers of land. Just before the 1870 land bill gave qualified protection to tenant-right, he wrote: 'I am inclined to and admit upon my Estate the *Custom* of Tenant Right. But I agree with the witnesses [heard by a Lords' committee in 1867]...who denounced its Enactment by Statute.' For that, he had always maintained, would be 'confiscation'.[61] The policy on an estate might change with a new owner. The 4th Earl Fitzwilliam, who succeeded to the family properties in 1857, spent over £300,000 up to 1879 in improving his 90,000 acres in Wicklow.[62] The otherwise exemplary treatment of his tenantry did not save him from being attacked for setting his face against tenant-right and refusing to continue to permit its sale. The moderate chairman of the county farmers' club, a tenant of his, complained to the Bessborough Commission of 1881 that the Earl 'claimed all the right of absolute ownership. He has endeavoured...to introduce English ideas, contrary to the feelings and rules of the Irish people...there should be a right of sale – the free sale of the tenant's...goodwill.'[63] A landlord might recognize tenant-right on one of his Southern estates and not on another. The Marquesses of Lansdowne allowed it in Kerry, not in Queen's County, Dublin or Meath.[64]

On efficiently administered properties like the Fitzwilliam and Lansdowne estates, a ban on tenant-right may have been enforceable: generally it was evaded. W. E. Forster, speaking on the 1881 land bill when Irish secretary, said: 'It is an undoubted fact that, notwithstanding all the attempts that have been made in some parts of the South and West of Ireland to prevent it, tenant-right has been sold...over and over again on estates where its sale has been forbidden. It has been done under the rose, but sometimes more or less with the acknowledgement and consent of the landlord or agent, and sometimes against the nominal prohibition of the landlord but in reality with his knowledge.'[65] The nominal prohibition and qualified assent to which Forster referred were, however, seen by landlords as important safeguards. Preservation of the power to disallow tenant-right, or to limit its price, was vital to their economic and social position. Giving evidence to the Bessborough Commission, the 5th Marquess of Lansdowne explained why he would not have tenant-right on his lands outside Kerry: 'The effect of...the right of sale...is... to confuse inextricably the interest of the landlord and tenant, and...the consequence of that confusion would be that the landlord's interest would tend to become a diminishing one. The expectation of the tenant...would be that his interest should be saleable at a competitive price...also...that the landlord's interest as against his should be limited by the action of...the law and otherwise.'[66]

In Protestant Ulster the extent of racial and religious unity enabled landlords and tenants to adjust their respective interests under the established tenant-right of the province. But even there, disagreement arose when falling agricultural prices sent down the price of tenant-right and occupiers pressed for commensurate reductions of rent. That was the reason for the Protestant farmers' widespread dissatisfaction in the late 1840s and early 1850s and the involvement, such as it was, of some of their spokesmen with the Tenant League. The Protestant Ulstermen were appeased by returning prosperity but again complained of the depreciation of their tenant-right during the recession of the late 1870s and the 1880s, although they held aloof from the Land League of 1879 with its obvious Fenian and Ribbon associations. Likewise before the 1870 Land Act they had been watchful of their own interests, while keeping apart from an agitation expressive of Irish Catholic nationalism. In the South, where the antagonism between owner and occupier was never far below the surface at the best of times and on the best of estates, the landlords were understandably pessimistic of achieving a mutually beneficial adjustment of interests if they were no longer able to use a legal monopoly of ownership to check the inveterate tendency of the tenants' interest to encroach upon theirs. The Bessborough Commission saw here 'a conflict of rights, legal and traditional [which] has existed...for centuries', despite 'strenuous efforts' by the landlords.[67]

TENANT-RIGHT AND NATIONALITY

RELIGION, CLASS AND LAND

Institutional Catholicism frowned on Ribbon lodges in accordance with the Universal Church's ban on secret societies: but the lodges were exclusively Catholic. The Ribbon oath, in the version given by Michael Davitt, the nationalist land reformer, to the Special Commission of 1888–9, ran: 'In the presence of Almighty God, and this my brother, I do swear that I will suffer my right hand to be cut from my body and laid at the gaol door before I will waylay or betray a brother, and I will persevere and not spare from the cradle to the crutch, and from the crutch to the cradle, that I will not bear the moans or groans of infancy or old age, but that I will wade knee-deep in Orangemen's blood, and do as King James did.'[68] The language was as archaic, in the nineteenth century, and ferocious as that of the Orange oaths and expressed a similarly invincible sense of religious and racial identity. O'Connell once declared of Irish Protestants, 'they are foreigners to us since they are of a different religion.'[69] The remark proceeded from his emotions rather than his intellect: but it stated what the peasantry, if not the whole Irish Catholic people, felt.

'How is it possible for men who call themselves Catholics...to enter into combinations productive of such awful and irreligious effects [?]' asked Paul Cullen in a pastoral of January 1851 directed against agrarian outrage, when he was Archbishop of Armagh.[70] That question was frequently asked by Englishmen who wondered that outrage was compatible with the peasantry's high standards, in most other respects, of personal morality. In their defensive evidence before the select committees of 1852 and 1871 on Ribbonism, clerical witnesses acknowledged the weight of such censures as Cullen's. They went on to explain how at the start of the century Ribbonism had been a protection against militant Orangeism, and they conveyed, clearly enough, that it still had a protective function against landlords after the Orange Order had ceased to be a serious force outside Ulster. Orangeism and the landlords were only different aspects of Protestant Ascendancy. While there is no reason to suppose that both the higher and the lower clergy were less sincere than Cullen in deploring the commission of agrarian outrage, they sympathized with its motives. The common belief that an agrarian killing was

23

'technical murder' – the phrase is O'Hegarty's[71] – found some encouragement in moral theology for popular consumption. It could not have been otherwise. The peasantry's convictions about their rights rested on a view of history and natural justice by which few Catholic Irishmen were unmoved. The parish clergy provided local leadership for the political agitation for statutory tenant-right, for that which violence asserted and maintained outside the law.

With individual exceptions, the bishops normally displayed the caution and moderation which are very proper episcopal characteristics. The British government was repeatedly misled into thinking that the prelates did not share national feelings about Protestant Ascendancy in all its forms. The dominating ecclesiastical figure of Catholic Ireland in the nineteenth century was Cullen. 'We are bishops, but so are we Irishmen,' said a faithful ally of his, Archbishop Leahy of Cashel, in public discussion of the land question.[72] Cullen himself was accused of being an enemy of land reform. The accusation was justified only in so far as he was pragmatic about the issue. During the early 1850s and again in 1869–70 when the demand for legal tenant-right was backed by organized and powerful constitutional pressure, he let it be known that he approved. He withdrew his approval of the Tenant League in the former period because he believed its Parliamentary tactics were self-defeating, and not because he objected to its primary purpose. In 1859 and 1864, when the constitutional pressure was much weaker, he called for legislation – compensation for improvements – which he thought the British Parliament might be induced to pass. Cullen was no friend to the landlords. The Synod of Thurles in 1850, over which he presided as Apostolic Delegate, elicited an indignant protest from Lord John Russell, the prime minister, by its references to the land and the Famine clearances. 'I must say,' Russell told the Commons, 'no language was omitted which could excite the ...peasant class against...owners of land...who...enforced the process of the law against their tenants.'[73]

The religious element in the conflict between landlord and tenant was clearest where Orangeism remained a force, and where landlords were actively anti-Catholic. The core of Orangeism in an agrarian context consisted of the small Protestant farmers of Ulster. They regarded the Order as a mutual protection society against Ribbonism. Historically, the Order was a defensive response by the embattled Ascendancy against the Ribbonmen's late eighteenth-century forerunners in those areas of Ulster where the Catholics were a large minority, or a majority. Orangeism rapidly spread to other parts of Ireland, but, where it lacked the popular roots it had in the North, its power was destroyed in the 1820s by the irresistible movement for Catholic Emancipation. The landlords, with their relatively numerous households, were able to defend themselves. The scattered Protestant farmers of the South suffered severely in the agrarian disturbances that accompanied the political progress of Catholics, and many emigrated as a result. The Protestant tenantry of Ulster did not intend to be driven out, and saw to it that holdings occupied by Protestants rarely passed into Catholic hands. The landowners and Protestant clergymen who led the Order had their determination stiffened by pressure from the rank and file, as when the Grand Lodge of County Tyrone, meeting at Dungannon in April 1832, resolved that 'mutual support...means to encourage Protestant tenants on the one hand, and to defend Protestant landholders on the other; to preserve a Protestant population, and to keep at its head an aristocracy truly Protestant.' The landlords in the Grand Lodge pledged themselves to give the desired encouragement and could see no reason, according to the last of these resolutions, why Protestant colonization should be confined to reclaimed wastelands.[74] This uncompromising attitude to Catholics in the North naturally added to the suspicion and resentment with which the Southern peasantry were liable to view the introduction of Protestant tenants. Their feelings were inflamed by the handful of Protestant landlords in the South who attempted to proselytize among the tenantry. The efforts of Lord Plunket, the Protestant Bishop of Tuam, on his Mayo estate earned him notoriety. 'By no means a fragrant affair' was *The Times*'s uncomfortable comment on the bitter dispute that erupted there in 1858–60.[75]

The Catholic middle class of Ireland was growing in wealth and influence long before Emancipation. They were sometimes the victims of agrarian outrage. As speculative buyers in the Encumbered Estates Court, they took risks which exposed them to peasant retribution. They sided, however, with the peasants against the landlords. On a schematic view, the class interests of traders and lawyers may have been logically opposed to the peasantry's.[76] In practice, they were not necessarily antagonistic. Apart from the pull of national and confessional loyalties, in the countryside and the smaller towns this middle class lived much more by their dealings with the occupiers of land than by those with the landlords: and stood to lose heavily if rural opinion turned against them. Their sons were a major source of ecclesiastical recruitment, and their attitude to the land question resembled the clergy's.[77] They did not take a hand in violence. They supplied the national and shared the local leadership of lawful agitation, and, to articulate its demands, they supplied something else of the first importance – the newspapers friendly to peasant aspirations.

The appetite of Irish country people for newspapers grew with the spread of literacy after the system of National Education was set up in 1831. The Dublin *Freeman's Journal*, owned by Sir John Gray and often understood to reflect Cullen's thinking, had been the chief of these for years when the 1870 land bill was in the making. It had its provincial counterparts throughout Ireland. The *Dundalk Democrat*, which upheld tenant-right over an extensive area of North Leinster and South Ulster, was one of several that acquired a reputation. These newspapers were frequently extreme in their partisanship. After the killing of a land agent near Dundalk in 1850, the *Democrat* announced with undisguised satisfaction that 'the murder of Mr Mauleverer has been attended with very good effects' – on the landlords in the district.[78] 'The press was the great palladium of their liberties; it scourged the tyrant and dragged his deeds before the public gaze,' said a respected local parish priest, a member of the Tenant League, proposing a toast to the paper at a dinner in the neighbourhood where the assassination had occurred.[79] Lord Clarendon, a former viceroy, who had gone on to experience, as foreign secretary, the abuse of British and Continental journals, wrote feelingly: 'There is not in Europe such a press as the so-called national press of Ireland – the people look to it alone for guidance and these pestilent newspapers are constantly read aloud by the priests at the Mass, and they thoroughly believe that the rights of others are theirs.'[80] Parliament and public in Britain did not relish interference with the established freedom of the press in a part of the United Kingdom, and it was left to Gladstone's powerful ministry in 1870 to introduce special curbs on newspaper incitement to agrarian outrage.[81]

'It is our duty and our interest...to walk in the footsteps of the great Liberator, Daniel O'Connell,' was how Cullen described his approach to the land question.[82] O'Connell must rank high among the moderate men who are said to have been predominant in Irish politics under the Union. He shrank from resorting to arms, and denounced agrarian outrage on many occasions. Yet he hinted broadly at the possibility and legitimacy of rebellion. The message of his speeches was that the Irish Catholic people had been humiliated and dispossessed. It was quite true, and the peasantry interpreted it in their fashion. Political excitement in nineteenth-century Ireland always resulted in the intensification of agrarian strife. O'Connell, himself a landlord, may never have set out to incite that strife, but it served his purposes, and never better than in 1828-9. It was a great wave of agrarian unrest that induced the Duke of Wellington to go for a complete reversal of policy and to impose Catholic Emancipation on his King. Besides the violence, the incidence of local refusals to pay rent was alarming. The Catholic Association had aired, though it had turned down, the idea of boycotting Protestants. In October 1828 Wellington told George IV that a general rent strike could not be ruled out. In November it was impending, according to the Duke's information, and he wrote: 'The state of society in Ireland is daily becoming worse. In the South the worst evils, excepting actual civil war, exist...Nobody can answer for the consequences of delay.'[83] Whether the issue was Catholic Emancipation, the abolition of tithe to the Anglican Church, or repeal of the Union, O'Connell's agitations brought agrarian outrage in their train. This peasant response was not controllable by the propertied Catholics who led the open national movement.

The concession of Catholic Emancipation, together with repressive measures, contained the situation that filled Wellington with apprehension. At intervals during the next decade and a half, reform and repression quietened the peasantry. Their collective reaction does not bear out the view that they were 'politically illiterate'. The agrarian element in O'Connell's programme grew. From opposing the Sub-Letting Act in the 1820s and 1830s he moved in the direction of fixity of tenure during the 1840s.[84] The expression, 'fixity of tenure' was taken to cover what became known as the three Fs. As formulated by the Tenant-Right Conference of 1850, they were *fair rents*, to be fixed with provision for periodic revaluation on the principle that the tenant's interest in the land was greater than the landlord's; *fixity of tenure*, indefinitely, subject to due payment of rent; and *free sale* of the tenant-right of occupancy. The conference of 1850 insisted on the occupier's freedom to sell 'at the highest market value'.[85] It was the third F that mattered: the other two were intended to secure it from being undermined by arbitrary eviction or enhancement of rent. O'Connell spoke of fixity of tenure and also, in a major speech of 1846 in the Commons, of the legalization and extension of Ulster tenant-right.[86] In Ulster, where the claim to tenant-right was openly admitted by the landlords, the *right* was protected by an *understanding* that its value ought not to be appreciably reduced by rent increases, which should be related to the general movement of prices, and that the occupier ought not to be disturbed so long as he paid his rent. The Ulster landlord invariably reserved the right to veto a new tenant but seldom exercised it save to prevent subdivision.

One tenant-right of occupancy resembles another, and that of the Protestant North, although not Celtic in origin, did not differ from the Southern kind except in the degree of recognition it enjoyed. It suited O'Connell, and many others after him, to ascribe good relations between landlord and tenant in the North to the quasi-legal status of tenant-right, and to draw the conclusion: 'Generally speaking there was a better feeling there towards the landlords, because the tenants were allowed to sell their tenant-right...Coercion...would do nothing...The remedy which he asked for was that the tenant-right of Ulster should be...adopted throughout Ireland.'[87] In reality, the good relations in Ulster were a cause rather than a consequence of the recognition given to tenant-right, and they did not exist to the same extent in districts of the province with a numerous Catholic tenantry. In the strongly Protestant areas of Ulster, the racial and religious ties with their tenants, and the added strength which those ties derived from the proximity of a common menace, reconciled landlords to the substantial abrogation of legal rights by custom. How far the extension of Ulster tenant-right, or recognition of tenant-right in the South as binding on the landlords, should be distinguished from fixity of tenure was a question which O'Connell avoided in his speech. It was answered, sooner or later, by most Irish land reformers who talked of Ulster tenant-right. They would not be content with anything less than fixity of tenure: the Ulster custom left the landlord too much that was his in law, and depended too much on the understanding between owner and occupier about security of tenure and rent.

THE YOUNG IRELANDERS, FENIANISM, AND THE PEASANTRY

The Young Irelanders of the 1840s lost patience with the Liberator's constitutionalism. Moved by the spectacle of the Famine, some of them far outstripped him in their ideas of land reform. Where, latterly, O'Connell had explicitly combined political and agrarian agitation, James Fintan Lalor announced that his aim was revolution, 'not to repeal the Union...but to repeal the Conquest'. 'That "conquest",' he wrote, 'is still in existence with all its laws...and results.' The landlords were 'not *Irish*, but English all, in blood and feeling...They got and keep their lands in the robber's right.' They were threatened with 'a social war of extermination' if they did not submit to the application of the theory of property in land which he preached. He employed the commonplaces of extreme radical thought in the service of Celtic nationalism. The land rightfully belonged to the people, not to individuals, to 'the present usurping proprietors', and a free Ireland would establish a peasant proprietary. Political revolution could not succeed without mobilizing the peasantry in a simultaneous social revolution.[88] Lalor's ideas made a deep and lasting impression. The failure of the Irish revolutionaries of 1848 to arouse the peasantry was due partly to the grim distractions of the Famine, but more to an understandable distrust of those who had fallen out with O'Connell and to a shrewd rural appreciation of the possibilities of successful rebellion. Despite the clearances that were going on, there was plenty of fight in the peasantry, as the returns of agrarian outrage in the summer of 1848 show. Indeed, Smith O'Brien, the leader of the rebellion, blamed the Catholic clergy for the peasants' refusal to rise. The clergy preferred the policies of the dead O'Connell to revolution, and gave extensive support to the Tenant League, initially.

When the League was frustrated by Parliament and its own

failings, an apparent lull ensued, during which the Fenians, the Irish Republican Brotherhood founded in 1858, were active. The Fenians were drawn, though very unequally, from all classes of Irish Catholics, except the gentry. For a secret society, they went to little trouble to hide what they were about. They ran a newspaper, the *Irish People*, as a thinly disguised vehicle for their propaganda, and trenchantly advocated peasant proprietorship. They were even bolder with the spoken word. In August 1863, a leading Fenian, Charles Kickham, advertised their plans at a gathering on the slopes of Slievenamon in Tipperary: 'The object of the meeting was, in the first place, to renew their vows never to cease until they had achieved the independence of Ireland. In the meantime, the Nationalists of Tipperary were ready to... aid...any non-Parliamentary movement which was likely to do good to the poor, oppressed and down-trodden tenants-at-will.' The editor of a local newspaper also spoke, calling the Irish aristocracy 'a set of bloodthirsty hounds' and looking to returning Irish-Americans, notoriously a source of Fenianism, for 'vengeance and deliverance'.[89] Unlike the followers of O'Connell, the Young Irelanders and the Tenant Leaguers, the Fenians penetrated the Ribbon lodges, without coming to dominate them until the 1870s. An article by Sean O'Luing in *Breifne* (1967) throws some light on this. He quotes a definition of the difference between Ribbonmen and Fenians given by a celebrated member of the I.R.B.: 'They were sectarian and defensive against the enemy; we were national and aggressive.' In fact, the Fenians were hardly less Catholic than the Ribbonmen. The ecclesiastical censures they incurred as a secret society, and one depicted by Cullen as hostile to the Church, culminated in a Papal rescript of 1870, for which the British government had worked. These measures do not appear to have been more effectual than those taken against Ribbonism. The Fenians were tinged with anti-clericalism but they had many friends among the lower clergy; in the Hierarchy they were favoured with the calculated benevolence of Archbishop MacHale of Tuam, and a certain ambiguity could be detected in Cullen himself. Catholicism was so much a part of Irish nationalism, and Protestants were so rare in the I.R.B., that Fenian recruiters among the large Irish element in the British Army used to begin by asking a likely man whether he was an Irishman *and* a Catholic.[90]

Nor, surely, was Ribbonism lacking in aggression. The real differences between them and the Ribbonmen were social and organizational. The Fenians formed, at any rate in theory, a highly centralized movement. Ribbonism was obstinately local or, at best, regional. That may help to account for the failure of the Fenian rebellion in 1867 to start a peasant rising, which is what the government really feared. The government had no illusions whatever about the dissatisfaction of the peasantry, and was clearly somewhat surprised, though immensely relieved, that they had hung back. It was thought that they would have risen had the revolt shown any sign of succeeding. In the event, the revolt was a desperate enterprise by an organization which informers, arrests and internal divisions had upset. The Ribbonmen who joined the Fenians were 'certainly actuated,' O'Luing says, 'by the desire to win possession of their ancestral lands'.[91] The manifesto issued by the 'Provisional Government' in the Fenian rebellion of 1867 declared: 'An alien aristocracy...usurped our lands...The soil of Ireland belongs to...the Irish people, and to us it must be restored.'[92] In a report that became a cabinet paper, Lord Strathnairn, commander-in-chief of the troops in Ireland from 1865 to 1870, stressed the consuming grievance of the Irish: 'The middling and lower classes...bewail the loss of... properties, which their traditions...tell them were taken from their ancestors and given to their conquerors. This is the theme on which the Fenians ring the changes, promising the redistribution of land amongst the descendants of the ancient inhabitants; and nothing has brought more recruits to Fenianism than these hopes.'[93]

Crushed in the field, Fenianism fell back on the well-tried methods of Irish protest. It was naturally involved in the movement for amnestying political prisoners, its imprisoned brethren, and Fenians helped with the Home Rule movement from the outset. They contributed to the steeply rising figures for agrarian outrage after 1868, to which the 1870 Land Act and two Coercion Acts were responses. The select committee of 1871 on Ribbonism was told: 'Fenianism has become engrafted on Ribbonism...and that has altered its character very much.'[94] How much was not clear until the 'Ribbon Fenians' of the Land League, set up in 1879 and proscribed two years later, constituted themselves the link with the aggressive Parliamentary nationalism of Parnell. With the tactical advantage of a deep agricultural recession, they carried on an agrarian struggle by openly organized demonstrations, refusals of rent and boycotting, and by the traditional anonymous violence. Parnell eventually acknowledged his debt to the Fenians and Ribbonmen. Appearing before the Special Commission of 1888–9 which inquired into the connexions between Parliamentary and revolutionary nationalism, he confirmed that a statement he had made to an American journalist in 1880 fairly represented his views. It ran: 'A true revolutionary movement in Ireland should, in my opinion, partake of both a constitutional and an illegal character'; and later in his evidence, he admitted to having misled the House of Commons about the influence, which he had sought to belittle, of secret societies in the Land War.[95]

The war got the three Fs on to the statute book in full with Gladstone's second Irish Act of 1881, completing the work begun by the 1870 Act. Afterwards the landlords and both the political parties in Britain turned to the state-aided purchase of their holdings by the tenants as the solution to the land question. Divided ownership, still less satisfactory in law than it had been in practice, was dogged by agitation and outrage. The landlords wanted the state to buy them out of a relationship that had become intolerable for their class. From 1879 Parliamentary nationalists and 'Ribbon Fenians' had treated a peasant proprietary as the second stage of land reform. There could be no realistic outcome to 'the conflict of centuries' but the total victory of the occupiers. Consummation of the policy of land purchase was delayed for twenty years by the failure to provide adequate finance and offer terms satisfactory to both landlord and tenant.

BRITAIN AND IRELAND

Between the Union and the Act of 1870, government and Parliament tried to uphold the legal rights of property, of landlords against tenants, by a succession of measures curtailing or suspending in Ireland, for varying periods, the ordinary liberties of the subject in the United Kingdom. The stream of legislation was required by the political nation in Britain. The legal rights of property were regarded as integral to civilization and progress such as Britain knew and Ireland ought to develop. A speech by the historian Macaulay, as a Whig minister, on the Suppression of

Disturbances (Ireland) Bill of 1833 expressed those convictions forcefully.[96] Short-lived but effective, the bill authorized trial by court-martial for agrarian offences, a drastic expedient not used again, besides the suspension of Habeas Corpus. Macaulay said it was with the greatest regret that he supported the temporary removal of Habeas Corpus and trial by jury: 'These were sacred portions of our Constitution...He touched those...bulwarks with trembling and awe.' He viewed O'Connell's disavowals of outrage with scepticism. Macaulay did not think that anyone who had paid attention to what was happening in Ireland could doubt that there was a connexion between political and agrarian unrest. He emphasized their community of aims – both were subversive of the constitution. He likened the O'Connellite complaint that liberty was being shamefully violated by the bill to the Kentucky slave owner's protest, '"Pretty liberty, when a man cannot wallop his own nigger."' 'Pretty liberty' commented Macaulay 'where a man is not secure of his property or life – where he is constantly obliged to go about armed.' Habeas Corpus and trial by jury, notwithstanding their sacredness, were 'the means, not the ends, of protecting life and property'. He compared the state of Ireland to that of the Scottish Highlands after the 1745 rebellion. The Highlanders now blessed, he asserted, the firmness with which government had broken native resistance and made possible the civilizing of the region. As things were, he would rather live under an Oriental despotism, or choose a visitation of cholera, the dreaded contemporary scourge, than be liable to 'this moral pestilence under which...men were exposed to the... midnight assassin, and to the noonday murderer, to having their houses burned by night, and to be shot as they fled'. Hostility to its motives did not lead him to exaggerate the moral climate when ruthless violence was rampant. The celebrated Catholic prelate, James Doyle, whose diocese lay in the area worst affected in 1833, was privately glad of a Coercion Act designated as particularly oppressive and insulting by nationalists and Catholics. The bishop's nationalist biographer remarked that his opinion in favour of the Act would cause surprise, as it did, when revealed long after his death.[97]

In the mistaken belief that the Famine clearances had started a continuing process long desired and predicted, *The Times* welcomed the disappearance of 'the native Irish...who held what were called "farms" of five or ten acres. Their condition and character has been so often described...that we need not prove the existence of such a class incompatible with civilization.'[98] It struck Parliament as inconsistent with this goal to hinder landlords in the exercise of their right by giving tenants a legal claim to the value of their improvements. Seven ministerial bills with that object, down to 1867, failed to pass. The bills were little more than placatory gestures. They were a necessary show of conciliation to contain separatism and for electoral reasons. J. B. Dillon reminded the Commons committee of 1865 that a candidate for an Irish seat 'seldom...addresses his constituents, in any interest or belonging to any party, without stating his intention to advocate...a change in the law relating to landlord and tenant in some form or other...Some state it vaguely... others more distinctly...They say they are all in favour of an equitable adjustment between landlord and tenant.'[99] This was perfectly true, and in his last sentence Dillon was quoting the conveniently ambiguous formula in which many candidates took refuge. Irish landlords might, and did, resort to more forceful means of persuasion in electoral contests than English landlords needed to employ. Voters and the voteless majority combined in Irish constituencies to exact some notice of their sentiments about the land from Whigs and Tories even when, as at general elections, in the 1860s there was no organized nationalist or agrarian party in the field. The thought behind the ministerial land bills of 1845–67 was the use of small, carefully limited concessions to diminish the Irish pressure for 'extravagant projects'. In 1847, for example, the government, in the person of its able viceroy, Lord Clarendon, was impressed by advice from members of the Catholic Hierarchy that legal security for tenants' improvements would 'do more than anything else...to knock Repeal on the head'.[100] Such arguments did not move Parliament before 1870.

It was quite clear that the tenants and the parliamentary advocates of their cause saw the thin end of the wedge in compensation for improvements made without the landlord's consent, or against his wishes, or permitted when he did not anticipate a retrospective liability. The most tenacious of those advocates, Sharman Crawford, said as much to the Devon Commission. He had started bringing in bills to secure compensation for improvements ten years before the first government attempt. His purpose was 'to produce a practical prolongation of...tenure, founded upon the tenant's improvement, without compelling, by any legal enactment, that prolongation...but, by giving the tenant the power of claiming value for improvements, he would, thereby, acquire a practical fixity'.[101] The alternative to paying the occupier for improvements was, of course, to let him sell his interest. To facilitate this, Crawford's first four bills of 1835, 1836, 1843 and 1845 did not base compensation on the sums that the occupier had actually expended, but gave it in the form of so many years' purchase of a fair rent for the improved holding. The flaw was that improvements would not usually have been worth enough to induce an unwilling landlord to sanction the free sale of tenant-right, something far more valuable to the occupier. Crawford's next bill of 1846 was more direct and intended to validate the tenants' claims 'in consideration of unremunerated improvements, or in consideration of the value of their right of occupation, known by the custom of the country in many parts of Ireland under the name of "Tenant-right"'.[102] Under his measure of 1848 – called simply 'a Bill to secure the Rights of Outgoing Tenants in Ireland' – the adjudicating tribunal was to award compensation against the landlord by ascertaining the value of the tenant's interest 'under the custom of the sale of Tenant-Right'. Where the sale of tenant-right had not been recognized, they were nevertheless to proceed 'on the principle of the said custom' and estimate the interest accordingly. In either case, they should assume a fair rent when making the valuation. The different elements in the tenant's interest were distinguished in order of importance: compensation represented 'the loss he would sustain by dispossessment from...occupancy ...taking into consideration any increase of value produced... by [his] industry, labour and capital'.[103]

This was the most ambitious of all the measures unavailingly devised by Crawford and, later, the Tenant League. Neither he nor the League ventured again to submit a bill providing directly for the extension of the custom to places where it was unrecognized, let alone a bill containing the three Fs defined by the Tenant-Right Conference of August 1850. The Tenant League's measure of November 1852, like Crawford's preceding ones of 1850 and February 1852, sought to promote the acceptance of tenant-right outside Ulster by an indirect method. The same provision reappeared in the League's bills of 1856, 1857 and 1858. It rendered the landlord liable to pay compensation for improvements and dispossession – assessed at a fair rent but without statutory reference to real or assumed customary payments – if he refused to let the tenant sell the occupancy.

The proposition commanded universal assent that it was wrong to confiscate the value of a man's improvements – either by an increase of rent regardless or at the termination of his tenancy. Parliament opposed compulsion on the landlord to compensate as an interference with freedom of contact and with the lawful power to control what was done on his property. The prejudices of the British landed and middle class very largely coincided on these points. For over ten years after 1855 ministries gave up introducing or supporting a compulsory security for tenants improvements. 'There is one principle which I have always maintained to be...fundamental...in regulating transactions between man and man – that those who have mutual relations should be left to deal with each other as they please, and that any law which tends to restrain the freedom of either party is most objectionable' – so Palmerston on Irish land in 1858, deploying in defence of landowners an economic commonplace which had a firm hold on the British radical mind.[104] Middle-class radicals were as uncompromising as Whigs and Tories towards the claim for tenant-right being advanced under cover of the plea for compensation for improvements. John Bright, notwithstanding his sympathy for the peasantry, considered it 'disgusting ...to see men of powerful intellect like my Cousin Lucas' involved in the Irish Tenant League.[105] Joseph Hume, who had helped to draw up the People's Charter of 1838, said of Crawford's Tenant Right (Ireland) Bill in February, 1852: 'The principle of tenant-right as expounded by the honourable Member was... nothing less than...communism...a principle which implied spoliation, and would lead to the robbery of all property...the very moment they destroyed property, they destroyed society.'[10 ?] Moreover, the prosperity that came to the tenants not long after the Famine suggested that they were doing well enough without the legislative assistance they were supposed to need.

These prevalent views in Britain seriously underrated the historical and political aspects of agrarian discontent. A future cabinet minister, G. C. Lewis, attributed its persistence to economic factors in his essay of 1836, *On Local Disturbances in Ireland*, although much of the evidence he cited did not lead to that conclusion. The essay became a standard work. It confirmed the explanation of agrarian trouble most acceptable to the people for whom he wrote. The explanation depended on a confident misjudgment of Irish nationalism, which was dismissed as superficial, the product of unrepresentative agitators, and something separate from the religious and economic problems they undeniably succeeded in exploiting. This interpretation of Irish nationalism was sustained by O'Connell's inability to carry a majority of constituencies in Ireland on an extremely restricted franchise, and was apparently vindicated by the collapse of the Repeal movement and of Young Ireland after the Liberator's death and the 1848 rebellion, respectively. Palmerston must have been one of the few Englishmen who never ceased to believe, privately, that nationalism had deeper roots in Ireland. The attitude of the Irish press to the distant Indian Mutiny in 1857 prompted him to alert the secretary of state for war in his first ministry. 'The Catholic party and its newspaper organs in Dublin,' he warned, 'are trying to do all the mischief they can. They are praising the mutineers, and calling upon the Irish to follow their example.' As a precaution, he advised sending the militia of Catholic counties over to England and replacing them with British regiments. The viceroy's assurance that the country was in little danger did not convince him. 'What I want to prevent,' he replied, 'is any, even the slightest outbreak, and this is only to be done by showing that we have in Ireland a sufficient Saxon force to make any movement on the part of the Celts perfectly hopeless, and sure to bring immediate destruction on those who take part in it.'[107] The spread of Fenianism over the next few years showed how right he was not to be complacent.

An extraordinary complacency about Irish affairs existed in Britain from the early 1850s to the middle of the 1860s, when the government moved against the Fenian leadership and newspaper. The one British radical of standing who had made fundamental criticisms of Irish land policy succumbed to this mood. Writing in 1861–2, J. S. Mill believed that the perpetuation of a Protestant church in Ireland was her 'only remaining real grievance', and referred to organized agrarian violence in the past tense. He compared the destiny of the Irish in the United Kingdom to that of the Bretons in France and justified their absorption: 'When the nationality which succeeds in overpowering the other is both the most numerous and the most improved; and especially if the subdued nationality is small, and has no hope of reasserting its independence; then, if...governed with tolerable justice... the smaller nationality is gradually reconciled to its position, and becomes amalgamated with the larger.'[108] A tradition of over-statement in the Catholic and nationalist press partly explains, no doubt, why its anti-British tone and reiteration of grievances were discounted to such an extent. Mill did not mention that the Irish administration had been unable to dispense with Coercion Acts. The situation remained as stated by Isaac Butt in the House of Commons in 1856. The founder of the Home Rule party in the 1870s was then a Palmerstonian Whig, sitting for the tiny, corrupt borough of Youghal. Butt said: 'Their whole experience of Ireland demonstrated that they could not safely govern that country without some power on the part of the Government to put a check on the possession of arms by the people. This necessity arose from the existence of secret societies.'[109] It was not realized in Britain how deceptive the *absolute* decline in agrarian outrage was, nor how far the secret societies relied on intimidation. 'The evil of the country is "Terror" – under terror juries acquit – under terror the farmers join the dangerous class – under terror no one can hope even to lodge the legal information that he is *in terror*.'[110] That was written in 1863 – in the relatively quiet years when Mill was so optimistic of an ideal solution to the Irish question – by Sir Thomas Larcom, the soldier who filled the post of permanent under-secretary at Dublin Castle with distinction for fifteen years, and of whom the Fenians used to say wryly that Larcom and the police ran Ireland.

A strong sense of nationality is pervasive, displaying itself in many ways. The Irish were historically conditioned to express it through religious and agrarian conflict. The intimidation that Larcom described required public support: merely criminal con-spiracies could not have maintained it so extensively and over such a long period. When Gladstone began to reshape Irish policy in 1866, he was hopeful that a modest land bill along familiar lines, in conjunction with religious, educational and local govern-ment reforms, would answer. 'We are...an united kingdom, made

up of three nations...welded politically into one': and within
the limits of that unity, there ought to be a shift of emphasis
towards 'not making the opinion of the one country overrule
and settle the questions belonging to the others, but dealing
with...the interests of each as nearly as we can in accordance
with the...sentiments of the natives of that country'. The policy
should apply to 'religion, or...to political...or social arrangements'.[111] After twenty years of applying it – after Irish disestablishment and the two Land Acts had been balanced by half
a dozen Coercion Acts from the Liberals alone – Gladstone proposed
to relinquish it and the internal government of Ireland. He had
satisfied himself of what 'all men do not perceive, all men do not
appreciate, ripeness'.[112] The consideration he put first was 'the
great subject of social order in Ireland'. If serious agrarian
offences had never again risen to the figure for 1832, outrage
retained 'a fatal capacity of expansion under stimulating circumstances', as in the 1860s. The fall was, in fact, misleading – certainly
not an encouraging response to the Gladstonian policy. 'Nothing'
he said 'has been more painful to me than to observe that in this
matter we are not improving, but, on the contrary...are losing
ground.'[113]

They were losing ground because the measures of conciliation
and concession had not elicited a corresponding diminution of
outrage. In only two of the previous fifty-three years had the
country been free from the operation of Coercion Acts. 'Is not
that of itself almost enough,' he asked, 'to prove that we have
arrived at the point where it is necessary that we should take
a careful and searching survey of our position?' The violence
might be stamped out by investing government with absolute
powers and banishing publicity for its actions. Given those
conditions, it was possible for coercion to succeed: but not 'in the
light of day and...administered by the people of England and
Scotland...by the two nations which, perhaps...best understand
and are most fondly attached to the essential principles of liberty'.[114]
This was an awkward truth for his opponents. It had been hard
for Earl Grey's ministry to enact their Draconian bill of 1833.
Since then the popular base of British political institutions had
expanded enormously with the Reform Acts of 1867 and 1884,
and a press catering for the enlarged electorate had come into
being. The new electorate and the new press were not as critical

of aristocracy and property as was feared initially. After experiencing Gladstone's busily reforming ministry of 1868–74 they gave Toryism a pleasant surprise and renewed confidence. But neither they nor the unbroken landed and monied monopoly of British Parliamentary representation had the stomach for repression involving, say, courts-martial.

With the exception of the measures of 1848 and 1866–8, all the Coercion Acts to which Gladstone referred were aimed at agrarian outrage. It was agrarian outrage that led him and his loyal colleagues to conclude that Ireland was ungovernable by Britain save at a moral and political cost too high for a liberal state. It was agrarian outrage that elicited from a statesman notoriously careful with public money the vast land purchase scheme which accompanied the first Home Rule bill and perished with it. As he said at the start of his opening speech on the Home Rule bill: 'The two questions of land and of Irish government are...closely and inseparably connected, for they are the two channels through which we hope to find...effectual access to that question which is the most vital of all...social order in Ireland.'[115] He declared for Home Rule because he had the backing of colleagues who did not share his emotional commitment. The work of the secret societies – Fenians and Ribbonmen – converted men like Lords Spencer and Kimberley, two former viceroys. It made Kimberley tell the Lords why coercion could not pacify Ireland in the long term: 'The only way...is by paying respect to the strong feeling of nationality...a feeling so strong that it overpowers every other in that country.'[116] The Parliamentary nationalists' capture of nearly every Irish seat outside the Protestant North-East following the Franchise and Redistribution Acts of 1884–5 completed the case for Home Rule accepted by a majority of the Liberal Party.

As early as 1870, Lord Bessborough, who was well acquainted with Gladstone, remarked prophetically on emerging from a conference with him about Ireland: 'I do believe he is capable of repealing the Union.'[117] This was the likely result of the fervently sympathetic insight which Gladstone had gained into the historical and actual grievances of the peasantry during the last six months of 1869 when he framed his land bill of the next year. He grasped that bad landlords, as the English understood them, were not the cause of agrarian unrest. They must realize, he told the Commons in February 1870, that in Ireland 'the old

Irish ideas and customs were never supplanted except by the rude hand of violence and by laws written in the statute book, but never entering into the heart of the Irish people...the old Irish notion that some interest in the soil adheres to the tenant, even although his contract has expired, is everywhere rooted in the popular mind.' He was the first minister to extenuate agrarian outrage by pleading, not the poverty of the offenders, but the hold that tenant-right had on them: 'No small portion is to be traced to an interference with the fixed usages of the country... with what the people believed to be their rights.'[118] This was far milder and less explicit language than he had used to the cabinet and individual members of it. He termed his second Land Act of 1881, which embodied the three Fs, 'a perfectly frank acceptance of Irish custom'.[119] The belated vindication of tenant-right did not blunt the sharpness of the racial memory that lay behind the custom. Gladstone hoped that legislation for tenant-right would reconcile the peasantry to their alien landlords, whom for social and political reasons he sincerely wished to preserve, subject to entrenchment of the occupiers' traditional rights.

When finally disappointed in this hope after the second Land Act, he was ready to sacrifice the landlords. They were, he admitted in justification of his land purchase scheme in 1886, a foreign element in Ireland: 'We planted them there, and we replanted them. In 1641, in 1688 and again in 1798 we reconquered the country for them.' It was now England's responsibility to evacuate 'the imperilled class...our garrison'.[120] To undo the confiscations was to remove the compelling argument for British control of internal government. Full independence was ruled out because the Gladstonians agreed that Ireland should not have a degree of autonomy incompatible with the safety of the Empire in that age. The Conservative party and the dissentient Liberals would not trust her with Home Rule, and together they prevailed into the Edwardian era. They showed as much concern for the Protestant businessmen, industrial workers and small farmers of the North-East as Gladstone did for the landed class.

The interest and significance of the 1870 Land Act lie in Gladstone's awakening to the real nature of the Irish question, and also in the skilful use made of the position he enjoyed in British politics between the general election of 1868 and the early 1870s. Looking back in 1896, the historian Lecky thought the 1870 Act had been 'one of the most important measures of the present century'.[121] It was inconsistent with the conception of property-rights, and with the restraints on state intervention, which were then regarded as essential to Britain's prosperity. When Gladstone introduced the bill in 1870, he had to deny in his speech that private property and freedom of contract were untouchable. Both had, of course, been affected by previous legislation in various fields, but not on the scale of his bill. The 1870 Act was the United Kingdom's first major piece of class legislation at the expense of the landed interest, in the sense that it was the first to invade their property-rights too widely not to set a dreaded precedent. The cabinet obliged Gladstone to settle for the qualified protection of tenant-right, not that he then wished to go as far as the three Fs. It was still a struggle to get the bill through the cabinet and a predominantly landed House of Commons, not to mention the Lords. At the end of it all Gladstone had performed a considerable political feat.

2

IRISH LAND AND BRITISH POLITICS
IN THE 1860s

THE LANDED INTEREST, GLADSTONE, AND BRIGHT

It is not easy to realize, at this point in time, how strong the landed interest was in nineteenth-century Britain, and how vulnerable it felt itself to be. While the concentration of land-ownership was not nearly as great as it was in Ireland, close on sixty per cent of England and Wales belonged to 4,000 people, averaging over 4,500 acres each, and twenty-five proprietors with not less than 100,000 acres each had almost a third of Scotland, largely in the depopulated Highlands.[1] Everyone is familiar with Bagehot's dictum that between the first and second Reform Acts the entire structure of government rested on the deference of lower orders to the ruling landed class. Not until 1885 did the House of Commons cease to have a majority of landowners.[2] A condition of deference was the willing acceptance by the landed class of a very wide range of social and political duties. 'Today,' wrote *The Times* in 1864, at the start of the Parliamentary session, 'there will meet what has often been called a Parliament of Landowners. Fortunately, these landowners are very often something else; fortunately, to be a landowner implies a good deal more...land is the beast of burden on which everything is placed in this country. All local and social obligations, religion, charity, order, peace, all rest on the land...The greater the income...the loftier the position of a landowner, the more exigent and multifarious are the claims made on his money, his influence and his time.'[3] The eulogy was not undeserved. If the landed interest had not been accustomed to give its mostly unpaid services so freely to the state and society, ownership of well over half the land in Britain by several thousand people would have been quite intolerable to the population, rising rapidly above twenty millions, in a country such as it had become since the Industrial Revolution. Even so, the inevitable resentment of great possessions and of the influence that went with them would have led to the early dispersal of aggregations of landed property but for the socially unifying force of a shared religious faith which, despite denominational rivalries, inculcated mutual restraint and respect in an expanding political community.

The continuing acquiescence of the country in the position of the landed class seemed less problematical during the 1850s and early 1860s than it had for several decades. The stability of this 'age of equipoise' – the name given to it by a modern historian[4] – was not always so evident then. Radical critics of aristocracy like Bright and Cobden contended that its place in national life was an anachronism, and some prominent politicians incurred the suspicion that they did not disagree. Lord Clarendon, whose correspondence illuminates over thirty years the fears and prejudices of the Whigs at cabinet level, thought in 1860 that Gladstone was 'a very dangerous man...He runs in couples with Bright as to abolishing indirect taxation, and I verily believe... if he remained...in office we should have a graduated income tax.'[5] Clarendon entertained a stronger dislike and distrust of the Tory Disraeli, writing two years previously: 'We don't fight in the streets like the French but we can give ourselves a new constitution by law more effectually than by violence – The object of Bright and Disraeli is to americanize England and so to raise up the Middle Classes upon the ruins of the Upper that the latter shall never be able again to govern the country.'[6] Of course, neither Gladstone nor Disraeli was a fellow-traveller with the radical: but the soundness of politicians on matters affecting the primacy and security of the landed interest was a natural preoccupation with the conservatives of both political parties. As prime minister, Palmerston's vigilance extended to colonial measures which might furnish a precedent to be used against landlords in Britain and Ireland. When he intervened to make sure that the legislature of Prince Edward Island did not succeed in its designs on the small Canadian colony's landlords, he warned his colonial secretary, 'We must not be led by your Tenant Right Irish Under-Secretary...to establish a principle of authorised spoliation even in a remote corner of the Queen's Dominions... the owners have as good a right to their Property as you or I ...have to our Estates; and it would be as unjust and of as bad example to *extinguish* the Rights of these owners, as it would be to...fix the conditions on which we should be compelled to make over our Farms to the Tenants.'[7] While Palmerston lived, neither Prince Edward Island nor Irish tenants could obtain the concessions of principle they sought.

Gladstone's liberalism was aristocratic and Christian. Denounced by some for years past as an iconoclastic reformer, he set down in 1875 the advice to his son and heir quoted in Morley's biography to illustrate the depth of his attachment to political and social leadership by landed families like his own.[8] He did not hesitate to avow those aristocratic sentiments before popular audiences, and nothing is more revealing of the atmosphere of Victorian politics, so different from ours though not far removed in time, than the admiring cheers by which his declarations were rewarded.[9] After his Tory period, he advocated the measured enlargement of the electorate and other reforms of comparable significance when a genuine and substantial demand for them arose. As he said in a momentous speech on Irish policy in 1868, 'the deep, profound and lasting convictions of the people are never formed and never stand the test of time and circumstances, without containing much of the truth and...sacredness of justice.'[10] This, to his mind, was consistent with unwavering disbelief in democracy as it was, and is, usually understood. As he wrote in an article in 1887: 'The natural condition of a healthy society is, that governing functions should be discharged in the main by the leisured class ...whatever control a good system may impose by popular suffrage...yet when the leisured class is deposed, as it now is to a very large extent in Ireland, that fact indicates that a rot has found its way into the structure of society.'[11] It sounded strange, coming from the statesman whose legislation had destroyed the Irish landlords as a power in their country: but the Land Act of 1870 and that of 1881 were far from being violations of property in his eyes. By doing belated justice to tenant-right they were, he maintained when the 1870 bill was under consideration by the cabinet, 'most agreeable to...historical and traditional rights, a contempt or disregard of which is in the worst sense an innovating and revolutionary principle'.[12] The 'leisured class' in Ireland were creatures of conquest who, to his regret, had not atoned for the wrong done by their forbears and compounded by their own un-willingness to give tenant-right its due.

Like all intelligent members of the governing class, Gladstone was aware that if it ceased to dominate both British parties it would be placed at a grave and possibly fatal disadvantage. The coincidence of party with class divisions could have only one outcome in the long, or not so long, term. Gladstone was concerned to preserve and strengthen the landed element in Liberalism when he succeeded Earl Russell at the head of the party in December 1867. He needed to regain the confidence of the more conservative Liberals who had demonstrated their distrust of him during the struggle over Parliamentary reform in 1866–7. His courtship of popular favour – or sensitivity to public opinion – since he entered the Liberal party and cabinet in 1859 had already made him suspect to Liberals who were hardly, if at all, distinguishable from many Tories in their extremely cautious approach to change. His speeches and actions in connexion with the Russell–Gladstone Reform bill of 1866 fuelled the Adullamite rebellion in the ministerial backbenches that brought the government down in June. One thing that upset the Adullamites, and others, was his responsibility for the abortive Irish land bill of the same session, which, though restricted to compensation for improvements, had been concerted with the Parliamentary friends of tenant-right. It was Gladstone's first venture into that political minefield, and the first by government for some years. Robert Lowe, the Adullamite to whom the ministry's defeat gave a personal triumph, was not alone in seeing a bargain in the conjunction of the two bills. 'The plan of Government,' he told his brother in June 1866, 'is to bribe the Irish, who support them, with the spoils of the Irish landlords.'[13]

Gladstone inspired much uneasiness by his relations with John Bright, who in the 1860s was the bogey of landlords. Bright passed for 'the representative...of popular ideas'[14] in the Commons. He was actually the principal representative of middle-class radicalism after the death of Cobden in 1865. The middle class, from wealthy businessmen down to the £10 urban householders enfranchised in 1832, gave a critical support to landed predominance in government and Parliament. They exacted a price for deference. It was paid in fiscal and commercial policy and in the adaptation of British institutions – the Church, the law, urban local government, the ancient universities – to accommodate middle-class views of their equity and efficiency. The traditional openness of landed society to those who could afford to buy their way into it helped to stave off the challenge to its position. Cobden and Bright deplored the absorption of natural leaders by the enemy.[15] Middle-class radicals were a small minority, forced to ally with Whigs inside the loose framework of Parliamentary Liberalism. The alliance, and the habit of compromise it encouraged, inhibited militancy; and from their links with Protestant Dissent, the radicals derived a sectarian character which their opponents were able to exploit, Church being stronger than chapel in England. But these radicals' greatest handicap was, perhaps, their profound respect for property, although some younger men, disciples of J. S. Mill, claimed to have freed themselves from it. When Cobden and Bright mounted their intermittent assaults upon aristocracy, they refrained from directly attacking its economic foundations. 'I am as careful as any man can be...of doing anything by law that shall infringe what you think and what I think are the rights of property,' Bright assured the Commons in the Irish debate of March 1868.[16] He admitted, on that occasion, to a sensation of constraint when speaking on land to a land owning House. When he spoke outside the chamber, he was capable of sounding as though he actively wanted to set class against class.

His speeches on Parliamentary reform in the autumn of 1866 excited lively apprehension, and a burst of indignation and alarm followed the first of two on the Irish land question delivered in Dublin at the end of October and beginning of November. He was seeking to further the collaboration between British and Irish reformers which he had urged two years before as the current agitation over the franchise started in Britain.[17] On 30 October his wording did not make it altogether clear that there would be no compulsion to sell under the scheme he unfolded for the state-assisted purchase of their holdings by some Irish tenants. After unsparing condemnation of Irish landlords and approving mention of the enforced redistribution of land on the Continent, he proposed 'a Parliamentary commission empowered to buy up large estates in Ireland belonging to the English nobility for the purpose of selling them on easy terms to the occupiers'. He stressed that the price received by these landlords should be fair and negotiable: but did not seem to envisage the possibility of a refusal to sell.[18] *The Times* led the ensuing outcry with an editorial written by Robert Lowe, which accused Bright of being 'a leveller ...but...not a liberal' and said it was 'a small step from compulsory sale to compulsory expropriation'.[19] The charges elicited an injured clarification from Bright on 2 November: 'I am not speaking against the aristocracy...or...property, or...anybody ...I do not propose a forced purchase, or any confiscation.'[20] His fellow radical M.P., James Stansfeld, defended him, as best he could, to a perturbed elder statesman: 'That Bright's speeches are, as a matter of fact, producing...bad effects...I don't doubt; but really people are very easily alarmed and disgusted just now.' His Irish scheme had 'nothing agrarian really in it'.[21]

With Irish land as with the franchise, Bright's methods were those of a demagogue. He was, remarked a leader-writer memorably, 'a sort of sheep in wolf's clothing'.[22] His object in trying to play on people's emotions as he did was to extract reforms from Parliament that were less radical – far less in the case of land – than he appeared to wish. While the tactics were not peculiar to him, no one else used them to such effect. His explanation of 2 November was greeted with relief and some reserve. The land purchase scheme, wrote the Duke of Argyll to Gladstone afterwards, was 'absurd enough but...not quite so revolutionary, as explained in his last oration, as the Tory papers make it out to be'. Although more sympathetic to Bright than dukes generally were, Argyll thought he was 'frightening all Whiggish Liberals into absolute Toryism'.[23] For Bright's scheme was an advance on his previous idea of land reform – 'free trade in land', the removal of legal restrictions on the freedom of bequest and sale which kept estates together from one generation to the next. In consideration of pressing economic reasons, free trade in land had been partly implemented in Ireland by the Encumbered Estates Act of 1849. The operation of the Act suggested that unshackling market forces would not have the impact on landownership feared by the landed interest. While Bright's new proposals were confined to Ireland, they constituted an admission of the inadequacy of free trade in land as a social policy for radicals.

THE INFLUENCE OF J. S. MILL

The Commons that passed the Second Reform Bill contained another great radical, who also raised a storm by his proposals on Irish land. J. S. Mill's career as an M.P. began and ended with the Parliament which sat from 1866 to 1868. His victory in the large constituency of Westminster gave the radicals their most notable success at the general election of 1865: but his radicalism was not that of John Bright. The attention paid to Mill as a politician was a reflection of his intellectual standing. The educated public, whatever their political sympathies, had registered his considerable influence from the 1840s. His *Principles of Political Economy* went through six editions between 1848 and 1865. Its target was 'the old school of political economists'; he set himself to demonstrate how wrong they were in supposing 'private property...the *dernier mot* of legislation'.[24] On an abstract plane, he entirely rejected the legitimacy of absolute private property in land, adopting the argument that land, as a vital commodity not produced by man and limited in quantity, rightfully belonged to the community. It followed that 'the claim of...landowners to the land is altogether subordinate to the general policy of the state.'[25] They had an indefeasible title only to compensation in the event of being dispossessed. The doctrine enunciated by, say, Palmerston, in an Irish land debate of 1863, identified natural right with existing property-rights; utility was a subsidiary argument employed to show the harm to society that would result from any serious infringement of those rights.[26] According to Mill, utility could be held to justify, at least for some time to come, social arrangements incompatible with an egalitarian interpretation of natural right applied to land.[27] In the *Principles'* famous chapter 'On the Probable Futurity of the Labouring Classes' with its distant view of economic life transformed by the spread of the promising co-operative movement, he refrained from postulating any kind of compulsion to that end.

When it came to the actual distribution of landed property, Mill did not read here – or anywhere else in his writings and speeches – as if he wanted to implement changes remotely resembling an upheaval in Britain's law of tenure and structure of landholding. He believed people would not toil and lay out money to benefit others than themselves and their posterity. To meet the requirements of progressive agriculture, he accepted that 'a holder...must have a sufficient period...to profit by them: and he is in no way so sure of having always a sufficient period before him...as when his tenure is perpetual.' He was simply repeating the view of the classical economists from whom he professed to differ on property, that its security was the fundamental condition of prosperity. But his vindication of 'perpetual' tenure was not special to peasant proprietors, on whose merits, moral and economic, in Continental Europe and, where they survived, in England, he spent two chapters of the *Principles*. The landlord, the large landlord, was permissible 'in an economical point of view', so long as he showed himself to be an 'improver', a stipulation which Mill granted was 'not unfrequently' met in Britain. He desired 'free trade in land', without setting such great store by it as Bright did; he asserted that tenant farmers needed the encouragement of leases, without suggesting that they should be obligatory, and deplored the agricultural labourer's lot: but he evidently thought the system as he found it a better guarantee of social progress than any alternative.[28]

In the four editions of the *Principles* to 1857, Mill excoriated Irish landlords in well-known passages, and insisted on the need for legislation to convert the tenantry into peasant proprietors, as they would effectively be, he observed, under fixity of tenure. This brought an invitation from the council of the Tenant League in 1851 to stand for an Irish constituency under its aegis. Declining, he pleaded his work at the East India House.[29] He could not have stood without discounting, as the League had done, another passage that appeared in each of these four editions, where he substantially withdrew the harsh criticism of Irish landlords and retracted the endorsement of fixity of tenure. The objections to fixity of tenure detailed there were thoroughly orthodox. Firstly, it would be 'a complete expropriation of the higher classes of Ireland' – an exaggeration revealing the strength of his misgivings. Secondly, it would prevent the creation of large farms by men 'of the best education' able to furnish the capital for their development. He recognized that 'many such landlords there are even in Ireland; and it would be a public misfortune to drive them from their post'; whereas in an earlier chapter he had referred to 'individual exceptions' to his pungent generalizations about Irish landlords. Lastly, Mill made two admissions that were particularly welcome to the landlords. Irish holdings – too many of them – were not of a size to ensure that the tenants would make a success of peasant proprietorship, and he continued: 'Nor are the tenants always the persons one would desire to select as the first occupants of peasant-properties.' While this latter remark did not contradict his previous indignant denial that the Irish race was innately lazy and feckless, it echoed complaints of the Celtic peasantry's alleged indifference to betterment. He went on to rule out any interference, except in respect of wastelands, with the rights of landlords. Giving tenant-right the precision and rigidity of statute law and enforcing it universally, as some wanted, would be tantamount to fixity of tenure, and he considered that the same objections applied. Compensation for improvements seemed to him an irrelevance: the primitive improvements of Irish tenants were 'incapable of judicial appreciation'.[30]

No stronger action was necessary on the part of the state than the acquisition of wastelands. Settling them with peasant proprietors and their families would remove enough people from the existing cultivated area to make its conversion into large tenanted farms possible. 'Very moderate' emigration would help. The scheme was a bold, if not a fanciful, one: its suggested proportions – one and a half million settlers on as many acres – and the element of compulsion ensured that it would be so regarded. Yet the wider aim was to facilitate 'the introduction of English capital and farming' over the greater part, by far, of Ireland.[31] In the *Principles*' third and fourth editions of 1852 and 1857, although Mill took an even stronger line against the landlords to begin with, his second thoughts were little changed. The massive emigration of the last few years of famine and severe distress had shocked him. 'To the owners of rent,' he exclaimed, 'it may be very convenient that the bulk of the inhabitants, despairing of justice in the country where they and their ancestors have lived and suffered, should seek on another continent that property in land which is denied to them at home...but justice requires that the actual cultivators should become...what they will become in America – proprietors of the soil.' Here, as before, he designated fixity of tenure as proprietorship. Once more, however, Mill listed, in words almost unchanged from the first edition, the cogent reasons against imposing fixity of tenure. It was quite plain that, on reflection, he still believed Ireland's hopes of amelioration depended mainly on the landlords, with their legal powers intact, and on the investment of British capital.[32] Subsequent editions of the *Principles* in 1862 and 1865 exaggerated the changes in rural Ireland after the Famine, and elsewhere Mill went on record as completely mistaking the underlying political mood of the Irish people. 'Heroic remedies' – that is, fixity of tenure – were now definitely not needed. Indeed, if the very small tenants were not 'rooted out' in the course of the next thirty years the landlords would have failed to accomplish 'the only real, permanent...reform in the social economy.' As in the first edition, he did not expect that these occupiers could benefit from compensation for improvements, which in the *Principles* of 1865 he concluded would assist those whom he described as 'small capitalist farmers'.[33]

Mill's practical conclusions about the British and Irish land questions were thus very much the same as Palmerston's.[34] Mill had lamented, Palmerston had welcomed, the volume of emigration from Ireland during the Famine and afterwards. By the 1860s the radical also regarded the exodus as salutary, if he could not suppress his regret that it had been necessary. A number of the economists who had been formed by him were radicals. Henry Fawcett, professor of political economy at Cambridge, saw nothing incongruous with his radicalism, and Mill's, in the remarks on tenant-right in his *Manual of Political Economy* when it first came out. 'The fact that such a tenant-right, which is neither just nor legal, can be maintained,' he wrote in 1863, 'is...sad evidence that the social condition of Ireland has been so deplorable, that a right could be established by terrorism with as much certainty as by law.'[35] Mill and Fawcett were, reasonably, understood to have conferred the approval of radical economics on Irish landlords. Lord Dufferin, the Whig politician who made himself the literary champion of the landed class in Ireland, quoted Mill happily. 'I have...frequently appealed to the authority of Mr Mill,' stated the preface to his *Irish Emigration and the Tenure of Land in Ireland*. 'It is curious to contrast the view which Mr Mill seems to take of the extinction of very small tenancies with the language of those who hold up the landlords ...to obloquy,' he commented later in that work.[36] Dufferin paid a discerning tribute to the author of the *Principles* when he spoke, in his presidential address to the Social Science Association's annual congress in 1867, of 'thoughtful and responsible statesmen, like Mr Bright, Mr Mill...and others who have exercised their ingenuity in suggesting remedies...compatible with...those rights of property which are the basis of civilization'.[37]

There was still plenty even in the *Principles* of 1862 and 1865 to inspire someone who was hostile to landlordism and not convinced that the rejection of fixity of tenure was justified on grounds of expediency. These editions reproduced Mill's exposition of the theory of property in land, to which he kept, and his strictures on the Irish landlord down to 1857, modified by the substitution of the past tense, not wholly consistently, but sufficiently. Retained too, and in the present tense, was the passage turning on the sentence, 'the case of Ireland is similar in its requirements to that of India',[38] although followed by the clear statement that it was no longer relevant. The Indian ryot – the term loosely employed to denominate tenant-cultivators comparable to the Irish peasant – was in general assured of the three Fs under the British land settlements. In that passage Mill deliberately ignored the all-important consideration that the British found no real equivalent in India to the Western institution of private property in land, and were consequently free to deal with tenure in a way unthinkable at home. British radicals who were separating themselves under Mill's influence from the creed of Bright and Joseph Hume could see the Irish situation of the 1860s differently from him, and some did. They preferred the outspoken reformer in Mill to the pragmatist. The *Spectator,* one of the journals which gave expression to their advanced radicalism, was urgently recommending, on the authority of the *Principles* and in its words, 'a valuation and a perpetuity' at a time when Mill excluded the possibility.[39] An article of 1866 on 'Tenant-Right in Ireland' in the *Westminster Review* claimed to put forward the ideas of those 'of whom Mr Mill is the coryphaeus'. It asserted that they wanted to limit landlord rights drastically and 'confirm certain spontaneous aggressions...habitually practised by tenants...establishing on a firmer basis the actual and hereditary position of tenants-at-will.' The writer argued that this proposed intervention was entirely consistent with the true rights of property, his explanation of which was the same as that given in the *Principles.*[40] The theory of property in land disseminated by Mill was only one aspect of his thinking about land reflected in advanced radical journalism. Another was the superiority, in a broader context than the British Isles, of peasant proprietorship over tenancy-at-will and large farms. Reviewing one of Dufferin's publications in 1866, a critic in the *Spectator* said that his 'diatribe against small farming, relied on arguments 'so fully demolished by Mr Mill...that we are somewhat surprised to find them resuscitated in a work of authority'.[41] 'It is in a great measure the countenance which Irish misconceptions and unjust claims have met with from benevolent but superficial sympathizers in England which has given them so fatal a tenacity' complained the *Pall Mall Gazette*, a liberal conservative paper. 'If there had been no *Spectator* and no Mr Mill to vitalize their errors by...sanctioning them, they might possibly have been greatly weakened, if not extinguished, long ere now.'[42]

The complaint was justified to the extent that the Irish made selective use of the *Principles* in their struggle against the obstinacy of his country's rulers. J. B. Dillon's evidence before the Commons' select committee on Irish land of 1865 affords an example: 'I suppose the highest authority in England upon the subject is Mr Mill: no man, I think, has given a stronger opinion in favour of security of tenure and the only objection he has to compensation [for tenants' improvements] is, that it is not quite adequate.' To illustrate the actual condition of the Irish tenant, Dillon quoted what Mill had written at one point in the earlier editions of his book and had preserved in the later as being of historical interest: 'The inducements of free human beings are taken away...against this he protects himself by the *ultima ratio* of a defensive civil war.'[43] The *Principles* were similarly exploited by Isaac Butt who was, with Sir John Gray, the leading exponent of fixity of tenure in Ireland during the later 1860s. His pamphlet, *The Irish People and the Irish Land* published in 1867, appealed to what 'this great thinker' said, 'not in any political discussion, but in a treatise from which many educated Englishmen will learn the principles of social science'. He took his quotations from the editions of 1848 and 1852, ignoring both the far-reaching qualifications of those statements at the time and the recent revisions of the book. Readers of Butt's pamphlet were led to assume that Mill was, and always had been, a firm believer in fixity of tenure for Ireland.[44] The clergy invoked Mill at the demonstrations they helped to organize in the Irish countryside, as at Navan, county Meath, in 1865, when the president of the local seminary read out a petition to Parliament incorporating those words on the justice of 'a defensive civil war'.[45]

In Britain it was Mill's conclusions that mattered, not animadversions of which he had, anyway, thought better. He imparted something of his outlook to younger men who were not radicals. Through the medium of the *Principles*, which established itself in the universities, he contributed to the disposition of intelligent Liberals and Tories of the right age to look at social and political institutions with more of critical detachment than their elders managed to attain.[46] His politics were tolerable to people who accepted a continuing need for some change and liked to think of themselves as progressively minded but were disinclined to jeopardize the fundamentals of society as it was. His well publicized anxiety about the dangers to intelligence and property inherent in democracy seemed to confirm that he was a safe and responsible radical. So his pamphlet, *England and Ireland*, of February 1868, caused amazement and indignation by the terms in which it called, wholly unexpectedly, for the immediate concession of fixity of tenure to the Irish, citing the British Indian example. The pamphlet unsaid – though it did not refer to – virtually everything about Irish land in the latest editions of the *Principles*. Irish tenants, it now appeared, lived under an active and unwavering landlord tyranny. The economic objections to fixity of tenure which had always been decisive for him were dismissed as obscurantist: 'Those who still believe that small peasant properties are... detrimental to agriculture...are discreditably behind the state of knowledge on the subject.' The propertied classes, and not the landed interest alone, were threatened with a dire prospect, to which the political atmosphere just after the Second Reform Act lent a degree of credibility. Mill suggested that, in default of an admittedly revolutionary measure to reconcile Ireland to the Union, the British working class, 'the rising power in our affairs', and the Irish peasantry would make common cause.[47]

THE DEVELOPING SITUATION IN BRITAIN

'An age when delegates of working-men meet in European Congresses to concert united action for the interests of labour,' wrote Mill in *England and Ireland*, 'is not one in which labourers will cut down labourers at other people's bidding. The time is come when the democracy of one country will join with the democracy of another, rather than back their own ruling authorities in putting it down.'[48] The Congresses were those of the First

International, founded in London four years earlier.[49] Mill was attempting to take advantage of the nervousness among the propertied classes as they contemplated the future with an electorate doubled by household suffrage in the towns. The apprehensions voiced by Robert Lowe and Lord Cranborne in the debates on Parliamentary reform of 1866–7 were the emphatic expression of a general fear for property. The landed interest, naturally, felt peculiarly exposed. Lord Kimberley, a moderate and sensible Whig soon to be a member of Gladstone's cabinet, confided his view of the situation to a future colleague, Lord de Grey: 'We are entering...upon a new and unquiet era of politics which will require very wary walking, especially for those who like ourselves are liberals by conviction, and large landowners.'[50] The newly enfranchised working-class voters, it was feared, lay ready to the hand of the radical who discarded Bright's scruples about property. The Whigs had to try and keep any such move from succeeding in the party that normally set the pace of change. The socialists and trade unionists of the International were mostly obscure figures, with little apparent support, but disturbing against the backcloth of the vividly remembered insurrections of 1848 on the Continent. They openly sympathized with Fenianism, and were well represented on the council of the Reform League, the popular radical organization which made an extraordinary public impact, whatever its real effect on the 1867 reform bill may have been. Within a few days of the publication of Mill's pamphlet and to the displeasure of its middle-class members, the council of the League passed a resolution in favour of nationalizing Irish land and redistributing it in leaseholds of up to 30 acres. The weakest point in the defences of landed politicians did look like being the agrarian problem in Ireland. Irish landlords had been an embarrassment to them at times in the past: now they became a distinct liability. Gladstone exploited the awareness of that fact in 1869–70. The radicals whom he overshadowed tried before him, over the years 1865–8, and failed.

W. E. Forster was the first to try the gambit in this period. He presented the Irish claim for tenant-right as 'simply...the right of the farmer to carry on his business in the only way in which he had a chance of doing it with success', namely, with security from being ejected or having his rent raised 'until at least reference has been made to some impartial tribunal'. 'It only needed the refusal of such reasonable demands for a few years to raise far more awkward questions,' he said, and those who wanted social harmony to endure between landlord and tenant in Britain had 'good grounds most earnestly to hope that such questions should not be even mooted in Ireland'.[51] There was a political calm, and Palmerston was still prime minister. The House of Commons in March 1865 did not find it opportune to suppose that insecurity of tenure was an impediment to Irish prosperity, nor did M.P.s believe that the recurrence of Irish agitation would turn the comfortable farmers of England against their landlords. The English chambers of agriculture were landlord-dominated bodies, the opposite of Irish tenant societies.[52] Compensation for such improvements as the landlords did not pay for had been talked about, but it was not an issue. The game laws – an entire code fortifying the landlord's rights of pursuing game on tenanted land – were an irritant.

Scotland and Wales, by contrast, provided clear indications that the habit of deference was weakening among the tenantry. The greater emphasis placed on a commercial return from agriculture in the Scottish Lowlands had evolved an independent breed of farmer. These Scots complained more loudly of the game laws, and they had another grievance in hypothec. Hypothec was a feature of Scottish law by which the landlord enjoyed extraordinary privileges as the preferential creditor: it was alleged to encourage 'political subserviency'.[53] The small tenants of Wales were more akin to the Irish peasantry than to the substantial farmers of England and Lowland Scotland.[54] They expected a holding to remain in the occupier's family and reacted with hostility to consolidation: but there was no customary tenant-right in Wales, no inveterate claim that the occupancy was saleable property, and no tradition of agrarian violence. The trouble between landlord and tenant was of recent origin. It arose when, after decades of political quietism, Welsh Nonconformists started to try the electoral strength latent in their numerical superiority in the Principality.[55] They quickly emerged as a fervent addition to the Dissenting radicalism of England which inspired and assisted them to organize. In rural Wales the attempt to assert themselves politically, if only by supporting Whig and Anglican candidates against Tories and Anglicans, was strongly resented by some landlords used to electors who had been more docile than most in English counties. A small number of political evictions and punitive increases of rent followed the defeat of the Nonconformists' candidate in Merionethshire in 1859. The rarity, hitherto, of such incidents made these more shocking. They helped the radicals, and hardened their determination to break the landed monopoly of Welsh Parliamentary representation. Nor was that all. 'No one wants to call in question the rights of property,' wrote Henry Richard, the Welsh radical leader, in his newspaper articles of 1866, *Letters on the Social and Political Condition of the Principality*, 'but...there exists almost as urgent a necessity for a Tenant Right law for...parts of Wales as for Ireland.'[56]

Soon after taking office, the Derby–Disraeli government decided that the British political climate was undergoing a transformation which allowed them to forget their outright opposition to the Liberals' Irish land bill of 1866. The Tories' chief spokesman on Irish affairs, Lord Naas, attacked the bill as 'entirely repugnant to all principles of British law and...fatal to the rights of property'.[57] Within a year of that speech Naas proposed to do what he had condemned, compensate tenants for improvements made without the landlord's consent, and hinted that it was only a beginning. 'He would not describe the bill as a settlement,' he said of the measure in February 1867. 'In a free country, and in an age of rapid change, it was presumptuous to affirm that any great question, political or social, was absolutely settled.'[58] The Liberal *Daily News* accused the government of employing the same tactics that it was using on Parliamentary reform, of exploiting 'the conscious weakness, not to say fears, of both sides of the House of Commons'.[59] On the second reading backbenchers narrowly carried an amendment rejecting compensation for improvements to which the landlord had not consented, and the bill was dropped. The Tory country gentleman who moved the amendment argued that ministers were really saying: 'Property should be enjoyed and administered not in the interest of the few who possessed it, but for the many who had it not, and...the state, being the best judge of the matter, had the right to step in and administer it for the benefit of the nation at large. Those doctrines were not new...They were the principles of Blanqui in the language of Proudhon...he did not expect to find them brought forward by a Conservative government.'[60] Tory ministers, like the Liberal government shortly before them, believed they were being realistic and prudent. They overestimated the adaptability of the Commons, where land was concerned, to 'an age of rapid change'. The House was convinced by the argument that to give way in Ireland would not only be wrong, but would encourage all those who wanted to diminish the rights and the influence of landed property in Britain herself.

The idea that property-rights were indefeasible was extremely tenacious in mid-Victorian Britain. It was normal to conflate natural and existing rights of property. Most lawyers and politicians held that the omnipotence of Parliament, in law, stopped short, in justice, of infringing those rights, except in marginal instances like provision for the effective operation of public services. The obvious example to contemporaries was the power of compulsory purchase available to railway companies for the construction of their lines. Such provision was regarded as the legitimate exercise of the state's inherent function of making adjustments when the public interest and the rights of individuals had to be reconciled. The legislature drew what seemed to its members a self-evident distinction between the exercise of this function of the state and class legislation. Restrictions on freedom of contract favouring those without property against its owners were few and plausibly seen as special cases. When the Parliamentary reform agitation undermined the confidence of landlords, Lord Dufferin approached one of the leading lawyers of the day, Sir Roundell Palmer, to discover 'how far, consistently with the recognized principles of English law and equity, can we go in controlling a landed proprietor in the management of his property.'[61] Palmer cited the use of compulsion in the commutation of tithe, the enfranchisement of copyholds and the purchase of land for railways and similar public purposes.[62] None of the examples was adequate to support the wholesale transfer of property-rights from one social class to another that fixity of tenure would involve, but he advised Dufferin not to rely on the history of real property. It could be deduced from these precedents that the principles to which Dufferin referred were not 'so fixed and absolute, as not to yield to a certain amount of pressure from reasons of public policy'. As to how far the state might go in thus yielding, Palmer did not see 'guide-posts or land-marks' in law and equity in the Chancery sense. For law and equity were there 'to accomplish all the objects, for which, in given circumstances, a sound political system ought to provide'. What happened when circumstances, the system and its objects changed was a question of 'policy and expediency' rather than of legal or quasi-legal principle.[63] On reflection, Palmer felt this was cold comfort. He wrote again to emphasize that nothing could justify fixity of tenure, except 'a plain case of great public evil to be redressed, or great public benefit to be obtained'. He did not think that any such excuse could be upheld, finding the economic objections, from the standpoint of the welfare of the Irish themselves, conveniently insuperable.[64]

Mill's call for fixity of tenure had been anticipated by another radical M.P., Thomas Hughes, speaking to his constituents of Lambeth in December 1867. Best remembered as a literary man, he was closely associated with trade unionism. *The Times* gave his speech a first leader, written once more by Robert Lowe, charging him with having proposed a 'flagrant...act of iniquity'. Hughes defended himself by the argument that Mill had promoted in the *Principles*: absolute ownership in land was inadmissible, and the state had every right to modify the terms of tenure at its discretion.[65] Lord Stanley, the foreign secretary, told a party rally at Bristol next month to beware of 'quacks' peddling drastic solutions to the Irish land question: 'If the principle is good for Ireland, it is good for England also.'[66] The Tory leadership had learnt its lesson, for the duration of the current Parliament, from the reaction of the rank and file to Naas's bill. Much thoughtful upper and middle-class opinion was unhappy with this negative stance. The pressing reasons for a more flexible policy were candidly stated in the journal edited by Walter Bagehot, who was not an alarmist. Commenting on Stanley's speech, it urged the government not to leave Irish land to the succeeding, reformed Parliament, 'a body sure to be more undisposed to compromise'. Legislating on the tenure of land bristled with problems: 'There is in the whole range of politics no subject upon which it is so easy to be violent, and so difficult to be at once statesmanlike and conservative.' Alluding to the idealists of the Constituent Assembly in revolutionary France, it said they had been 'quacks too', and treated accordingly in their beginnings, but had brought about a revolution in landholding – the dispossession of princes, nobles and the Church – over a vast area of Western Europe. The government's attitude was 'not prudent...just as a new power, whose wisdom or unwisdom is unknown, but whose strength is irresistible, is coming into existence'.[67]

By then *The Times* was equally alive to the desirability of neutralizing Irish land as an issue in British politics. John Walter, the paper's proprietor, owned 7,000 acres in Berkshire and sat for the county. A conservative Liberal, he had definite views on land, and on Irish disaffection. Some land legislation for Ireland looked unavoidable to him – but not primarily to appease her people. 'The great point to be gained is unanimity *here*' he informed the editor, J. T. Delane. 'If we could satisfy the British public, we might snap our fingers at the Irish.'[68] Delane, an astute and adaptable Palmerstonian, concurred. Fixity of tenure was excluded. So was Bright's scheme. When Bright advertised it in a speech at Birmingham on 5 February, the paper beheld the prospect of a 'process of confiscation, disguised under the title of a voluntary sale...The end of the wedge looks very thin; but a few stout blows from an excited tenantry, aided by a strong Democratic party in a Parliament half committed to the principle, would very soon drive the wedge home.'[69] Delane favoured the expedient of a royal commission, telling Stanley that justice had never been done to the Irish landlords' case.[70] That aspect of an inquiry appealed to Stanley, who liked to make speeches proving that large landlords were a blessing. Disraeli, who became prime minister in February, saw other possibilities in the course which Stanley pressed him to adopt.[71] So, no doubt, did Delane. When the government announced its intention of appointing a commission, Disraeli spoke of issues, 'very vague but...of considerable magnitude', lying beyond compensation for tenants' improvements, which should be reserved for the inquiry.[72] The tendency of these remarks in the Commons' Irish debate of 10–16 March was clear from the preceding discussion of principle by Sir Stafford Northcote, a cabinet minister close to the new premier. Denying that the commission was solely intended to exculpate the Irish landlords, Northcote sought to prepare his party, and the House, for the inevitable: '*Salus populi suprema lex*...To a certain extent the rights and...privileges of the possessors of land must cede to the wants and advantages of the people at large.' British legislation had frequently demonstrated this, he argued. They should expect something more than a compensation for improvements bill – after the commission reported: 'I say...we must proceed delicately.'[73] A somewhat less pliant Tory, Gathorne Hardy, the home secretary, struck a different note and maintained that fixity of tenure would be a revolutionary measure.[74]

In a leading article of early February headed 'The Attitude of the Liberal Party in the Coming Parliament', the *Pall Mall Gazette* had analysed the change that was taking place in the party's thinking about Irish land, and therefore about the practical immunity from legislative interference enjoyed by landed property in the United Kingdom generally: 'Too many of our Parliamentary politicians are holding language which implies... that "fixity of tenure" should be conceded...or that the State shall become "middleman" on a great scale, and purchase... estates...to create a "peasant proprietary"...Herein lie the danger and wrong of such language...the politicians we speak of are giving a parliamentary status to projects hitherto entertained only by irresponsible agitators and reckless doctrinaires...They are acting', the paper protested in a reference that conveys its feeling exactly, 'as the Conservatives acted when they first pronounced the words "Household suffrage"; they are doing what can never be quite undone.'[75] For those prosperous and responsible radicals, Bright and Hughes, followed by Mill within days of the *Pall Mall* article, were not as isolated among parliamentarians as the direct response to their plans suggested. Disraeli and Northcote carefully avoided mentioning fixity of tenure in their speeches of March – significantly, when the expression was heard repeatedly in a debate in which Mill's pamphlet rivalled the disestablishment of Irish Anglicanism as a topic. Both parties were, however, divided over compensation for improvements, let alone the momentous next step or steps which would carry them towards fixity of tenure.

Gladstone was very conscious of the division in the Liberal party when he was meditating his Irish policy at the close of 1867. The passing of the reform bill had freed the politicians to concentrate on the next business that insistently demanded their attention. Fenianism ensured that it would be Ireland. 'The Irish question, which has long been grave, is growing *awful*,' thought Gladstone. He was anxious that the Liberals should make 'every effort' to agree on a new land bill with J. F. Maguire, M.P. for Cork, the last leader of the defunct Tenant League's Parliamentary group and subsequently a comparative moderate in agrarian politics, and through him with others. Gladstone confessed he did not know how the party could attempt to legislate except, as in 1866, to secure compensation for improvements. In 1866 their proposals had not been put to the test of a second reading vote. 'It would have been with the utmost difficulty,' wrote Gladstone, 'that we should have got that Bill well supported by the Cabinet and our friends, and a more ultra measure would only mean more splitting.'[76] 'More splitting': this was a factor he could not ignore with the Adullamite revolt fresh in his mind. Land figured in his Southport speech delivered some days afterwards, on 19 December 1867, which signalled that he was taking up Ireland's grievances in earnest. But at Southport he discussed the agrarian problem as one of compensation for improvements, nothing more. More was implied, though, in the statement that 'here is a subject which, depend upon it, is of vast importance.'[77] In the Commons' Irish debate of March he did as expected and finally pronounced that the time was ripe for Irish disestablishment. He declined to go with Mill in 'what appeared to me to be the dismissal of the landlords of Ireland'. This was not quite fair to Mill but it went down well with the House.[78] The Commons would not hear of fixity of tenure even from Mill, who deferred to them and to an overwhelmingly bad press by watering down his demand in a speech of which the *Pall Mall Gazette* not unjustly observed: 'Mr Mill himself completed the work of demolition.'[79] Lowe's attack on him so pleased the Liberal backbenchers – and indeed the House – that he was thought capable of repeating his achievement over Parliamentary reform and dividing the party if its leaders undertook a stronger commitment on Irish land than that contained in the bill of 1866.[80] Gladstone carefully avoided any such commitment in his contribution to 'this remarkable debate'.

The attack on the Anglican establishment in Ireland united the Liberal party with few exceptions. It commanded Lowe's enthusiastic assent and healed the breach over Parliamentary reform. The first complete Irish religious census of 1861 had dispelled hopes that Anglicanism was slowly gaining ground there because reformed in its structure and spirit after Catholic Emancipation, and because of the Catholic Church's assumed vulnerability in Ireland to the modernizing influences affecting her adversely elsewhere. Whig and Liberal M.P.s were preponderantly Anglican, but in the Erastian tradition that was historically a distinguishing characteristic. The activists among their old political clients, the Nonconformists, swung the weight of the sects behind Irish disestablishment. It was irresistible to Nonconformists as being at once an act of magnanimity and of vengeance – magnanimity to Catholics distanced from them by the Irish Sea: vengeance on the Established Church in England which the Act of Union of 1800 had declared indissolubly linked to the Irish Establishment. But overthrowing the Establishment in Ireland appealed more widely than to Irish Catholics and British Nonconformists. Though basically conservative with a small 'c', the expanded British electorate had been stirred by the Parliamentary reform agitation, and looked vaguely for some satisfying demonstration of its power. The Irish church question was ideal for the purpose: disestablishing Anglicanism in Ireland represented an historic withdrawal of religious privilege and a reverse for the closely associated landed interest, but it was also a politically profitable retreat from an outwork of privilege awkward to defend. An element in the Tory cabinet, including Disraeli himself, seriously considered the partial disendowment of Irish Anglicanism – the policy of concurrent endowment. Irish Catholics and British Liberals refused to entertain a compromise of that kind. In April and May 1868 the reunited Liberal majority in the Commons defeated the Tory government on Gladstone's resolutions in favour of disestablishment. Compelled to fight the first general election for the new voters on this issue in the autumn, the Tories fell back on vigorous denunciation of what some of them half-accepted in private. 'This measure,' said Gladstone drily of the disestablishing legislation next year, 'has been...the object of very hard words – sacrilege, spoliation, perfidy.'[81]

The Liberals held that the property of the Established Church was a public trust which they were entitled to terminate – with compensation. The Tories did not really think otherwise: but contrived to sound as though they did. Their indignation about this aspect of disestablishment was largely inspired by the prospect of the Irish land bill, dealing with private property, which must follow as much the most important instalment of the remedial policy that Gladstone had adumbrated at Southport in December 1867, filled out in the Commons next March and reiterated in his speeches during the electoral campaign. He spoke little about

Irish land in the campaign. In his opening speech he confirmed that of the two questions, Irish Church and land, the latter 'is in the rear while the other occupies the front'. He promised that when a Liberal ministry came to deal with the land question they would give the Irish tenant 'a fair and rational provision for his security'. 'And,' he added, '...it is my firm conviction that this may be done with the fullest regard to the rights of property...in the due observance of which, not property alone, but the entire community has a vital interest.'[82] The second undertaking was interpreted to render the first harmless. At Liverpool on 14 October, however, he enlarged on an agrarian incident in county Tipperary.[83] The tone of this speech rather than its content troubled keen-eyed observers, at Court and among the Whig magnates. General Grey, Queen Victoria's private secretary, drew her attention to the 'only objectionable part of his speech...being the seeming endorsement of...opinion ...that the laws in Ireland were partial and unjust as regards... the tenure of land'.[84] Lord Bessborough and the Duke of Argyll wrote to Gladstone with the frankness their political intimacy allowed. Bessborough thought the Liverpool speech 'might have been...going rather near the wind as to the rights of property... I know that at election times a little pull of the rein is sometimes advisable or the support of moderate men may be endangered.'[85]

Gladstone's side of the correspondence that ensued with the Duke is not extant. Argyll, who knew his man better than most did, wanted him to remember three things. Firstly, the danger of encouraging the Irish people in 'extravagant expectations... which can never be satisfied except by measures which will never be carried unless as the result of a struggle of almost a revolutionary kind'. Secondly, the Liberal leaders were as yet bound, in principle, only to a land bill resembling the one of 1866 – and Lowe, who must sit in a new cabinet born of victorious Liberal unity, was not committed even to that. The Duke was quite warranted in admonishing Gladstone that he had no wider mandate on Irish land from past and likely future colleagues in cabinet.[86] Their caution was exemplified by the election address, dated 5 November, of Chichester Fortescue, who had been Irish secretary in 1866 and was to hold the same post under Gladstone. Fortescue confined himself to telling the electors of county Louth, where he was heir to 20,000 acres owned by his brother Lord

Clermont, that 'the laws relating to the...occupation of land still await amendment, with a view to the security of the tenant farmer...'[87] Argyll did not agree, thirdly, that the long delay in legislating for the Irish tenants was attributable to 'Proprietary Instincts in excess, or that these have been always clearly and sharply opposed to "Reason and Justice"'.[88]

Gladstone had to balance intra-party reactions like these against his formidable popularity with plebeian voters that had been growing for years and turned the 1868 election into a personal triumph. In his remaining campaign speeches – including the famous 'upas tree' speech against Protestant ascendancy in Ireland at Wigan on 23 October – he referred to Irish land with prudent vagueness. To talk of disestablishment as the prelude to an attack on private property was integral to the electoral strategy which the Tories had been forced to adopt: but they were not eager to drag the land question as such into the centre of controversy. They refrained from appointing the royal commission announced in March, which would have saddled any government that emerged from the election with a review of Irish land policy when handed a report unlikely to be as negative as that of the select committee three years ago had been under Palmerston's ministry. Gladstone's attachment to the landed interest and the basic conservatism of the British electorate were not so obvious as they are a century later. As the election ended, Clarendon, about to become foreign secretary for the third time in the first Gladstone ministry, put his thoughts to Lord Granville who from the outset was Gladstone's confidant in and emollient helper with the cabinet. 'Among all the people I see,' wrote Clarendon, 'there is great fear of G[ladstone] and a notion that he is not *quite* sane enough for the leadership of affairs.'[89]

The climate of politics was felt, rightly in the short term, to have been transformed, although the new Parliament differed little from the old in its social composition. Gladstone's success in inflicting a symbolic defeat on privilege – although at the head of what was nearly as much a party of privilege as was the Tory party – won over the popular radicals in the Reform League and isolated the tiny handful who proved to be genuine socialists. Gladstone's standing with the popular and the parliamentary radicals made him potentially a dangerous man indeed. As long ago as 1865 John Walter had expressed to Delane a common view among sensible Liberals, that they must not alienate Gladstone 'who, if he were to turn nasty and to join the Rads, might break up the Liberal party, and do a deal of mischief'.[90] That consideration was now an extremely powerful one. Good judges thought there was enough combustible material lying about with which Gladstone could set out to radicalize British politics and not merely to pass items of radical legislation. Apart from the enthusiasm for him in the big towns, the farmers of Wales and, to a lesser extent, of Scotland displayed more independence of their landlords in the election than ever before. The consequent evictions in Wales, few but well publicized, did the landed class no good. Gladstone did not wish to radicalize British politics, but for the next couple of years he was able to take advantage of the belief that he might do so if thwarted. It was relatively easy to break down the Lords' opposition in July 1869 to the size of the compensation awarded by the Irish Church bill of that session. Irish land was to be a far harder problem.

This may be the place to dwell briefly on Gladstone's awareness of the imperial and international aspects of the Irish question, and therefore of Irish land. 'In my opinion,' reflected Gladstone in December 1867, 'this Empire has but one danger. It is the danger by the combination of the three names, Ireland, United States and Canada.'[91] It was the achievement of Fenianism to have fashioned out of the naturally anti-British sentiments of millions of Irish-born and Irish-descended immigrants in the United States an active and organized hostility to the British empire. And this when Anglo-American relations had been strained by resentment of the sympathetic attitude and actions of the British governing class towards the South in the recently concluded Civil War. Her mood exacerbated America's dislike of the new confederation of British colonies in Canada as strengthening the empire. The Fenians did everything they could to embroil Britain and America – as by their forays across the Canadian border, the most serious being in 1866. Both the Tory government of 1866–8 and Gladstone's after them strove to conciliate the United States – whose present and future greatness Britain could not afford to have arrayed against her – and they gave away a lot on the various points in dispute between the two countries. The eradication, or mitigation, of Irish discontent was inseparable from a conciliatory policy towards the United States. Irish Americans, or the non-Irish majority in America, must be persuaded of Britain's good intentions in Ireland. With that in mind, among other things, Gladstone determined to follow Irish disestablishment with as good a land bill as he could devise, although he did not know what he might put in it. He was also resolved to avoid yet another Coercion Act after the Tories allowed the suspension of Habeas Corpus, passed by the Liberals in 1866 and continued under Derby and Disraeli, to expire on the approach of the general election.

THE IRISH REACTION

The Irish national press in the 1860s and before was given to asking the rhetorical question why the agrarian reforms of Continental Europe – especially since the 1848 revolutions – had not been vouchsafed to their country. There was frequent mention of the earlier Prussian Stein–Hardenberg laws tardily rounded off in 1850. One reason was that on the Continent the peasantry usually had rights in the land as well as obligations to landowners which were both unknown in Britain and Ireland. The Irish were not serfs like the Russian peasants emancipated by Tsar Alexander II in 1861 or subject to labour services and other feudal dues like those in the Austrian empire prior to 1849. When the Continental peasantry became proprietors they had to surrender part of their land to the former lords. The Irish had no such obligations and no corresponding rights. Their position was quite different. The law ignored their tenant-right. Palmerston's second ministry of 1859–65 passed Deasy's Act (1860), called after the Irish attorney-general responsible for it, to reaffirm the principle that the relationship between landlord and tenant rested upon express or implied contract and not upon the fact of the latter's tenure. As Deasy said, there was nothing new in this codifying measure.[92] The Irish secretary, Edward Cardwell, believed that reaffirming the principle would stand as 'a real settlement of the tenant law of Ireland' combined with the Tenure and Improvement of Land (Ireland) Act – named Cardwell's Act – a permissive measure of which he said: 'We should not interfere with the power of the landlord...we should reserve to him the right of objecting to improvements...we cannot violate the law of property.'[93] J. F. Maguire accused the government of promoting eviction by their refusal to legislate less restrictively.[94] But evictions had fallen so

steeply after the Famine that their political value lay chiefly in
the susceptibility of British opinion to allegations of inhumanity,
which were, however, easily disproved in most instances. The
issue was tenant-right – 'totally subversive of all...social order',
Palmerston held. 'For myself, I am for landlord-right,' he proclaimed in the Commons. 'In...1860...we went as far as I think
it was possible to go consistently with...justice.' That was said
in 1863.[95] He remained inflexible down to his death two years
later, when the Liberal government lost their determination not to
compromise at all over land.

A run of bad seasons in the early 1860s aided the rebirth of an
organized political movement to express constitutionally those
aims which the peasantry enforced by violence or the fear of it
to an extent seldom understood in Britain. Fenianism aided this
movement in more than one way. Apprehensiveness of the disaster
into which the revolutionary nationalists might lead the Irish
people induced moderate nationalists to put pressure on British
Liberalism. A manifestation of the pressure was the National
Association – disrespectfully christened 'Cullen's Association' by
some – founded in December 1864 to work for the disestablishment
and disendowment of Anglicanism in Ireland, for the minimum
of agrarian reform and the changes in the Irish state educational
system that the Catholic Church wanted.[96] The priorities were
those of Archbishop Cullen and of all Irishmen who appreciated
that their aims must be related to what British opinion – or a
powerful section of it – thought right or not unreasonable. Nothing
was achieved as to land until the Russell–Gladstone ministry
formed on Palmerston's death. To assist the Liberal party in
Irish constituencies at the general election in the summer of 1865
Palmerston offered a small, illusory concession several months
ahead – without suggesting, to be fair, that anything would come
of it. This was a select committee into the working of Cardwell's
Act; its optional machinery of compensation for improvements
agreed between landlord and tenant had been disregarded by
both. Under J. F. Maguire's chairmanship the inquiry ranged
widely over the Irish land question: but its British membership,
as much as the Irish landlords on it, decided against any weakening
of the principle that the landlord must have consented to improvements for which compensation was claimed.[97] The committee
reported before the general election which nevertheless saw a

relatively easy victory for the government in Ireland. 'The late elections show great sobriety of understanding on the part of the farmers,' reflected the *Freeman's Journal*. 'They know that so long as England and Ireland are to receive their laws from the same Parliament, it is quite impossible that their principles [the three Fs] should succeed, and to press them would only prevent any settlement whatever.'[98] For there was hope of obtaining something – envisaged as compulsory compensation for improvements – when at the age of eighty even Palmerston's days were plainly numbered. Notwithstanding the report of the committee on Cardwell's Act, a British government would then be inclined, as in the 1840s and 1850s, to take more notice of those public pressures, about which Sir Thomas Larcom had written warningly: 'The Altar and the Press...are all in all when they pull in the one direction, as now they do, in the land question.'[99] Without mentioning the land or committing himself to anything specific, Gladstone had already responded openly, and in his own time, to Irish appeals directed to him personally, as the coming man.[100]

Palmerston's disappearance; the concern aroused in Britain after September 1865 by the exposure of Fenianism's ill-organized but extensive penetration of Ireland; Gladstone's willingness not to be bound by the very recent conclusion of the committee on Cardwell's Act; the government's need of every Irish vote for its Parliamentary reform bill – these considerations produced the mild Liberal Irish land bill of 1866, which reversed, but not retrospectively, the presumption of law that, in the absence of agreement to the contrary, improvements were the landlord's property.[101] From then on the expectations of the Irish rose. They discounted the Tory bill of 1867.[102] The talented lawyer and disappointed politician, Isaac Butt, once a Tory, then a Whig until he lost his seat in 1865, transformed himself into the Fenians' counsel at their trials and the advocate of fixity of tenure in three eloquent pamphlets. Dean O'Brien and the numerous signatories of the clerical Limerick Declaration of January 1868 calling for repeal of the Union wanted 'a land tenure compatible with the rights of property and the existence of freedom'. What the priests meant by this was indicated in the preceding statement that 'the very nature of...the remedies required to make Ireland rich and contented make it impossible for a British Parliament to adopt...them.'[103] The agitation that led up to Gladstone's

Land Act of 1870 was launched on the decisive phase of its career by a speech in January 1868, and furthered by an affray in the following August which counts as one of the fateful incidents in nineteenth-century Irish, and Anglo-Irish, history.

The speech was that made at Kilkenny on 3 January by Sir John Gray, the proprietor of the *Freeman's Journal*, the ally of Cardinal Cullen (as the Archbishop became in 1866), the recipient of a knighthood from Palmerston as Lord Mayor of Dublin in 1863, and a man who had been imprisoned for his nationalism in the 1840s. Mere compensation for improvements, Gray said, was 'confiscation' from the tenant's point of view and he applied the same word to short leases, even leases for thirty-one years which constituted a good long term in Irish practice. He demanded the enforcement of Ulster tenant-right throughout Ireland, defined to secure the tenant a 'fee-farm lease' – that is, an indefinite, saleable right of occupancy at a fixed rent. He paid tribute to Hughes, to the *Spectator* and to Bright: they had prepared Britain for Irish land reform. Gray credited Bright – quite wrongly – with having suggested the forcible sale of absentees' estates, and he broadened the scope of the idea: 'Give a fee-farm lease or sell – take your choice.' That was the message he wished the people and Parliament to send Irish landlords. There was a chorus of approval from the Irish provincial press that spoke for the tenant.[104]

The affray was at Ballycohey in Tipperary. A small local landlord, William Scully, tried to evict some tenants in the village of Ballycohey. He was a man with the reputation of encountering the peasantry head on in his disputes with them, and burdened with the added unpopularity of being an apostate Catholic. The tenants met Scully and his party of bailiffs and police with armed resistance, shooting two dead and wounding others, Scully himself among them. The landlord's party retreated, leaving the tenants in possession. Individual assassinations of landlords and their employees were a feature of Irish life, but a clash of this sort had none but rather distant precedents. Unfortunately for the landlords, it transpired that Scully had attempted to evict his tenants for refusing to accept fresh agreements which provided for three weeks' notice to quit instead of the six months that the law presumed under tenancy-at-will, and which included provisions subjecting them to intolerable conditions. Scully at once became a byword.[105] Very few Irish landlords indeed behaved remotely like him in the nineteenth century – not even the almost equally notorious Earl of Leitrim on the borders of Ulster and Connaught. But the landed class of Ireland suffered irreparably by their involuntary association with Scully. For the incident could not have happened anywhere else in the United Kingdom. Where else would the tenants have resorted to arms? Where else did an historic enmity between landlord and tenant exist, regularly punctuated by acts of sanguinary violence? The Conservative government conspicuously failed to bring the men of Ballycohey to justice: partly because the community declined to give evidence against those who had fired from concealed positions – they were the heroes of the countryside – and partly because the moral and political position of the attackers was a very strong one.[106]

The reluctant tolerance displayed by government encouraged the peasantry to assert their claims with a new confidence and by lawful and unlawful methods.[107] Parliament had prudently refrained from widening the county franchise of a discontented country in the Irish Reform Act of 1868 and had not redistributed even the preponderantly small, venal boroughs where the franchise had been enlarged without significantly affecting their character. The Irish Liberal majority returned at the autumn election was again drawn heavily from the landlords. They had got themselves elected with no more than the usual imprecise pledges on land reform to a narrow electorate on which the voteless mass had exerted less pressure than might have been brought to bear. The Irish people were exhorted by the moderate nationalists and the Catholic clergy to place their trust in Gladstone for this election and support most of the candidates, however Whiggish, who stood as Liberals. The symbolism of disestablishment exercised a great attraction.[108] The results were less than ever a reflection of peasant sentiment about the land, which agrarian rallies and the incidence of outrage demonstrated with mounting emphasis in the ensuing months. The Protestant tenantry of Ulster watched and waited, reasonably sure that no government would leave them at a disadvantage if the Southerners obtained legally what they enjoyed by convention. The educated public in Britain was deeply disturbed by Ballycohey and anxious that nothing like it should happen again. In that climate of opinion, Gladstone, profoundly moved by the Ballycohey incident, referred at Liverpool to 'the painful and heart-rending...attempts at eviction on the part of Mr Scully', and to the conditions of the agreements which he had sought to impose. Gladstone said that because Scully's actions had been perfectly legal 'everyone of us...cannot indeed justify, but can excuse, or if we cannot excuse, can at least understand...this deep and sullen feeling of...passive estrangement, sometimes arising into active and burning hatred,' which confronted Britain because Ireland had 'unjust laws regulating the tenure of land'.[109] That passage in a campaign speech was the Irish tenants' charter.

3

THE APPROACH TO LEGISLATING,
JANUARY TO AUGUST 1869

GLADSTONE'S POSITION AND TACTICS

Gladstone's speeches in 1868, and particularly that of 14 October, with Argyll's protests following it, seem to indicate plainly that he was bent on introducing an Irish land bill when he took office. Yet in conversation with a reliable witness – the Liberal journalist, G. C. Brodrick – at the close of his first ministry, he is reported as denying that he came to power with any settled aim but the disestablishment of the Irish church. After succeeding so well in that aim, he then, in the words of Brodrick's account, 'utilized his surplus of Parliamentary energy for the Irish Land Bill, the Education Bill and other legislative tasks'.[1] An explanation of the apparent contradiction may be that Gladstone was distinguishing between his personal wishes and his commitment as leader of the Liberal party. There can be no doubt that he wanted to bring in a land bill, and probably a strong one, when he attained power. His ability to do so was subject to the concurrence of prominent Liberals like those who, from December 1868, made up his cabinet. It is clear that in the early part of 1869 some members of the Liberal cabinet did not regard themselves as irrevocably committed to a land bill, and the majority of that body seems to have expected that nothing more would be attempted than another compensation for improvements measure. The position of the former is perfectly comprehensible: the long succession of tenants' compensation bills had all failed to pass; and one powerful member of the cabinet, Robert Lowe, now chancellor of the exchequer, had not retracted a word of his persistent and very hostile criticism of any such proposals, including Gladstone's and Fortescue's of 1866. In this situation, Gladstone acted circumspectly when the land question came up, within the administration and in Parliament, before he was ready for it, as happened repeatedly between January and May 1869. He pledged the government to nothing but consideration of the problem in due season, once the Irish Church legislation had gone through. At the same time, however, he stressed the gravity of the land question in private and in public, using language which hinted broadly that the result of the promised consideration ought to be a strong bill.

Gladstone's conduct should be viewed in the light of a scrap of autobiography quoted by Morley. In this fragment the man who was so much abused for his political silences wrote that if he possessed 'a striking gift...it has been shown in what may be termed appreciations of the general situation and its result... This must not be considered as the simple acceptance of public opinion...it is an insight into the facts of particular eras, and their relation one to another, which generates in the mind the conviction that the materials exist for forming a public opinion and directing it to a particular end.'[2] He was not what is usually meant by an opportunist. He did not utilize the 'striking gift' indiscriminately as the occasion presented itself: its employment was determined by his sympathies. Perhaps he never made use of his special talent with greater subtlety and patience than in his handling of the Irish land question in 1869–70; although, for reasons that will become apparent, he did not look back on this at the end of his life as one of four episodes which he thought illustrated his ability to get the timing of political action right. There was no question in 1869–70 of 'the simple acceptance of public opinion'. Gladstone was accustoming his party and public opinion to the idea of far-reaching legislation on Irish land, while he avoided giving the predominant conservatism of cabinet and party sufficient cause to rebel. With the passing of the months the idea took root, and was reflected in the newspapers' growing tendency to assume that the land bill vaguely foreshadowed by the prime minister would comprise more than compensation for tenants' improvements. In this way, Gladstone brought about a situation in which the opponents of a strong land bill found themselves placed in the position of challenging a fairly well-established if very recent assumption.

They had also to challenge Gladstone's unprecedented authority in British politics during the opening years of this ministry, which derived primarily from his hold over the lower middle- and working-class electors. He had shown himself capable of waking their enthusiastic support for the causes of his choice by means of rhetoric that sounded disturbingly radical to conservatives of both parties and moderate men in his own. He had presented the disestablishment of the Irish Church as an onslaught upon privilege rather than as rational reform in the Whig tradition. The result of the 1868 general election had confirmed and greatly enhanced his popular influence. The passage of the Irish Church bill through the lower House by large majorities was the Parliamentary consequence of his success with the plebeian voter under the post-1867 dispensation. Many Liberal Members were believed to entertain considerable reservations about the bill's details but his influence in the country made it hard for them to oppose the prime minister: because their enlarged constituencies manifested a loyalty to Gladstone which transcended personal and local ties. This novel discipline was one factor conditioning the attitude of the party when the seriousness of Gladstone's intentions in the matter of Irish land became apparent. Another was the Liberals' growing desire to see the policy of conciliation and concession succeed in Ireland, despite persistent misgivings, now that they had been launched upon it. Their tendency to acquiesce in Gladstone's aims was strengthened in the middle of the year following his crowning victory on the Irish Church, over the House of Lords. The peers' capitulation was induced by the fear, of which Gladstone did not fail to take advantage, that it was in his power and in his mind to arouse popular feeling and threaten 'the security and the stability' of the upper House.[3] Before long he was to exploit the same sort of apprehension as a weapon against Liberal opponents of Irish land reform.

Nevertheless Gladstone was acutely sensible of the political risks attendant upon the agrarian phase of 'Justice to Ireland'. It was without optimism, indeed with unwonted despondency, that in August he read and remarked upon the plan which, in a modified version, he subsequently induced Fortescue to put to the cabinet. On reflection, he saw that inherent in the plan was a unique combination: it went a very long way towards fixity of tenure, and it offered hope of circumventing the fatal objection to infinitely milder schemes, encroachment upon the rights of property. This way out of the impasse which Gladstone's conscience and Irish unrest had created was not one that he immediately adopted, but the possibility grew on him. In an indirect fashion, at least, he drew the attention of his colleagues to the central feature of the plan when, as the session was ending, the cabinet committed itself to attempting to frame some sort of Irish land bill in the later part of the recess. That deliberately and necessarily unspecific decision was, in the circumstances, a success for Gladstone. The difficulty thus sought to be postponed was at once raised by the cabinet's action in seeking from British diplomats and consuls information about foreign models of tenure. Gladstone and those who were ready to resist him concurred in the leading questions that were asked, because they expected quite different conclusions. In this situation he was naturally attracted by the plan that has been mentioned. All the more since the liberal press was moving towards, not fixity of tenure, but a compromise between that demand and the rights of property as they stood.

IRISH LANDLORD FEARS

The rising tide of agrarian agitation and violence in Ireland after Ballycohey and the general election was an embarrassment to the ministry from its inception. The things said by Gladstone and other members of the government in the course of the campaign were coming home to roost. The announcement, and then the appearance of the disestablishment measure, the realization that the Church of the Ascendancy really was about to be cast down, naturally gave the peasantry hope that the Liberal animadversions upon the Ascendancy and the land would have a not dissimilar outcome – fixity of tenure. No one was more alarmed by these developments than Lord Dufferin, appointed chancellor of the Duchy of Lancaster, outside the cabinet, in the new ministry. In January he was writing anxiously to leading members of the administration and the party, urging strong action to counter the agrarian threat to order. He addressed an appeal to Argyll, for the cabinet in which his close friend sat as secretary for India: 'Do any of you fifteen Deities, sitting in your ministerial Olympus, cast an eye towards these forlorn regions?... Not an unimportant function of government is the preservation of life and property. Joking apart, matters are looking very ugly in this part of the world.' The recent 'crimes' and the demand for fixity of tenure put forward by the popular leaders and newspapers were 'the natural consequence of all...being said about the inherent rights of the Celtic race to the soil of Ireland'.[4] Dufferin knew the bitter truth, that 'a man may come from a stock rooted for six hundred years in the soil of Ireland: unless he be a Catholic and his name begin with an O', he is to be denounced as an alien, declared incapable of holding landed property, his title...considered as an usurpation; and the fee simple of the soil is to be adjudged to a set of thriftless squatters...' So he saw the outcome of fixity of tenure, 'introduced under the euphonious guise of a proposal to deprive landlords of their right of capricious eviction'.[5]

This letter Argyll immediately forwarded to the prime minister, saying that he thought the Irish government should act to contain 'so dangerous a spirit' manifested by 'the Irish "Liberal" Catholic Leaders'.[6] Gladstone's reply vouchsafed nothing, and gave the clearest indication to date that he meant to tackle the land question by quite other means than repression, means which, if as yet unspecified, Argyll and Dufferin would not find easy to swallow. 'I can very well believe,' he wrote, 'that after the obstinate and most selfish resistance which has now for so long been offered to reasonable measures in relation to the land in Ireland, we shall find it difficult when the time comes to keep within the limits of a true modification.' He evaded Argyll's point about the language of the Irish popular Liberals, with the observation that no one holding office had overstepped 'due bounds' in this respect. He professed not to see how the Irish government could be expected to denounce such language, any more than it could 'engage to notice with censure acts and words which very often deserve it in an opposite sense', a reference to the landlords and their political friends.[7] To appreciate the full significance of his intimation that something more than 'a true modification' of the law of tenure might be anticipated, it must be taken with Dufferin's complaint that the land bills of the very recent past were now regarded in Ireland as 'puerile expedients'. Gladstone had evidently decided to work for a fundamental agrarian reform, and not merely to try and get a compensation for improvements measure through Parliament. He refrained, however, from such comparative frankness in his public statements on government policy.

Argyll does not appear to have pursued the topic of Irish land reform with Gladstone then and perhaps for months afterwards, but the Duke's continuing correspondence with Dufferin in January shows that the latter at any rate now began to revise his notion of what might be acceptable in dealing with the question. He was rather taken aback to learn that the prime minister had seen the text of the letter in which he had expressed himself so freely, and offered suggestions which were clearly intended to correct the impression that he was obstinately opposed to widening the scope of previous governmental attempts to legislate. If the cabinet were favourably disposed to the idea, he was ready to make a speech which 'would do good at the present moment' but would not bind them, since he was not of their number. This speech 'should be quite liberal enough about the land to please our most fervent friends, such of them at least as still remain in their senses on the subject'. Another Devon Commission might be appointed but not simply in the landlords' interest: for its membership should embrace radicals, and it should be furnished with 'a special instruction to examine and report on the "Customs of the country"'.[8] While these suggestions as to the inquiry's composition and terms of reference were most significant emanating from the landlords' champion, they did not come to anything. Dufferin was genuinely afraid that the worst – namely, fixity of tenure or something like it – might happen. A few days later he was telling Argyll that he had left off certain agricultural improvements on his estate until he knew whether Parliament was likely to interfere with contractual obligations. Illustrating the crisis of confidence which had beset the market in Irish estates, he instanced the advice received that same day from his own solicitor not to sell a part of the property 'unless you think legislation is likely to make the owner's position worse off than it is at present'. Outside Ulster, he pointed out, matters were even more unsatisfactory. In the circumstances, he did not conceal his sympathy with landlords who – Argyll was disturbed to hear, though incredulous – were reported to be evicting tenants in order to safeguard themselves against the enforced concession of fixity of tenure. He warned the Duke that since their opinions on this question went unchecked, 'some of our cleverest members of Parliament' were tending to view with favour the prospect of a 'revolutionary' Irish land bill.[9] All this apparently failed to move Argyll again. The Duke was a little inclined to think that his correspondent exaggerated the seriousness of agrarian discontent in Ireland.

At the same time as he was unburdening himself to Argyll, Dufferin approached John Bright, Lord Bessborough and their former leader, Earl Russell, about Irish land. He seems to have written to encourage Bright, whom Gladstone had brought into the cabinet, to persist with his land purchase scheme. From now on Dufferin increasingly felt its political and financial attractions. He wrote to Bessborough in the strain of his letters to Argyll. That realist about Ireland and good party man reminded him of assurances in respect of the land question which he, Bessborough, had received from Gladstone the previous year, adding with a perceptible shade of doubt, 'I hope he adheres to his text.' Bessborough agreed with Dufferin that the Irish Liberal newspapers were having a bad effect in building up hopes of fixity of tenure, and he thought 'the Government ought to bring out their land bill shortly – & declare that they are not prepared to adopt the Communistic views advocated by the Press.'[10] Despite his ownership of an estate in Ireland, Lord Russell did not take seriously Dufferin's account of the insecurity of property in that country. 'Never fear,' he wrote cheerfully, ' – a Jacquerie never did, and never will succeed against all the possessors of property, and all the holders of the armed force of a modern kingdom – Solicitors may be frightened. . . but property is safe enough.'[11] The suggestion that he was a prey to unreasonable and unbecoming fears stung Dufferin into replying warmly that the support of 'the English philosophers' had encouraged nationalists and the Catholic Church, always wishful to encompass the landlords' destruction, to agitate for fixity of tenure, and fixity of tenure, 'a mortgage which I cannot foreclose', was 'infinitely more cruel and unjust than. . . a forced sale of Irish Estates'.[12] Russell assured Dufferin that 'of course I agree with all you say about transferring the property to the tenant, & so will large majorities in Parliament – *non obstante* Stuart Mill.' The pattern of Irish unrest was unchanging: agrarian crime succeeded political insurrection, and only the gradual improvement both of landlords and tenants could remedy this state of things. Russell had never entertained a good opinion of Irish landlords and he accompanied these remarks with an anecdote which he had obtained from an impeccable source, 'an Irish squire who keeps fox hounds and hunts them', and which implicitly justified the peasantry's resort to violence.[13]

The anxiety of Dufferin and Bessborough was matched by the

disquiet of another Irish member of the administration, Monsell, expressed to Lord Granville at the beginning of January. He wanted 'strong declarations of the determination of the government not to parley with assassins'.[14] These Irish ministers had little success with their colleagues. They belonged to the Ascendancy[15] and were involved in the collective guilt imputed to it so memorably in Gladstone's recent speeches. An administration, the chief of whose proclaimed objects was 'Justice to Ireland', was understandably loath to begin by disappointing the Irish people's hopes of sweeping land reform, impracticable though these hopes undoubtedly seemed to most English Liberals. The worried Irish Whigs were at a further disadvantage in that they, like all Irish landlords, were suspected of being ready to cry out for extraordinary measures to keep public opinion in check. During January the cabinet discussed the maintenance of law and order in Ireland: but the public statement, by Gladstone, of ministerial intentions as to a land bill was not what Dufferin and the others thought was needed.

'CAREFUL AND ADROIT RETICENCE'

The prime minister referred to Irish land next month during the Commons debate on the speech from the throne, in which the land question was not mentioned. The omission was solely due, Gladstone explained, to an insuperable obstacle, the lack of Parliamentary time and of time for mature consideration. It was 'a subject...which...occupies a very high place in the estimation of Her Majesty's Government as to its importance and necessity'.[16] Asked a few days later by an Irish Liberal whether the government would announce the principles on which it meant to legislate in due course, Gladstone replied that any such statement 'would be extremely difficult to make intelligible unless...accompanied by...details and particulars...'[17] Meanwhile Lowe, speaking at Gloucester on 27 January, had categorically stated that '"Justice to Ireland"' was 'not to be sought in overthrowing the social structure of the country, nor in the raising of one class at the expense of another', but in religious equality.[18]

On 18 March, after Ballycohey and its consequences had been raised in the House earlier that month, the Lords held a debate on the recent agrarian killings in Ireland, which were blamed by the Opposition and by some Whigs on the government's policies in disestablishing the Irish Church, releasing Fenian prisoners and on the use by very senior ministers of 'strong language with reference to the oppression endured by the tenants.'[19] Lord Granville, the Liberal leader in the House, maintained that both Bright and Gladstone had 'carefully guarded themselves against any proposal...inconsistent with the sanctity of property.'[20] Winding up for the government, Lord Kimberley assured the chamber, as had Dufferin and Granville, that the law would be fairly enforced against 'crimes...I regard...with the utmost abhorrence', and he finished with some words which suggested that those of Gladstone in the Commons were perhaps optimistic. 'Successive governments,' said Kimberley, 'have failed to carry Land Bills, and it seems to me it is infinitely better than exciting expectations to disappoint them.'[21] Whether or not these cabinet peers convinced themselves, they did not convince members of their House who knew what was happening across the Irish countryside.

The apprehension felt by Dufferin, Bessborough and Monsell in private and voiced in the Lords by Whigs outside the ministry was justified by the course of the agitation in Ireland. The viceroy, Earl Spencer, inexperienced and relatively youthful, showed here at the start of his long official career the fairness, the sensible liberalism and the courage which characterized it throughout. He was to be one of the very few representatives of grand Whiggery who did not leave Gladstone in 1886. Although the chief secretary, Fortescue, was in the cabinet, Spencer remained the head of the Irish government, and was not disposed, as he might reasonably have been in the circumstances, to confine himself to a largely ceremonial rôle. His strong sense of duty and marked taste for responsibility won him the respect of Dublin Castle. Untried and junior though he was, his personality and hereditary position gave him a standing in the party which neither Fortescue nor Dufferin, with their greater experience of government and knowledge of Ireland, possessed. Like so many Englishmen when first put down in Ireland, he was surprised and disturbed by the bitterness of Irish conflicts, whether agrarian, political or religious. These feelings of his emerged in the anxious letters which he wrote in March and April of 1869.

On 26 March Spencer told the prime minister that while he appreciated his reasons for postponing legislation, 'I see every day more and more the immense importance of a measure being passed on the Tenure of Land in Ireland.' He found it 'very appalling' to contemplate the recurrence of behaviour like that of Scully and Lord Leitrim. 'To leave Landlords such as these,' he wrote, 'with power to madden a people who have deluded notions about their rights to land into acts of revenge, is very serious.' Giving a sombre account of the successes achieved by agrarian combination, he warned that the 'outrages' and the overt agitation for land reform exercised a reciprocal influence. Intensified agitation would make a difficult task harder when the government came to legislate on the land question. 'It seems to me therefore of the greatest importance,' he concluded, 'that a Land...Bill should be passed which will be taken as a settlement, as soon as possible.' Lord Clanricarde was the sponsor of a very limited measure designed to help landlords as much as tenants by the substitution of written contract in cases of parole tenure with its inevitable uncertainty about mutual obligations. Since it was claimed to meet with general approval 'as far as it goes', Spencer suggested adopting and amending it, conceivably with 'the best clauses' of the ministerial bill of 1866. He was not blind to the possibility that Clanricarde's proposals, thus reinforced, would fail to prove an acceptable settlement. He firmly believed that 'whatever is done should be done completely'. The latter ended with the assurance that whether his suggestions were followed, or 'a Bill of your own' introduced, 'it would be a great boon to the country to get it done at once.'[22] Gladstone sent the viceroy's letter of 26 March to Lord Granville, asking him if he was aware of its contents.[23] Granville, who enjoyed the confidence both of Whig peers and of the prime minister, left the question unanswered, but in his considered advice came down against Spencer. While Spencer's letter was 'a good one', Clanricarde's bill would require 'considerable additions', and it was not clear that Parliamentary time would be available. Granville nevertheless suggested that Gladstone might ascertain from J. F. Maguire and Sir John Gray 'whether it would be possible to get their adhesion to any Bill which the Cabinet could properly adopt'.[24] He thus raised the crucial difficulties attendant upon the promised land bill, difficulties in which Gladstone had no intention of being caught up at that juncture. The prime minister sent Spencer's letter on to Fortescue, with the endorsement that he saw no chance of a government bill that year,[25] and the chief secretary duly replied that he did not think Clanricarde's bill an acceptable substitute, although he and the attorney-general for Ireland would go over it. He advised consulting Kimberley, and Gladstone did so.[26] In a short memorandum, Kimberley stressed that Clanricarde's bill was really irrelevant to the tenant-right agitation and quite unacceptable to its Parliamentary friends.[27]

The reintroduction of Clanricarde's proposals in the Lords now forced ministers to define their position more clearly, to themselves as well as to the world. The Marquess was not optimistic about its prospects; but his indignation was overflowing against the government's handling of the whole Irish question, and especially of the agrarian problem, and he wanted to force a confrontation in Parliament.[28] Writing to Granville on 12 April, Spencer asked him what line the government would take on the second reading of the bill.[29] The viceroy understood the difficulties of legislating but reiterated his conviction that it was necessary. The loss of its property by the Irish Church under the measure going through Parliament, after many years' tenacious resistance, had led the people of Ireland to 'apply without discernment the same doctrine to other lands'. Spencer showed that he was in close touch with Clanricarde and his associates. They would be content if the government intimated its willingness to let the bill have an unopposed second reading and be fully discussed in committee. Otherwise they would invite Conservative support, which would be forthcoming.[30] The cabinet's decision on Clanricarde and his bill at its meeting of 17 April was succinctly recorded in the prime minister's notes: 'Not to oppose, but it does not settle the question.'[31] Gladstone told Spencer some days afterwards: 'It is I think very sanguine indeed to assume that any Land Bill we could produce at this moment would have a soothing effect. A compound controversy is like a compound fracture; and the Church is enough for today.'[32] This was clear enough: the prime minister wanted such a measure as the cabinet could not be expected to sanction quickly and without dispute. After the glimpse he had been given of Gladstone's thinking, Spencer readily revised his idea of what was practicable. Typically, he did not disguise the moral implications from himself. At the beginning of June he stated his general position to Dufferin, following a conversation they had had. What Dufferin said is not recorded, but it is likely to have been that compensation for improvements represented all that was more or less consistent with justice. 'I sincerely trust,' wrote Spencer, 'that the views which you hold go sufficiently far to form the basis of a satisfactory settlement of the question: for I admit that one step further and some injustice must be committed. If however I were convinced that nothing but a more radical measure would set the question at rest, I should be disposed [to] make that step in the Public interest.' He hoped and believed that Gladstone could satisfy the greater part of Ireland. He was hopeful, too, that Irish extremism was not a deep-seated phenomenon. His optimism was based on an exaggerated estimate of Gladstone's popular success in that country. 'They trust him', he said simply.[33]

The debate on the second reading of Clanricarde's bill on 20 April provided another opportunity for the Whig critics of government on the issues involved to ventilate their misgivings, and for the Opposition to make a little capital out of those discontents. 'All that could be done by legislation,' said Clanricarde, 'was to facilitate and enforce contracts; and he would appeal to the Government to accept this Bill, or in some other way show their determination to maintain the law of the land with regard to property, so as to check the extravagant opinions which at present prevailed.'[34] Granville made it clear that in the eyes of ministers the bill was inadequate for their purposes, namely 'finally to settle the question and to produce...contentment among moderate persons'. The ministry was not pledged to Fortescue's bill, although, like Clanricarde's, it contained provisions which 'moderate men of both parties' might adopt. Granville said that he would not vote against the bill before the House, but that to proceed with it in the absence of government support would be futile.[35] *The Times* quoted, approvingly, the criticism by Earl Grey, a former Whig cabinet minister: 'My noble Friend's balanced phrases, one for the landlord, and another for the tenant, can do nothing but unmixed mischief.'[36] The subsequent remarks by Kimberley, the Lord Privy Seal, did not help. On the one hand he stressed that Mayo's bill 'went exceedingly far in principle', saying: 'Challenged...to state the principles on which we think it would be wise to legislate...it would be in the highest degree indiscreet for me to do so', for the Irish land question required careful deliberation. On the other hand, he gave the

House the following assurance: 'I am sure I speak the feeling of my colleagues...we should not consent to a measure upsetting the rights of property and inconsistent with the just rights which must be maintained throughout the United Kingdom...I have thought it proper to say this much, because it is said that vague expectations are entertained in Ireland on this subject.'[37]

The chief antagonist within the Tory party of Disraelian conservatism – that eloquent pessimist, the Marquess of Salisbury – was sufficiently convinced to say: 'I believe myself that the Cabinet are what we should, on this side, call "sound" on this question of property. I do not believe they will interfere with the liberty of landlord and tenant to contract...as to...land, and... labour.' At the same time Salisbury complained that there was enough ambiguity in the speeches of Granville and Kimberley to sustain the Irish agitators – 'it is upon this careful and adroit reticence that the disaffection of Ireland leans.'[38] The Conservative leader in the upper House, Lord Cairns, endorsed Salisbury's comments as expressing the Opposition's view of the Government's handling of the question, and harked back to language held during the election by Bruce, the home secretary, at Merthyr Tydfil and Gladstone in South-West Lancashire, which might mean that the Protestant landlords of Ireland were to suffer the same fate as the Established Church of that country.[39] Clanricarde's bill was given a second reading, but on 26 April the committee stage was postponed and the bill consigned, in effect, to the Parliamentary equivalent of limbo, speeded on its way by Argyll's remark that it would have been 'perfect madness and folly' for ministers to take on the Irish Church and the land questions simultaneously.[40]

There was no general expectation yet in political circles that the Gladstone government would go to the lengths it did in the land bill of 1870. If *The Times* was troubled by the 'vague and elastic utterances' of official spokesmen, it was concerned about their effects on agrarian crime, rather than about the possible provisions of a measure which it saw as, at most, limited to compensation for improvements. Moreover, the paper still felt able to prefer Clanricarde's bill to that.[41] But the observations of Kimberley and Salisbury bore witness to the intensification of the uneasiness to which Irish land had given rise. The press correctly surmised that the cabinet did not know its own mind on this most delicate of subjects. An opinion which was amply vindicated when an extensive and acrimonious discussion of the question began a matter of days after the demise of Clanricarde's bill.

BRIGHT'S INDISCRETIONS

Lord Derby did not share the relative complacency with which Salisbury viewed the Liberal government's probable behaviour. Writing to a prominent Scottish Tory early in April, Derby was afraid that 'under present guidance, a combination of the most discordant elements has succeeded in establishing a policy which must lead to an entire social and political revolution in the three Kingdoms.' In a political life of nearly fifty years, he had never before felt such apprehension.[42] The focal point of this conservative disquiet continued to be Bright rather than Gladstone. The Dissenting radical and critic of aristocracy who had loudly proclaimed himself the friend of the Catholics as well as the tenant-farmers of Ireland, and sat in the cabinet with Whig peers – thus seemed to illustrate perfectly in himself the dangers of an unnatural alliance such as the Gladstone ministry appeared to many less partisan than Derby. The outcry was understandable when on 30 April Bright repeated, in somewhat more emotive terms than usual, his familiar arguments for Irish land reform. As a result of this episode, Gladstone's broad intentions in the matter of Irish land could be sensed, rather than seen, by the perceptive and the apprehensive.

Speaking in a debate on the state of Ireland in the Commons, inspired by the continuing agrarian agitation and violence, Derby's son, Lord Stanley, took up the Tory peers' demand and pressed ministers to make it plain where they stood on the land question.[43] Acting on his own initiative, Bright responded by saying, apparently without thought for the restraints of cabinet membership: 'There can be no peace in that country...till the population by some means or other – I am prepared to propose a means, and believe it can be done without injustice to any man – are put in possession in greater numbers...of the soil of their own country.' 'The time has come,' he declared, 'when acts of constant repression in Ireland are unjust and evil...no more...should...pass this House unless attended with Acts of a remedial and consoling nature.' The language went far to confirm the fears expressed about his land purchase scheme since he first put it forward – fears reiterated in this debate. Nervous people had always found it difficult to believe that Bright did not intend the scheme to be in any way compulsory upon landowners. Now it seemed to hostile and frightened minds that he actively sympathized with the aims of the perpetrators of those agrarian crimes which were exercising both sides of the House.[44]

In Ireland Bright's remarks were received as feared. The *Irishman* observed: 'Mr Bright appears to catch a glimpse of the future. Next year his message to the British Parliament may be that Ireland and its landlords cannot both be preserved. The bulk of Irish landlords...fatten on confiscated property. They are still aliens in sentiment.'[45] Daniel O'Sullivan, the mayor of Cork whom government had compelled to resign early in May for flaunting his sympathy with Fenianism, was even more sanguine. He was loudly cheered when he told a large and excited gathering in the city on 21 May: 'Let any man look to the meaning of Mr Bright's speech...What is the meaning of that speech? It is this – that the land of Ireland is to be handed over to the people of that country...I believe every inch of the ground confiscated 200 years ago was confiscated improperly...I believe we are coming [sic] to do away with that...wrong...violence...fraud.'[46] Gladstone might remark to Granville that Bright was scarcely to be blamed for O'Sullivan's 'misconstructions', which he thought were probably inspired by some English reactions to their colleague, but in Ireland the damage had been done.[47]

As tactfully as he could, but unmistakably, Gladstone disowned Bright and on behalf of the ministry denied any prior commitment to his scheme, while he emphasized that it did not threaten property and its rights. Gladstone declined to meet the demand for clarification of the ministerial position on Irish land save by citing the views he had expressed in the Commons the previous March: and he saw fit to add that he did not suppose 'they would have the influence, which the noble Lord was inclined to assign to a declaration made by the Government on this subject at the present moment'.[48] This studied evasion, coupled with Bright's ill-considered statements, constituted an important stage in the growth of a conviction that the ministry was moving towards the kind of measure which had so recently been unthinkable for the government of this country.

Bright was condemned in and out of Parliament for the popular reaction in Ireland where his speech would surely be taken 'as a promise...on the part of the Ministry...to give the land to the peasantry and to treat with indulgence all offences which may be committed by them until the scheme...is accepted.' 'It may be doubted,' continued the *Pall Mall Gazette*, the organ of a moderate and rational conservatism, 'whether it would have been easy, or been possible for a practical statesman to have crowded into the the same quantity of words a greater amount of mischievous indiscretion than Mr Bright put into these sentences.'[49] With greater perception, Lord Salisbury, who acknowledged Bright's respect for property and its rights, was more disturbed by the implications of Gladstone's remarks. Speaking in the Lords on 7 May, he pointed out that what Gladstone had said came to this: 'Fixity of tenure should not be adopted till other measures had been tried...He did not disavow – as we might have expected he would disavow – an unabashed assault upon the laws of property...This vacillation...these intimations that they [ministers] will be prepared to yield to increased agitation are...the means of exciting men of violence to continue their intrigues against property.'[50] Salisbury's confidence in the 'soundness' of the cabinet had received a mortal blow.

There was an undeniable contrast between the speeches of Granville and Kimberley on 20 April and those of Bright and Gladstone on 30 April. On 13 May Lord Russell, who in January had cheerfully assured Dufferin that 'property is safe enough', rose in the upper House to ask the government about its policy on agrarian crime and land tenure in Ireland, and to complain that it had allowed 'every kind of hope to be held out to the tenantry...which could tend to shake...property.' He described Bright's action in stating his aims from the Treasury Bench as 'with a people like the Irish...extremely dangerous' – while acquitting him of any desire to invade the rights of landowners. Russell avowed he was afraid that if the present session ended without ministers defining their policy on Irish land, without their disowning 'every such visionary plan' as Bright's, Parliament might find itself faced, on reassembling next year, with proposals repugnant to it, which government would proceed to justify on the plea of necessity before an agitation left to assume unmanageable proportions.[51]

Russell's reference to 'the great anxiety which exists on this subject' was echoed in other contributions to the debate. Lord Derby delivered the notable speech mentioned earlier in this study, setting forth how and why Irish landlords, himself included, did not possess, and had never in his long experience possessed, anything like the freedom of action which British landlords took for granted. He explained what Irish landlords well knew, that at a time such as the present the Irish peasant was fired by the hope of coming into his own again, of obtaining by law the land which ancestral memory taught was his. Derby made it clearer than anyone had succeeding in doing why Bright's language would have the feared effect. Absolving the government of any intention to adopt Bright's scheme, let alone expropriate the landlords, Derby, too, wanted an unequivocal disclaimer of 'revolutionary' suggestions.[52] Kimberley retorted by inquiring whether Derby's observations were any wiser than Bright's: for they would 'lead many people to think that although the Government may not advocate such measures as fixity of tenure, yet... practically fixity of tenure prevails at present in the South of Ireland, and is likely to prevail there.'[53]

Yet neither Kimberley nor Granville would be more specific than they had previously been about the likely shape of government policy, except to state that Bright's scheme was not a substitute for any ministerial bill. Why they were not more forthcoming emerges clearly from a letter written on 5 May by one of their cabinet colleagues, Lord de Grey, to another, H. A. Bruce, the home secretary. De Grey, although in outlook more open to change than most of the Whigs in the ministry, was one of their number, while Bruce was not, representing that element in the cabinet which was neither Whig, nor radical like Bright. De Grey's letter was prompted by the wish to impress upon Bruce, as the responsible minister, the need for circumspection in dealing with the Scottish game laws, a problem exacerbated by the emotions and candidates' pledges of the general election. Bright had also ignored the limitations of collective responsibility in respect of this awkward topic, and reasserted long held and embarrassing opinions. Three days before his controversial remarks on Irish land, he had made a short speech, in his most radical vein, during a debate on these laws, describing the game laws in Britain, and not in Scotland alone, as a great social evil, particularly for the tenant-farmers 'degraded' by the restrictions to which they were subject. He had looked forward to the farmers of England emulating those of Scotland and organizing themselves politically, with the object of securing the return of farmer candidates or forcing the gentry to pledge themselves to reform the obnoxious laws.[54] This was what land-owners meant when they accused Bright of setting class against class. De Grey thought that the resentments already stirred up by the whole issue in the Liberal party might be considerably increased if the government did not exert its influence against certain proposed additions to the membership of a select committee on Scottish game laws. The additions promised to reduce the chances, such as they were, of avoiding recommendations which the upper House would never stomach if embodied in a bill.

'There is one last consideration,' wrote De Grey, 'which appears to me to outweigh all the others...We shall in all probability have to take up, as the principal question of the next session, the subject of Land Tenure in Ireland. Whether we shall be able to agree among ourselves as to the measure to be proposed may be doubtful; but if we do, we shall certainly have to make large demands upon the forbearance of the moderate section of the Party, and especially over that of our supporters in the House of Lords.' Accordingly it was 'of the very greatest importance' meanwhile not to antagonize these elements in the party 'with whose support we shall not be able to dispense'. Not even the most radical Scottish Member would claim that the game laws and the Irish land question were of equal moment. 'Surely,' he went on, 'it would be the part of a wise Government to abstain as far as possible from creating alarm among landed proprietors from a variety of questions at the same time. Already, such speeches as Bright's have had a mischievous effect upon many of our supporters, and the task of the Government in the House of Lords is already sufficiently difficult, and more than sufficiently dis-agreeable, to make it most undesirable to cast fresh obstacles in our way.'[55]

At the beginning of May, then, the cabinet not only had no clear idea of how to proceed in the matter of Irish land: they were still unsure whether they should take up the question in 1870. They were, moreover, conscious that it would be difficult for them to agree on any proposals. After the Lords' debate of

13 May, Kimberley observed in his diary that Lord Russell was merely offended by ministers' failure to take him into their confidence and Lord Derby was moved by 'party bitterness'. 'All the taunts of our opponents,' wrote Kimberley, 'have failed to drive us into the suicidal folly of attempting an Irish Land Bill.'[56] De Grey nevertheless expected that if the cabinet did succeed in arriving at a measure for next session, it would be one so unpalatable to many of their followers as to impose a severe strain on the cohesion of the party. He was certainly right in thinking that if it was to get such a bill through Parliament, the government should in the interval eschew anything else which might upset the landed class. As Russell pointed out to Granville after the debate of 13 May, *The Times* supported his initiative in urging the ministry to spell out its intentions on Irish land. Russell spelt out his fears to Granville: 'A Government that has not made up its mind whether it will accept a plan destructive of property, or not, seems to me to be abandoning the rudder, and allowing the ship to drift on the rocks.'[57]

The advanced radicals noted these symptoms of alarm with satisfaction, if they could hardly bring themselves to believe that the English tenant-farmers were going to emerge from their strange passivity. Following the debate in the Lords, the *Spectator* inquired: 'What if within five years "tenant-right" as the Irish call it, that is, the legal relation of the occupier to the owner of the land, should become *the* question in the internal politics of the Empire?' There were indications of a different mood in the English countryside, and the Scottish farmers had become very independent in their political outlook. Derby's speech, showing how his tenantry had behaved towards one of the greatest noblemen, should be taken as a warning by English landlords.[58] Gladstone, too, saw the 'feverish and fidgetty' speeches in the Lords as manifestations of weakness. 'The great possessors of property', he told Granville, 'can surely not expect to act much upon opinion on behalf of property.' He even suggested to the leader of the House that the inevitable misinterpretation in Ireland of Bright's remarks of 30 April had its origin in the attacks made on them in the Lords.[59]

Bright persisted in advocating his scheme, but not again in public. He pressed it on Gladstone and his other colleagues during May. Robert Lowe thought 'Lord Russell's attack had a little ruffled the charming serenity of Bright's temper...and he talked something very like nonsense.' The 'statesmen' of Cumberland and Westmorland formed the best-known, if not the sole, concentration of peasant proprietors in England and they, wrote Lowe from Grasmere with characteristic *brio*, were 'drunken, improvident, lazy, wretched cultivators...very immoral and disappearing very fast...from their own vices...If these things happen on the green tree what will they do on the dry?' Needless to say, this portrait reflected his vigorous prejudices and should be set beside Mill's enthusiastic reference to the 'statesmen' in the *Principles of Political Economy,* where he quoted a long extract from Wordsworth's truly poetic description of their way of life. According to Lowe, who had of course no illusions about the discontent in Ireland, what the Irish really desired was not peasant proprietorship but 'occupation of the land by the sept – tribal right.'[60]

Undeterred by this kind of reception, Bright appealed to Gladstone on 21 May: 'When the Irish church...is out of the way, we shall find all Ireland united in demanding something... much broader than anything hitherto offered...in "Compensation Bills". If the question is to go on without any real remedy for the grievance...measures far beyond anything I now contemplate will be necessary. I am most anxious to meet the evil before it is too great for control, and my plan *will meet it,* without wrong to any man.' Asking for 'a quiet hour' to discuss Irish land comprehensively with the prime minister before the end of the session, he told Gladstone that he had gone into the whole question 'from a point of view almost inaccessible to the rest of your Colleagues, and from which possibly even you have not had the opportunity of regarding it.' 'It is a great question for the Government,' he wrote; continuing: 'what is wise and necessary for Ireland now...may be also in Great Britain at some future time.'[61]

This letter was typical of Bright in that it envisaged a really radical goal to be achieved by studiously moderate means; typical, too, in a certain naïve assurance that the vision of upper-class politicians could not be as clear and true as his own. The eventual aim was nothing less than a transformation of the British as well as of the Irish scene. The mention of Britain was significant; like the *Spectator,* the veteran agitator seemed to scent the most fundamental of social changes in the air. It was nevertheless essential to him that the means of realizing a most controversial aim should be morally unexceptionable. Conscious rectitude on this score showed in the repeated assertions that the operation of his scheme would deprive no one. This feeling was undoubtedly one reason why he found the peers' recent criticisms more wounding than he allowed.

Bright presented Gladstone with a distinctly embarrassing problem, one which caused Granville to warn the prime minister that 'this question may break us up'. In terms of popular reputation and influence Bright carried far more weight than all the rest of his colleagues, save only Gladstone. If such a figure left office, as Granville thought was possible, out of disappointment over the cabinet's certain refusal to sanction his cherished scheme, it would be a serious blow to the ministry. There was, however, no alternative to that refusal, in Granville's view, even without reckoning on the hostility to the scheme of Lowe and others.[62] Behind the cabinet, moreover, stood the Parliamentary party, the large majority of whom were unsympathetic to Bright. The government's leaders in both Houses had indicated the official view of his conception of land reform. It was entirely predictable that Gladstone would make no concessions in replying to him on 22 May.

As he acknowledged in the letter, Gladstone might have been expected to word his rejection of Bright's appeal less critically than he did. He put his finger on the weakest link in the attractively simple reasoning of the scheme which had been so earnestly recommended to him. The proposal was to tender the landlord something more than the market value of his property as an inducement to sell, eventual payment of the full purchase price by the tenant being assured. 'How then,' asked Gladstone, 'is it to give contentment. . .to men who make the necessity of paying the market value a subject of complaint?' He thus mentioned for the first time in his correspondence one of the major difficulties he met during his exhaustive consideration of Irish land later that year – the tenants' conviction that their stake in the land should be reflected in the value placed upon the landlord's interest. Gladstone put it to Bright that Irish land was an issue as delicate as it was important: 'We must all take this question to heart as our No. 1, the moment that we see our way out of the question of the Irish Church.' He gave an exhortation and a warning which were to figure repeatedly in correspondence with his cabinet: 'We must anticipate both more difficulty and less support [than in disestablishing the Irish church] and we shall have nothing to set against this expectation except our own hope of combining together in the formulation of our measure the qualities of circumspection and resolution. If we succeed with the Church, and fail with the land, we shall have done less than half our work.' He justified the tone of his letter by the value of frankness in 'early friendly and confidential communication on subjects of great public interest'.[63]

Gladstone judged his own power rightly. Bright was attached to his scheme – he reverted to it later at a most inconvenient time for the prime minister. Until then he subordinated the conviction that he had the answer to the question perplexing his colleagues, to the need to support Gladstone. Bright cared too deeply about Irish grievances to refuse his backing to a man whom he admired and trusted to advance the real interests of the people. That backing was essential to Gladstone if he were to carry a reform which he knew would encounter strong resistance from other cabinet ministers. United, he and Bright were a host in themselves. Although in the coming months the prime minister told him far less than he did Granville, on this as on other matters, he was concerned to keep Bright in touch and in sympathy with the trend of his thinking. Hence the satisfaction with which Gladstone penned a note to inform Granville on 27 May that he had seen Bright and their talk had 'comforted me greatly with respect to Irish land and given me good hope that no impediment will arise on his side of a nature not to be surmounted'.[64]

Bright's scheme was not understood to have been completely ruled out by all that his colleagues had said in public and in private. He had, however, been brought to accept, with the aforementioned lapse months afterwards, that there was no possibility of his scheme being adopted by the cabinet to the exclusion of a major reform of land law.

Still, his efforts in April and May had these results for the land bill of next year. In the first place, they strengthened the government's commitment to a bill, which had been by no means inescapable. Secondly, with the public statements which he elicited from other ministers, and against the background of growing agrarian unrest in Ireland, he created the impression that the legislation thus vaguely foreshadowed would be more considerable than anything previously supported by either front bench. It should be said that this impression was not shared by one of those responsible for diffusing it, Granville. After seeing Gladstone's letter of 22 May to Bright, his idea of a land bill was a combination of Clanricarde's bill with Fortescue's.[65] There were others who sensed the way the situation was developing. Particularly well placed to judge the trend were Delane and John Walter; although far less intimate with the prime minister than was Granville, they had a better idea of what the government was likely to find itself proposing.

THE POLICY OF 'THE TIMES'

In April and May *The Times* had supported the moves by Lords Grey, Clanricarde and Russell to get the ministry to define its policy on Irish land, and had reiterated its approval of Clanricarde's bill. By the latter part of May such a very moderate measure struck the paper's chiefs as unrealistic, and so did one restricted to compensation for improvements. They set out to influence and contain what apparently had to be.

On 18 May a leader, for which G. C. Brodrick was responsible, selected the moderate advocates of tenant-right before a Lords' committee of 1867 as representative of the tenantry in their outlook, and maintained that, except on the length of leases, they 'claimed little, if anything, more than a good landlord would do and does of his own accord. What they demand is...that proprietors should be deprived by law of powers which only a harsh proprietor would exercise. This...is something widely remote from a demand for spoliation.' He thought it wiser to concede that much, 'taking its supporters at their own word'. The people, the article finished, should be made to feel that the land question was going to call forth 'true statesmanship... superior to lawyer-like prejudices and to...purely English conceptions of proprietary rights and to conceptions which have no justification but the imperious instinct of rapacity'.[66]

It was novel stuff in such a place. The advocates of tenant-right whose reasonableness Brodrick defended were of course far more advanced, even in 1867, than *The Times*, up to the appearance of this leader, considered was tolerable. Not surprisingly, John

Walter at once sent his unfavourable comments: 'The article...
talks loosely about *statesmanship*, as something distinguished
from lawyer's prejudices and English ideas of property. This is
not very encouraging.' The weight of evidence before the Devon
commission and two recent inquiries was, as he thought, against
compulsion upon the landlord to grant leases and the insertion
of compulsory provisions in contracts. The tenants' outstanding
claims for compensation were hard to accept, but with these
settled 'there ought to be no difficulty whatever in laying down
a few simple and equitable rules for the future relations between
landlord and tenant – the first and foremost being that of written
agreement.'[67] If Walter still believed that no more than this was
required to dispose of an intractable and embittered question, it
was not for *The Times* to gainsay him. On 21 May the reliable
Tom Mozley wrote a leader that went some way towards offsetting
Brodrick's. As so often before, it was argued that the peasantry
must inevitably continue to leave the land, and the article continued: 'The Legislature will do what it can to mitigate results,
to soften griefs and alleviate sufferings; but it cannot commit
itself to the hypothesis that England and Ireland are to be
always naturally...different and discordant.'[68]

The reversion to the paper's usual views on Irish land was
deceptive. In fact, on the day after his disapproving reaction to
Brodrick's leader, Walter was readily considering a suggestion
from Delane which had important consequences for the development of the question: a special correspondent to tour Ireland
and report on the land question.[69] Delane had approached his
choice for the mission some days, at least, before publication of
the leader of 18 May. Brodrick's article may have reflected the
opinions of the man chosen, William O'Connor Morris, an Irish
barrister and landowner, who emphasized to Delane how strongly
he felt 'the advisability of settling this question generously' by
going to the extent of a concession suggested by two Irish M.P.s,
which *The Times* had roundly condemned, W. H. Gregory's and
Sir Colman O'Loghlen's proposal to convert tenancies-at-will
into leases for twenty-one years.[70] While John Walter wanted to
know on what principle this treatment of the landlord could be
justified, he observed that the document submitted to Delane in
which the potential special correspondent expressed himself thus,
'promises well'.[71] He invited O'Connor Morris to his country seat,

97

Bearwood in Berkshire, where they talked Irish land with Sir Roundell Palmer, whose influence on the government back-benchers was considerable.[72] Palmer's reputation had recently been enhanced by the selflessness and dignity which he had displayed in fighting for the Established Church of Ireland. O'Connor Morris gave a short space to these conversations in his memoirs. As might have been expected, the lawyer found the equity of the matter and general legislation hard to reconcile. In O'Connor Morris's understanding words: 'Had we lived in the days when legal sages were able to effect great social reforms, by wise and far-reaching judicial decisions, he would have gone a long way to solve the problem.' Walter's views Morris described as 'shrewd, reasonable and liberal in the true sense'; and the emphasis should be placed on the first two adjectives.[73] For Walter's close interest in Irish land from this moment until the cabinet had settled the general outlines of their bill, was governed by his recognition that the social order in Ireland had now to be defended pragmatically and not by standing on principle.

Walter was quite satisfied with the talks. He wrote cheerfully to Delane: 'We are very much pleased with our new Irish friend, who is an agreeable and clever man...With so redoubtable a Cabinet, it is very hard if we do not manage to settle the Irish land question.'[74] In his memoirs O'Connor Morris claimed that Walter and Delane 'did not seek to fetter or direct my judgment'.[75] The claim is not borne out by Walter's letters in *The Times* archives. The proprietor carefully watched the tone and trend of Morris's articles as they appeared week by week during the special correspondent's tour of Ireland commencing in July; and when he did not like what he read, Walter intervened through Delane. One may cite a letter from proprietor to editor in August commenting on the opening piece of the series: 'I have altered a line or two...The great point is to keep him as much as possible, to the collection of facts, leaving us to draw the inferences for ourselves.'[76] O'Connor Morris was not inclined to adhere to the understanding as faithfully as Walter desired, and the latter had subsequently to insist on maintaining the division of labour.[77] Palmer made no reference to the conversations at Bearwood in his memoirs, but, looking back, he had no doubt of the importance which should be attached to the articles written by O'Connor

Morris. The series had, he wrote, 'an effect hardly less than if it had been set on foot by public authority'.[78]

For the next two months *The Times* was preoccupied with the ministry's efforts to get the Irish Church bill through the Lords substantially unchanged. Clearly, the ability of the government to deal with the Irish land question, and indeed its continued existence, depended on the outcome of this struggle. So did the Anglo-Irish relationship under all its aspects. Late in July the attempted assassination of a landlord in the Queen's County prompted the paper to declare that the disestablishment measure must be carried. 'The gravest results may well be apprehended from even its temporary postponement, and heavy, indeed, is the responsibility that lies on those who still have the power of rescuing it from delay.'[79] The appeal was an echo of that recently made in the House of Commons by John Walter.[80]

When the Irish Church bill was safely passed, *The Times* impressed it upon readers that an even graver legislative matter lay immediately ahead: 'A more difficult task has never been undertaken by any Government...The mere facts of Irish tenure are so distorted, as repeated from witness to witness, that the utmost patience is often baffled...To settle the Irish Land Question must, in the ears of many, sound as the wildest of promises. It has been the dream of statesman after statesman, yet no one has realized it; for in addition to the combination of qualities the Minister must possess...He must be supported by an intelligent and resolute public opinion.' In securing the disestablishment of the Irish church 'the especial fervour of voluntaryism' had been decisive. There was no such feeling within the Liberal party on the subject of Irish land. The articles by the paper's special correspondent were intended as a fresh attempt to answer the perennial inquiry from Englishmen 'why there should be any Land Reform in Ireland at all'. The long succession of government bills on Irish land was in itself 'a sufficient reply'. On a deeper level, the inescapable truth was that 'while nations differ laws must differ also'. *The Times* was emphatic that 'we do not mean to imply...and we do not in fact believe that it is common for the landlords of Ireland to outrage the proper claims of their tenants.' On the other hand the paper made a still guarded but now definitive admission which laid down one of the guidelines of its policy on the land question in 1869–70: 'If it is found as a matter of fact that there is a proportion of Irish landlords – although the proportion may be so small that their joint acreage may be even comparatively contemptible – habitually disregarding laws which on any principle of justice must be admitted to be rightly put forward by their tenants, a case for the intervention of the Legislature, by way of stricter definition of mutual rights, is established.'

This simply meant that a man like Scully could not be allowed to inflame the hostility to landlords which existed in Ireland quite independently of any oppression by members of his class. *The Times* had not weakened in 'the most unqualified belief that in the highest development of our social organization the relations between landlord and tenant must be determined by free contract...' The forthcoming legislation should have that freedom as its ultimate goal, and legislative interference on behalf of the Irish tenant should not foster 'the injurious notion that he and the soil he cultivates are indissolubly connected'.[81] These remarks were underlined by the following leader in the same issue. There *The Times* commented on a speech delivered by Lord Stanley in Lancashire two days previously, in which he had aired a favourite theme, the fatal unwisdom of trying to diffuse small holdings.[82] Like Stanley, the leading article made no direct reference to Ireland, but it warmly welcomed the speech 'at a moment when land questions threaten to become the most urgent of the hour. Whatever we do, we ought not to move in a retrograde direction, or encourage desires which...are simply barbarous. The man is not happy, "whose wish and care a few paternal acres bound", and a nation "that is content to breathe its native air" is content with stagnation.'[83]

Taken together, the two leading articles of 13 August depict the fundamental attitude of the paper, with its evident anxiety to see the *status quo* upheld while conceding that some appreciable degree of land reform had now become unavoidable in Ireland only. In his letter of 8 August to Delane, quoted above, about the beginning of O'Connor Morris's series, John Walter had written: 'We must not expect to satisfy the Irish; but if we can succeed in applying English principles of justice, as between landlord and tenant, to this case, we shall have done enough to satisfy ourselves, and all reasonable people.'[84] This was the primary concern of most Englishmen well placed to influence policy on Irish land: to prevent or at least to keep within bounds the sympathetic reaction to Irish agitation that was a disturbing prospect in Britain. The proprietor and editor of *The Times* were trying to arrive at a formula to encompass simultaneously these conflicting aims: to safeguard landlord rights in one part of the United Kingdom and to justify their partial sacrifice in another. This was the whole policy of the newspaper for the next six months.

FOREIGN AND IMPERIAL EXAMPLE

Gladstone's letter of 22 May to Bright confirmed that he understood the relative importance of his Church bill and the as yet problematical land bill. On 3 June, when in sight of victory on the former, he observed to his old acquaintance, Manning, the Catholic Archbishop of Westminster, that the Commons had behaved in a most encouraging fashion: 'The House has moved like an army, and an army where every private is his own general. Such a house will be well calculated to face the land question for which we must lay our first parallel the moment we are out of the Church.'[85] These are extremely revealing comments, especially the military metaphor. An Irish land bill which vindicated the language of his more significant public references to the subject needed to be undertaken with the forethought and thoroughness of a properly conducted siege. To pursue the metaphor, the prime minister started what may be likened to siege operations against the fastnesses of prejudice which existed in his cabinet. If the cabinet could be won over then the Parliamentary Liberal party might mutter unhappily but would in all probability follow the leadership, as it had just done in the case of the Church bill. Not that he was inclined to underestimate the risks of a cabinet split and a backbench rebellion: he proceeded with marked caution, and at one point seems to have hesitated. He did not again seek to influence public opinion directly, but left the Parliamentary statements mentioned earlier in the chapter to do their work. Accordingly, he refused to let himself be drawn by Disraeli when the latter accused the ministry, in the course of the Church bill's third reading on 31 May, of proposing to adopt 'Socialism' for their Irish policy and of having diffused 'the impression that a great revolution is about to take place in the tenure of land'.[86] The previous section dealt, and the next section will deal further, with the press as the reflector and the manipulator of public opinion. This section is devoted to what was happening in private, inside the government.

The evidence for its deliberations during these months is exasperatingly thin, but the cabinet took Irish land at meetings in July and August. The decision was reached, apparently unopposed, to embark on drawing up a land bill in the autumn, without any attempt being made before then to define the scope of the measure. While the affirmative decision was a distinct gain for Gladstone, in the light of the consistently sceptical attitude manifested by Lowe and widely shared among the Liberals in both Houses, it should be stressed that nothing at all had been settled as to the bill's provisions. It was, however, agreed to institute an inquiry by British diplomatic and consular representatives into the law and practice of landholding abroad. Where the idea of the inquiry originated is not clear. In his letter of 21 May to the prime minister Bright had wanted someone reliable sent to report on 'the great *land reformation*...effected, and... now in progress' in Prussia.[87] Gladstone put no obstacle in the way of a renewed attempt to direct the government's attention to the advantages of promoting the small-scale ownership of land. His jottings for the cabinet of 31 July contain the note: 'Bright's suggestion: mission resp[ecting] land abroad. Fortescue to inquire.'[88] In fact, the Foreign Office circular of 26 August covered much more than the familiar controversy which Bright hoped would be determined in his sense by the answers to the relevant questions for him. They were accompanied by more significant questions.

The tenor and purpose of the inquiry were clearly indicated by its preamble. The questionnaire was divided into two sections, 'Small Proprietors', and 'Tenants and Sub-Tenants under Landlords'. In particular, detailed information was to be supplied 'as to the limitation in other countries of proprietary rights, as they exist in Ireland – whether the granting of leases and compensation for improvement have been enforced by legislation; how far, if at all the positive law is modified by custom; and... such custom is recognized by the Law Courts; and what are the precise relations between Landlords and Tenants, and their mutual Rights and Duties.' Under the innocuous subheading 'Miscellaneous' these pregnant questions rounded off the inquiry:

'Are there any tenures resembling the copyholds of England, in which the rent or services have become, *or are becoming*, fixed by custom, and [the] tenant irremovable? What is their nature and mode of growth?'[89] Clarendon certainly approved of the circular for which he was, of course, the minister responsible. The preamble and the second section of the questionnaire suggested that a far-reaching Irish land bill was in contemplation. How could he accept an inquiry in such terms when he thought that Clanricarde's anodyne measure went quite far enough?[90] The answer falls into two parts. Firstly, Clarendon surely anticipated the response to the circular, which was predominantly unfavourable to any extensive interference with property-rights. Secondly, it seems clear that the important concluding questions were added by Gladstone's wish.

Replies from the officials abroad came in slowly. The earliest were not available to the cabinet until after it had begun to deliberate in earnest upon the provisions of the Irish bill, and after Gladstone, having drawn up differing outlines of the legislation, had come down in favour of one type of solution. No reference has been found to these Foreign Office reports in the abundantly documented discussions which absorbed members of the cabinet, collectively and severally, between October 1869 and January 1870; and when laid before Parliament following the introduction of the land bill they met with little notice from M.P.s, although some reference was made to them in the press. The evidence amassed in the reports was irrelevant to the problems with which cabinet and Parliament had to wrestle: the example of continental Europe and of the United States pointed either to maintaining unfettered freedom of contract, or to change of a nature which government and the Houses rejected out of hand, and which, moreover, had been realized in a legal and social context quite different from that of Ireland.

These conclusions were predictable, given the facts of tenure overseas and, one might add, the sympathies of those who wrote the reports, drawn as they mostly were from landed families. Yet Gladstone had not lost by agreeing to the inquiry: as a result of its terms he had succeeded in widening the scope of the discussion when the cabinet got down to considering Irish land. That this was his intention seems to be shown by his letter of 25 August to Fortescue, who had gone over and amended the questions asked. 'I agree with you about the F.O. circular,' he wrote, 'and I think you have made a great improvement. One thing I should yet a little desire, that some cognizance should be taken of those who are neither tenants in one sense nor proprietors: but who have holdings more in the nature of those which gradually grow into copyhold.'[91] Hence, evidently, the addition of those significant questions at the very end of the circular under the misleading heading 'Miscellaneous'.

When and how did Gladstone grasp the significance of tenancies like those under Ulster custom which could be viewed as being in the process of becoming copyholds? The first reference to them in his correspondence comes in a letter of 7 August 1869 to Granville. He there referred to the Earl of Portsmouth, with whom, he said in passing, 'I have had heretofore the real pleasure of communicating about Irish land, and I hope before our measure has been passed to enjoy that advantage again.'[92] The rules of the Portsmouth estates in Co. Wexford incorporated the custom in a form as comprehensive as that generally allowed on many estates in Ulster. This was the most remarkable feature of Lord Portsmouth's Irish estates; and it is a reasonable deduction that he told Gladstone about the custom, and explained the satisfaction which in his case both landlord and tenant derived from its operation subject to certain restrictions. Sir John Gray had, of course, publicized the extension of Ulster tenant-right as satisfying the Irish people. Portsmouth was shortly to advertise in a letter in *The Times* the mutual contentment on his Wexford property and the practice in respect of tenant-right to which he gave the credit for those feelings.[93] Moreover, in October the Earl was recommending tenant-right as he knew it to Lord Granville, and was certainly consulted by Gladstone on the subject afterwards.[94]

It was neither Portsmouth nor Gray, however, who persuaded Gladstone that custom was feasible as a basis for the land bill. That was the achievement of a pamphlet printed for private circulation at the beginning of the summer. The author was an Indian administrator and judge, George Campbell, just returned from the first of two visits to Ireland, and it was put into Gladstone's hands by the eminent civil servant, Sir Charles Trevelyan, who had begun and ended his official career in the subcontinent.[95] Campbell utilized his Indian experience of customary tenures and the notions underlying them, which were quite alien to the

Anglo-Saxon mind, and the re-examination of the familiar parallel between Ireland and India displayed a novel insight. His approach to the problem deserved the encomium, 'singularly able and ingenious', bestowed by a competent authority, O'Connor Morris, on the short treatise of which this pamphlet formed the first part.[96] While everyone with more than a superficial understanding of the Irish land question knew that the importance of custom was not confined to Ulster, it is Campbell's peculiar distinction, not simply to have publicized the fact in Britain, but to have laid bare its implications to those who had so obstinately seen in the perennial discontent only what they wished to see. He demonstrated that the Irish peasants' alarming behaviour was as much the expression of right as were the statutes and rulings of Parliament and the Courts. In advocating the literal imitation of Indian land settlements, Mill and others had dwelt on the economic and social arguments and the political benefits to be anticipated and, save for incidental references, had not gone further into the popular basis of either the settlements or the demands which the application of their principles to Ireland was to meet. Campbell went behind the legislation and showed how it rested on customs which the British found to be, like Irish tenant-right, integral to the *mores* of the natives and consequently did their best to translate into colonial law with fairness to all interested parties – government, the local equivalents of landlords, and European planters in addition to the ryots themselves. He thus illustrated a point that Mill had made but failed to expound the year before: a truly conservative policy in Ireland involved recognizing the force and virtuousness of the peasantry's historic sentiments towards the land. Campbell succeeded where Mill failed: he presented the Indian solution in a way that brought it into British politics as a serious proposition. He thought Mill's plan a desirable but unattainable aim.

Campbell recommended setting up a commission and under it 'simple courts, with an untechnical procedure...power to do justice between man and man on the general principles of equity and good conscience as interpreted by the customs of the country'. On the one hand, he believed, 'this would practically lead to something like fixity of tenure in a large number of holdings.' On the other, he argued that the landlords would retain a greater freedom and influence for good than under fixity of tenure *tout court*: 'Well-managed and peaceful estates would be managed as they now are; badly managed estates would be brought under a certain public control.' Control should extend to the power of eviction and of increasing rent. That was to begin with: he looked to see Irish holdings turned into 'well-established peasant properties...copyholds in fact' over a period of years, as the upshot of rule of thumb judgments handed down by the commission and its tribunals in the light of their very general directions. He ended with a renewed plea that contained a telling observation about the policy affirmed in Deasy's Act: 'If anything effectual is to be done for the mass of the land-holding people...Whatever is really held by "tenure" should be regulated by the customary law – what is held by genuine contract only should be regulated by contract law – one holding should not be falsely disguised in the garb of another.'[97]

Gladstone did not have to learn from this pamphlet that the mood of the Irish peasantry, in the aftermath of Ballycohey, was formidable. He learnt of a possible approach to legislating, one that was not virtually assured of failure – like fixity of tenure as such, because the latter, in Campbell's words, 'is more than the landlords would accede to, or the Houses of Parliament, in which landlord and capitalist influence is still so strong, would be likely to grant'.[98] If Gladstone had heard from Lord Portsmouth the advantages of permitting the full custom of tenant-right, he got from Campbell what shortly became the *idée mère* of his memoranda and exchanges about Irish land. Campbell wrote as a disciple of Mill, and one who had stood for a Scottish county in 1868 as a 'good radical'.[99] Gladstone did not share those sympathies: but his troubled conscience where Ireland was concerned made him extremely susceptible to the case that Campbell made for the Irish tenant. For that case did not depend on the application of Mill's teaching, although influenced by it. Campbell saw the Irish land question as essentially the conflict between 'two sets of laws – the English laws, and the laws or customs of the country, which, enforced in a different way, are as active and effective. In the clashing of the two systems lies the whole difficulty'.[100] Campbell further explained that the Irish 'laws or customs' were the modern form of Celtic tenure superficially abolished by the English law many generations previously. The affray at Ballycohey, which had made such a marked impression on Gladstone

106

at the time, was not only what he had seen in it – the desperate reaction of poor men to outrageous abuse of legal rights – but at a deeper level 'a simple and clear issue between the law on the one side and the custom of the country on the other'.[101]

Campbell might be an 'Indian radical' – so the Duke of Argyll dubbed him.[102] The interpretation of the Irish land question in his pamphlet and the means of solving it there adumbrated, were, or were susceptible of being presented as, quite compatible with a standpoint that was the opposite of radical. This aspect of Campbell's plea that the small farmers of Ireland, like Indian ryots, should be treated according to indigenous ideas of justice and not according to those of Englishmen was omitted from the pamphlet and its sequel in October, but Gladstone saw and developed the implicit argument. His imagination was captured by the vision of the 'historical and traditional rights' of the Irish peasantry: so he described them in a very full statement of his views composed when the cabinet discussions on Irish land came to a head. In the same memorandum he emphasized that those who wanted to preserve the rights of property in this country should not refuse to recognize similar claims on the part of the Irish tenantry which were largely justified by moral and historical considerations left out of account under the existing law. He tried to turn his opponents' most powerful arguments against them, by representing that they, not he, were lacking in respect for property, and that his proposals were essentially conservative.[103] There, for Gladstone, lay the value of Campbell's approach to Irish land. Gladstone's confidant and biographer, John Morley, acknowledged long afterwards – privately, not in the official *Life* – that 'a little book by...George Campbell... on Indian tenure as applied to Ireland...first inspired the thought underlying the Irish Land Act of 1870.'[104]

Gladstone was already convinced in a general way that the Irish peasantry were the victims of landlord oppression: it was now revealed to him what that oppression chiefly signified – the attempt to erase or ignore the tenacious popular ideas of right as to the land. Nevertheless, he was at first inclined to doubt whether Campbell's plan was feasible in terms of British problems. He told Trevelyan in the middle of August that he had read 'Mr Campbell's very able paper' and commented: 'Its effect is on the whole disheartening: but nothing can be more desirable than to know the worst of every question and I believe a vein of truth runs thro' the pages of this pamphlet.' At the same time, he asked Trevelyan to procure a copy for Granville.[105] A fortnight later, as was noticed above, he suggested to Fortescue the insertion of those significant concluding questions in the Foreign Office circular on agrarian legislation: questions which were an echo of Campbell, who had argued that the Irish tenant was well advanced under custom towards being the copyholder he would become with the operation of the plan described in the pamphlet. The more he thought about it, the more Gladstone was drawn to Campbell's solution: there is an acknowledgment of this at the start in a letter written the day before that to Fortescue. John Lambert, a well-known civil servant, who enjoyed the prime minister's confidence, was going to Ireland, and Gladstone asked him 'to look as much as you can at the question of Irish land'. He sent Lambert his annotated copy of Campbell's pamphlet with the comment that it 'seems to open up many of the sources of difficulty'.[106]

First among 'the sources of difficulty' on which Gladstone's mind was running, was the attitude of the Liberal party in the Commons, which in time was to be conditioned by its reading of public opinion. On 12 August he referred thoughtfully to these preoccupations in a letter to the Speaker, J. E. Denison: 'It is I suppose a matter of speculation how much of the credit which the household suffrage Parliament has earned should be set down to its own qualities in their average state, and how much to the definite character of the chief work it has been engaged upon, and the thorough comprehension of that work by the country. It will become difficult for the majority to hold together on the question of the Irish land but I hope we may frame a measure which will satisfy reasonable men.'[107] Denison had many friends in the Liberal party, especially among Whigs, and Gladstone was clearly inviting understanding and sounding him out.

Gladstone now watched the press attentively, for signs favourable to the land bill that was beginning to take shape in his mind. He well knew, as his letter to Denison indicates, that the Commons would be influenced by the trend of opinion as it appeared in the newspapers. On their side, the leading papers were, by the end of August, discussing the principles of the expected land bill constructively in response to the spreading belief that the most powerful ministry ever known was preparing to follow Irish disestablishment with a measure of comparable significance on the land question. This was in keeping with the practice of the weightier journals, which tended to echo the hopes and fears of the politicians rather than to shape them. Both politicians and press were worried about the reaction of Gladstone and Bright, committed as they to some extent were by their warm and vague declarations, to growing public agitation and violence in Ireland. If both politicians and press were coming to think that something fairly radical must be done about Irish land, they thought in terms that were still negative at bottom, of giving so much in order to avoid worse. They wanted to contain not only the Irish but also those ministers whose propensity to overdo reform was a source of anxiety. The danger apprehended was always that to landed property generally; Irish land could not be isolated from British concerns.

THE MOVEMENT OF THE PRESS

The line followed by *The Times* in 1869 down to the end of August has been described. The paper changed its tactics to meet the situation created by the emerging probability that the government intended a more ambitious land bill than any previous ministerial effort. Other journals did not all start from the same position as *The Times* early in the year, but they were arriving at similar conclusions by August. In this general movement, some conservative papers outdistanced all but the most advanced liberal organs: which seemed to heighten the impression that a fundamental revision of social verities was in train.

The *Daily News*, as before, sounded more critical of landlords, and their political friends, than it really was. In April an editorial on Clanricarde's bill warmly defended the government's refusal to announce a policy, explaining: 'They could not define their precise attitude...without sketching the larger scheme which they contemplate.'[108] The *Daily News* had its own conception of a 'larger scheme'. Instead of 'experiments' like the schemes of Bright and Mill, it suggested, 'much might be done by simply applying to the soil the principles of free trade.'[109] Such automatic resort to its brand of conventional wisdom shows how little this paper envisaged the nature of the legislation that was to be introduced within twelve months. Following the speeches of 30 April in the Commons, the realization dawned that, to quote the first leader in the issue of 3 May, 'a superficial solution would be no solution at all'.[110] Fixity of tenure was specifically mentioned as almost unthinkable because impossible to reconcile with either political economy or the rights of property. The alternative favoured seemed to be Bright's scheme, the attractions of which were now more prominent. Russell's attack on Bright moved the *Daily News* to observe pertinently: 'The country has suffered some inconvenience from not considering Mr Bright's schemes in time...The Irish Church would...be thankful for the terms which Mr Bright proposed more than a dozen years ago, and not a few Conservative peers would have preferred to have advanced towards household suffrage in two steps within a quarter of a century to following Lord Derby in his leap in the dark.'[111] The first leader in the paper of 24 August implicitly acknowledged that it was no longer possible to evade the issues raised by Irish land to the extent that Bright's scheme did so. Instead, this editorial argued, those issues should be seen in perspective, and treated pragmatically, although it was admitted that 'the great court of public opinion' had not decided on Irish land and, moreover, that 'no definite and responsible proposal' had been submitted for consideration by that tribunal. The English land question must not be allowed to impede disposal of the Irish Land Question. To illustrate the difference between the two, the *Daily News* instanced the studious moderation of the newly founded Land Tenure Reform Association with Mill at its head. The intended reassurance could hardly have survived the next few lines: 'Make the Irish tenant secure and content if you can, but do not go far enough to make English tenants feel discontented ...This...argument is not only dangerous – it is self-destructive. The Irish Land Question can never be settled on such terms and the reason for attempting so to settle it might rouse in England the very agitation which is feared.' This supported the conclusion that 'fixity of tenure is the one thing the Irishman needs, whether it be freehold or leasehold matters little.' The reasons so lately adduced against such interference with property and free contract were ignored.[112] The *Daily News* spoke with a certain authority, as a recognized voice of Liberalism, and it was giving a clear lead to the party.

The Liberal *Manchester Guardian* broke a long silence on 31 August to spell out what was involved in the question which its contemporary had thus doubtfully tried both to open up and make safe. 'It seems...to be agreed,' wrote the *Guardian*, 'that ...Irish land...is to be the great topic of the next twelve months, and if so the relations...between those who toil and those who possess the land in other parts of the Kingdom must also come in for consideration. Nothing can be more preposterous than to imagine that grave interests...directly connected with all our ideas of property and private right, and rooted in the very foundations of the social fabric, can be dealt with according to one set of principles in Ireland, and on diametrically opposite principles in England and Scotland...It should be clearly understood that whatever is done...in regard to that right in Ireland will supply a precedent for the adjoining island which we may be sure no time will be lost in transplanting thither.' The *Guardian* looked forward to seeing the influence of English landlords curbed as a result: if Irish landlords were the worse offenders, 'in England ...a despotism prevails very alien to the temper...of the times ...The position which the landowners aspire to hold is altogether a relic of the past, and must be modified.' There was no indication, however, of the form which the restraints upon landlords might take.[113]

In April the *Spectator* had remarked à propos of the government's noble critics in Parliament, 'If Irish landlords are too bigoted to believe in Mr Gladstone, they may at least believe in a House in which the strongest Radicals are also the strongest adherents of the doctrines of [political] economy.' In May this radical journal dared to hope that opinion was shifting. At the end of July it wrote that Gladstone would be careful not to go too far, 'especially when he knows that from the moment the words come out of his mouth retrocession is impossible, except at the price of the reconquest of Ireland; that whatever he says they ought to have, that the Irish, and Scotch, and Welsh tenantry will have, if they have to fight for it.'[114] This special interest in Irish land, particularly as a means of undermining the English social system, had understandably no parallel in *The Economist*, which, on the contrary, all but ignored the question. *The Economist* did not underestimate the potential disturbance of the British political and social equilibrium. It made that absolutely clear a little later, but prior to September the only leading article to make any worthwhile mention of the subject in 1869 adverted not to the government's aims but to Disraeli's. This article, like one of the same day, 31 July, in the *Spectator*, but with more emphasis, expressed the widely held suspicion that Disraeli looked to exploit Liberal disunity when the Parliamentary majority got down to considering the land bill. *The Economist* alleged that Disraeli had helped the Church bill on its way, because there was no gainsaying the verdict of the constituencies and he so freed himself to pursue 'a policy of *divide et impera*', commencing with a measure which no one could claim had been authorized by the voters.[115] Two discerning journals gave contrary indications of conservative thinking; they obviously wanted to find the agreed elements of a land bill. The *Saturday Review* had upheld the government in April when Whig and Tory peers failed to obtain satisfaction with regard to Clanricarde's proposals or any alternative. Subsequent comment maintained the same tone and spoke of 'remedial measures of a moderate and sensible kind', but recognized that the Irish tenantry wanted their land, or at least fixity of tenure. Then on 21 August the first pages of that number were given to a full discussion of the choices posed by Irish land. Bright's scheme, the only method of transferring the land to the natives 'which would not involve downright, wholesale confiscation', was uncertain to work successfully. With one option closed, the only other, 'so far as at present appears', was fixity of tenure. Here it was stressed that 'when we ask whether it would be desirable, we cannot leave out of sight the interests of Great Britain or omit to weigh well the consequences to our whole social system of such an enactment...for although the interests of Ireland are to be studied up to the last possible point, there is a limit beyond which it is impossible to go.' The article was in favour of taking a look at the Continent, India and, closely, Ireland herself, to assess the viability, in every way, of fixity of tenure. None the less, the *Saturday* concluded by avowing its predilection for the existing land law under which – by universal consent, it supposed – Ireland had made 'vast strides towards prosperity' over a generation. The onus of proof rested on those who inclined to a different order of things.[116]

Another conservative voice spoke out sooner and less ambiguously than the *Saturday Review*. On 23 August the *Freeman's Journal* observed that applying the Indian model of tenure to

Ireland 'has obtained the powerful advocacy of the *Pall Mall Gazette*'.[117] The *Pall Mall* had shown itself prepared to revise conventional judgments with expressive suddenness. When Clanricarde's bill focused attention on Irish land again after some months, the paper wished compulsory and retrospective compensation for improvements to be included, which was new on its part, but did not move forward from that point until August. Bright and Gladstone were taken to task for their dangerously misleading language: the tenants could not possibly receive what they coveted from government and Parliament, and ministers should say so. These articles gave no hint of compromise: 'The tenants, in plain English, want the land to be confiscated for their benefit...Phrases about "fixity of tenure" protection against "undue", or "arbitrary" power of raising the rent, and others of the same sort...are only soft phrases which...mean that a part of that which the law at present gives to the landlord should be taken from him and given to the tenant.' On 4 August the first leader struck an altered note. The *Pall Mall* was now willing to recognize the custom of tenant-right more or less for what it was, besides supporting compensation for improvements. Forsaking empirical arguments advanced the previous year against the lessons of Indian experience, the paper referred to their practical value in defining tenant-right where that was to be found. The reply to 'the great question of all', whether or not to do away with the landlord's power of eviction, treated it as to all intents an open one: 'To decide...against the landlords would involve nothing less than an attempt to redistribute property in general...to decide...absolutely against the tenants...has its own dangers.'[118] When nearly a fortnight had passed, the paper published the first of two articles entitled 'Ireland and India'. The position of Irish and Indian tenants was legally and historically quite different; Irish landlords were entirely within their rights when acting in a manner which rendered them liable to assassination by an implacably opposed peasantry. 'If, however, we suppose that Parliament should determine to enforce a compromise much might be learnt from Indian legislation as to the sort of terms which might be imposed upon the parties.' Promising to return to the subject, the *Pall Mall* explained that Indian methods of valuing rent were 'well worthy of consideration with reference to Ireland': but permanent occupancy-right was implicitly ruled

113

out. The second article, appearing on 18 August, confirmed the suggestion that the state should intervene to fix rents, without granting perpetuity of tenure. The validity of the peasantry's hereditary claims was 'mere antiquarianism or speculation misplaced'. Fixing rents was 'no doubt...interfering with the rights of property; but the misfortune of the whole matter is that it will be impossible to settle the Irish question without a certain... interference with these rights, and the question really is in what form interference would be least offensive and injurious.' What the *Pall Mall Gazette* was trying to lay down was 'the sort of direction which...legislation might take without involving any ...attack upon the general security of property'.[119]

The *Saturday Review* and the *Pall Mall*, like the *Daily News*, arrived quite suddenly at a new outlook upon the Irish land question, and this took place in August. The timing is significant. Gladstone had carried the Irish Church bill and ridden down the opposition of the Lords. The July number of the *Quarterly Review* was repeating the stock criticisms of his handling to date of the land question and predicting his failure to settle it, and the leading Conservative daily, the *Standard*, refrained from following the *Pall Mall* and the *Saturday*.[120] The latter journals, less orthodox though they were in general, did typify the pretty thorough readjustment which many Conservatives were rapidly making to their idea of what it was right and advisable to do when landed property was at stake. In September the Liberal pamphleteer and clerical admirer of Gladstone, the Rev. Malcolm MacColl, summed up what had happened to the rival party in a letter to him from a house party at the seat of a Scottish Conservative, Alexander Baillie-Cochrane: 'The house is full...principally Tories, and I have been interested to hear their views on the Government Land Bill. The prevailing opinion is that your Bill will be liberal, but wise. It is wonderful what a conversion the... Church Bill has already wrought among the Tories. It has lifted them forward a whole generation.'[121]

THE PROGRESS OF A WAITING GAME

It was not merely Conservatives who, as a result of the Irish Church bill, underwent the experience of which MacColl wrote. The first nine months of the Gladstone administration were decisive for the Liberal party when it turned to Irish land. That, as his letters to Archbishop Manning and Speaker Denison plainly show, was Gladstone's hope. If he does not seem to have had a clear picture of the agrarian reform on which he was going to embark when the omens were propitious, his letter of January to Argyll reinforces the very strong impression conveyed by his speech at Liverpool the previous October and the ensuing correspondence with the Duke, that he intended to offer the Irish tenants not just compensation for improvements but some form of protection against the likes of Scully. In April he manifested such determination not to be pinned down to a premature declaration of policy that expectations were inevitably heightened on one side and apprehensions on the other. These reactions were powerfully stimulated by Bright's impetuous reaffirmation of faith in *his* plan. Gladstone benefited all round from his colleague's blunder. Firstly, he was able to put Bright in his place, namely still in the cabinet, where Gladstone badly needed him, but submissive to the restraints of collective responsibility. Secondly, Gladstone was given the opportunity to exclude the adoption on a large scale of a plan which he disliked on several counts and believed was unlikely to satisfy the Irish tenants if carried into effect with such fairness to the landlords as Bright desired. Thirdly, it looks as if only after Bright had made his declaration in Parliament and followed it up by pressing the necessity of legislation on Gladstone and other colleagues, was the cabinet prepared to undertake a commitment to *try* and frame an Irish land bill. To have that decision taken on Bright's account as much as on his own suited Gladstone very well politically.

Gladstone and Bright were helped, not hindered, by the uneasiness of landed men, British and Irish, about the deteriorating situation in Ireland and the impact which legislation, especially if belated and ill-considered, might have on the position of their class in Britain. Pressure now came strongly from this quarter where it was hoped that a land bill of calculated moderation would avert the dangers that threatened. The question was, how moderate should the unavoidable measure be. Old opponents of any genuine compromise, like Dufferin and John Walter, watching all the signs within and without the Liberal ministry and party, thought it best, in a spirit of realism, to consider how the limits of previous government bills might be exceeded with least cost to the landlords. Influential journals caught up the politicians with a rush when the Lords gave way over the Irish Church, and Gladstone was well placed to realize whatever his public and private statements added up to. He was perfectly well aware of the formidable difficulties he still faced. Hence the increasing value he attached to Campbell's perspective of Irish land, a novelty to him as to most Englishmen. All in all, however, the prime minister was justified in the thinly disguised satisfaction he was to indicate with the progress of opinion during the late summer – progress that vindicated, and surely was partly contrived by, his tactics.

When in September the philanthropist Edward Denison, nephew of the Speaker and a Liberal M.P. whose social conscience weighed more heavily with him than party or class, set down his hopes of the Irish land bill as a factor in English politics, he was describing exactly what so many of the people he knew dreaded. 'The flower of our workmen,' he wrote, were emigrating from Britain where 'the whole structure, industrial, as well as political, is ingeniously framed to keep the bulk of the people in a state of serfage...This Irish Land Bill is a good lever; it is stirring the dregs. Ireland is not the only country where there is land. Interfere but by a finger with the legal rights of the Irish landlord, and you show the British Philistine that his idol, "Property" is a fiction and a nonentity: that it is the creature of political expediency.'[122]

4

FIRST THOUGHTS AND
REACTIONS IN THE CABINET,
SEPTEMBER AND OCTOBER

INITIATIVE AND RESTRAINT

'This Irish Land Bill is a good lever...Interfere...with...the Irish landlord, and you show...that..."Property" is...the creature of political expediency'[1] – these words of a Liberal M.P., deeply sensitive to the social ills which afflicted England, evoke the atmosphere of September 1869 when the rumour circulated that the government had been converted to fixity of tenure. The truth did not emerge in Gladstone's lifetime, nor for a couple of generations afterwards: that not the government but the prime minister had drafted the outline of legislation intended to make the Irish tenant all but irremovable and to fix his rent. This chapter examines the secret document in which Gladstone first detailed the provisions he hoped to see in the land bill.

These proposals were stillborn. Despite the continuing onward movement of opinion in the press, it was sufficient for certain members of the cabinet to declare both in confidence and publicly that there could be no capitulation to Irish demands, for the price, it was broadly hinted, would be the dissolution of the ministry. None of these colleagues, it seems, knew of the secret memorandum and its startling contents: but they were understandably alarmed in view of the newspaper speculation, the unmistakable hints which Gladstone dropped in his correspondence, and their acquaintance with the working of the man's mind when a popular cause enjoyed his sympathy. They rightly thought that he needed to be restrained.

Finally, the chapter investigates the relationship between Gladstone and Chichester Fortescue with regard to the credit inside the government for originating serious consideration of a novel land bill. The prime minister – not the Irish secretary, as is sometimes said – took charge of the enterprise from the beginning; he did not fail to consult with the tenants' leaders, and he was throughout the main source of inspiration. This was particularly the case when they started their consultations in September. Gladstone was not indebted to Fortescue either for the initial plan which he felt compelled to drop or for the alternative that attracted him, the approach to investing the tenantry with a species of proprietary right which was unfolded in Campbell's pamphlet.

Lord Clarendon had taken his gout to a Central European spa in late August, and on 4 September introduced Irish land into his correspondence with the prime minister. Mentioning his concern at the 'poison' being disseminated by Irish newspapers, he added bluntly: 'Legislation to some extent may be necessary for enforcing the duties of property, but if its rights are not steadily upheld it will in my opinion go hard with your Government next Session.'[2] This set the tone of the exchanges between the two men during the next few weeks. In replying, and subsequently, Gladstone was at pains to eschew the vigorous language of his colleague; he took as his theme, not the rights and wrongs but the evolving political realities of the question, both in Britain and Ireland, and intimated that pragmatism should dictate their attitude. Seemingly quite impressed, Clarendon was much disturbed, especially to learn that Gladstone had not discouraged an overture from Sir John Gray and was inclined to favour the legalization and extension of tenant-right. Clarendon communicated his alarm to other members of the government, and the prime minister was warned of the fact by the chief whip, Glyn.

Gladstone answered Clarendon's letter of 4 September at length on the 7th: 'The Irish Land question,' he informed him, 'appears to me to be assuming formidable proportions and to have altered its aspect a good deal since you left England.' He believed he could detect a shift in the comments of *The Times* and its itinerant special correspondent in Ireland, and Bright, who had sent Lord Bessborough a very satisfactory assurance of the moderation of his views on the land question, was 'now afraid lest the subject should have outgrown them'. Gladstone had heard that the Dublin Conservative newspapers were, for the most part, supporting 'large measures, such as giving the force of law to the custom of tenant-right and making it universal', which was openly recommended by the Earl of Granard, a great Irish land-owner. There followed a paragraph that possibly exceeded Claren-don's worst fears: 'I certainly had thought two months ago that the elements were shaping themselves in such a way as to present the subject hopefully. I do not at present feel by any means so sure. Sir John Gray has written to assure me that he is only "going for" the tenant right custom. In my reply, without committing myself, I have asked him in what method and form he proposes to give to that custom the force of law? A question to which I await his reply with curiosity.' In the circumstances, he felt the cabinet should assemble earlier than usual in the autumn.[3] Gladstone's cool announcement that he had invited Gray to explain precisely how he would implement a revolutionary plan implied that Clarendon was liable to find himself politically isolated. To the hint of a crisis for the government if it did not behave according to Whig tradition, he returned the hint of a crisis for those who might try to stand in his way.

Clarendon answered on the 11th: he was 'unfeignedly glad' to hear that the cabinet was going to meet earlier than had been thought necessary, and continued: 'The land question has doubt-less altered its aspect since I left England, but not...to cause me the least surprise, for I did not share your opinion that the elements were shaping themselves...hopefully – I knew all along that the Agitators, the Priests, and the National Press were going for Socialism in its most dangerous form and they are now throwing off the mask.' The Dublin Tory papers were surely inspired by 'the hope of alluring [sic] the Government into a pitfall'. He dismissed Lord Granard, a Catholic proselyte, as a '"booby"...a convert of the blindest order...does nothing now but at the dictation of some priest'.[4] He would like to ask Gray *why* Ulster tenant-right should be extended, which was equivalent to giving tenants in the three provinces half the purchase of the land. What troubled Clarendon most was the firm belief that the treatment of landed property in Britain and Ireland could not be dissociated, and he laid great stress on the peril he foresaw: 'Not agitators alone but successive Governments,' he observed sharply, 'have so long sought to glean popularity off...this question that great measures are...looked for with certainty, but there can be no great measures if the *just* rights of property are to be respected and if they are to be dealt with nonetheless the process cannot be limited to Ireland.' Nothing was needed except compensation for improvements and the enforcement of written contracts – 'If we are to go further it will be necessary to prove that the Irish Tenant has other rights and claims than English and Scottish Tenants, and that Irish Landlords can be despoiled with more impunity than their fellows in England and Scotland.'[5]

Gladstone declined to take umbrage at Clarendon's outspokenness, and kept pressing on his notice selective evidence of a changing climate of opinion. 'You know much of Ireland and I know little and I feel it to be an assumption if I add or take from what you say,' replied Gladstone soothingly on the 14th. 'But I think that perhaps you have hardly been able to follow the events of the last few weeks. Before deciding that there is nothing in them pray read Mr Fitzgibbon's "Land Difficulty of Ireland".'[6] Fitzgibbon was an Irish Tory lawyer who resignedly counselled the statutory grant of long leases, contingent upon the tenants' improving their land. The following day he wrote again to Clarendon, sending cuttings from the Tory *Irish Times*; then on the 16th he drew his attention to the Earl of Erne's declaration to his tenantry that he was well satisfied with the operation of tenant-right on his Ulster estates;[7] and on the 22nd came the advice: 'If you want more signs about Irish land – signs which I admit are of little significance except in combination – observe the elbow-room the *Times* is giving itself: a very "wide berth" indeed.'[8] Clarendon was unimpressed by any of it, remarking on the 19th that he had to face a much worse agitation than the present in 1847. He made three points in letters of the 21st and 24th. 'The agitators,' he said, '...are illogical – they argue from a particular case to a general rule, they dress up a case in hideous colors [sic] which may or may not be true or...have extenuating circumstances, and then leave it to be inferred that all tenants are similarly oppressed, and all landlords...equally inclined to be oppressors.' Secondly, while 'gross injustice' to tenants no doubt occurred, it happened far less frequently than twenty years ago. As for Lord Erne, his statement – 'just what I expected from a benevolent Northern Landlord' – did not remove the objections to legalizing the custom, still less to extending it.[9]

On 23 September Lord Granville, who had not had anything to

say about Irish land to Gladstone since his very limited suggestions in May, told him that Clarendon really wanted Clanricarde's bill 'and nothing more – and...he has talked so loudly in that sense, that any other course is difficult for him'.[10] The day before Glyn had written to inform the prime minister that Clarendon had been telling Fortescue's politically interfering wife, Lady Waldegrave 'that the land question would upset the Government', and the chief whip, who did not regard her as a good witness, yet feared that the foreign secretary was genuinely alarmed.[11] Undeterred by these revelations, Gladstone proceeded to clarify the intention which he had hitherto hinted. On the 24th Gladstone had sent him Gray's response to the inquiry as to what legalizing and extending custom would mean in practical terms, with the comment, 'Does it not make the landlord a tithe commutator?'[12] Nor was this the first indication Gladstone had given that he found Gray unhelpful. On 7 September Gray had called for naked fixity of tenure in a speech at Skibbereen which Clarendon mentioned to Gladstone as confirmation of what he had just written in his candid letter of the 11th, and extracted an acknowledgment that the speech was 'most mischievous and outrageous'.[13] Yet on the 25th, Gladstone wrote: 'The Ulster tenant right is doubtless very imperfect, yet probably the best thing would be to legalize and extend it, if only this were possible. I have puzzled and puzzled over it and cannot for the life of me see how it is to be legalized without being essentially changed. It is like trying in Algebra to solve a problem of two unknown quantities with only one equation.'[14] This meant: Gray's solution was deemed the best in principle, but it was unacceptable if in practice it worked as that veteran advocate of tenant-right desired.

Where the custom was strongest, it was still extra-legal and, moreover, the product of organic and largely unrecorded growth: as a result, and especially if landlords and tenantry were not separated by race and religion, the former possessed an influence which it was improbable that they would have to anything like the same degree once their powers had been delimited and circumscribed by statute. There was, however, the possibility suggested by Campbell: enforce the custom quite simply by erecting courts charged to do justice in accordance with the accepted rules of equity. This would obviate the necessity of defining the custom in an Act of Parliament; establish 'something like fixity of tenure', as Campbell put it;[15] and leave the landlords with rather more of their old authority and prestige because subject to less explicit restrictions. Gladstone's dilemma was that the advantages of Campbell's plan made it suspect to those for whom Gray spoke: 'something like fixity of tenure' was too indeterminate; Gray had said so, in effect, at Skibbereen.

Clarendon could not know the extent of Gladstone's reservations about extending tenant-right. Gladstone did not properly know himself. The ex-viceroy was only aware that the prime minister and the detested Gray were in broad agreement. That was enough for Clarendon, whose fears had been inflamed by a highly un-satisfactory conversation with the Irish secretary. On 27 September he related to Granville how he had disturbed Fortescue and his wife by saying that Irish land might break up the government. That ominous remark may well have been provoked by Fortescue, who, Clarendon told Granville, admitted that the draft proposals which he had forwarded to Gladstone went far beyond the Liberal bill of 1866, but was otherwise evasive as to their nature.[16] Clarendon resolved to take a public counter-measure on the occasion of a speech he had to deliver at an agricultural dinner in Hertfordshire on the 28th. His correspondence with Gladstone and others afterwards amply testifies to his indignation at the thoughts about Irish land within the cabinet which had been partially revealed to him. He had not let his audience into these ministerial secrets, but the speech was an endeavour to whip up English feeling against such schemes as those being matured by Gladstone and the Irish secretary.

Clarendon was the only member of the cabinet to remonstrate with Gladstone over Irish land at this early stage, although not the only one to make warning noises in public. He learnt as much as he did because as foreign secretary he was in regular touch with the prime minister, raised the question in their cor-respondence, and persisted with it. He did not know that Gladstone was consulting J. F. Maguire in addition to Gray, and on the same problem of what tenant-right should be understood to imply if adopted by law to regulate tenure throughout Ireland. It is not true that, as J. L. Hammond stated, the Liberal leader neglected to ascertain the view of the tenants' spokesmen.[17]

Gray wrote to Gladstone on 31 August, opening with a reference to their previous consultations over disestablishment. He wanted to push his Irish land scheme and maintained that since the practice of Ulster allowed for 'an occasional increase of rent... if it be based on improved prices and _not_ on the improvements made by the tenant...the landlord is not as is represented by some reduced to the condition of a _rent-charger_'. Give fixity of tenure, he urged, and control the advancement of rent 'so as to render it altogether...based on the increased averages of prices ...and make all Ireland what the agricultural part of Ulster now is – peaceable, loyal, wealthy, and happy'.[18] There was a pertinent objection to these proposals of Gray's: they were not quite consistent with Ulster tenant-right as known.

Gladstone's answer was encouraging and an acknowledgment of Gray's influence: 'I shall truly regret it, if, after our free and cordial co-operation in regard to the Church question, which you did so much to help forward, we should stand reciprocally...in a less happy position, with respect to...Land Tenure.' He then put the questions already mentioned.[19] Gray took his time about them. Meanwhile, he made the speech angrily condemned by Gladstone in his letter of 16 September to Clarendon. He had faith in Gladstone, said Gray at Skibbereen, but the prime minister 'was not an Irishman and did not understand the Irish tenants' case and therefore could not deal with it unless the tenant-farmers told him what they wanted. A long lease did not meet the case: they wanted...fixity in the soil.'[20] Gladstone's wrath is understandable. The unwarranted reflection on his ability to grasp the essence of this Irish grievance must have been annoying, but mattered little. The speech looked like a bid to exploit the vulnerability of a reforming government whose head had just given what amounted to a confidential assurance of its willingness to listen to and its hope of being able to work with Gray. There was an air of political blackmail. When the fuller explanation of his scheme which had been requested of Gray on 2 September eventually arrived, Gladstone's comment to him was, 'it might be held to place the landlord on the footing of a Tithe Commutator? What would be the reply?'[21] There does not seem to have been a reply: obviously, it would not have been very easy to compose. Gladstone's letter amounted to a polite rejection of Gray's claim that extending Ulster tenant-right as he conceived it was to be sharply distinguished from fixity of tenure.

FIRST THOUGHTS AND REACTIONS

At Skibbereen J. F. Maguire, M.P., had been the least insistent of several speakers: he had demanded 'a settlement, not an adjustment of the question', but avowed 'the fullest confidence' in those who had passed the Church bill.[22] He wrote to tell Gladstone of the proceedings, who thanked him for 'renewing my early and full knowledge of them', and added that he was reading Fitzgibbon's pamphlet and found it 'of no small significance'.[23] On 17 September Maguire sent the report of the previous day's conference of the Munster farmers' clubs in Cork, which had acclaimed perpetuity of tenure and official valuation of rent on principles that decidedly favoured the occupier, and agreed on the formation of a National Tenant League. 'Take it from me,' he entreated, 'as a simple, naked truth, that...meeting was in the highest sense...representative...and exposed the feeling of the country – of all save the owner class – as to the measure required, and what would be acceptable. It is nearly impossible to stop agitation. To many it is now a duty – for it is commonly said that if Ireland do not make her demand known to the statesmen and people of England, they will legislate in ignorance of her feelings and wishes.' He asked 'whether it would not be well to delay the final consideration of your measure to the last moment, until the opinion of the country is thoroughly expressed? In that time you will have the *landlords* themselves...putting forward advanced schemes, from which valuable assistance may be obtained. But believe me that the country looks for a large bill and...none other can satisfy.'[24] Maguire's letters provided corroboration of Gray's remarks at Skibbereen which had angered Gladstone. At the Cork conference Maguire had chosen his words carefully and avoided tying himself down to a programme that was still unrealistic. Still – but for how much longer? The advice to Gladstone, to bide his time and keep the options open until the landlords should have made his task easy, was sound, if unnecessary.

Gladstone had a higher regard for Maguire than for Gray, and accordingly went into the problems of legislating with a considerable, though by no means entire, lack of reserve. He began a lengthy answer to Maguire on 20 September by complaining that the report of the Cork conference had not really helped him: 'I find the end in view described by different appellations, which, perhaps for want of knowledge I am not well able to bring into harmony. Sometimes it is security: sometimes it is perpetuity: sometimes it is Ulster tenant-right.' True of the Irish land question a short time before, this observation was really no longer justified. The resolutions of the Cork conference were quite distinct: but Gladstone did not want to discuss them, though he could not avoid indicating why. He was interested in actual tenant-right, to which the letter was mostly devoted. He mentioned the question he had put to Gray, and asked it of Maguire in much more detail and accompanied with reflections on awkward or obscure points. What was 'goodwill'? 'I want a guide and a rule for approving it.' He said that he had never seen it defined as compensation, but sketched how it could be utilized to give an evicted tenant a sum over and above the price of his improvements. Whatever 'goodwill' might be – 'if...a thing fit to be recognized at all, would it not be better to attach to it some definite and certain, though only approximate measure ...of value, than to leave it to be determined by persons who would go to work with a bandage on their eyes, I mean with no uniform practical standard, and with no legislative light or aid?' In other words, were this somewhat puzzling, but very likely convenient, customary payment made law, its size must be regulated, in the landlord's interest.

Gladstone's reluctance to weaken the landlords seriously as a force in Irish life comes out strongly: 'To say that the Landlord's rent shall vary hereafter only according to the prices of produce as determined by a public authority, is not only to alter but, perhaps to destroy the relation between *landlord* and *tenant*, and to declare...that the continuance of that relation is incompatible with justice, and with security to the tenant.' Only days earlier, he had himself drafted proposals for handling the landlords very roughly – and one wonders whether his correspondent ever had an inkling of that – but there is no reason to doubt the genuineness of his social preferences. He found, however, another, more cogent motive for resisting such drastic interference with the rights of property as official valuation of rent. The principle was good for the United Kingdom: 'It is therefore a principle essentially *imperial*: and the position of Ireland might not be very strong in the face of the world, if her agricultural population should commit itself to demanding the adoption of any rule which would fundamentally change the structure of society throughout the rural districts of the three countries...' Clarendon's remonstrances, and other warning signals, had had some effect and Gladstone was conveying this message to the most reasonable of the tenants' leaders.

If fixity of tenure under the name of Ulster tenant-right were therefore to be considered improbable, taking up the custom in something like its present form was not. That was the deduction from the letter. Gladstone thought that Gray, who had not yet replied, might have understood his questions about custom 'as a merely controversial challenge. It was not so meant...I am stating difficulties "without prejudice".' Helpfully summarized, these were the criteria to which he was working: 'I suppose this argument...that all the circumstances determining the relation of landlord and tenant in Ireland, including even the law in its practical application, have been so different from those of the sister island, and that evils, acknowledged...by public authority, have been treated for a quarter of a century with such obstinate neglect that extraordinary measures must now be adopted for... an inveterate mischief. This is a broad proposition. But supposing it to be admitted...[and] it were found necessary to introduce into the law some provisions more restrictive of *liberty of contract* than are in force on this side of the Channel, or in themselves desirable...would there not remain strong arguments in favour of stopping short of any permanent and fundamental change in the landlord's position, perhaps even of inquiring whether a temporary character would be imparted to such of the remedial enactments as could fairly be called exceptional?'[25]

The choice of the tenant-right solution – not Gray's version, but as faithful a copy of the reality as one could get – would not threaten to undermine English society, and would be kinder to Irish landlords than competing plans. Yet Gladstone felt uneasy even about that prospect: hence the suggestion of some other legislation, 'temporary', as recognition of custom could hardly be. This letter to Maguire shows that Gladstone's mind was far from settled, but that he leant ever more towards adapting Ulster custom to the requirements, whatever they might turn out to be exactly, of the land bill. He must have been strengthened in his intention by Fortescue's first outline of the bill, received less than a week earlier. Maguire did not provide some of the answers which Gladstone was seeking until over a fortnight had elapsed. By which time Gladstone knew better still how formidable were the objections to any but a specifically Irish basis for the awaited reform.

Of the three members of cabinet who referred publicly to Irish land during September, the first was Lord Hartington, the Duke of Devonshire's heir. The others were Cardwell and Clarendon. Between them they made the government's task appreciably harder, which was their intention.

Speaking at the Cutlers' Feast in Sheffield on the 3rd, Hartington uncovered his sense of an impending crisis for his order in Britain and Ireland, as the inexorable consequence of embarking upon the reform of tenure in the latter. He presented the question as 'one of the greatest and most important affecting our future'. He saw two vital concerns involved: 'On the one side may be... the future pacification of Ireland and the immense gain...to our national strength...[and] happiness...on the other hand...the enormous damage which might ensue to the interests of property of all kinds, not only in Ireland, but throughout this country, if this question is settled or attempted to be settled, on principles which are unsound or ill-conditioned.' His appeal for the suspension of party warfare in this regard was perhaps foreseeable but his succeeding words were of portentous gravity. He invited the continuing co-operation of classes, 'between the representatives of the land and the representatives of commercial and manufacturing enterprise', saying pointedly to the prosperous middle-class audience: 'Never was it more important than now, and will be next Session, that...these cordial relations should be maintained. It is not only the property of Irish landlords which is at stake, it is not only the property of English landlords, but it is property of all kinds...do not suppose for a moment that any discussion will arise next year...any measure can be passed, without principles and doctrines being enunciated equally hostile not only to the interests of landlords but of capitalists of every description.'[26]

It was in every way a remarkable speech, bringing abruptly to the surface all the fears that had been gathering for many months. The unmistakable meaning of Hartington's words was that landed and business wealth should alert themselves to the united defence of property; and against whom but those in the

Liberal government and party, and very likely on the Opposition front bench as well, who, by implication, could not be depended upon? Although Hartington was a comparatively junior cabinet minister and the youngest, his Parliamentary standing was out of all proportion to his experience. He enjoyed the instinctive liking and confidence of many Liberal M.P.s, if outside the House he was the target of some disparaging comments about his ability. *The Times*, set on containing the Irish land question, tried to insinuate that Hartington's judgment was seriously at fault, and administered a stern rebuke: 'To combine, under the influence of a panic, Irish landlords and English landlords, and capitalists of all kinds and parties, in a...league against possible extreme demands is not to prepare the way for the moderate and equitable arrangement which Lord Hartington doubtless has himself at heart.'[27] The *Pall Mall Gazette* was more open and fairer: but reached practically the same conclusion as *The Times*. Which, in the *Pall Mall*'s view, made it imperative not to ignore party, as Hartington so earnestly desired: for only party discipline could hold in check the class feeling of M.P.s that in the past had drawn them together, and created a 'landlord phalanx' very difficult to break when once allowed to form. Gladstone's bill, the paper was confident, would, and should, be innovating and comprehensive and therefore certain to upset landowners as a class. 'Under these circumstances,' it wrote, 'to bid them forget that they are Liberals or Conservatives is to bid them discuss the subject, not, we fear, like statesmen or patriots, but like landlords.'[28] The *Spectator* believed that Hartington's speech would please Disraeli, who might see him as Earl Grosvenor in a new Cave of Adullam.[29] The *Daily News* said outright :'The Post Master General has, we fancy, been taking lessons of Mr Disraeli'; his remarks were 'broken echoes...of the great Conservative.'[30] To such criticisms Hartington's speech of 23 September conceded quite a lot.

Addressing the Lismore Farming Society in a part of Ireland where his family held broad lands, he dwelt on the improvement in Ireland and local conditions over nearly twenty years' acquaintance with them – farms; livestock; dress; the general state of farmers and labourers were all much better. He emphasized that he did not speak as a member of the government. His purpose was to give 'one word of warning'. He denied regretting that the farmers' clubs should have taken up the land question.

These were the points on which he insisted. First, and very positively: 'The clubs have been very explicit in explaining what they want for themselves...let them remember this, that if there is one thing more than another they should bear in mind, it is this – that Englishmen will never consent to deprive, without compensation, persons of any rights and advantages which they may possess...have legally acquired...and have not palpably misused.' For the rest, the tenants must show that the legislation they wanted would benefit the agricultural labourers as well as themselves, and would enable Ireland to produce as much as she ought under the best agriculture. If they failed to satisfy Parliament on these points, whatever else it might do for their country, it would not make a law in the interests of one class alone.[31]

In this speech Hartington was apparently ready to sacrifice much for the sake of pacifying the tenants. Even fixity of tenure was conceivable, if demonstrably the most satisfactory expedient and granted subject to the landlords' right to compensation. Hartington patently expected radical reform of some sort. If the land question in Ireland could be settled peacefully and with reasonable despatch, then there was less chance of its exciting unwelcome controversy in Britain about the rights of property. And if he, the heir to one of the greatest Anglo-Irish magnates, were now prepared to try for a settlement, that made Gladstone's task a little easier. The *Daily News* was approving this time. It said shrewdly, if with rather offensive patronage: 'The tenant-farmers of Ireland have been listening of late to a good deal of wild and inflammatory language...Lord Hartington may unconsciously have done them as great a service in bringing before them in his own person a sample of the tribunal before which they will have to plead...With his good intentions, his plain and somewhat heavy common sense, and his inevitable pre-possessions of rank and fortune uncorrected by great keenness of apprehension or quickness of sympathy he is a truer type of the House of Commons than Sir John Gray or the O'Donoghue.'[32] This did Hartington less than justice: he was far more percipient and adaptable than the average member of the governing class, and these qualities were almost always put to good use.

Cardwell, the secretary for war, was due to speak to his constituents at Oxford in the last week of September. The swelling concern about Irish land would make it difficult to avoid referring to the question, which, Gladstone remarked to Granville on the 22nd, 'fills the public mind in an extraordinary degree'.[33] Evidently sharing the general uncertainty about his views, Cardwell asked what the prime minister thought of the terms in which he proposed to mention Irish land at Oxford. Gladstone's judicious advice, sent on the 21st, was: 'I am too much given to the note of superlative and you never err in it. Nevertheless I would not at this moment say "the strictest regard to rights of property" – were I choosing for myself I think I should say "a careful regard to the security of property and of the just rights belonging to it" or something of that kind.' He went on to offer Cardwell something resembling a brief for his speech: 'I wish...you may be able to follow closely what is going on in Ireland at this moment. There is a wild agitation for laws which as I understand them would destroy the relation of landlord and tenant. There is an opinion among a more sober class...that you cannot now retain confidence and get rid of the question simply by compensation for improvements, and that in a country like Ireland that does not really cure the loss and hardship attending on eviction. There is an extensive desire for...the Ulster tenant right...which does not seem to have developed itself into any perfectly distinct meaning. Lastly there are singular manifestations of conversions...among the landlord...class.'[34] What was being suggested emerges clearly. Fixity of tenure was impracticable – though Gladstone had not eliminated it from his private consideration. Ulster tenant-right was a possibility worth exploring. The old formula of compensation for tenants' improvements would no longer suffice. 'Just rights' embodied the moral nuance when revising an established policy. Cardwell put the phrase drafted by the prime minister into his speech, but talked of the question as one of compensating the tenants for improvements, and 'exceedingly difficult' at that. It was his belief that 'the guides and leaders of the Irish people will...induce [them] ...to accept that which equity and justice will give, and not to demand that which no Parliament and no Government can propose of themselves.'[35] There was little to encourage Gladstone here.

There was little to comfort the Duke of Argyll either, who wrote, 'You seemed delightfully hopeful at Oxford.'[36] No one said that about the speech delivered by Clarendon at Watford on the day before Cardwell's. The latter was almost completely overshadowed. Clarendon denounced the Irish clamour, but his real target was Gladstone. He told an old friend afterwards: 'As I am not and don't mean to be a spoliator, I thought the opportunity a good one to protest against wild schemes. Merrypebble [Gladstone] may think I went too far; if so I shall be glad to have it out with him. I have warned him that if he used the Irish landlords roughly, the English ones would assuredly fraternize with them, which would be more injurious to the government than dissatisfying the agitators.'[37] Part of the speech was a defence of the constitutional function of the upper House, a topical matter in the immediate aftermath of the Irish Church bill. To Clarendon, naturally, the Lords were a valuable institution, if in need of 'a little more steam'. The Lords' power to apply the brake might be required when government produced the land bill, or, as he expressed it, 'there is coming on an occasion when the two Houses may unite in harmonious action. The question of the tenure of land in Ireland is...momentous...vital.' Like Hartington, he declared that it was not a party matter; where Liberals and Conservatives had repeatedly tried and failed, they should come together and 'with calm moderation' contrive an entirely satisfactory result. His audience would not expect to hear what government meant to do about Irish land: indeed they would react with 'surprise and dissatisfaction' if he did tell them, for there had not been time in two months since the prorogation of Parliament to assemble the information necessary to a mature decision, and, he said, 'any determination...taken already... would be crude and imperfect.' He would, however, tell them what the government was not going to do. 'They will not adopt any of those wild, subversive schemes of which we have heard so much during the last few days' – an allusion to the Cork conference. For the prime minister this whole passage was a message of calculated defiance.

There was another side to the speech. He felt impelled to make certain admissions. He vigorously denounced as 'felonious' the action of a landlord who confiscated the value of improvements effected by the tenant's money and labour; an action which he thought occurred too often – though not on the large and well-run estates – and should be stopped as destructive of good feeling between owner and occupier. Unlike Cardwell, Clarendon hinted that compensation for improvements might not be all that was needed for an 'equitable settlement'. The opacity of his language reflected the misgivings which it cost him to acknowledge as much: 'I do not say that exceptional legislation may not be necessary with reference to the wants, the wishes, and the usages of an agricultural people like the Irish; but I believe that if the rights of property are scrupulously upheld and its duties rigidly enforced by law, a measure will be produced which will entitle ...Government and Parliament to say...they have fulfilled their obligations and entitle them to the support of every honest man.'[38]

The bid to restrict Gladstone's liberty to develop a new policy on Irish land did not succeed any too well. The press fastened on what Clarendon conceded rather than on what he refused. The speech was taken to herald a reform that broke with precedent. Far from affording the intended reassurance, his strictures on some landlords, and especially the use of the word 'felonious', neutralized his warm defence of property. 'I see you are fired into by both parties in Ireland about the land,' Gladstone wrote to him, with a pardonable touch of smugness.[39] Other colleagues in the cabinet were more appreciative of Clarendon. Argyll congratulated him on 'a "word in season" about the Irish fanatics *on Land*'.[40] So did Kimberley, heartily, but he did not, or preferred not to, understand the speech in the same sense as the orator. He commented, 'There *are*, as you justly said, real grievances to be redressed; but the sooner the Irish peasants know that we don't mean to hand over to them the *ownership* of the land the better. Short of that we may have to go a long way, and we have the pleasure to know [sic] that nothing we can do will satisfy any mortal being in Ireland.'[41] Kimberley was a more liberal Whig than Clarendon, but still very much a Whig. He believed he saw the future, the near future, with a clarity lacking in the older man. There was no sensible alternative to real compromise for the landed interest, and it was always in Kimberley's mind that Irish land must be tackled to avert the ill-effects which its exacerbation would have on the British public's approval of his class as landlords and rulers. Altogether more flexible than Clarendon, he was more typical of the cabinet.

Kimberley's letter, written on 1 October, told Clarendon what he would be forced to recognize. Clarendon wrote to inform Gladstone of his speech, and to vindicate it, on the day after its delivery. The more he considered the statutory enforcement of tenant-right, the more he was struck by the practical objections, but admitted, for the first time, that 'there would be advantage in making a standpoint of a usage...that works tolerably well and Landlords and Tenants *say* they are satisfied with.' He urged consultation with 'one or two honest, intelligent Northern agents'. Extending the custom must encounter strenuous resistance and, in fairness to the *landlords*, must involve a general valuation of rent and the numerous legitimate increases would be unpopular. 'I get many letters,' he warned, 'full of alarm at what the Government may be meditating.' He repeated his earlier warnings that if it did not show a proper concern for Irish landlords the ministry would be jeopardized by English landowning hostility, and that the leaders of the agitation in Ireland were worthless. Behind the wonted bluster, Clarendon had the sagacity of an experienced politician, including the ability to sidestep the consequences in the event of a mistake: 'I said...the Government would not adopt any of the wild schemes that were producing so much alarm – the applause at this was vociferous and I hope the rural reporter may not have made me go too far.'[42]

Clarendon hoped to 'have it out' with the prime minister, but Gladstone did not let himself be drawn, either by the speech or by the letter following it up. When Granville scribbled a couple of lines to say that he found the first 'good on the Lords, and not bad on the land, but the less Ministers speak on the subject the better,'[43] Gladstone replied: 'I doubt the wisdom of Clarendon's *voces ambiguae*...at this moment. But there is no great harm.'[44] Clarendon was obliged to pursue the matter himself. He told Granville on 5 October: 'The hubbub that these very commonplace views created proved the uneasy feeling of the public mind and the expediency of *some* declaration that the robber policy of the agitators would not be inforced [sic] on the Government.' He and Granville belonged to the inner circle of Whiggery and he was quite candid in stating his dire apprehensions: '...if we go in for fixity of tenure or peasant proprietors we shall have all the property of England as well as of Ireland against us,' adding, 'I doubt whether Merrypebble liked my saying as much and I have asked him to tell me frankly whether he did or not.'[45] His next letter of 5 October to Gladstone was largely a repetition of that to Granville: but a deliberate challenge, not the expression of anxiety to an understanding colleague. Clarendon professed himself surprised at the 'sensation' excited by his few words, which revealed 'the uneasy state of the public mind and the desirableness of someone saying that the robber policy of the agitators would not be imposed on the Government'. He announced, rather misleadingly, that he had had 'a letter of strong approval from Kimberley, who is as much alive as I am to the danger of allowing...Irish peasants to believe too long without contradiction that they are to oust the landlord'. Blandly confessing that he had 'a sort of notion, tho' I can't say why, that you disapprove of what I said', he invited Gladstone 'to tell me whether I am right or wrong in my instinct'.[46]

Gladstone sent back a masterly answer. Its purpose was to ensure that Irish land came before the cabinet as an open question. The cabinet was adjusting itself to a situation by which none of its members except Gladstone and Bright actively desired to profit, and a situation which the mood of Ireland acted upon that of British politics to create. The process of adjustment had been advertised in Hartington's address at Lismore and in the guarded reference by Clarendon himself at Watford to the uncertain prospect of 'exceptional legislation' on top of compensation for improvements. This process would assuredly be halted if Gladstone gave in to or quarrelled with the senior Whig in the cabinet, even supposing that the ministry survived the breach. For on Irish land Lowe, Cardwell and Argyll would also take 'a purely landlord view', as Granville had written to the prime minister on 25 September.[47] At this stage, with the conversion of more moderate colleagues to the need for a strong bill only beginning, it would be fatal to drive the four of them, or be driven by them, into a corner. Gladstone did not take offence and continued to avoid giving it while conveying a rebuke. He did not like 'putting on paper, sometimes, words which could be spoken with perfect freedom; for they look ugly, on paper, where they partake even gently of objurgation.' As Clarendon had asked for it, he should have '*all* that I can say against your speech...It does not come to much.' He softened this still further by avowing that he had himself sometimes erred in using exaggerated language, and by stating that he did not believe the speech had done 'any real harm'. The criticisms he offered were exactly suited to his intentions. He thought that Clarendon's '*gros mots*', distributed between condemnation of the tenants' demands and of landlord misconduct, balanced each other. But it seemed to him that in respect of both tenants and landlords Clarendon had overstepped the bounds of 'strict justice, regard being had to the history of the Land question in Ireland'. It was a shrewd thrust; the word 'felonious' applied to strictly lawful if morally dubious actions had been resented. Under cover of that unexceptionable and discomfiting comment, Gladstone slipped in his insistence that the tenants, too, were to be heard with sympathy.

He appealed to Clarendon's sense of responsibility: 'Though with no dogmatic assertion, my feeling is that the circumstances are extremely delicate...and that...the safety of the Government lies in a great reserve, and, where an occasion arises which forces ...speech of some kind, in the use of mild or general phrases.' In the case of an authentic popular movement like that in Ireland, Gladstone ventured to think that trying to check it by ministerial pronouncements before legislating was useless. He therefore propounded a 'rule of silence...[to] hold in full force until we knew our own mind as a Government, and could trust our language to it with precision'.[48] This was the crux, and Clarendon gave way. On his own admission Irish land might compel recourse to some extraordinary enactment. It would have been hard to deny that the cabinet's deliberations must gain from being spared the increased tension and misunderstanding that would arise from further public debate by its members on the eve of meeting to discuss that question.

Nor did Clarendon want to bring down the government – his talk of its disruption was not wishful thinking. There, always, lay Gladstone's strength, maintained by resisting the temptation to put too great a strain upon it. Clarendon was very much a party man, and that loyalty governed him, so he averred: 'No one can have a stronger sense of discipline that I have – it is as necessary in a Cabinet as on board a man of war...a Government cannot be carried [on] if its members pull different ways and thereby embarrass their Chief – I am accordingly sorry to have said what you disapprove.' In fact, he was scarcely repentant, as he explained: 'You have not...convinced me that I...was wrong, and, apart from my regret at having in any way annoyed you, I am glad that I said what I did because I believe that good has come of it.' He stuck to every word in the speech about both landlords and tenants: 'I have no predilection for *gros mots* but occasionally it is useful to call things by their right names.' He had spoken to allay anxiety which he knew existed, and had imagined that in disowning on behalf of the government schemes like fixity of tenure and the extension of tenant-right he was uttering a 'platitude', but a salutary one. Public reactions and his post vindicated him: he enclosed a letter from Kimberley and quoted another from O'Hagan, the Lord Chancellor of Ireland. 'Please bear in mind,' he wound up, 'the nefarious speeches of Sir John Gray who of course will have told everybody that he was in correspondence with you – *Dixi*.'[49] Clarendon kept to the spirit of this rejoinder, manifestly indignant notwithstanding the declaration that 'between friends nothing should ever be allowed to rankle.' He made no more speeches but he had no inhibitions about continuing to oppose Gladstone stubbornly within the government.

It is not clear what contacts, if any, there were between Hartington, Clarendon and Cardwell. They appear to have acted independently. The effect of their speeches was cumulative: they were the public expression of fears in his party which were also being privately communicated to Gladstone, and they surely helped to deter him from going ahead with the idea of establishing fixity of tenure *overtly*. Thus, he first cut down drastically the proposals in his secret memorandum of mid-September. Reviewing the outlook after the interval of a few days, he concentrated on securing fixity of tenure *covertly*, by means of extending custom – custom as it was, not as Gray wanted it defined. This was something he could hope to encompass, without being absurdly optimistic. While Clarendon had attacked extension of custom in his letters and it was included, as he told Gladstone on 5 October, in his general denunciation of 'spoliation' from the platform, he had indicated at Watford that compensation for improvements might not be an adequate concession. Hartington at Lismore seemed to invite suggestions for a compromise which would tend to favour the peasantry. Gladstone's strategy was to present tenant-right as a compromise – though he well knew that it was one-sided. If it served no other purpose, a plan sketched by Lambert on his return from Ireland showed Gladstone's to be moderate in comparison.

FIRST THOUGHTS AND REACTIONS

At the conclusion of his Irish tour John Lambert composed a long letter, dated 27 September, giving his impressions of the land question and its possible remedies. Gladstone thought this a valuable contribution to the case which he was engaged in building up and circulated the letter to Granville, Clarendon and Fortescue. 'Anything from him deserves to be carefully pondered,' he advised the Irish secretary.[50]

Lambert had kept Campbell's pamphlet by him and had twice met the author in the course of the latter's second visit to study Irish land on the spot. The two of them had talked at length with the viceroy about 'the difficult "conundrum"', which occupies so much attention' – how to legislate. Campbell, it transpired, had modified the views in his pamphlet; he was now for establishing 'some kind of fixity of tenure' in a more positive fashion. Lambert's understanding of the situation and the scope of his proposals promised to be helpful with the cabinet. He had been educated by events in the eighteen months since a memorandum on Ireland composed for Tory ministers.[51]

In complete contrast with his assumptions in that memorandum were the first two of three factors which he considered must be taken into account when trying to form a judgment on Irish land. The practice, and not the legal theory, of tenure and the state of public opinion, British and Irish, counted for much more with him than the third factor, Parliament's record on the question. There was *de facto* fixity of tenure under custom in the Northern province, and 'under the fear of the Blunderbuss' in other parts of the country. He had met with almost universal backing 'for fixity of tenure in its extreme form', and he agreed with Fitzgibbon that the landlords were isolated in resisting it. As a Catholic himself, unusually for a high official in England at this period, Lambert was well qualified to report on the attitude of the Cardinal and clergy. Cullen was for fixity – this was ascertained in a long conversation – and Bishop Moriarty of Kerry was believed to be the only member of the episcopate who disagreed, because afraid that 'all the educated class of Gentry' would leave Ireland. Against this background, Lambert drew a moral from the Parliamentary history of Irish land: 'The mistake...we have hitherto made is this; we have based our measure[s] upon English law and feeling, and not upon Irish custom and the sentiments of that people.'

He was unwilling, however, to recommend the extension of tenant-right, as distinct from legalizing the usage where it flourished. He called the custom 'the strong lever of those who advocate permanent fixity of tenure' and, consistently in this respect with his memorandum of March 1868, he was opposed to permanent legislation, maintaining that Ireland's present condition, though serious, was transitional. Nor was it practicable, in his judgment, to extend a custom which varied so much locally. There remained the ineluctable consideration: how to proceed 'without offending English notions as to the rights of property', or, rather, without offending blatantly. Only fixity of tenure with a built-in but generous time limit could meet both this requirement *and* offer a hope of contenting the Irish tenantry. That was what Lambert proposed: the assurance of continued occupation for between twenty-one and sixty-two years. His plan was an adaptation of Fitzgibbon's, to whose pamphlet he was heavily indebted, but differed in that he included past improvements. No interference was envisaged with the small minority of occupiers with written agreements for a term of years. Thus the sanctity of contract was preserved.[52] Like Gladstone's in his ten-day-old secret memorandum, which it closely resembled, the plan was politically unrealistic. The claim that it saved the rights of property was ingenuous, or disingenuous. Lambert's letter nevertheless aided Gladstone's missionary efforts among the cabinet. The testimony of such a witness pretty well demolished Clarendon's allegation that the unrest was the work of the 'professional agitator'. Not less impressive was the length to which an eminent and level-headed civil servant thought it right to go in order to try and dispose of the question.

THE PRIME MINISTER AND IRISH SECRETARY

Chichester Fortescue had been overshadowed by Gladstone during the preparation and passage of disestablishment. His dominating spouse, the political hostess, Frances, Countess Waldegrave, was resolved that it should not happen again with Irish land, and he did assert himself. This was not an embarrassment to Gladstone because he wished to continue monopolizing the limelight – he was above such common jealousy, and knew, besides, that should the new measure be warmly contested, he was bound to find himself in the forefront. Nor was Fortescue thrusting and unreasonable, like his lady. Difficulty arose mainly because the Irish secretary and his wife were more conservative than the prime minister, although at the same time Fortescue was slow to perceive where his plan would lay the government open to attack by guardians of property and individual freedom, and how the method he wanted to adopt of proceeding with the draft bill would probably turn the cabinet against him. Gladstone's own first ideas were far more generous to the tenants: but he was so doubtful of their acceptability to the other side that he seems to have been very careful not to let anyone, with the possible exception of Granville, see the memorandum in which they were stated. If he could not carry Fortescue with him, there was little hope of persuading a majority of the cabinet: for the Anglo-Irishman did not belong to the strict sect of landlordism represented by Lowe and at least three more. He had perforce to coax the Irish secretary along, encouraging him to expand his conception of what was desirable. Fortescue, with his long experience of the question, followed and Gladstone, who had never set foot in Ireland, led. The former did not like the reversal of their proper rôles, as they appeared to him, in this of all Irish matters: and he was not easy to move, but move he did.

Glyn told the prime minister on 22 September that Lady Waldegrave 'is much annoyed, or professes to be, at the idea of a Land Bill being discussed in Oct[ober] by the Cabinet *unless a Bill prepared* by *the Secretary* is before the Cabinet. She is loud in *her* determination that "the Secretary" shall not be put in the background...' Had the chief whip known of the exchanges between Gladstone and Clarendon about Irish land, he would probably have been less surprised than he was to hear Lady Waldegrave declare that she trusted Clarendon and others unnamed not to allow 'revolutionary ideas' to prevail. Fortescue had indeed asked Glyn not to take what his wife said too seriously: but the whip, worried by Clarendon's involvement, thought the husband was 'entirely in her hands and she...in a temper to do mischief'. Moreover, Fortescue himself had been 'inclined to complain that his offer...to have a scheme ready had not been *suggested* by you'.[53]

FIRST THOUGHTS AND REACTIONS

It was not until the middle of September that the prime minister received from the Irish secretary the first of a protracted series of letters and memoranda. Glyn remarked on the 22nd that if the bill were to be prepared by Fortescue, he had been spending too much time with his wife on her Somerset estates.[54] Gladstone's letter of 15 September commenting on Fortescue's memorandum of the 13th shows clearly that this was the beginning of the interchange of their views. By then Gladstone had made considerable progress with his study of Irish land and was ready to formulate conclusions.

In the memorandum of 13 September Fortescue's first proposals were to legalize Northern tenant-right in the apparently simplest way by making 'the usage or usages *legal customs*'; and to require similar recognition by the courts of tenant-right – of the sale of 'goodwill' – constituting 'established "customs of the country" in any part of Ireland'. Elsewhere, there should be 'similar protection...so far as circumstances allow'. This was confined to tenants-at-will. At present the law gave them an implicit right to hold from year to year, terminable at six months' notice. The yearly tenant's implied contract should henceforth confer additional rights, to compensation not only for improvements, retrospectively, which was an advance on his bill of 1866, but also for 'Disturbance'. Fortescue wondered, doubtfully, whether this category of tenant might not be presumed to hold, not for one year, but perhaps for as long as seven years. Compensation for disturbance, he wrote, was 'very novel and important, and I am working at it very carefully'. There must be a limit on the sum which the occupier could claim, under this head, and he thought only those should be eligible 'who farm not for profit but existence...say all holding land below £30 a year'. The £30 line presumably represented rateable valuation, which in Ireland seriously undervalued the land. Fortescue must have been aware that in many parts of the country the line took in men occupying well over thirty acres of good land and definitely farming for profit. Present and future leaseholders were not to be affected by anything so far described. To discourage exploitation by means of such agreements they should be registered with a local authority, possibly the clerk to the poor law guardians.

These were Fortescue's main proposals, and they bore a marked resemblance to Gregory's and O'Loghlen's (p. 97 above). Like

140

theirs, his could be circumvented by the landlord's giving a short lease, which was just what the tenants did not want. Registration of leases locally, and opening them to public scrutiny, might work against the inclusion of harsh conditions: but it would hardly deter landlords from restricting the length of agreements to, say, the seven years officially considered to be a fair, if not excessive, maximum in Fortescue's opinion where tenure-at-will was concerned. Unlike Gregory and O'Loghlen, the Irish secretary would deny to bigger occupiers the extensive protection envisaged for tenants not enjoying leases, thereby omitting, as a knowledgeable landlord like Bessborough was later to point out, the natural leaders of the class. They were forcible objections, seen from the tenants' angle, and Fortescue was aware of them. 'The Bill,' he said, 'cannot go to the extent of the popular demand.'[55]

Gladstone's first memorandum on Irish land was mostly written a week before he got Fortescue's. It enumerated the main contrasts between the English and Irish systems of tenure. At the beginning stood a truth which he fully grasped, unlike many Englishmen who, knowing Ireland at first hand, tended, consciously or not, to minimize it: 'Traditions and marks of conquest, and of forfeiture, still subsist.' Sweeping generalizations very damaging to Irish landlords characterized the document. He assumed that they were the exact opposite of English landlords; that they – still – neither contributed to improvements, nor, outside Ulster, credited the tenant with their value; also that the landed class played no part worth mentioning in Irish local government. With more fairness, he listed absenteeism, the religious and political differences separating owner from occupier and the reluctance to grant leases. Lastly, he noted: 'Ireland. Occupier (yearly) holds by Custom. England. By Contract.'[56] Since the identity between yearly tenure in the two countries was obviously known to him, what he meant must have been that the English farmer accepted the contractual relationship postulated by law, whereas the Irishman did not. The latter clung to his traditions, which O'Connor Morris was currently describing in the *Times* articles attentively read by Gladstone. There is evidence in plenty that Gladstone did not think so badly of Irish landlords as he would seem to have done from this memorandum. The deliberate oversimplifications represented the bare bones of a case for legislating which, as he pointed out to Maguire in his letter of 20 September, must not be applicable to Britain. Hence the exaggerated contrasts between landlordism in the two countries.

Gladstone's reply to Fortescue started: 'I see...that your mind has been going through a process, which I too have to some extent undergone.' He wished that they might have had preliminary talks, with Sullivan, the Irish attorney-general, participating. That being hard to arrange, he and Fortescue must proceed by correspondence. He warned the Irish secretary that they faced 'difficulties of a kind...we had not to encounter in the case of the Irish Church Bill...I anticipate that many members of the Cabinet will find it hard to extend their views to what the exigencies of the times, solely considered, now require.' He intended to summon the cabinet for late October, and set up a committee of their colleagues, picked with due care, to prepare the land bill. As to Fortescue's initial draft, he encouraged him to elaborate it, observing of compensation for disturbance, 'this is indeed... full of difficulty. It is very desirable to prevent using augmentation of rent as a method of eviction. I shall be most curious to see the means and provisions you may devise, without at present being too sanguine.' He wanted to know whether legalizing Ulster custom in the way proposed by Fortescue would work – 'I mean as a practical rule in the Courts.' He saw, what was later to help defeat his own scheme before the cabinet, that 'the very recognition of the custom where it prevails will be *adverse* to its extension.' The point was of course, that custom, by definition, cannot be invented; it must grow. He had subsequently to convince himself that it *had* grown beyond Ulster. In this letter, however, he did not discuss the custom further. Instead, he reiterated his unwillingness to accept the most moderate of the plans with any real appeal for the Irish – Bright's – and singled out Fitzgibbon's, 'a very important sign of the times'. 'I have arrived at no positive conclusion...,' he wrote, 'yet I lean to think [it] well worthy of consideration.' This was a direct intimation that Fortescue should raise his sights, while not forgetting the uncertain temper of the cabinet.[57]

Gladstone was understandably more open with the Irish secretary than with either of the other two cabinet ministers to whom he was writing about Irish land in September. None of the three, save perhaps Granville in October, was shown his memorandum dated 15 and 17 September. This was fuller and more finished, as well as very much bolder, compared with Fortescue's, and the leading provisions were a distinctive version of those in Fitzgibbon. As from 1 January 1870 – that is, with retrospective effect, since the next session of Parliament would not begin until after that date – any tenant-at-will could give notice to his landlord, recording it in a public office, of his intention to pay half-yearly an increase of not less than ten per cent on the present rent: and in return the tenant should be 'deemed to have received a lease... for 31 years certain'. At the end of that period the tenant was entitled to a further lease of the same length, conditional upon another increase of rent. It was sought to protect the landlord from suffering unduly by these arrangements. Where he could show, with reference to prevailing values, that his land was underlet by at least ten per cent, then the tenant, on claiming, not the first, but the second term of thirty-one years must pay an increase of ten per cent on the market rent, and perhaps the further term should depend on mutual agreement. Tenants-at-will who did not claim under these provisions had their presumption of tenure extended to seven years; this, too, was retrospective. If the landlord tried to dispossess such tenants and failed to pay for improvements, they could not be removed until, if they withheld the rent, arrears exceeded the compensation owed. To soften the blow to the landlord, government would advance money towards the cost of meeting retrospective obligations. The state was enabled to acquire wastelands and settle them with leaseholders for thirty-one years at low rents. Bright's plan got a mention. Tenants might receive three-quarters of the price of their holdings at $3\frac{1}{2}$ per cent interest from the Treasury: but a ceiling – not specified – was to be placed on total advances for this purpose, and the scheme was only to operate for, possibly, five years. The last of twenty clauses in the draft was incomplete, and read 'as to custom of tenant-right.' For the moment Gladstone was unable to see his way round the objections to recognizing the custom, let alone extending it.[58]

The ingenuity of the secret memorandum is as noteworthy as the other qualities it displayed. Desiring to give the Irish peasantry substantially what they were asking for, and believing – or persuading himself – that it was politically necessary to do so, Gladstone cast about for the means of making it acceptable, if not palatable, in Britain. It had never been easy, or, rather, comfortable, to raise rents in Ireland. If the right to claim fixity of tenure for two generations were dangled before tenants-at-will, the vast majority of occupiers, they might consent to pay a reasonable price for it. On their side the landlords would surely be grateful for increased rents and the cessation of agrarian strife and thus reconciled to the loss of rights awkward and dangerous to exercise. And if they, or enough of them, accepted Gladstone's plan in this spirit, British critics, those most to be apprehended, would find themselves outflanked. However skilful the plan was as an abstraction, it did not make political sense in terms of either British or Irish opinion. Not only in their excited mood of the moment, but at any stage in the middle of the nineteenth century, the tenants would have refused to pay an immediate and general increase of one-tenth on their rents, no matter what the duration of tenure to be obtained thereby. The demand for a just valuation of rent was popularly understood as the euphemism for a reduction all round. Gladstone himself had pointed out to Bright in May that they were dealing with men who complained when the market price was exacted. Yet now he hoped that these same men would be ready, whatever they might be paying, to offer more, not towards the gradual purchase of the freehold or for a perpetuity, but for a mere thirty-one years' lease, which could only be renewed by a further enhancement. Disposed to compromise though many of them were, the response of Irish landlords would most certainly not have been sufficiently enthusiastic and united to sway British opinion. Gladstone already had a good idea of the cabinet's likely attitude from Hartington's public forebodings and Clarendon's letters. What is surprising is that he nevertheless conceived this revolutionary plan. The change in newspaper sentiment probably misled him as to the extent and pace of the underlying shift; and he earnestly wanted to do the fullest justice to the peasantry. Belated reparation ought to be unstinted: he had already warned Argyll of that in January. The secret memorandum of mid-September exposes the significance of his words to the Duke: 'After...obstinate and most selfish resistance...we shall find it difficult when the time comes to keep within the limits of a true modification.'[59]

Fortescue did not take Gladstone's letter of 15 September as he was intended to do. His wish was to frame the bill before the cabinet came to discuss Irish land. He would have satisfied his wife's insistence that he should have the central rôle in preparing the legislation. Gladstone believed that the cabinet would not swallow even such a measure as Fortescue contemplated, if it were presented to them in a definitive shape. It would require much skill in argument and persuasion to bring them round. The task was not one for the Irish secretary. Glyn had written of Fortescue and Lady Waldegrave in this context – 'the party will not stand dictation from her or cares much about C. Fortescue.'[60] Another reason, of course, why Gladstone was not agreeable to submitting a bill to the cabinet, instead of outline proposals, lay in his hope of winning acceptance for greater concessions to the tenants than were contained in Fortescue's draft of 13 September. It was going to take a little time to make the latter see the desirability of improving on that draft, which therefore must not be allowed to furnish the basis for a bill. Lastly, it seemed that the draft measure could not in fact be ready for October. 'I do not think,' Gladstone observed to the chief whip, 'that we can expect Bright, Lowe, Granville &c, &c to sit silent till December.'[61] Clarendon's outburst at Watford a few days later proved the point.

Fortescue's letter of the 20th was not answered for a week. 'I postponed my reply,' Gladstone told him, '...being anxious to consider the matter carefully. But the conclusion I have arrived at is this: that if an Irish Land Bill were to be prepared by you, and our colleagues in Ireland, without further and weightier indications than correspondence with me could afford you, we should much increase the risks with which the subject, at every stage, is beset.' He evinced a caution that had not hitherto oppressed him. He reminded Fortescue of the misgivings felt by two members of the cabinet at 'my limited declaration of policy' in Parliament (p. 81 above). When discussing the question, they had not 'as a Government' agreed to any advance on compensation for improvements: 'Naturally enough, I am apprehensive,' wrote Gladstone, 'of the effect of producing some time hence a *measure* drawn upon a wider principle without previous authority.' An early cabinet must resolve whether to make the decisive advance; with assent to 'this general proposition' secured, Fortescue might set to work with the Irish government on 'the particular proposals'. 'I agree,' the prime minister advised the colleague whose responsibility he was eroding, '...in thinking that you must take charge of the drawing of the main proposals into the form of a plan: but authority to the extent I have described seems to me indispensable.'[62] What actually happened was rather different. The general and the particular were telescoped in the plan laid before the first of the cabinets on Irish land. This resulted from a stream of advice and criticism directed at Fortescue by Gladstone over the intervening month.

On the 27th Gladstone repeated his inquiries of the 15th about Ulster tenant-right – in such a way that they could not be overlooked. Gray's answer to them was enclosed. Fortescue's long reply by return dealt with points raised in both letters from the prime minister. He had seen Gladstone's letters to Maguire, and they were covered by his discussion of the custom of tenant-right. He quoted and saw the advantages of following the Irish judge Keogh's recommendation to Monsell, 'legalize Tenant Right in general terms, and leave us [the judges] to make the law for you': but he could not support it. Fortescue was at pains to emphasize how in the greater part of Ireland, compared with Ulster, 'the customary claim is very much fainter, weaker or more irregular', and he showed no disposition to legislate the full custom of tenant-right into being all over the country. Hence compensation for disturbance was required: but he confined it, as before, to occupiers under the £30 line. Regarding custom in Ulster, he wished to reinforce it when legalized by stipulating that the value of the occupancy-right should be assessed in the courts by calculating the amount it would fetch at a fair, and not the actual, rent. This introduced a cause of protracted disagreement between Gladstone and Fortescue, the wisdom of bringing rent within the range of legislation. Fortescue tried, and failed, to find good in Fitzgibbon's pamphlet. When he summed up what was firm in his own ideas, even compensation for disturbance was prefaced by a significant 'perhaps'.[63] All that the Irish secretary would commit himself to, in respect of tenants outside the Northern province, was compensation for improvements, the familiar and inadequate response of successive governments to the land question. He had grown more cautious over the last fortnight, during which he had heard Clarendon's ominous talk and been warned by a firm friend of land reform like W. H. Gregory[64] that the agitation was becoming dangerously unreasonable. Granville guessed rightly in remarking at this moment that he would not expect 'anything very novel' from Fortescue.[65]

Faced with the opposite tendency to that which he was striving to encourage, Gladstone became more insistent and his tone a little sharper. On 1 October he gave up hinting, and propounded a scheme, concluding tersely: 'The suggestion I have put goes to the very heart of the problem.' He would allow a tenant-at-will under notice to quit, or to pay an unacceptable increase of rent, to choose from three options. First, to leave his holding and have the benefit of Ulster custom under such circumstances, with the value of the occupancy-right settled by the price it commanded at either the actual rent or the rent paid before the increase which prompted the tenant to go to the courts. The landlord should be permitted to show, if he could, that the occupancy-right's value had been enhanced by his underletting of the land, and so to obtain a proportionate reduction of the sum due from him – supposing the tenant's replacement did not pay whatever was asked. Secondly, the tenant might leave and require payment for improvements together with fifteen or twenty per cent of what they were worth superimposed as compensation for disturbance. Finally, he might opt for a thirty-one-year lease conditional upon a five or ten per cent increase of rent, and 'possibly' be given power to require a second term of equal length, subject to the same rise in rent. The landlord's right to prove that his land had been underlet was reserved in respect of the first such lease, a substantial alteration in the plan of 15 and 17 September. In combining his own and Fortescue's reflections, Gladstone had strengthened the latter's compensation for disturbance, making it not only applicable to all tenants-at-will but profitable to the deserving; and had modified the proposals of the secret memorandum, of which Fortescue seemingly remained ignorant.[66]

After the first of the three options – Ulster tenant-right – Gladstone inserted a query: 'This could only be available where the custom prevails?' In his letters of 20 and 25 September, to Maguire and Clarendon respectively, he had shown his deep interest in the tenant-right solution. Payment for occupancy-right was the essential feature of the custom: and it was the enforcement of that over the whole country which Gladstone was now considering, as an alternative to his version of Fitzgibbon's plan. He was hopeful of having found how to solve the quasi-mathematical puzzle of which he had complained to Clarendon. Now, rather uncertainly, he thought he saw the means by which the tenant, with minimal adjudication upon rent and without fixity of tenure, could yet become virtually a co-proprietor. In this letter of 1 October Gladstone wanted Fortescue to have the procedure for valuing occupancy-right 'well turned about and sifted to see whether it will hold water. If it will, we shall have made some way.'[67]

Spencer learnt from the prime minister on 21 September that 'something may have to be paid for the long and obstinate neglect of this question by Parliament: if so we must try to limit and guard that something, so as to prevent a general and permanent disturbance of the relation between landlord and tenant.'[68] Ulster tenant-right would serve the twofold purpose better than compulsory leases for one or two generations. As Gladstone worked on the question and on his Irish secretary, the press fed him with facts and opinions that were most useful. *The Times* played an unusually important part in furnishing both.

THE 'TIMES'S' SPECIAL CORRESPONDENT AND THE PRESS

Asking Spencer on 21 September to have a record kept of the views on land coming from 'Conservative or quasi-Conservative quarters' in Ireland, Gladstone commented that these statements indicated 'a great stirring of the waters',[69] which is also a description of the activity in the British press during September. *The Times* and its special correspondent were the centre of attention: their impact was wonderingly described by the *Spectator* on the 18th, which inquired: 'Is the reform of...Land Tenure in Ireland to be effected without an argument in defence of the present system?'[70] This was an exaggeration, but a pardonable one.

'I think our...Commissioner has not made much of a case as yet against the Landlords,' wrote John Walter to Delane on 23 August.[71] By that date the first four of O'Connor Morris's articles had been printed. The series opened with a survey of the Irish land question before and since the Famine which, with studious detachment, recited the allegations commonly made against the landlords and went on, with rather less detachment:

'Schemes, accordingly, of the most revolutionary character...
have been propounded...and are known to find favour in the
eyes of some at least of the Roman Catholic Hierarchy. Even
statesmen of the highest distinction...seem to think that the...
system...must be changed in some way that shall augment the
interest of the occupier in his holding, though with the exception
of Mr Bright perhaps, their language has hitherto been vague
and undefined.'[72] The former of these two sentences read quite
differently when the articles were republished in book form early
in 1870. It was reworded to sound neutral, and the reference to
the Catholic bishops disappeared.[73] In the original, the whole
quotation did convey the purpose and limits of O'Connor Morris's
investigation, as seen by his employers.

The next seven articles, out of a total of twenty-nine, all
carried Tipperary datelines – Tipperary town; Cashel; Clonmel;
Nenagh. They were written between 26 July and 21 August, and
came out between 14 August and 3 September. The noticeable
time-lag was evidently dictated by the wish to get at the British
political mind when the echoes of the battle over disestablishment
had had a chance to fade. County Tipperary received such extensive
treatment because of its notorious, and fresh, association with
agrarian violence. The clash at Ballycohey was recounted in
detail. In Tipperary and as he moved on to Westmeath through
the King's and Queen's Counties, O'Connor Morris steadily recurred to the sale of 'goodwill' and its connotations. 'It is
impossible,' he wrote from Maryborough in the article appearing
on 6 September, 'not to see that this practice is, on estates where
it is sanctioned, slowly eating away the freehold...and converting
the tenant into a copyholder, and [leaving] the landlord...with
a right to little more than a rent charge, and it is difficult to
suppose that in this age Parliament will not, in some measure at
least, follow the example of the judicial legislation of our tribunals
in the days of the Plantagenets, and confirm the equitable title
of the occupier.'[74] Since O'Connor Morris had recorded that the
'goodwill' was bought and sold very generally, the *Spectator* had
reason to hail this passage as a signal portent: 'The mere citation
of an English precedent for legally recognizing moral rights should
help to show that "revolutionary" measures may not be inconsistent with the rights of property.'[75]

The special correspondent maintained a line of retreat if the expectations he was fostering proved to be mistaken. Indeed, he spoke with two voices. '...Observe,' remarked Gladstone to Clarendon on 22 September, 'the elbow-room *The Times* is giving itself – a very "wide berth" indeed.'[76] O'Connor Morris repeatedly stressed that the great majority of landlords were not guilty of oppressing their tenantry in any sense. Rents were not, as a rule, too high. The reverse was nearer the truth. In relative terms, they were appreciably lower than at the epoch of the Devon Commission, and still falling.[77] Writing on 17 September from Meath, with its rich pastures, O'Connor Morris depicted its agrarian society as a conclusive refutation of Mill or any other advocate of fixity of tenure. The graziers were capitalists and for Parliament to intervene on their behalf would be quite superfluous, and wrong. He inquired rhetorically: 'Are we to divide Ireland into a land of Egypt under the influence of the Common Law, and into a land of Goshen, rejoicing in the divine light of the new philosophy?' and reflected that the history of England bore out the lesson of Meath and illustrated the futility of trying 'to baffle the irresistible energies of commerce, to keep the small tenants in their holdings...'[78] When he looked at the Portsmouth estate in Wexford, in the subsequent article printed on 30 September, O'Connor Morris changed his tone again; he warmly approved of what he saw there. This example of how advantageous the custom of tenant-right could be to both landlord and tenant was presented as most instructive. On such evidence, if the custom were enforced by law, he asked: 'Would not the suspension of ...shadowy sovereignty be more than compensated by the increase of property and of substantial benefit to the proprietor that, from analogy, would be the certain consequences?'[79]

The *Times*'s leaders in September set beside the special correspondent's reports were somewhat confusing to those anxious to establish exactly what the paper's policy was. 'Have you any power of making out what Delane is after on...Irish land?' wrote Lord Stanley to Disraeli on 16 September.[80] The editorial of 1 September was concerned about the effect on British opinion of agrarian crimes in Ireland. It rightly discerned 'the secret of the murderous temper of so many Irish tenants' in the presence, as related by its special correspondent, of the custom of tenant-right, 'more or less developed', throughout the country. The failure of the law to define and protect the tenant's interest was the root cause of all the trouble.[81] Glyn promptly sent this leader off to Gladstone lest he should miss it.[82] On 6 September Hartington earned an editorial reproof for alarmism obstructing necessary reform.[83] A week passed and *The Times* was distinctly pessimistic: 'What fearful obstacles impede the course of the publicist and statesman.' The demands just aired at Skibbereen – not sharply distinguishable from the conversion of tenant-right into copyhold tenure seen as fair and reasonable by O'Connor Morris in his article printed on 6 September – were roundly condemned. In language very familiar from past editorials, Sir John Gray's speech was called 'irreconcilable with all theory of proprietary rights over land', and, intentionally or not, rabble-rousing. If a minority of landlords abused their powers – the name of Scully got a mention – the overwhelming mass of tenants was unfit to be entrusted with fixity of tenure. But, though entire freedom of contract must remain the goal, for the present Gray and other Irish patriots might bend their energies to devising 'some organization of Local Tribunals of Conciliation', before which landlords and tenants could cite each other. 'Is there virtue enough in Ireland to perform the task?' asked *The Times*. 'If the answer to the question were satisfactory, we believe that the opinion of Great Britain would approve such a settlement as we have in principle suggested.'[84] The first leader a fortnight afterwards attacked Irish advocates, lay and clerical, of land reform for their intransigence. Discernible, however, were 'the lineaments of a wise and just measure', which readers were left to deduce was that adumbrated on the 13th.[85] Of fixity of tenure as such, John Walter wrote to G. W. Dasent on the 29th that the *Freeman's Journal* 'overlooks or ignores the...owner of the soil, he has a right to change as well as choose his tenants. I should like to know on what grounds the pretended claim...to permanent occupation...distinguished from...compensation for improvements – is really based...The thing is manifestly absurd.'[86] Walter's interventions were usually followed by a leader echoing their gist, and that of 30 September was no exception. [87]Yet *The Times* had moved so far forward, in submitting its plan for 'Local Tribunals of Conciliation', that it was hard to turn back.

The *Pall Mall Gazette* and the *Saturday Review*, which had had so much of consequence to say the previous month, were oddly circumspect in September, after the former's article on Hartington's

Sheffield speech. They seem to have felt it was best to leave the government press to make the running at this stage: and their later comments bear this out. *The Economist*, too, kept silent, but not for the same reasons. The *Daily News*, rather surprisingly, had second thoughts about recommending fixity of tenure, and proceeded to argue against it. 'Whatever plausible analogies may be pleaded,' said the first leader of 25 September, 'we distrust the application of Indian precedents to Ireland. The best economic organization of that country, to be permanent, must be in harmony with modern and European ideas.' The principal distinctively Liberal newspaper asserted, even now, that compensation for improvements, with free trade in land, possibly helped out at the start by a scheme like Bright's, 'would probably meet...justice and necessity'.[88] Leading articles on 29 September and 1 October on the speeches by Clarendon and Cardwell described compensation for improvements as that 'which needs to be done next Session.' Irish farmers should not be too ambitious: 'It will be unwise to loosen their hold of the bird in the hand on the chance of capturing some very shy birds...still in the bush.'[89]

The *Daily News*, patently, feared for the unity of the Liberal party, and swerved away from a policy that threatened grave discord, trying nevertheless to sound more favourable to reform than it really was. The *Manchester Guardian* was less afraid and more honest. The organ of provincial business interests, it was not so intimately concerned with the fortunes of the party. The first leader of 4 September displayed very little sympathy for the perpetrators of agrarian crime; and that of the 14th compared the *Times* special correspondent with W. S. Trench's *Realities of Irish Life*, to the former's disadvantage.[90] A more reflective leading article on the 20th granted that in certain districts fixity of tenure might work well, if government took the place of the landlords and provided 'just and fair administration': for the *Guardian* thought that Irishmen probably required a controlling hand, under any system of tenure. Trench's book, by contrast, showed what good landlords could do and had done.[91] Two days later a leader considered the Irish question in its entirety as a problem of nationalism. While the sentiments of the Irish should be taken into account, their country could not be treated like the Ionian Islands or Canada but, for better or worse, must remain bound to England and Scotland. From that premiss the *Guardian* continued: 'The greatest happiness of the greatest number is the only fit and reasonable rule of government, and...Ireland shall be administered so as not only to please the Irish, but also the English and Scotch.' Irish land must be related to these principles. The *Guardian* conjured up dreadful possibilities if exceptions were to be made for Ireland: an Irish tariff, or a refusal to contribute to the upkeep of the British Army unless a force were despatched to help guard the remnant of the Papal States.[92] In the last days of September, the *Manchester Guardian* became less negative in its approach, but still extremely cautious. As a compromise, so called, it was prepared to think about going to the length of Fortescue's bill of 1866. After Clarendon's speech at Watford, the *Guardian* referred to 'a middle way between revolutionary projects and stolid adhesion to a system...always unjust', but did not tell its readers what the course might be, beyond saying that it would conform to the lines indicated by Clarendon.[93] This illustrates how Clarendon's speech had an effect contrary to the one intended. With reluctance, the paper was registering an influence of which it had complained – that of Englishmen using the language of Irish agitators.

This partial survey of the press, following those in previous chapters, should explain the mixture of gratification and doubt in the *Spectator*'s first leading article on 25 September: 'There is something perfectly astonishing in the progress made by the Irish Land Question within the last few months. It is almost too great to be trustworthy.' The *Spectator* recalled how its advocacy of a perpetual settlement for Ireland had been judged 'political eccentricity not far removed from lunacy', and when Mill published his celebrated pamphlet extreme radicals had shrunk from its argument for fixity of tenure as 'monstrous'. The radical weekly was equally right to wonder if the phenomenon reviewed were really so substantial as it looked at first sight.[94] Only the landlord press in Ireland furnished clear instances of conversion to fixity of tenure in the period mentioned. *The Times* was pulling other English journals in the direction of a more thorough land reform than they had been willing to support, but they were a prey to strong misgivings. The silence of some of these journals was as expressive as the fluctuating opinions of others.

Gladstone's correspondence, he cautioned Fortescue on 1 October, did not lead him to believe that he had overestimated the difficulty of Irish land.[95] He was more optimistic than that remark, taken out of context, suggests. On the same day, he put out a feeler to Lord Halifax, the most co-operative and influential of the old Whig politicians outside the cabinet.[96] On such as Halifax, men whose conservatism was prudent and benevolent, the fate of an Irish land bill and of the government would depend. Gladstone wrote that he would have liked to talk over the question with him and recommended reading Fitzgibbon.

Halifax had recently been discussing Irish land at Raby with his Whig host, the Duke of Cleveland, and a couple of former Tory ministers, one of them being Lord Stanley; he told Earl Grey afterwards that they were agreed 'the dividing point is between compensation for improvements carried even to extremes, and everything giving right of occupation, except as a mode of compensation, i.e. a long lease.'[97] Halifax could not have been surprised to receive from the prime minister a strong, though general, hint that a drastic measure was taking shape in his mind. 'On the one hand,' observed Gladstone, 'it is vital not to *carry* the question, but to do enough to settle it. On the other hand, it would be an unpardonable error to divest the landlord of his character as a landlord, for with his rights would go the last hope of his performing his duties.' He went on to say that if 'general rules' were to be infringed, it should be only temporarily.[98] This was the language he had held to Spencer nearly a fortnight earlier. It could describe a scheme like his of mid-September, which was theoretically based on the principle of compensation, but hardly tenant-right. The latter gave, even if in a qualified sense, 'right of occupation', to which Halifax and the others objected.

In the event, Gladstone's letter did not make a favourable impression. Writing to Grey on 5 October, Halifax said that he would go as far as compensating the tenant for improvements carried out with the approval of the state. He believed that the condition of the Irish farmers was getting steadily better; and that a few years' respite from agrarian agitation would have stilled it for ever. His experience of Irish affairs had, however, convinced him that 'what is required...is more to produce a moral effect on the people than a mere improvement of the law.' Some concession, he assured the unbending Grey, was imperative.[99] This realism was to prove the best support for Gladstone's idealism within his administration and party, and had already induced certain of the prime minister's colleagues in the cabinet to moot changes with which Halifax's could hardly stand comparison. The cumulative tensions of many months in Britain and Ireland were yielding positive results. At long last, public debate and agitation and private apprehension were driving several quite unsentimental politicians to a shared rethinking of Irish land. That is the principal subject of the next chapter, together with Gladstone's adoption of custom as the basis of his reform.

5

THE ADOPTION OF A PLAN

Granville, Lowe, Kimberley; the noticeably divided Tory party; and, of course, the press – these, deliberately or otherwise, helped Gladstone in October by preparing the mind of the cabinet, and preparing it specifically, for the plan unfolded at the meeting on the 30th of the month. The prime minister continuously fostered several of these influences.

His main efforts were directed to reaching agreement with Fortescue on Ulster tenant-right as the form that their legislation should take, to which end he enlisted the co-operation of Edward Sullivan, the Attorney-General for Ireland, who has been credited with inspiring the plan revealed on 30 October. In fact, he cannot have been responsible for the conception, only, at most, for helping to encourage the Irish secretary to develop a wide ranging plan, and for expounding it persuasively to the cabinet. Between them, Gladstone and Sullivan destroyed Lady Waldegrave's hopes that her husband would distinguish himself when Irish land was considered there.

In Ireland, the situation increasingly dismayed landowning Liberals who genuinely wanted a settlement, but jibbed at fixity of tenure and valued rents. As for the leaders of the tenant agitation, and newspapers supporting it, they were further emboldened by the movement of opinion in Britain.

LORD GRANVILLE

As early reactions had shown, Gladstone was separated from the majority of his colleagues by suspicion, dislike, and sheer lack of understanding when he and they faced very delicate decisions about Irish land. He needed an intermediary between himself and those who, as anticipated, opposed him strongly over this legislation. Granville was the man. During nearly twenty years of political intimacy with Gladstone he perfected the rôle. His charm was famous; his characteristic air, *un peu moqueur*, was disarming instead of aggravating. These amiable qualities never won him the reputation of being a lightweight in politics, as might have been expected; he achieved the feat of being considered both amusing and sound. He had the art of listening sympathetically to the disgruntled and the anxious, and giving without offence advice other than they had hoped to hear. His outlook was that of the kind of conservative often invidiously called 'intelligent'. His instinct was to deflect rather than meet a challenge, to look for the possibility of accommodation. A man of this stamp had much in common with Gladstone. Moreover, though himself completely wanting in the moral energy that gave Gladstone his astonishing authority, Granville seems to have understood very well that the prime minister was in himself a daemonic force, at once the most powerful defence and the most dangerous menace above the contemporary horizon to established institutions in Britain. As intermediary between his leader and the others, he favoured the first: that was obvious during the period from September 1869 to January 1870 when his tactical help with Irish land was invaluable to Gladstone.

It was a tribute to his special abilities that one side did not resent Granville's loyalty to the other. For the opposition in the cabinet believed it was they who were loyal – to the Whig and Liberal, to the English, traditions of property and freedom. Commencing some little while before he knew with any certainty how far the prime minister meant to go, Granville advised him how to take the noises of dissent emanating from Clarendon and Lowe, and what to expect on the part of other cabinet members likely to give trouble. Gladstone was slow to reveal his mind when in September Irish land again figured in their correspondence after a long interval since they had considered the problem of Bright in May. He let fall a couple of passing references – to the attitude of the Dublin Tory press and to Fitzgibbon – and then, on 14 September, forwarded Clarendon's letter of the 11th with a comment that Granville would appreciate, and did, to judge from his own subsequent use of it. 'We shall need a great deal of nice steering,' he wrote, 'and the worst of it is that if we fail much more will have to be done by others.'[1]

No reply from Granville to this letter exists: but writing to him on the 22nd Gladstone discussed an important move in a way that implied a shared purpose. Sending Fortescue's proposal to frame a bill by the time the cabinet met, Gladstone suggested that the question should first go to a committee of their colleagues. 'A Committee keeps a Cabinet quiet,' he remarked dryly. His full explanation for thinking that the committee might be a rewarding stratagem is instructive. Irish land was 'arduous and critical' in terms of both the cabinet and public opinion. General interest had attained 'an extraordinary degree'. The government could not postpone some sort of move. These were not the factors that weighed most with him; he reasoned: 'It is highly necessary that we should be quite ready when Parl[iamen]t meets, and yet there is so much mental movement...from day to day...that it is desirable to keep final decisions open.'[2] It was sensible to want to leave the cabinet uncommitted for as long as possible and so exposed to being further conditioned by the wider debate outside their select and critical body. Granville began his answer by agreeing with the idea: but pointed out two serious objections. A committee on Irish land must include Lowe, whom Gladstone had omitted from the membership enumerated in his letter of the 22nd. Secondly, although he confidently asserted that none of them would break up the government, Granville wondered if it really were advisable to face the expected opposition in a committee instead of the assembled cabinet.[3] Gladstone, on the 27th, showed that he was hesitating between the alternatives.[4] In the event, no such committee was set up.

Granville's advice, given with misleading diffidence, was good. It was impossible to shut out of the committee colleagues with pronounced views on Irish land who promised to be specially awkward: they would have to be prominently represented, since they might fairly lay claim to particular knowledge of its business. The prime minister's list of seven comprised two of the five who, Granville thought, would devote themselves to upholding the landlord's rights – and there was Lowe to add. The committee would probably have arrived at recommendations quite inadequate in Gladstone's eyes. It was wiser for him to do what he did, and take the question in full cabinet, where his more determined opponents were thwarted by the whole number of those who, whatever their real feelings, were willing to travel much, though not all, of the way with him.

This little episode is typical of the relationship between Gladstone and Granville which was cemented by their co-operation over Irish land in 1869–70. Despite his civilized scepticism of men and motives, Granville held Gladstone in perceptibly increasing respect and affection. On the other side, Gladstone admitted this contrasting personality to his confidence, when Granville's advice on how to tackle the cabinet on Clarendon and, particularly, Lowe had proved his reliability. Not until 5 October did the prime minister send a box, and an additional packet, of papers and correspondence with Fortescue and others 'in case you should like to know all I can tell you'.[5] The secret memorandum of 15 and 17 September may have been included. Gladstone's debt to Granville was appreciable: the latter's diplomacy, his persuasiveness and tact may have made the difference between a reluctantly accepted compromise and several resignations fatal to the ministry.

ROBERT LOWE

On 27 September Robert Lowe wrote to a sympathetic friend, the dowager Lady Salisbury: 'I am quite at a loss about Irish land, never having been able to understand the grievance of holding people to their contracts, nor able to find a better plan than leaving every man to do as he likes with his time and labour.'[6] While there can be no doubt that this continued to be his fixed belief, he produced two days later a sketch of legislation involving a complete break with his notorious attachment to doctrinaire laissez-faire. Nothing, perhaps, brings out so well the compulsion now felt to modify even the most obstinate hostility to tampering with the rights of property. Lowe symbolized and had articulated with apparently unshakable confidence the objections and prejudices that blocked agrarian reform in Ireland for a generation.

His quite short memorandum of 29 September belatedly acknowledged that the peasants' sense of justice could not be left out of account if there was to be peace in the Irish countryside.[7] Not that the present and future state of Ireland was Lowe's chief concern. His aims in the memorandum were to explain how to legislate effectively for that country and how to do so without, or with the least possible, risk to property in Britain – and it was the second that mattered. At the start, he laid it down that the grievance which government was to take up must be

defined as peculiar to Ireland, and therefore 'not, I think...
precarious tenure...for that would go straight against the whole
system of England'. He preferred not to notice that the same
criticism applied in part to his chosen definition of the tenants'
complaint. The tenants did not have 'fair play', as he put it, in
a country where they had to find a holding or emigrate, where
landownership was concentrated in the hands of a few, and where
landlords had not been much disposed to make the improvements
on farms. The terms in which he justified his proposed remedy
showed what he feared; he said of his scheme: 'It does not shake
the foundation of property, but broadly recognizes the rights of
the landlords, while it controls their alleged abuse. It fosters no
wild hopes; it favours no revolutionary designs...'

He proposed not to alter permanently 'the existing law which
is founded on sound principles and will become every day better
suited to Ireland as she improves, but...a temporary appeal to
the principles of equity, used in its moral and not its Chancery
sense'. He wanted to establish throughout Ireland 'Courts of
Conscience or Conciliation'. These were to be guided 'simply by
the consideration of what is fair and just between man and man'.
In following that rule of thumb, they were to 'range over the
whole relation of landlord and tenant', with retrospective jurisdiction, wherever there was no written agreement at issue, to
award compensation for any proven injury. Such compensation
might be given either as a money payment or as prolongation
of tenure. The landlord of a tenant-at-will could escape from this
tutelage by entering into a 'sufficiently comprehensive' contract
in writing. The courts might be empowered to annul oppressive
provisions in the agreement: and Lowe mentioned those which
Scully was reported to have tried to impose. In spite of their
very wide powers, no appeal should be allowed from the judgment
of these courts.

Lowe wished to deny his courts some of the marks of ordinary
tribunals with a view to emphasizing their temporary nature.
They should have 'no formal procedure and be bound by no
technical rules of Evidence'; nor should lawyers be required in,
or perhaps even admitted to take part in, cases heard before
them. He was envisaging what amounted to standing courts-
martial on Irish landlords for the duration of a state of emergency
in their island. 'I think this species of judicial dictatorship very

much preferable to any attempt to remodel the law,' he wrote. The most a landlord might suffer, he argued, was an unjustified fine, and the tenant, too, could be arraigned for transgressing the sweeping, simplistic interpretation of equity. The tenant, for his part, would benefit from an 'impartial, gratuitous, well-informed and friendly adviser', as well as from the types of compensation available to him. Lowe added mordantly that the scheme 'will do something towards lengthening Irish life by presenting an alternative to the blunderbuss'. He added, too, a postscript stressing his preference for these proposals over Fortescue's of 1866, which he thought would be either ineffective or if strengthened, 'a heavy blow at property'. Contrasting the two plans, he finished: 'A man need not be ashamed that he will not have tenants at all but will turn his estates into a sheepwalk rather than submit to such a law, but no one calling himself a gentleman can plausibly object to having his treatment of his inferiors tested impartially by the rules of equity and fairness.'[8]

The obvious and serious objection to Lowe's extraordinary idea was that the very general instruction to adjudicate solely on the basis of 'what is fair and just between man and man' placed an impossible responsibility on the courts to be set up. Anomalous judgments or a bias against one class must have resulted. It was, too, sufficiently apparent that Lowe's notion of 'fair play' did not coincide with the Irish peasant's. It is more than doubtful whether the landlords would have appreciated the scheme. They were certainly not tyrants, but neither were they the men to consent with equanimity to official scrutiny of their relations with tenants. The investigation to which those relations were to be subjected could easily become an intolerable inquisition. Lastly, the rights of property had not been saved in this memorandum, and it is surprising that Lowe should have thought so. His lawyer's intelligence misled him into thinking that others would concede and be equally anxious to preserve the separation which he had laboured to establish between law and this exceptional statute of his devising. He had violated the sanctity of property with a thoroughness that undermined his position in the approaching cabinets on Irish land.

Granville, to whom Lowe disclosed his scheme in the first week of October, informed Gladstone, Spencer and Cardwell that he did not regard it as viable.[9] The prime minister, in an apposite comment, replied: 'It seems to me that we should as far as possible aim at even a rather rough settlement by Act of Parliament... rather than smooth down our...difficulties by passing what would either be a dead letter or else set every body [sic] by the ears.'[10] Lowe was sure that his memorandum expounded the right policy, and the safest one; he sent it to Cardwell and Kimberley.[11] Cardwell was still loath to accept that the situation demanded such strong action as the document urged, and on 18 October Lowe was obliged to describe what they were up against. He agreed that if the ministry sought to impede by legislation the slow process of agricultural change in Ireland, this would be 'counteracting the symptom which relieves the disease'. He told Cardwell that the politics of the question were largely the creation of English Liberals: 'Certain members of the Government (neither you nor I) have chosen to admit the existence of grievances and to excite hopes which cannot be ignored...You write as if our problem was to do what is best for Ireland while the problem really is how to deal with a storm which we have done much to raise.'

In this letter Lowe presented his scheme as having a wider scope than the memorandum seemed to imply. He wanted to protect the 'sentimental rights' as he called them, of the peasantry – 'quasi-customs and reasonable expectations which it is though it ought not to be in the power of the Landlord to disregard at will'. Thus interpreted, his proposals came near to realizing the tenants' desires. That this interpretation was actually an enlargement may be a valid inference from the tenor of the letter as a whole. Far from repeating the intemperate criticisms of Fortescue's bill in the postscript to his memorandum, he said that he did not insist on them, because such moderation, though emphatically right, was no longer practicable. The government must embody those 'sentimental rights' in the law, or else they must erect 'a temporary dictatorship...according to natural justice'. He concluded: 'I think the latter the lesser...though still a great evil. To do neither one [n]or the other in the present crisis of affairs seems to me impossible.'[12]

Gladstone was as desirous as Lowe to prevent the intended legislation from seeming to be applicable to Britain, and he said so in his reply of 12 October. Although he was then turning finally towards the Ulster tenant-right solution and that explicit

and lasting acknowledgment of native Irish rights which his
colleague hoped to avoid, he said that he, too, wanted the
government's measure to be temporary. Lowe's memorandum
fully warranted this conciliatory reception and the prime minister's
request to let it be printed and circulated to the cabinet:[13] its
admissions greatly strengthened Gladstone's hand. Lowe consented
to the circulation of his paper and, in deference to the prime
minister, withdrew his postscript on Fortescue's bill. He explained
to Gladstone, as to Cardwell, that its manifest inadequacy and
irrelevance constituted his main objection to that measure,
whereas his own was 'addressed exactly to the thing complained
of instead of...giving something because they want something
else'. 'Your last letter,' he finished, 'gives me every reason to
believe that the settlement of the question is not out of reach.'[14]
The letters that passed between the two men testified to the
soundness of the advice which their mutual confidant, Granville,
had offered Gladstone when first reporting Lowe's state of mind
about Irish land at the end of September, before the Chancellor
of the Exchequer had made his plan known. Granville predicted
then that Lowe was not one 'to be bound by cobwebs' when
high office and the disillusioning experience of his recent indulgence
in rebellion combined to deter him from sticking to his principles.
The recommended 'firmness and mildness' on Gladstone's side
did work, thus far – but Granville had thought fit to add that
Lowe might prove obstinate if the remainder of the cabinet were
frightened by 'something extreme' from their leader.[15]

Both before and after he had unfolded his plan, Gladstone and
Granville overestimated Lowe's pliability. When he visited
Granville at Walmer Castle, the latter wrote to the prime minister
that their angular colleague seemed 'ready to stretch his conscience
as far as it can legitimately go...[and] very anxious to know how
the cat will jump in the Cabinet'.[16] Lowe was certainly not
emotionally reconciled to the abandonment of that policy on
Irish land which he had upheld in Parliament and in the editorial
columns of *The Times*. His letter of 18 October to Cardwell laid
the blame for the condition of Ireland and of the land question
on the administration to which they belonged. During the summer
recess of 1869 Delane had described the Chancellor of the Exchequer
as openly abusing Gladstone on all occasions.[17] When Gladstone
expected to have more success than he actually enjoyed in isolating

and persuading Lowe, that degree of optimism found support in Lord Kimberley's reaction to the plan to save property by riding roughshod over it.

In his letter of 1 October to Clarendon, Kimberley had shown that, notwithstanding his detestation of what was going on in Ireland, he was ready to give a lot to restore a greater degree of social peace there. This was in accordance with the view expressed in his Lords speech of August 1866. When Lowe sent his plan for exceptional legislation to Gladstone, written on the document were Kimberley's remarks in which the former viceroy commented on that plan in terms of qualified approval, and offered a more precise definition of its scope. These remarks were, by Lowe's wish, printed for the cabinet together with his memorandum. Shortly afterwards, Kimberley developed his comments in a paper for the prime minister. Gladstone's decision, reached around the middle of October, to go for the statutory enforcement and diffusion of tenant-right was one towards which his colleague's opinions seemed to be evolving.

Kimberley told Lowe on 3 October that 'what is wanting in Ireland is a fair custom, by which, in the absence of written agreements, the terms on which land is let shall be regulated.' Ulster tenant-right was such a custom, and recognition would be merely equitable where the landlords had allowed it. The variations of tenant-right in Ulster alone presented, to his mind, an insuperable objection to its enforcement by a simple statutory declaration. Outside the province, the problem of ascertaining custom's strength was worse, but, equally, could not be shirked: 'It would be as unjust to recognize it indiscriminately,' he wrote, 'as to refuse to recognize it altogether.' In both parts of the country, Lowe's special courts seemed to answer the need described. Kimberley saw those weaknesses in the plan on which others fastened – its vagueness and the consequent margin for disagreement over the interpretation of right. He considered that, from a landlord point of view, the defects were not comparable to the prospect of 'a confiscation, disguised as "fixity of tenure" ...and in the end things would adjust themselves' under a measure like Lowe's: but by shifting the point of reference for the new tribunals from 'what is fair and just between man and man' to the native conception of tenant-right, the implications of the scheme were significantly altered.[18] Lowe was grateful for these friendly observations and attached great importance to them.[19] He showed later that, if there had to be legislation more specific than his draft, he preferred it to be based on Irish custom to exclude, as nearly as possible, general principles which were arguably valid for Britain.

Kimberley expanded his remarks in a memorandum to Gladstone at the end of the month just before the subject of Irish land was opened in cabinet. He thought the prime minister might be glad to learn in advance how the question, 'so exceedingly perplexing' as it was, appeared to him.[20] 'The Irish "national" party asks for fixity of tenure.' Kimberley was under no illusion about that. Fixity of tenure was equivalent to copyhold in England; it would make the tenant the dominant partner and must therefore be rejected as involving 'a transfer of the real ownership'. Going on to discuss whether 'greater security of tenure' was practicable, he looked at the idea of compulsory long leases, like those which, unknown to him, had featured in Gladstone's thinking until a couple of weeks earlier. To interfere thus with property-rights would be grave, but Kimberley was against it chiefly for other reasons. The best interests of Irish agriculture and small farmers would not be served. This large concession would be politically ineffective, indeed self-defeating, and irresistible pressure for unlimited fixity of tenure the only outcome.

He did not approve of the custom: but it worked in so far as Ulster was the only province with, broadly speaking, good relations between landlord and tenant, and it was spreading to other parts of Ireland. '...The value of Ulster custom to the tenant is this,' wrote Kimberley, 'that he becomes in fact though not in name, joint owner of the soil...It seems to me that such a system is at all events better than a general lease for a long term.' Lowe's extraordinary jurisdiction – or, better, the chairman of quarter sessions – might be authorized by Parliament to inquire into any dispute between landlord and tenant and bind the former to observe tenant-right in full where the tenant could show that it was 'the custom of the country'. Where the custom could not be proved, Kimberley proposed to encourage its diffusion. The landlord should be forced to pay compensation for improvements, retrospectively, on the presumption that they were the tenant's, with the option of conceding either a lease for thirty-one years or the right to sell the occupancy of the holding.[21]

Kimberley's suggestions came fairly close to what Gladstone wanted at the time of writing: but the gap, it turned out, was unbridgeable. To encourage the extension of custom was not the same thing as extending it: for the second implied a transfer of property. When the line between the two was reached, Kimberley hung back. That, however, was by no means the prospect before he heard his assembled colleagues. For the moment, his memorandum seemed to promise endorsement of Gladstone's desire to give fixity of tenure, decently, but not too heavily disguised. The ex-viceroy's opinions had progressed to such an extent since his days in Ireland that their further radicalization was likely. A moderate Whig of his essentially reasonable type could be expected not to lag behind Irish landlords and Tories.

THE TORIES

From the government's point of view things continued to worsen in Ireland. Thomas O'Hagan, the Irish Lord Chancellor, told Dufferin on 19 October that 'the Land Question is desperately difficult...Giving and taking...gathering the good out of endless schemes and speculations, I think we may get through.'[22] Another Catholic Liberal, Sir Rowland Blennerhassett, a landlord and M.P. in the West of Ireland, elucidated these remarks for Dufferin. He wrote that O'Hagan, whom he had recently met, seemed to believe 'nothing will satisfy the extreme party but government arbitration between Landlord and Tenant and fixed rents. If this be so,' he exclaimed, 'I cannot see how that party is to be taken into consideration at all. Such a proposition being nothing in principle different from the maximum prices of the Reign of Terror.'[23] Blennerhassett's concern illustrates perfectly what O'Hagan meant when he said that 'the people whom it is most sought to serve have, certainly, been very active in intensifying the difficulty of serving them.' Despite his position, the Irish chancellor was not consulted by either Fortescue or Gladstone while they were arguing over the land bill, but his judgment was sound. The ministry would have to make 'compromises and concessions' hard to stomach if it was to have any measure of success politically, and the undertaking was being severely complicated by the declarations of Gray, Butt and others.[24] Halifax, that tried and sensible politician, who was approaching Irish land in a realistic spirit, was nevertheless provoked by the tenants' leaders to tell Granville: 'I confess to feeling a little hardhearted about the Irishmen...it does not seem to me that there is the slightest chance of satisfying the agitators on the land question by anything...not...fatal to the future prospects of the country.'[25] Since this attitude was so marked among English and Irish landlords in the Liberal party, the Tories might have been expected to unite in the warm defence of landed property. On the contrary, they made no attempt to conceal or reconcile their divergences.

Gladstone maintained from September 1869 onwards that should his government come to grief on Irish land, the Opposition leadership would then bring forward a more nakedly radical bill than he contemplated. In the *Quarterly Review* for October, Lord Salisbury obligingly testified to that effect. His article 'The Past and the Future of Conservative Policy' besought Tories not to repeat what then looked like the disastrous blunder of 1867 and make common cause with radicals against the Whigs. The outcome of such alliances, he insisted, must always be destructive of the interests that both Whig and Tory wanted to preserve. It was Salisbury's gloomy conviction that 'the recess which separates the Irish Church Bill from the Irish Land Bill makes a change of supreme importance in our politics.' Hartington's Sheffield speech left Salisbury in no doubt that their common forebodings were firmly grounded. The Tory Marquess agreed with the Whig that Irish land ought to be regarded as too serious a matter for party politics. The Whigs, should they find the Opposition adopting radical policies for the sake of office, would of necessity follow that unnatural example, the more readily because they dreaded a repetition of those Tory manoeuvres which had been their undoing in the struggle over Parliamentary reform. 'Atoms of opinion mutually so repellent must fly asunder,' wrote Salisbury of the Liberal party, 'if they were not bound together by some strong aversion...This vote-compelling power which ensures... union...we believe to be the recollection of recent Conservative tactics.' He was quite right: unhappy memories of Disraeli's agility gave Gladstone an argument that was useful with recalcitrant Liberals in the cabinet and on the backbenches. Whereas in April and May he had considered that the government was hiding moderation behind its vague public statements, Salisbury now thought Gladstone capable of espousing the most advanced views.

Like many others, Salisbury obtained comfort from the presence in the cabinet of Lowe, Hartington and Clarendon; rather unusually for a high Tory, he was also glad Bright would be there to help draw up the land bill. It was reassuring that the two Whig magnates should have been at such pains 'to show...they are not prepared to commit social suicide'. Colleagues of this temper were a check on the prime minister, as was the character of his majority, too diverse in its composition, though so large, for him to risk with safety the withdrawal of influential supporters. Salisbury anticipated that the operation of these conservative forces within the Liberal party would restrict the land bill to compensation for improvements made with the landlord's knowledge and 'some harmless adaptation' of Bright's scheme. If, as might be predicted, the government thus alienated a number of Irish Liberals and English radicals, he warned the Tories against trying to bring about its fall. Ministers were entitled to the Opposition's backing in the circumstances. Not that it was open to the Tories to join with the other extreme in demanding a radical Irish land bill: but the two might well combine to defeat the government on some incidental question, blown up into an issue of confidence. Once in office, the Tory party could be made to afford 'the use of a Conservative organization for the achievement of Radical triumphs': a fatal course with the rights of property at stake. As Salisbury saw it, there must be unswerving adherence on the Tory side to a self-denying ordinance: 'To act the part of the fulcrum from which the least Radical portion of the party opposed...can work upon...friends and leaders, is undoubtedly not an attractive future...it may well end in the moderate Liberals enjoying a permanent tenure of office...Yet it is the only policy by which the Conservatives can now effectively serve their country.'[26]

The anonymity of the article was, of course, transparent. It contained uncomfortable truths for both parties, which the *Manchester Guardian* tried to refute as far as the Liberals were concerned. The *Guardian* declared that there was no danger whatever of a split in the Liberal ranks. The reason given for the absence of any such threat was, however, one that confirmed Salisbury's diagnosis of the tensions brought to the surface by Irish land in English politics. 'Nothing could be more foolish and futile' than the union of landlords to fight for their vested interests regardless of party: because there would be no better means of destroying their popular esteem.[27] Salisbury may have been as close to the mark when he protested against an apprehended Disraelian *coup*. The Tory leader's thoughts can be gathered from the speculations of Lord Stanley in correspondence with him.

Until the autumn the Opposition was on occasion loudly critical of the Liberals' reticence about their intentions with respect to Irish land, suggesting that it concealed a disposition to surrender to revolutionary demands. The obvious tactic was to exploit the question when it gave rise to public dissensions on the government side. It was in the hope that a waiting game was going to be crowned with success that Stanley retailed the latest political gossip to Disraeli in mid-September: 'The report that reaches me is, that Fortescue and Lord Spencer are ready to go all lengths, even to complete fixity of tenure: but nothing is known, or thought to be known, of Gladstone's views. Will the Whig party stand a forced sale of their lands? for it comes to that.' Stanley regretted that old Lord Russell, who when encountered the previous month had avowed his determination to resist an extreme bill, was 'past being of much use'.[28] The *Saturday Review* said a few weeks afterwards that the Opposition had seen in Irish land the ministry's certain undoing.[29] This was no longer true after the end of September. Stanley's garbled information, although heartening, preceded a new appreciation among the Tories of their prospects, however Gathorne Hardy, in a private reaction to the ministerial speeches, continued to relish the 'trouble ahead for those who have so long traded on statements by their friends which now they begin to find too strong'.[30] Tories had always resented the Whigs' success in using the Irish, like the English radicals, for their own ends.

Disraeli's animus against the Whigs was keener, and restrained by fewer inhibitions: the suspicion that he would like to buy an Irish alliance was not new.[31] In 1867-8 Mayo (as Lord Naas had since become) and Northcote had put on record the distinct possibility of a sharp break with the hitherto accepted limits of Irish land policy. Now, when he set himself to deal with the land,

Gladstone tried a direct approach to encourage the tendency to compromise among leading Conservatives. On 30 September he met the least partisan of the former cabinet, Wilson-Patten, and discussed Irish land, leaving him Campbell's pamphlet and Fitzgibbon's.[32] In its number of 30 October the *Saturday Review* remarked how prominent Tories were telling public meetings that they did not disapprove of suggestions certain to have incurred their condemnation a year earlier.[33] It was a very recent development. In the middle of September, an extreme Tory, C. N. Newdegate, used an address to the Warwickshire Agricultural Society to imitate Hartington at Sheffield and warn the businessmen of Birmingham and Coventry that principles subversive of landownership in Ireland must undermine the security of property. He was not afraid to assert that the Irish farmer had no real cause for complaint.[34] Lord Carnarvon was a far more considerable figure, Salisbury's ally who had resigned from the cabinet with him over Parliamentary reform in 1867, and, unlike Newdegate, a sympathetic figure in the eyes of opponents. On 23 September Carnarvon spoke out with what the *Daily News* described as 'a...contribution to the worse understanding of the Irish Land Question'.[35] He argued at some length that all relevant foreign experience told the same story: small farms ran counter to the economic trends of the age. Compensation ought to be forthcoming for tenants' improvements carried out with the landlord's tacit consent: but he believed that problem, and others that were sources of agrarian ill-feeling, best solved by the use of written contracts and not by curtailing the freedom of either owner or occupier. Upholding the aims of Clanricarde's bill, Carnarvon outdid Hartington, whose speech was also mentioned, in the seriousness of his warning to everyone in Britain who had something to lose, 'whether invested in the funds...the stocks ...the railways, or in the savings-banks', if rights indistinguishable from theirs were not to be protected in Ireland. This was his message: 'No property which the humblest man owns can escape the application of the same principle...you are prepared to apply to land.'[36]

Speaking to the Conservative working men's association in Glasgow in April, Lord Stanley had said that he did not think any British parliament would ever admit the claim of 'the Celtic national party...[to] a moral right to the possession of the land itself, subject only to some fixed...payment to the owner'. The claim, he contended, was as unreasonable on the part of an Irish tenant-farmer as it would be if put forward by the Glaswegian tenant of house property or lodger, or if a workman were to maintain that he had a similarly indefeasible title to his job. Stanley was sure that the government and the majority of Liberals would resist fixity of tenure.[37] In August he delivered another of these speeches attacking dangerous ideas on land and society, but without alluding to Ireland.[38] Not long afterwards, he was apparently more flexible when Halifax talked over Irish land with him in private, although he held that, do what they might, nothing could prevent discontent from swelling into a general cry for an Irish parliament.[39] The Conservatives began to temporize: and this was signalled in a speech warmly welcomed by the *Daily News* in a leader of 4 October.[40] Lord George Hamilton was not only a son of the Duke of Abercorn, the last Irish viceroy, but a well regarded young backbencher, whose victory in the popular constituency of Middlesex had been one of his party's consolations in the 1868 election. He granted that there were bad landlords in Ireland, and that the tenants were sensitive to their legal insecurity. While he avoided being too definite, he intimated that Ulster custom showed the advantage to every one of allowing tenants to put a price on their holdings.[41] The *Daily News* greeted Hamilton's remarks as witnessing to 'the general concurrence of opinion that has been brought about'.[42]

It may be doubted whether his views carried much weight with English Tories; like Lord Erne's they reflected the outlook of Ulster landlords reconciled to living with practical restrictions thought intolerable elsewhere. Far more valuable as evidence of Conservative thinking were the addresses of James Round and Colonel S. B. Ruggles-Brise, the members for East Essex, to a party rally in the county. They were, according to *The Times* of 28 October, representative of solid Tory and landlord reactions to a developing situation. Round and the Colonel did not specify agreement to any measure other than compensation for improvements, they rejected fixity of tenure, and denounced the agitation in Ireland: but there was nevertheless a conciliatory note in their remarks, especially in the Colonel's final words: 'The Irish land question would require the best and most careful deliberation ...in the ensuing Session, and it would be the duty of the

Opposition to give all the support they could to the Government.'[43] *The Times* gave an editorial to these two M.P.s at their rural gathering because they helped, however modestly, to further the policy that the paper was doing its best to promote: 'If Conservative county members and their constituents will go so far in aiding the Liberal party in Parliament...there is a large section of the...party which will accept thankfully their promise of assistance to resist any really dangerous interference with the rights of property.'[44]

The Conservatives were responding to the appeals of Hartington, Clarendon and Salisbury. It was so obviously in the interests of the landed class, which both parties had at heart, to avoid a genuine conflict in English politics over a question the socially disruptive effects of which were being demonstrated more frighteningly in Ireland with each day that passed. There was also the sense of being left behind by public opinion, as they had been when the Irish church was the issue. The Conservative leadership, from which Salisbury and Carnarvon had separated themselves, remained silent: they had to reckon with a great deal of continuing hostility in the party to touching landed property; and they could still hope, as was eminently reasonable, to see the cabinet break up.

THE CONTRIBUTION OF THE PRESS

On 9 October *The Times* printed a report of John Walter on the Irish land question at an agricultural association meeting in his county. He stressed the value of the newspaper debate and the information that was being gathered to feed it.[45] *The Times*, under its proprietor's influence, took, as hitherto, easily the chief part in this educational process. It was the only paper with which Gladstone seems to have intervened, saying in his letter of 6 October to Delane about Irish land that 'any error committed by the Government on that subject, would in all likelihood be irremediable.'[46] *The Times* knew more or less what it wanted. Other English journals, leaving the *Spectator* aside, were as convinced as was the prime minister of the hazards surrounding the question: but they were much less clear how to advise their readers. This relative uncertainty was perhaps not less effective than the *Times*'s planned persuasion in forming the climate of opinion in which the cabinet began to consider what the land bill might do.

John Walter was not too optimistic about Irish land; and he emphasized to G. W. Dasent that their special correspondent should not be given more latitude. If O'Connor Morris desired to know what Printing House Square was thinking, said Walter in a letter of 7 October, he should be answered in conformity with the division of responsibility indicated by him, the proprietor, early in the assignment. There could be no answer until all the facts were before them: 'It is *his* business to furnish us with every particular that can help us to draw a sound conclusion; but it is *our* business to draw that conclusion.' He agreed with O'Connor Morris, as he understood his articles to date, that either tenants' improvements or the custom of tenant-right, where allowed by the landlords, should have the protection of law administered by '...some Court of Equity'. Walter was positive, however, that these arrangements should extend only to existing tenancies; future contracts ought to be left quite alone, and no landlord forced to compensate the tenant except if he had failed to object on receiving proper notice of an intended improvement. In the event of compulsion to hand out leases or settle rents 'with a view to meeting the wishes of the Fenians and Papists, who want to improve the Protestants off the soil and keep Ireland for the Irish', the least that Britain could do for Protestant owners would be to buy them out at a price in excess of the market value. This letter evinces the deep concern to which Irish land gave rise in a man who was very experienced politically and not prone to nervous fears. He was not only disturbed but also unsure of his bearings when the possibility had sprung up that, as he put it here, 'the modern idea of landed property is to be abolished in Ireland.'[47]

What he had written to Dasent was restated in John Walter's speech to the agriculturists at Maidenhead, in much more general terms and with the natural omission of the pessimism and bitter references to the motives behind the Irish agitation. The government would not, he said, propose anything revolutionary, nor would the House of Commons 'submit to the preposterous demands which a large portion of the Irish people are setting up'. He attributed the 'miserable' relations between landlord and tenant in Ireland to the practice as to capital expenditure on holdings, and endorsed Clarendon's use of the epithet 'felonious' to describe an owner who appropriated the occupier's improvements. 'The

best thing that could happen,' he assured his hearers, 'would
be for the system...in England to be adopted in Ireland...the
next best thing...is to make such equitable arrangements as the
case requires during the interval which must elapse.' This policy
was feasible if both parties would unite in its support and 'not
set up...claims which no English landlord would grant for one
moment'. Although Walter said that Irish land, unlike the church,
did not excite political passions in England, his remark did not
harmonize with the defensive and worried note struck by the
speech as a whole.[48] He patently wanted to believe the strange
assertion of the second leader in his paper on 14 October: 'It tells
much for the soundness of public opinion in this country that...
the tendency of argument on all sides is to contract rather than
extend the sphere of reform.' *The Times* compared the 'practical
propositions' emerging from the discussion of Irish land with the
'revolutionary nonsense' uttered on property in land at the
recent congress of the First International at Basle. The lesson
of history was that socialism applied to the land could not be
reconciled with freedom and order. The French revolutionaries
in 1793 had made the advocacy of agrarian reform a capital
offence.[49] When John Walter and *The Times* denounced revolutionary measures and maintained that, in this as in other
matters, Ireland's salvation lay in conforming to the English
model, and in the same breath spoke of making 'equitable
arrangements as the case requires' for the tenant and of 'compensation for all claims connected with his tenure'; when it was
editorially asserted, contrary to all the evidence, that public
discussion was not broadening but diminishing the scope of
legislation – there was no disguising their perturbation. Their
promotion of moderate reform to avoid worse was being put to
the test. Whereas they had helped in recent weeks to sway
responsible opinion in favour of an Irish land bill that would not
be ineffective, the movement of ideas in such circles was becoming
disconcertingly rapid. The first leader of 20 October cautioned
that no bill 'which Parliament would be justified in passing'
could satisfy the peasantry.[50]

On the day following Delane wrote to Dasent: 'I will take
care of Gladstone next week. The first Cabinet is on the 26th.'[51]
Whether he was referring to a meeting arranged with the prime
minister, or to an understanding already reached after the latter's

approach to *The Times* on the 6th, is not apparent. That the first leader of the 27th was composed from inside information cannot be doubted, and it hinted broadly at such direct inspiration: 'Without pretending to lift the mysterious veil which shrouds all cabinet deliberations, we should not despir of forecasting the probable direction of...policy on Irish Land Tenure...there are not wanting indications of a principle upon which a safe cure may be applied.' To add conviction to the message, the article had earlier stated: 'It may be assumed that most Cabinet Ministers have matured their views, at least so far as principles are concerned.' An assumption which *The Times*, with its contacts, must have known was highly questionable, but the semi-official announcement of unity was calculated to hamper Gladstone's certain opponents among his colleagues. What the cabinet had settled on, it was intimated, as a means of giving the tenant *security* of tenure – 'a sentiment' the paper explained '...not in itself anarchical, though very capable of anarchical abuse' – and a means of reconciling the peasantry's 'interest' with the landlord's 'right', was a new law based on 'these deeply rooted usages exemplified by Ulster tenant-right...on the ancient structure of Irish custom'. Simply to legalize and extend Ulster tenant-right would be 'at once an heroic and an inadequate remedy': but the answer to the government's legislative problem dwelt in the custom.[52] It was an accurate, if in places less than explicit, account of Gladstone's reasoning in opting for this solution. When the second leader of 28 October had noted the welcome development in the Conservative party of a bi-partisan attitude to Irish land, the first leader on the 30th reminded readers where the paper stood. Security of tenure was the proclaimed objective, but 'in closing accounts with the past it may be necessary to recognize prescriptive rights of doubtful origin...it cannot be just or necessary to foster the growth of similar rights in future.'[53] *The Times* was a very doubtful convert to the utility of Irish custom.

The letters from O'Connor Morris that appeared in October could be used, as previously, to support either a reform founded on the custom of tenant-right or a lesser change in the legal relations between landlord and tenant. He pilloried the Earl of Courtown, whose agent in County Wexford had advertised a holding as one on which the buildings would be erected by the landlord for 'a solvent Protestant tenant'. O'Connor Morris observed that the Earl's Cromwellian forbear would have been gratified by his attitude. The nevertheless favourable verdict on Wexford stressed that it was an exceptional area.[54] The counties of Waterford and Kilkenny were much more like the other parts of Ireland that O'Connor Morris had visited. There his interest centred on the extensive Bessborough estate in Kilkenny, which he remembered as it had been in the 1840s. He gave Lord Bessborough, who had succeeded his father in 1847, full credit for having got through the Famine with 'not a single notice to quit', and for having developed the estate into 'a beautiful specimen of small-farm husbandry promoted and stimulated by the proprietor'. Such benevolence, however conscientious and constructive, could not make sufficient headway against the feeling of the countryside that the landlords did not belong. Not that O'Connor Morris gave this bald explanation. Instead, he argued, ignoring the agrarian history of Britain, that 'the civilization that comes from above is not likely to be so permanent as that ...from below.'[55] In the two letters that he wrote from County Cork, O'Connor Morris's findings were that too few landlords ever tried to live up to the ideal typified by Bessborough: farms were quite commonly overrented, and their owners had done little to improve them; there were complaints of baseless evictions and oppressive treatment of tenants in other respects. He had a good word for the great absentees of whom the Duke of Devonshire was a local instance. 'Just and princely', the management of his estates stood out in the county. As he travelled into West Cork the land got poorer and the peasantry worse off, but, taking the county's more fertile districts into account, it seemed to him that the state of Cork was depressing when it was not also depressed. Had the rising of 1867 met with only brief success, the local people's Fenian sympathies and agrarian discontent, both strong, would probably have set off 'a wild rising against the upper landed classes'. Fixity of tenure, 'in its essence an indefensible wrong', had aims which were attainable in another way.[56] O'Connor Morris ended the second of these letters from Cork with a paragraph in which he said that, without for the moment being more specific, he was convinced property's 'true rights' could be upheld and tenant-farmers given all reasonable security on 'enlightened principles'. This was printed in *The Times* of 23 October. Its correspondent had left the leader-writers with as much freedom as the proprietor and editor wanted.

The *Daily News* followed the trend in ministerial thinking; it abruptly discovered that it was good sense, as well as legitimate, to diminish appreciably the strength of the landlord's position in law; and it was afraid for the Liberal government. It was in receipt by the end of October of a degree of official guidance as might be expected once the government began to know its own mind. No longer was a bill on a broader basis than compensation for improvements deemed 'an evasive and impalpable shadow'.[57] As was noticed above, Lord George Hamilton's speech in Middlesex provided the occasion for the change. On 14 October another speech on Irish land by an M.P., a Liberal this time, prompted a first leader. Addressing the National Reform Union at Manchester, Sir Thomas Bazley, one of the Members for the city, had misrepresented Ulster tenant-right, in which the *Daily News* – pointing out that the custom had really to do, not with improvements, but with 'a kind of right of user in the soil' – thought 'wise statesmanship would recognize a *point d'appui* for new and general legislation.'[58] To this suggestion the paper added, on 20 October, an outspoken attack upon Irish landlords, which was inspired by the publicity being given to Lord Leitrim's dealings with his tenantry. In 'Shooting Niagara and After?' it was recalled that Carlyle had taken the defence of aristocracy to the length of wishing that every landowning nobleman would act the part of 'a complete king' on his estates. The editorial said that 'Mr Carlyle's beautiful ideal' found expression in 'many an Irish landlord's ugly practice' and went into an aspect of Lord Leitrim's dealings with his tenantry which was currently the subject of censure by the British press. The Earl's conduct was quoted as exposing the other side of Carlyle's ideal, 'the tenant shall be a complete serf...a degradation of human nature which fortunately cannot with safety be reckoned on as permanent'; and readers might have inferred that Leitrim was a typical specimen of the Irish landed class. Should there be an agrarian revolution in Ireland, it would be due more to abuses like the ones alleged of Leitrim than to agitators.[59] This hostile radicalism was not entirely a temporary deviation from the responsible way in which the paper liked to set forth its opinions. The outburst was indicative of the anti-landlord feeling that lay near the surface of liberalism, however moderate, when it was based on interests other than the land. The first leader on the following day looked for a moment beyond an Irish bill to reform of British land law, saying in passing that 'the English farmer may require time before he perceives that the Irish tenant is simply an extreme instance of a dependence and a restriction which exist on this side of the Channel as well...and which are almost inseparable from the present land system.' For the rest, this editorial of 21 October was really about the room for manoeuvre which ministers possessed. The *Daily News* invoked the authority of none other than Sir John Gray and led up to the statement that 'the concession... of a legal guarantee for a certain continuity, not necessarily perpetuity, of occupation, would not, perhaps, be unjust, and might prove to be expedient'. The government, however, was bound only 'to propose or give effect to the improvements for which public and Parliamentary opinion is ripe'. A bill – a good one – limited to compensating tenants for their expenditure of money and labour was not certain to pass. It should be accepted for what it was worth, although it would not dispose of the Irish land question. The leader thus ended on a far from hopeful note, after extending the range of possibilities to include fixity of tenure.[60]

On 28 October, two days before Irish land was opened in cabinet, the *Daily News* gave its support to those who looked for a solution in the practice of tenant-right. The wealth of Irish experience among ministers in the cabinet and outside it promised well: they were unlikely to be deceived by false analogies with English agriculture. Ulster custom invested the tenant 'with a certain status, independent of contract', besides protecting him against capricious and uncompensated eviction. Lord Derby's admission to the Lords in May was quoted, that *de facto* fixity of tenure of this kind existed on his Irish estates. The *Daily News* believed that the Irish government approved of the idea of legalizing and extending the custom, with whatever restrictions and safeguards might seem proper; here the name of Lord Leitrim came up again. 'Legislation respecting...Irish land tenure must be based on the recognized, but often precarious and often violated customs and on the common understanding of the country.'[61] The editorial was undoubtedly inspired.

The *Manchester Guardian* was less well informed, but observant.

It was also far more reluctant to give up its previous opposition to extensive statutory changes designed to benefit the tenants. Its attitude was summed up in a sentence by the first leader on 19 October: 'The Irish priesthood objects to landlords as Protestants, and extreme English Liberals object to them as Tories; but prudent people will not abolish the aristocratic system without being prepared to put something in its place.'[62] The Manchester journal's comments resembled those of *The Economist* in their unemotional preoccupation with what would do some good politically, in terms of the Irish situation, and, economically, as little harm as possible; and in reacting sharply against attempts, from the Conservative or the radical side, to involve English landlordism in the controversy. On 4 October the *Guardian* reviewed O'Connor Morris's article on the Portsmouth estate. The advantages which Ulster tenant-right could demonstrably have for the owner of land yet did not remove the obstacles to its legal definition and enforcement.[63] A week went by and the next first leader on the subject remarked astringently 'how entirely contradictory are the opinions expressed by recent visitors to the country'. An English radical economist, Thorold Rogers, had asserted in the *Freeman's Journal* that since the owners had done nothing for the land in Ireland, they had no valid claim to compensation for a lost investment in the soil should fixity of tenure be enacted. 'Vast sums,' said the *Guardian*, had been spent by landlords on improving their estates over the last twenty years. 'A writer who does not know this fact, or omits to notice it, is unlikely to guide his readers to any trustworthy conclusion.' The *Guardian* suggested instead a board to supervise or, should the need arise, to assume the management of estates within the framework of regulations contained in the Act of Parliament. The board would secure against eviction the tenant who paid a fair rent regularly and farmed his holding well. Property would, at any rate, be liable to suffer less than under fixity of tenure.[64] First leaders of 19 and 26 October reiterated the plea for 'a Board of Control': good landlords in Ireland were advised to help in finding a formula by which offenders might be constrained not to imperil the whole class by their actions. The paper of 27 October replied to Salisbury's *Quarterly Review* article with the warning that for landlords, English and Irish, to put class before party would be self-defeating.[65]

The Economist was carefully inconclusive when on 9 October it detailed some of the facts of the Irish land question, 'one of the most difficult ever discussed in Parliament'. This only could be stated: 'Whatever we enact should be as *flexible* as possible... we should as far as we can enlarge men's choice and opportunities ...and not counsel them to this or that specific course.'[66] There *The Economist* left the matter for a fortnight before submitting 'A Practical Plan for Dealing with Irish Land Tenure', the basic premiss of which was not economic. 'It is not good for the welfare of Ireland, it is still less good for the British Empire, that the ownership of land should seem to belong exclusively or mainly to any single race...or religion.' Lord Leitrim got one more mention – but that did not touch the central problem: – 'how are we to give the...Catholic or Celtic Irishman any share in the ownership of what he thinks his own soil?' The answer, a little surprisingly in the light of what had been said, was that in general he ought not to be entrusted with the responsibilities of proprietorship. The probable impact on the Irish character would have a fatal economic result: rampant subdivision and all that that implied. *The Economist* narrowly restricted the transfer of land to the native Irish which it held was advisable politically; none but '*particularly* industrious' tenants should be lent the money to purchase their holdings. Even at this late stage, an attenuated version of Bright's scheme was the only advance upon the old, though now more widely drawn, formula of compensation supported by perhaps the most discerning of contemporary British journals.[67]

The *Spectator*'s astonishment and pleasure of September was compounded by Hartington's and Clarendon's 'call for help to the Conservatives in putting on a drag to check the velocity with which this question is moving'. On the other hand, the prospect of a united front of landlords induced, momentarily, greater realism than usual: it was argued that 'at the very least' the state should do away with tenancy-at-will and prescribe a minimum term for all parole tenure.[68] The following week the *Spectator* was again insisting on 'that great social revolution' which it had preached for years.[69] In the knowledge that the idea was being officially considered, the issue of 30 October objected to extending Ulster tenant-right because it did not provide the security of tenure furnished by Indian land settlements. The prime minister would have 'directly or indirectly' to resort to the principles of the latter.[70]

Like all these liberal papers, with the exception of *The Times*, the conservative *Saturday Review* and the *Pall Mall Gazette* were waiting on events rather than trying to mould them. Irish land was in 'a totally new phase' the *Saturday Review* commented on 2 October, and Clarendon's speech had been 'exceedingly injudicious'.[71] Perhaps nothing, it was said on the 23rd, could have such an educative effect on Englishmen as the revelations concerning Lord Leitrim's agreements. The proposals to extend Ulster tenant-right now being heard in the English debate were 'worthless in themselves' but significant of the readiness to enlarge the dimensions of an Irish land bill. There was every reason to think that in the event the legislation would bring 'law and fact' into line and underpin 'the existing scheme of government and administration'.[72] The leading article of 30 October on the question thought it was not one to split the Liberals: the Conservatives were coming round, and the probability was small that the Whigs would part company with their party for as far ahead as the *Saturday Review* cared to predict. Tackling the problems of the day individually was the way to keep the Whigs on the popular side.[73] These articles showed that the government's position looked stronger to some Tories than to its friends.

In October the *Pall Mall Gazette* started by going into reverse on Irish land, causing the *Freeman's Journal* of 13 October to complain: 'One day it has a glimpse of truth – another, and it is in black ignorance.'[74] Irish agriculture and Irish landlords had so improved, the *Pall Mall* argued on the 11th, that England should hesitate before imperilling the prosperity by 'daring and hazardous experiments'.[75] Then on the 14th the paper criticized *The Times* for, it said, persistently regarding the relationship between landlord and tenant in Ireland as contractual and for talking of modifying a hard bargain. This was a dangerous misconception: the tenants were really claiming that 'their moral right...is as sacred...as the landlord's.' How should government treat the sentiment? The *Pall Mall Gazette* could not say, but knew that nothing less than the right to remain on their holdings as, in fact, joint owners would satisfy the peasantry.[76] Like other journals the *Pall Mall* was taken aback by 'Lord Leitrim's Leases', the heading of its leading article on the 20th; its very recently expressed confidence in Irish landlords was quite dissipated. Caution should, however, be exercised in devising the remedy. Compensation for the tenant's improvements, on which nearly everyone agreed, ought to be passed in a form that assured him of an absolute title to them, and given as 'a pledge of further measures' which would take time, but must be worked out.[77]

It was the uncertainty of most of the press, with regard to anything but undisguised fixity of tenure, that helped Gladstone. There was a willingness to co-operate if and when the government's wishes could be comprehended. *The Times* was in a unique position. The special correspondent's letters diffused an idea of the approximate limits of state action in a horribly delicate situation. The deliberate ambiguity in the letters and in editorials did not obscure the admission that however deplorable their present behaviour was, the tenants had some valid claims: and to the reiteration of that fact by the paper Gladstone owed part of his liberty to discard the old restraints on Irish land bills. The mysteries of tenant-right were considered for what they were worth to prospective legislators, and not explained to be condemned. By being so reasonable, *The Times* was better able to oppose surrender to the demand for fixity of tenure, the possibility which was the subject of rumour among the Tory leadership besides figuring in Gladstone's secret memorandum of 15 and 17 September. Submission to extremism in Ireland carried the threat, resisted by anticipation in the leading article of 14 October, that the 'revolutionary nonsense' of Basle would be encouraged. While Gladstone was, and *The Times* was not, zealous for justice for the peasant, his reservations were near enough to those of the newspaper.

ARRIVING AT THE PLAN

Between 6 and 9 October Gladstone drew up three memoranda on Irish land. They watered down his plans of mid-September and 1 October to place fixity of tenure for at least a generation within the tenant's grasp, at a price, and, unexpectedly, were not concerned with the extension of Ulster tenant-right which had increasingly occupied him during the last three weeks. If the September memorandum and the letter to Fortescue of 1 October were much too ambitious, from the standpoint of British politics, the resulting modifications were open to the contrary objection.

Thenceforward Gladstone concentrated on the idea that already exercised a very strong attraction, on exploiting the custom of tenant-right as holding out the sole hope of reconciling English landlordism to Irish agrarianism. Only then on 9 October did he get in touch with Edward Sullivan, whose legal and political talents had struck him when the Irish church bill was being drafted and got through Parliament. He contented himself with putting a couple of questions about the custom to Sullivan, who after replying had apparently no further contact with the prime minister until, as requested in the letter of the 9th, he came over from Ireland to help present to the cabinet on 30 October a plan built upon custom. Meanwhile Gladstone personally laboured to convert Chichester Fortescue to that design for a land bill.

Of Gladstone's three memoranda one was dated the 6th, and both the others, the 9th. The first of the two latter was devoted to general observations, which guided him in the composition of the second and were also applicable to the memorandum of the 6th. The intervention of government between landlord and tenant should be kept to the minimum possible under the circumstances; and legislation should nevertheless cover its area thoroughly and confine judicial discretion to construing the statute in a straightforward fashion – the point, of course, made in his letter of the previous day to Granville when referring to Lowe's scheme. Secondly, he wrote: 'It has been suggested that what we have now to provide for is a transition from a state thoroughly vicious to a better one, and that the remedies which the time requires may not be well suited to a permanent land law.' Consequently, existing and future tenants should be treated differently – the way to meet the former's claims was by a lease and not a money payment – and a time limit might be put on the sections of the contemplated statute that were 'decidedly exceptional' – Fortescue's compensation for disturbance, awarded in inverse proportion to the size of holding, and financial assistance to occupiers who had the opportunity of purchasing their holdings. Thus the landlord–tenant relationship would continue 'in its essence without interruption' – the five words of the quotation need underlining – and would in due course be restored to normality as defined by the Act. Of fixity of tenure in its accepted meaning, understood to include fixing rents by law, Gladstone said in this memorandum: 'My present impression is that it radically alters and subverts the relation of landlord and tenant, and involves a principle which could not be limited to Ireland.' Ulster tenant-right did not here appear as the means of securing the benefits of fixity of tenure without its disadvantages, but only as a side-issue: 'It will be convenient,' he actually observed, 'to carve the difficult question of the...Custom out of the general question, and if the time be come for legislating upon it, to make separate provision for those parts of Ireland.' A jury, he added, would presumably decide where those parts were.[78]

The document was an appreciation of the situation as well as a statement of principle. The political weaknesses in the plans of 15 and 17 September and 1 October were seen to be too grave: but since Gladstone could not perceive a workable alternative, it survived with modifications that lessened, almost to extinction, its appeal to the peasantry without ceasing to offend seriously against British prejudices. He shared these prejudices, and particularly the attachment to social leadership by the landed class. While he was sure that the peasantry had been grievously wronged, he did not want to destroy the landlords as such, which was what the mid-September plan and that of 1 October came near to doing. He did not want to be responsible for justifying an assault upon the landlords of the United Kingdom. His misgivings were reinforced, there can be no doubt, by what colleagues were telling him and the public. As to the tenant-right solution, he had before him two conflicting interpretations – the one he had discovered in Campbell and the one that Gray and the *Freeman's Journal* were disseminating. Gladstone feared that if he took up the first, he would himself be implementing the second and fixity of tenure.

The memorandum of 6 October was a variation of the proposals in his letter of 1 October to Fortescue, with the future occupier now barred from their benefits except for compensation for improvements and disturbance. The detail omitted in the letter and now filled in tended to be to the landlord's advantage. Over three weeks Gladstone steadily cut down the scale of his ideas. They still rested on the use of the principle of compensation for improvements to vindicate the grant of extended and secure tenure: but by 9 October the tenant had lost, even if unfairly evicted, the power to exact a thirty-one years' lease which had been his absolutely in the original set of proposals, while the choice of compensation for disturbance was now taken away from tenants currently in occupation, who were to have had it so recently as the 6th. Moreover, the detailed proposals of 6 and 9 October deprived a tenant evicted for non-payment of rent of the right to any compensation whatsoever – a severe drawback in Ireland where many occupiers were habitually in arrears.[79] The memorandum of general observations was, under one aspect, an apologia, addressed by Gladstone to himself, for this retreat. His desire to redress the historic grievances of the peasants was wholly undiminished: and his search for a means, frustrated in other directions by his estimate of the difficulties, came back to the custom.

In the second memorandum of 9 October there was a paragraph with the marginal note against it: 'Most difficult and prospective.' Its subject was the procedure under custom when landlord and outgoing tenant made financially conflicting demands for rent and 'goodwill', respectively, upon the incoming tenant. This was the problem, affecting the custom whether extended or merely legalized where operative, about which Gladstone and Fortescue had hitherto corresponded inconclusively. Here Gladstone proposed to resolve it by arbitration, either upon the amount of the 'goodwill' at the rent which the outgoing tenant had paid, or upon the rent to ascertain what it would 'fairly' be in the open market. He had been driven into adjudication upon rent. The precision of the drafting testified to the prominence of the custom in his reflections on the whole question of Irish land. He wrote to Sullivan that day, inquiring into the soundness of statements by Gray and Lord Granard, which, he was told in reply, were not accurate in their picture of the tenant's security under custom.[80] In his letter to the prime minister of 28 September, Fortescue had said that he would enlist Sullivan's help in examining custom as the form of legislation which he, Fortescue, thought, however, should be intended primarily to ensure compensation for improvements and for disturbance only in the case of small farmers.[81] It may therefore be supposed that the Irish attorney-general knew of Gladstone's lively interest in the tenant-right solution before he heard from him on Irish land for the first time on 9 October.

Answering on the 12th, Sullivan's remarks indicated that he had been considering the matter and was optimistic of devising a bill which would 'substantially' succeed. Landlords who acknowledged Ulster tenant-right, he advised Gladstone, increased rents 'constantly' but 'within moderate limits'. He went on: 'This is one of the anomalies of the...Custom which nevertheless works well and if we can by apt legislation procure...tenants elsewhere the security of occupancy which they have in most parts of Ulster we will go far to meet a good deal that is required.' He could not see a court at present allowing an insolvent to reckon the 'goodwill' as property and for that reason Granard had put it *'on too high a ground'*.[82] On the same date Sullivan took 'a very favourable and hopeful view' of Fortescue's September proposals, so their author informed the prime minister.[83]

It looks as if the attorney-general was as yet no closer than Gladstone to being able to translate the practice into statutory law, and was not clearly inclined to prefer this course to another. That Fortescue did get the attorney-general's skilful assistance in preparing the adaptation of tenant-right for the whole island is certain: it was the latter who, effectively, took the leading part in expounding the scheme to the opening cabinet on Irish land. This does not mean that Sullivan was responsible for persuading Fortescue to propose the diffusion of custom by an Act of Parliament which would enable the tenant to claim the price of 'goodwill' and not just compensation – for improvements, and also for the disturbance of smaller tenants only – as conceived by the Irish secretary in September. The pressure on Fortescue to submit this scheme for extending tenant-right in the sense in which it was properly understood came, on all the evidence, from Gladstone, who made a direct request ten days after the memoranda of 9 October. When Gladstone and Sullivan consulted again on Irish land, it was the eve of the cabinets on the question, and the Irishman had travelled to London at the prime minister's invitation. By which time the policy had been determined: its presentation to the cabinet needed to be arranged, and Sullivan's professional advice was particularly necessary on a subject that to many of Gladstone's and Fortescue's colleagues was baffling in its superficial likeness and underlying dissimilarity to British landholding.

On 7 October J. F. Maguire, replying to Gladstone's long exploratory letter of 20 September, missed or was unreceptive to a lot that it had tried to convey. This moderate of many years' standing was a survivor of the Repeal Party and the Tenant

League: his hopes and his apprehensions had been excited by the pace of developments in Britain and Ireland. He wrote with emotion and repeated underlining, impatient of Gladstone's solicitude for the landlords of England and Scotland: 'I do not speak of Fenians – I refer to honest and logical Nationalists... let it be said that Ireland is not to have what she has been asking for for half a century and now universally demands, *because it may prove inconvenient to England*; and what is the lesson thus taught? Is it not...that union with England means...the denial of justice...of...her national improvement and redemption?' As to the aims of the land agitation, he assured Gladstone that the different names given to it denominated the same 'giant want': 'The tenants and their sympathisers (meaning all not landlords) ...cry out as it were from the depths of their hearts...They naturally desire *irremovability* – and they describe it as fixity, or perpetuity, or sometimes as tenant right.' He showed how the people had taken the attitude of ministers in the way foreseen by their fearful critics: 'Your Government declares that the land question must be dealt with; and those who are mainly interested ...see only what they want – what would be a settlement...and ...in their strong and passionate conviction, jump over and disdain all obstacles, whether political or class.' Maguire's account of the tenants' wishes was virtually indistinguishable from Gray's version; they must have '*security against capricious rise of rent*'. His unhelpful message in response to Gladstone's appeal for cooperation in aiming at a compromise – and a compromise that would be a good one for the peasants – was: 'I cannot reduce the popular demand to anything more exact or less vague than I have done.'[84] The whole letter afforded not the slightest hope that those who spoke for the tenants would try to smooth Gladstone's path. If custom were made law, it must be fortified by that which Gladstone was so keen to avoid, though forced to entertain in the second memorandum of 9 October, arbitration upon rent and the size of the 'goodwill' payment, backed by an appellate tribunal.

Gladstone was not to be dissuaded even by Maguire's wilful blindness, from what was beginning to resemble a search for the philosopher's stone. He sent Fortescue his two memoranda of 9 October, and a covering note which said: 'I think the question seems to open by degrees.'[85] The Irish secretary approved the suggestion that compensation for disturbance should be but a temporary right, weakening the main feature of his plan in deference to the prime minister. He also agreed that state intervention to regulate rents was undesirable. He could not agree that compensation for disturbance should apply to future occupiers only, nor that, when in excess of a year's rent, it should be proportionate to the value of a tenant's improvements. The second of these restrictions, he wrote, would be 'an entire departure from the analogy of the Ulster Custom, and...defeat the object of getting rid of bad, unimproving tenants, without extreme hardship to them, or danger to the landlord, the succeeding tenant or the public peace'. These words epitomize Fortescue's approach to the land question, that of an Irish landlord, though an unquestionably liberal one. When he said compensation for disturbance was 'the adoption into...law of a system...deeply rooted...in the habits of the people', he was thinking of its efficacy 'as a mode of tempering the hardships of eviction, providing for emigration, facilitating consolidation of farms, &c'.[86] Eviction, emigration, consolidation – these were dreadful things to the peasantry – and Gladstone did not want to 'facilitate' them. 'Irish Land is very hard of digestion,' he confided to the Speaker on 18 October.[87]

Gladstone had called his second, detailed, memorandum of 9 October 'a kind of rough first outline to serve at any rate to draw the matter to a head'.[88] On the 18th he had an amendment to the memorandum of the 9th while still awaiting Fortescue's observations upon them. It was, in order to eliminate 'needless disturbances', to transfer to the category of future occupiers all existing tenants worth £100 a year and more, or whatever the valuation was that reflected the ability of tenants to fend for themselves and the type of farm for which the landlord found capital.[89] The modification – better political economy than sense – was put forward after a letter from Bright which, as Gladstone reported to Fortescue, was 'very moderate indeed'.[90] Gone was Bright's earnest assurance of the summer that he knew how to set about curing this running sore. 'I have my own plans,' he wrote, 'but I am not sure they would content the Irish expectations ...I have great faith in political economy, a science unknown I suspect in Ireland, and as far as it will carry me, I am willing ...to go...but I shrink from nearly all the propositions which are offered.' He looked on Fitzgibbon as too extreme for him.[91] Two or three days after hearing what Bright felt, the prime minister at last gave up the centrepiece of his draft schemes, the long lease established upon the principle of compensation for improvements, the plan which had been propagated by Fitzgibbon and had been attractive because, *inter alia*, he was an outspoken partisan of the opposition. Gladstone had, first and last, to carry his colleagues with him. On the 18th Fortescue was writing that 'I don't think any scheme will do for "overriding the landlord" in the matter of improvements...for enabling a tenant to improve in spite of him, guarded from ejectment.'[92] How could anything satisfy the tenants if the landlord were not 'overridden', not permitted to escape with a fine, being compensation for disturbance? The Ulster tenant-right solution raised the problem equally acutely, if the custom were to be imposed where it did not flourish; and Gladstone confessed his perplexity once again when he had read a letter from Lord Portsmouth to Granville: 'What I should like to know from him is his view of the *mode* of legislating upon "tenant right" in Ireland, if, as it seems, some legislation on that subject has become necessary. I cannot see my way to making it by compulsion universal.'[93]

That was also written on the 18th: but on the 19th Gladstone made up his mind to make a law, somehow, out of custom. 'Fortescue' he told Granville the day after, 'is apt to be tenacious. I have incited him to draw out a plan for extending the Ulster custom over Ireland.' He added, reassuringly, that he thought Granville would not disapprove of the Irish secretary's ideas as they had been revealed to him thus far.[94] 'I cannot doubt,' Gladstone put it to Fortescue, 'that if anyone can devise a set of good or fair provisions, first for legalizing Tenant Right, secondly for extending it throughout Ireland, there would be much to be said for such a course'; and he asked for a draft from which they could decide whether to proceed.[95] Fortescue's compensation for disturbance fell well short of Ulster tenant-right: but he, Gladstone, and Sullivan between them enlarged it, and transformed it. Granville and Bright would also seem to have been involved: Gladstone wanted them to meet him and Fortescue '*before* the question is touched in Cabinet'.[96]

Fortescue was quite ready to extend tenant-right – though it must not be forgotten that his attitude to it was never the same as Gladstone's – but in his eagerness to show himself in command of the question he did not realize that the cabinet must be handled with great tact and induced to discuss, not immediately to agree to, a plan. Gladstone explained how they had to start: '...I do not think you can safely reckon on obtaining the definitive approbation of the Cabinet for any land tenures...at its Oct[ober] sitting. The distance between cup and lip is in this case considerable. The first part of the operation will...be by no means the least delicate.' He did expect their colleagues to give their views on Lowe's scheme: but it was safe to say that, since he knew what those were likely to be.[97] Fortescue was slow to understand, and sought a week's postponement of the first cabinet on Irish land, so that he could perfect the clauses of his measure. 'For weighing and examining the form of heads as a first step is far preferable to that of clauses,' came the reply. 'I apprehend the preliminary steps are more serious than you seem to anticipate.'[98]

Gladstone, Fortescue and Sullivan – these three, certainly, and perhaps others – were to have met on the afternoon of 29 October to prepare for the following day's cabinet. So the prime minister wished.[99] Sullivan's position was embarrassing; Gladstone, who had already written, now telegraphed for him. The attorney-general informed Fortescue – after Lady Waldegrave – he had been summoned in this fashion, and had telegraphed back that he could not leave Dublin before the night of the 29th. 'I write [sic]...by this post' continued Sullivan's letter to Fortescue '...telling him I was thoroughly satisfied you were complete master of the Land question in all its bearings and that your ideas if carried out by apt legislation would settle the matter and you and I had discussed the question in a most satisfactory manner.' He did not assume he was going over to attend the cabinet himself, saying: 'You know if you have the *slightest wish* I should be at the cabinet...I will be with you.'[100] Gladstone's interest and his authority, and Fortescue's dependence on Sullivan to devise and articulate the statement of suggested policy that the prime minister desired made Lady Waldegrave fear for her husband's performance on the day: 'Pray take care,' she urged him, 'that when the proposal for the Land Bill is laid before the Cabinet...*you* are the *person to do it* – I am delighted to see that the Papers now treat you as *the* person in this matter – This makes it all the more easy for you to stick to your rights.'[101] Poor Fortescue failed to rise to the occasion. The Irish attorney-general went to the cabinet, too, and after listening to them both Kimberley noted in his diary: 'Now, having heard Sullivan... I see light. It is evident that Sullivan is the real author of the plan. Chichester Fortescue shows much less mastery of the subject.'[102]

Sullivan was not, of course, the real author: but Gladstone plainly tried not to be identified with the plan from its commencement in the cabinet: a certain detachment would improve his chances of being able to sway those who were hostile or sceptical. Moreover, he had to have this freedom because it could not be known how the majority, possibility the great majority, of the body would react to the boldness of the initiative he had instigated. Clarendon, for example, who was sent Gladstone's correspondence with Maguire of 20 September and 7 October, was as full of objections to extending the custom as he had originally been: returning the letters, he argued that it would lend itself to the organization of 'a system of terror' against landlords with the purpose of obtaining complete liberty eventually to dictate rents.[103] 'I am glad,' responded Gladstone diplomatically, 'you did not find in my letter to Maguire any disposition to ride roughshod over the difficulties of the case.'[104] Bright was just as unhappy, though less combative. 'If we knew what was right to be done, and what it is possible to do, we might proceed with courage,' he said to Clarendon, 'but courage in the dark may turn out to be only rashness and mischief.'[105] With powerful members of his government in this mood, Gladstone was grateful to Sullivan whose achievement on the 30th rated Granville's discriminating praise: 'It was impossible to open the question...in a more acceptable manner to the Cabinet, than he did.'[106]

Sullivan's submission to the cabinet was subsequently printed over Fortescue's initials in a memorandum dated 2 November for circulation to that body and, Kimberley recorded in his diary, 'amounts practically to extension of tenant-right to the whole of Ireland'.[107] 'Practically' is the word to emphasize. 'The custom of tenant-right, commonly called Ulster custom, or any similar custom' received the force of law, without being defined, wherever operative 'by common consent of landlord and tenant', which took in the scattered localities in the South that knew tenant-right in its Northern vigour. 'Compensation of an analogous character to be secured,' the memorandum continued, 'in parts of Ireland where the courts shall not recognize the existence of a custom of tenant-right, to...tenants whose occupation shall be disturbed by the landlord, subject to the conditions of the Act.' Disturbance meant eviction, arbitrarily or consequent upon unacceptable demands for higher rent or for some other revision of the conditions of tenancy. That is, the custom was artificially reproduced under limitations not applied to the natural growth. If the occupier claimed under the artefact he should get 'such a sum as a solvent tenant would give for a farm under its actual tenure, in its actual condition, and at a fair rent, having regard to all improvements executed by the tenant or by those from whom he purchased or inherited'. The presumption of law as to the property in improvements was changed in the occupier's favour, but his improvements were subsumed under the market price of the occupancy-right, as happened with Ulster custom. The tenant also had a claim against the landlord if not allowed to sell his interest to a new occupier. Someone evicted for non-payment of a previously agreed rent was restricted to this claim to dispose of his interest. If the landlord refused to permit a sale to a solvent and respectable new occupier or, having consented, was held by the court to have contrived to defeat the sale, then the tenant was entitled to compensation from him as though turned out for some other and valid reason. There was a ceiling, left undecided in the memorandum, on the landlord's financial liability, to which the court might add if satisfied that certain major improvements – buildings and wasteland brought into cultivation – were worth more than the valuation of the occupancy-right. At the discretion of the court, up to two years' arrears of rent might be deducted from the sum paid for the tenant's interest. It was the easiest and least contentious way of extracting arrears from the Irish peasant. The limit of two years was kind to the tenant and good for the landlord.[108]

By the device of the hypothetical offer which the court considered someone would make for the succession to a particular tenancy, by thus simulating the sale of occupancy-right, with the alternative of an actual sale, the idea of custom as the native and proper resort in agrarian disputes was everywhere acknowledged and fostered by the law. In that legal climate, artificial custom might be assimilated to the real within a generation or two. The tenantry were also to have, indirectly, valuation of rent. The court did not have the power, of course, to direct what an occupier should pay, but it would show him what he ought to be paying on a named holding or estate, in a neighbourhood, when computing a fair rent as integral to the assessment of compensation for a tenant 'disturbed', to use the memorandum's term, by the landlord. As Gladstone was conscious, it did not follow in these years of prosperity for very many Irish farmers that a fair rent was necessarily lower. Tenants on overrented estates might well profit by the moral effect on their landlords, and the surrounding countryside, of an official estimate. It was this exploited minority which Gladstone and Fortescue were so concerned to succour that they were prepared for the state to announce, though not to enforce, a fair rent – despite firmly agreeing in principle that they wanted to refrain from interference with rents.

The tenants were not to gain the fixity of tenure they were vociferously demanding. There was to be no unavoidable loss of control by landlords over their property; they might still exercise their rights, at some cost. If it were argued, as it was bound to be, that mulcting landlords for using admitted rights offered a dangerous example to the people of Britain, the operation wore an appearance and employed the mechanism of an exclusively Irish practice, so foreign as not to look susceptible of transplantation. Compensation for disturbance had been disguised. Among the controversial features of the plan was its failure to distinguish between large and small farmers, but the use of custom was the stumbling-block.

THE FERMENT IN IRELAND

Any government land bill must concede less than the tenants were hoping for – that was now true even of Gladstone's secret memorandum of mid-September. The reception of whatever emerged from the cabinet could not but be improved by a conciliatory step in other fields of Irish policy. On 2 August Maguire suggested to Gladstone that, with an eye to the welcome in Ireland of the land bill expected next session, he should not rest content with having liberated a batch of imprisoned Fenians earlier in March. Maguire believed that if these political prisoners were not freed, 'even a large measure would fail to propitiate a very considerable section of the country...Were I a minister, I would take a generous race captive by generosity.'[109] When Gladstone considered whether the government should act on this advice, he encountered resistance from within thead ministration which persuaded him to desist, not before he had written to the viceroy on 26 September: 'The question is rather subtly related to that other great matter of the land...Maguire observes with truth that feeling goes a great way with the Irish and that they will accept the gratification of feeling, to some extent, in lieu of what are thought more solid concessions. Such are my present impressions of the difficulty of the Land...that I should try... every other with reference to it...to smooth its passage.'[110] Apart from the complications of British opinion, the prime minister had to steer a course between frightened, angry landlords and belligerent tenants in Ireland. It was partly because the landlords were more frightened than angry, and resentfully aware of their dependence on British reactions, that Gladstone gave the tenants most of his attention.

The letters of Blennerhassett and O'Hagan to Dufferin quoted earlier showed a willingness to compromise up to some point that would preserve them from fixity of tenure. Similarly misled was the Earl of Limerick, with estates in the county of that name, who sent Gladstone an unsolicited letter on 27 October suggesting compensation, on notice to quit or increase of rent, to be estimated under two heads, improvements, and 'goodwill' when sanctioned 'by the custom of the estates or privity of the landlord', with a maximum on awards under the second head. These were ideas not so far removed from those being worked over for the cabinet.[111] A number of landlords gathered at Cork to take stock, wanting to organize themselves against the attack upon 'what they supposed to be their exclusive property'.[112] There were landlords who became converts to the people's cry as it drowned moderate voices. The *Freeman's Journal* of 30 October cited, among others, Sir Robert Gore-Booth, M.P. for County Sligo and one of the leading magnates in the West. A Conservative, he had been elected as supporting 'an equitable adjustment' of agrarian relations. About recruits like Gore-Booth, the *Freeman's Journal* inquired delightedly, thinking of the impression they would make in Britain, if they were 'Communists and Revolutionaries?'[113]

The Times reported on 13 October that the agitations for amnestying the Fenians and tenant-right were going 'hand in hand' in the South of Ireland, and the month saw them progressing in a rash of mass meetings.[114] The intertwining of agrarianism with nationalism, which was instinctive and had uncontrollable consequences when the peasantry were roused, naturally recurred in the despatches of the *Times* Dublin correspondent. Two extracts may be cited from his report appearing on the 18th. He quoted the *Freeman's Journal* of the 16th, which said: 'The great ground of complaint with the tenant farmers and all their true friends is that "property" is not respected by the landlords...power to act capriciously is incompatible with this solid marketable property – occupancy right...the tenant must by law have his property in the occupation of the farm as securely protected as is the landlord's...in his fee simple.' Gladstone kept a close watch on the *Freeman*, and it could have been that this article influenced his letter of the 19th to Fortescue. The rural form of this rigorous but calm presentation of the tenants' goal was a notice extensively distributed in Westmeath: 'PUBLIC NOTICE. TENANTRY OF THE SURROUNDING DISTRICT – SLAVES OF THE SOIL ...In few words, which must be complied with...you are requested to withhold rents until ample justice is done you...Justice, justice to Ireland! faith and fatherland! together, together!... the Scully landlord who refuses...honoured [sic] concessions to his tenantry shall be dealt with as Council may hereafter determine ...[signed] RED RORY.'[115] The editorials of the *Freeman* became more cogent as the threats and violence of the Ribbonmen and their imitators swelled. The number of agrarian offences notified to Dublin Castle rose from fourteen in September to fifty-nine in October, the highest monthly figure yet for the year and the highest compiled since 1854.[116]

The language at the tenant-right rallies was charged with emotion. Clarendon's use of the term 'felonious' was made to yield all it was worth and more in the speeches. The speakers recalled ancient dispossession as well as present wrong.[117] The Catholic clergy were in their accustomed place, to the fore, at these rallies. Fenians, or some of them, might entertain reservations about the primacy accorded to the land question: but the whole spectrum of Irish politics was represented in asking, with the old stridency but a new sanguineness, for fixity of tenure. The minority of landlords who joined in were, of course, the least prominent and enthusiastic element. They chiefly took part because they smelt capitulation in the air. They were too pessimistic, but it was excusable.

Those Englishmen in the ministry who were fully alive to what was passing in Ireland knew that in October and for several months afterwards they had to deal with the severest test of their professed intentions towards Ireland. Bruce, who was one of the most Gladstonian of the cabinet in his outlook, showed Dufferin that he understood his fears, and would not be turned aside from right and expediency by the sympathy which he felt for the Anglo-Irish landed class. '...The continued agitation,' he told him on the 4th, 'of such radical and exciting measures as the overthrow of Churches and the reconstruction of the bases of property, must have a serious effect...Act as wisely as we may, you Irish landlords have a *mauvais quart d'heure* before you... But the crisis was inevitable and must be met manfully.'[118] Attitudes like Bruce's contributed to the bitterness that Dufferin did not try to hide in a memorandum written for the conclaves on the land bill from which he was excluded. As Gladstone watched the *Freeman*, so that paper read the omens coming thick and fast from England. 'The wonderful growth of English public opinion within the past few weeks...' it exulted on the 27th '...points with certainty to the speedy triumph of...the downtrodden tenant farmers of this country.'[119] It displayed greater realism in the leading articles of the 28–9th when *The Times* and the *Daily News* gave out that the government was meditating the adoption of Ulster custom for the land bill's foundation. The *Freeman* warned the cabinet that nothing but the custom so interpreted and safeguarded as to be 'indeed..."fixity of tenure"' would satisfy Ireland and the farmers were exhorted to keep up the pressure of their movement.[120]

SIR JOHN GRAY AT MANCHESTER

Ireland had been worse hit by unrest during Clarendon's viceroyalty than she was in the late summer and early autumn of 1869, as he reminded the prime minister in a letter of September. It was England and the international dimensions of the Irish question that had changed conclusively. The Manchester-based National

Reform Union was the incarnation of moderate middle-class radicalism, if indeed many of its members could be called radicals at all. Its prominent figures were substantial men, who were not averse to aristocratic leadership but wanted to assert their mildly reforming tendencies and special interests within a party the inner councils of which their sort had just begun to penetrate. Criticism of the landed class at the Union's meetings was often real but its regard for property was ingrained. At the start of September the executive had considered Irish land along with familiar topics, when deciding what guidance the membership should have for several months to come. Of half a dozen speakers whose views were given some space by the *Manchester Guardian*, two suggested fixity of tenure or compulsory leases. A third ignored the question altogether for the ballot and educational reform. Of the remaining three one spoke of 'the difficult business' of ensuring fair play for the tenants and satisfying both them and the landlords; the government would require every assistance they in the Union could render. The next speaker said that Irish land – 'he looked upon it more as a social question' – should not take precedence over the aims in their programme. Summing up, George Wilson, the veteran of the Anti-Corn Law League and a person of note in the Liberalism of the industrial North, observed that there were as yet many differences over it and recommended the Union to devote itself to gathering and making known the facts. Among the resolutions carried as advice to branches those on the ballot and large cuts in taxation were followed by one to afford the government 'all possible support in passing a well-considered measure for the improvement of...land tenure in Ireland'.[121] Six weeks after this cautious and nondescript counsel had gone forth, an audience of the National Reform Union rewarded with 'loud cheers' an uncompromising but extremely skilful speech from Sir John Gray on 18 October.[122]

He played on the changes in England and the world since the epoch of the old Tenant League. He asked the meeting to dismiss compensation for improvements as a remedy and described the plan to invest the Irish tenants with an occupancy-right that should be absolute, subject to payment of rent – although when addressing the Union only the week before Sir Thomas Bazley had opposed the tenants' desire 'to have something like hereditary possession...to have the farms transferred from father to son'.

This hereditary possession was exactly what Gray appealed for. 'The English people owed it to themselves,' he said, 'as parties (and they would pardon him for reminding them of it) to the original confiscation of the Irish lands, to make restitution.' By such restitution he did not intend a literal restoration because, he assured those prosperous Englishmen, 'history taught them that when a man had been declared the rightful owner...his proprietary rights should not be lightly interfered with.' The comfortable reflection was one way of helping them to swallow what was so clearly the creation of joint ownership. The other ways were, firstly, to talk of landlord oppression – without identifying individuals or localities, except in the case of the marriage restrictions on Lord Lansdowne's property which Gray introduced as demonstrating 'a state of serfdom...disgraceful to any civilized country'. Secondly, and this was where he touched a sympathetic nerve, he claimed that rooting the Irish tenant in his holding would not only raise agricultural production by half, it would realize 'that unity of sentiment which all wished...between the people of England and...Ireland', would convert the Irishman into 'the ally of the Englishman, his brother, and the staunchest supporter of the empire and the throne of Britain'. A tactfully worded reference to the animosity of the Irish 'in another hemisphere' drove the point home. Gray was presenting the costs and benefits of his plan to end the Irish land question: and of the benefits, peace in Ireland and the removal of a serious danger to good relations with the United States were those to which the British business community and middle-class taxpayers worried about economy should look forward with a sense of personal advantage. The cheers were for the confident statement from so authoritative a source that a loyal Ireland was not an impossibility, rather than for the conditions attached to the promise of reconciliation.

Whether or not Gladstone read Gray's speech before writing as he did to Fortescue on the 19th cannot be known, but he surely read it at about that time and it must have encouraged him in his preference for the tenant-right solution. He was in no doubt that the implications of recognizing occupancy-right, even with the accompanying limitations in the plan explained to the cabinet on the 30th, were repugnant to moderate liberals, let alone Whigs like Clarendon. Bazley's conclusions following a rapid tour of Ireland which he had undertaken to study the land question were submitted to the prime minister. In them Sir Thomas advocated, as he did to the National Reform Union, a retrospective presumption that tenants-at-will held for twenty-one years: but payment for goodwill he termed 'a system of extortion'.[123] It was not superfluous for Gladstone to tell Bessborough on 30 October that, 'we are now proceeding to compare ideas a little on Irish land...We are not...you will readily believe, going for confiscation.'[124] The prime minister admitted to 'much difficulty', and Bright was correct in having surmised that the ministry's enemies were enjoying its doubts and divisions. Its enemies would have been surprised by the truth about the basic disagreement that showed up at the cabinet on the 30th and hardened during November and December until Gladstone gave way.

6

THE CABINET DEBATE, OCTOBER
TO DECEMBER

The cabinet jibbed at the proposed extension of the custom of
tenant-right: that was the extent of Gladstone's failure with his
colleagues between 30 October and 10 November, when these
meetings ended for a little short of a month. He did elicit considerable admissions. In the hope of forcing members of the
cabinet to think Irish land through as he had done, cover the
rest of the distance separating him from the majority of them,
and accompany him in the measured development which he
undertook of the 30 October proposals – they were then invited
to draw up, individually, their outlines of a bill to be circulated
in time for the resumed discussions in December. Altogether eight
wrote the desired papers, including those composed prior to the
general invitation. Only John Bright's, for vital reasons, was not
printed and made available to the cabinet. Disappointed in these
responses, Gladstone was constrained to accept partial defeat, and
the Irish secretary was emboldened to revive compensation for
disturbance *as such*, and in an amended plan for the December
cabinets it displaced the universal resort to custom. This did not
happen without strenuous argument on Gladstone's part, argument
which revealed how completely his mind was filled with the
historical wrongs of the Irish peasantry and the commanding
relevance of those wrongs to legislation. In his eyes, the diffusion
of occupancy-right by law had the merit of being seen as some
tangible restitution for the confiscations – had not Sir John Gray
said so? Gladstone's critics in a debate which they were all
anxious should remain private, found this aspect of his case
bewildering as well as alarming: they seem to have felt that his
judgment was unbalanced. For him justice to the tenants was
a moral obligation personally irresistible because of his responsibility in government. Inside the administration pressure was

gathering for a coercion bill, which Gladstone withstood out-spokenly, resolved to see first how the Irish greeted the planned reform of tenure.

When he aspired to win cabinet approval for the extension of custom, Gladstone wanted two kinds of evidence. One was sure knowledge that outside Ulster tenants-at-will habitually acted as if they were co-proprietors of their farms, and were everywhere acquainted with 'the idea, at least...(if not the practice) of Tenant-right, more or less corresponding with the Ulster custom'.[1] The other type of evidence was support that the most obstinate ministers must heed – landlord support. To get information about peasant wrongs, he had the civil servant, Lambert, detached from London to supervise the Irish administration in the work. Among the landlords he tried to convert Halifax, potentially more useful to him than any other Whig peer outside the cabinet. Halifax was understanding but critical and his advice of major value, as, no doubt, was his activity in persuading others in both parties to see the necessity for a new sort of legislation on Irish land. Spencer rightly received more than the attention that was his by virtue of the post he occupied. Of those who would be directly affected, owners of Irish estates, Gladstone consulted with Lords Dufferin, Bessborough, Portsmouth, Monck and the shrewd businessman with much personal and great hereditary prestige, the 7th Duke of Devonshire, to whom his son Hartington would listen. Bessborough's character, his reputation as an Irish landlord, and his place in the upper House and the party made him a good adviser who seems to have been firmly on Gladstone's side – the rumour at one moment of his resignation over the land bill was treated sceptically when brought to Disraeli's private secretary, who was eager to discern any break in the ministerial front.[2] Dufferin had to be heard, as a minister of some seniority and the Irish landlords' defender in the 'paper war' of the last four years: but he opposed extending custom until halfway through December when it was too late for his concession to be of use, although in his earlier papers for the cabinet what he yielded in principle was a definite contribution to the making of the bill. Monck, Devonshire, and Portsmouth who agreed, more or less, with Gladstone, were not political figures comparable with Bessborough and Halifax and not, therefore, allies to impress the cabinet.

THE CABINET DEBATE

A clear picture of what transpired with regard to Irish land at the cabinets of 30 October and 3 November, and particularly on the first occasion, is preserved in Fortescue's letters to Spencer in Dublin. For the meeting on 10 November there is no similar account. In the intervals between the three dates ministers' correspondence shows the stalemate developing which was reached on the 10th. Bruce told the Irish secretary on the 31st: 'I like much your plan of crystallizing customs where they exist, and creating them where they don't.'[3] It was a minority sentiment, but the majority were up against Gladstone.

'I need not tell what anxious work yesterday's...was to me' wrote Fortescue to the viceroy after the first cabinet. 'It is true that the able men who sit round that table approached the subject in an excellent spirit – yet one could not but feel that most of them had not that deep and lively sense of all that lies around us and before us in Ireland, which you and I must have, nor yet any full knowledge of the problems to be solved. The long discussion...which took place was as favourable, according to my view of the necessities of the case, as could be expected, and Mr Gladstone was quite satisfied...' The excerpt from the prime minister's diary in Morley's *Life* corroborates the last impression.[4] Gladstone had not allowed Fortescue to lay his proposals in writing, being 'afraid of anything so definite coming at this early stage from a member of the cabinet.' How right Gladstone had been in recommending such caution was evident from the description of individual reactions. Cardwell and Hartington – neither of whom was as ignorant of Ireland as Fortescue's remarks above implied – had been the strongest in their objections, and Lowe 'critical but moderate. The Chancellor, Granville, Bright ditto, though timid – D[uke] of Argyll questioning but reasonable, most of the rest silent.' 'A good beginning,' said Fortescue with the exaggeration of relief, but it was deceptive, even allowing for that feeling of his.[5] Lady Waldegrave warned her husband that Lowe might not be so restrained next time; she had often observed that he was a little while in gathering himself for the attack.[6]

Gladstone in his diary called the cabinet of 3 November 'stiff' on Irish land.[7] Fortescue told Spencer: 'We have had a very heavy Cabinet. Things looked ugly beforehand – a paper of objections from Cardwell – storms from Lowe &c. But the result though still uncertain was better than I had feared. Important admissions were made.'[8] The cursory record in Gladstone's minutes stated: 'Discussion on the Irish Land Tenures. Five questions as to tenancies at will.'[9] The five are detailed in a rough unsigned memorandum in his hand dated the same day. They went over the ground of the 30 October plan and more besides. The first reopened an issue assumed by now to have been determined in the tenants' favour: 'Shall we revise the presumption of law as to improvements?' The second bordered on the region of current controversy: 'Shall we extend the tenants' claim in respect of improvements already made?' The third and fourth came to the centre of the argument: 'Shall we admit any claim of the tenant at will in Ireland, on being evicted by his landlord or on a demand for the increase of...rent beyond what the tenant is willing to pay, over and above compensation for...improvements? If we admit such claim whether we call it of goodwill, occupation value, compensation for disturbance, or whatever it is to be, what is the best legislative form in which to clothe it?' The last of the five questions inquired whether Ulster custom should be legalized in that province.[10]

The first to the fourth of these questions were put in ascending significance. It would appear that this progression was deliberately arranged to elicit admissions from the stubborn conservatives within the cabinet which could be used to extract further admissions. Granville later reminded Lowe that the opponents of the bill 'have lost their immaculate reputations by consenting to retrospective compensation'.[11] Gladstone in a memorandum containing most of the points he adduced in arguing with colleagues laid it on more heavily still; by compensating the tenant for improvements retrospectively: 'We shall...take away from the landlord what ...belongs to him. This is a large, some might say a violent concession to equity as against law. It seems to me to be the camel of our problem: for one I assent to it reluctantly, and with a full sense of its gravity. I know of nothing else so grave, which any member of the present Cabinet is likely to propose or support.'[12] It looks absurdly like special pleading. It was quite effective: because the contemporary legalism made it so. Common sense, however, ensured that the transition from paying the tenant for improvements to paying him for 'disturbance' or 'goodwill' was an uphill struggle.

This memorandum tells how Gladstone had openly taken charge of Irish land. Fortescue said that 'things looked ugly' before the meeting. The prime minister could not leave their plan to be defended by the man to whom Granville and Argyll respectively referred shortly afterwards as 'our feeble Irish secretary' and 'a bit of a fool'.[13] They were rather unfair to Chichester Fortescue, but it is undeniable that he did not have it in him to talk round abler and politically more formidable men. Gladstone, moreover, in the face of the criticism already encountered, wanted to enlarge the plan, as will be explained further on in this chapter.

Fortescue summarized the outcome of the cabinet as 'still uncertain, though better than I had feared'. From memoranda circulated after the meeting it seems that the 'important admissions' covered some kind of compensation for eviction. The battle was fought over the form and extent of that compensation. Gladstone decided to force the cabinet to share the responsibility for finding an answer to problems the legitimacy of which they had been got to concede. The disadvantages of extending custom had come under fire: the advantages might be seen to outweigh them if ministers were to examine, at their leisure, possible ways of recompensing the tenant for his occupancy surrendered unwillingly. At the cabinet of 10 November, the last until discussion of the programme for the session of 1870 recommenced in December, Gladstone minuted: 'Invitation to offer *suggestions* or *queries* on Irish land.'[14] While these were coming in, Gladstone worked at the case for tenant-right and on those who could, or wanted to, prevent its acceptance and its controlled expansion beyond the limits of 30 October.

THE DUKE OF ARGYLL

Two members of the cabinet had anticipated the general invitation of 10 November and composed memoranda since the initial discussion on 30 October. The first was Argyll's, printed for circulation on 6 November.[15] He began with the assumption that 'in some form or other we must recognize "Goodwill", or "Tenant-right" or "disturbance of occupation"'. His opinions had advanced recently but he did not agree that compensation for eviction

could 'best be provided for on the basis of "Ulster Custom".'
He resisted the idea because it entailed more than such compensation or than impeding 'arbitrary' evictions: it was 'incapable
of defence...placing every tenant-at-will in Ireland, in the
position of a leaseholder'. This was the deciding factor – by
giving the yearly tenant a disposable interest the custom recognized occupancy-right, with greater permanency than under a
leasehold tenure and with undesirable political and historical
connotations which Argyll brought up, not in the memorandum,
but in subsequent correspondence with Gladstone. It was wholly
irrational to say to landlords, in or out of Ulster, who had bought
up the tenant-right on their estates or never permitted it to grow
up that, applying 'the "analogous" substitute...by the Act...
we must assume that it does exist where we have evidence that
it does not'. He also argued that the custom was economically
harmful, citing the usual grounds. The roundabout method of
estimating fair rent in the plan before the cabinet incurred severe
censure – 'altogether vicious in principle' – fairness being very
difficult to ascertain except by reference to the market.

Argyll advocated compensation for eviction as suggested by
James Caird[16] in a pamphlet and in a long memorandum written
by Dufferin for Gladstone and printed as a cabinet paper:[17] paying
the tenant for the loss of his expected profits and term in
occupation. It would not, he reasoned, expose ministers to the
charges that would be made in Parliament against legislation on
the basis of Ulster tenant-right – the custom being 'the confusion
of all principle and of all policy' as a method of giving compensation in addition to the value of improvements. The defensibility
of any plan was a point to which he recurred in this memorandum
and in his correspondence. 'I would be no party to asking the
House of Lords,' he declared to Granville on 12 November, 'to
assent to measures which Cairns or Bethel[l] would blow to
shreds, on the _merits_ – we having...in support...the argument
of the Plunderers.' Moreover, Argyll wanted, he told Granville,
to confine compensation for eviction to tenant-at-will '_below_ a
certain size _of Holding_' – a limitation not apparent in the memorandum. 'Beyond this,' he finished, 'I do not see my way to go:
and would rather see the Government broken up a thousand
times than be a party to the Universal Tenant Right so wildly
propounded to us – or any attempt to fix rents.'[18]

Starting on the Duke's side there ensued a correspondence with Gladstone in which they dissented warmly over both the provisions of the land bill and the spirit of its conception. After an exchange about a paper on Irish land from Hatherley, the Lord Chancellor, that was welcome to Argyll as resembling his own thoughts on custom and compensation expressed to the cabinet and Granville, but a disappointment to Gladstone,[19] the Duke wrote on the 26th: 'We shall have to "put our foot down" fairly soon about Ireland. They are a people who require absolutely not to be too much "made up to".'[20] Gladstone retorted: 'The Irish Land question...the Irish case generally...is very dark and I see neither truth nor policy in optimising on it. Indeed the people of this island neither know in any tolerable degree how bad it is in itself, nor do they feel as they ought how disgraceful it is to themselves.'[21] As the December cabinets drew nearer, Gladstone felt it was time to speak his mind and he proceeded to do so when on the 27th Argyll told him in a postscript that Spencer had found his memorandum unanswerable in its rejection of legislation based on custom.[22] 'I go with Lord Spencer,' he said on the 29th, 'if he accords to your argument on the Tenant Right, all the praise of clearness, vigour and decision. But forgive me if I say yet it does not and *cannot* conclude the question... it does not grapple with the main allegation, on which the advocates for Tenant Right found themselves.' He meant, as he confirmed in his next letter, that the custom of tenant-right was in some shape familiar and observed, if only by the tenants, extensively outside Ulster. Trying to widen the admitted breach in Argyll's defences, Gladstone continued on the 29th: 'My strong belief is that the main question must be whether we are prepared to go beyond compensation for improvements, and that if we are, there ought to be no vital difference going beyond your point.' He strove to bring the Duke to see Ireland as he himself saw it: 'For the last two months I have worked daily, I think, upon the question, and so I shall continue to do...We have before us a crisis, and a great crisis, for us all...and a great honour, or a great disgrace...I do not mean to fail through want of perseverance.' To underline the rampant disaffection in Ireland he enclosed a letter from Sir John Gray and his reply.[23]

'Gladstone writes under very high pressure steam,' was Argyll's philistine comment to Granville on his correspondence.[24] The

Duke, however, hardly less stirred by events in Ireland, was 'all against getting in perpetual sackcloth and ashes'. While the state of Ireland was undoubtedly to some extent due to 'old sins of England', for a couple of generations the latter had made amends. 'I feel quite sure,' he said candidly, 'that the language of self-reproach and lamentation may very easily be overdone... and I think it tends to make men already highly excited, expect sweeping changes – corresponding in importance to the depths of the repentance we express.' He would choose to be confronted with a wholly Fenian Ireland, were the option a land bill 'unjust in principle and... in its economical effects... certainly... disastrous – There is no argument for it – except... simply fear.' Gray was correct, Argyll believed, in saying that only fixity of tenure would placate the Irish: but as 'an absolute transfer of Property to the Occupier', it could not be. Government's efforts should be restricted to 'what is really just in itself'.[25]

At this stage, on the other hand, the Duke was encouragingly responsive when Gladstone urged that the custom of tenant-right had a significant presence in Ireland as a whole. Argyll did not object to recognizing tenant-right payments anywhere, presuming the landlord had known about and implicitly sanctioned them. A conversation with the prime minister on 8 December turned on the use to which custom outside Ulster might be put in the land bill.[26] 'I agree,' the Duke said on the 10th, following another letter from Gladstone on that aspect of the subject, 'the confirmation of existing customs clearly ascertained, is a safer basis of legislation than any abstract reasoning, however... if it can be proved that at least the idea of the Ulster custom is familiar all over Ireland, then of course it becomes the safest basis everywhere.' Notwithstanding the last sentence, he refused to agree to extending custom.[27] He was also highly sceptical of the astonishing claims which Gladstone made for the custom as a means of advancing the productivity of small Irish farmers, and consequently swelling the rental of their landlords. Argyll's experience of Highland crofters, who so closely resembled the peasants ministers were discussing, led him to tell the prime minister that he was flying in the face of facts: 'My firm belief is that to expect any such increase of produce as you contemplate, or indeed any material increase at all, from *this class* of Tenantry, is nothing but a vision and a dream.' Consolidating half a dozen or ten of these little holdings to comprise a single farm in the hands of a leaseholder, with his capital undiminished by having to purchase the occupancy-right, was the only way of securing the growth for which Gladstone hoped.[28]

The Duke took up Gladstone's argument that once compensation for improvements was agreed, there was no longer any barrier in principle to conferring further rights on the tenant. In his view, the sticking point would come after a further step – which he did not think anyone in the cabinet would oppose – the legalization of tenant-right payments wherever the landlords were cognizant of them. 'But in any attempt to go beyond this,' he warned the prime minister, 'there is room for the most serious difference of opinion on points involving fundamental principle.' Like compensation for improvements, which Argyll was quite willing to give retrospectively, such conditional recognition of tenant-right was at present morally binding on an honourable man. These were legal innovations that kept landed property morally inviolate. 'Everything beyond these two great Provisions,' it seemed to him, '. . . will be in the nature of a concession to the "Political Situation".' He told Gladstone, as he had the whole cabinet in his memorandum, that he was prepared for some concession of the kind: but, as in his letter of 12 November to Granville, he would not extend it to all tenants, only to smaller tenants. How to justify compensating them for eviction was one of the worst, if not the worst, of 'the Rocks and shoals of this question'.[29] On 2 December he reflected: 'Poor creatures, they have come into existence under a vicious system, for. . .which many parties have been responsible: and as a matter of expediency, perhaps even of justice I admit. . .there is much to be said for not allowing them to be removed without some compensation for the loss of their means of livelihood.' But he was a prey to doubt: 'This. . .Protection. . .most offends against principle and will be most difficult to defend. I do not know how to defend it, except on some such general and vague pleas as those alluded to by the Chancellor.' (The Lord Chancellor's memorandum is discussed below in pp. 211–12.) Argyll thus had a coherent, eminently defensible bill in mind, and summed it up in his letter of 2 December, under the three heads of improvements, custom, and special provision for those with what he graphically termed 'rights of semi-pauper occupancy'.[30]

It was not that Argyll failed to understand the Irish land question as well as Gladstone had learned, and was still learning, to do, but that he looked at it, though compassionately, from a landlord and British angle. His obstinacy was intelligent: he understood exactly what the prime minister was aiming at in trying to stretch custom. Gladstone 'most *earnestly*' asked him to read up the question and directed him to 'many matters of fact which had seriously modified my views, most of them connected with and branching out of the very wide extension of the idea and even the practice of tenant-right mostly perhaps *un*recognized beyond the limits of the Ulster Custom'.[31] The Duke retaliated with a pamphlet by Peter Maclagan M.P.,[32] 'following your advice to read as much as I can'. There he found confirmation that the landlords needed Parliamentary protection even more than did the occupiers; and he drew to Gladstone's notice the account in the pamphlet of discontent among Lord Portsmouth's tenantry in Wexford when an increase of rent was demanded at the end of a long period – proof of their 'utter unreasonableness'.[33] 'Do let us try,' wrote the Duke in his last letter before the December cabinets, 'to sow the seed of sounder Tenures than these bad old customs of a bad state of society.' He and Gladstone could agree, at any rate, on leases as an optional method of compensation, beside those which they had discussed. Gladstone saw in long leases a way of inclining the landlord to give under another guise, more attractive to their and to British eyes, the security and sense of property that went with the custom where it was strong. Argyll saw 'an alternative by which the owner escapes the "Black Mail" levied by the Occupier'.[34]

Argyll was able and eloquent. In this correspondence he had handled his side of the argument with skill and vigour, giving way enough, compared with his recent position, to make it hard for the prime minister not to oblige. Above all it was plainly going to be far easier for the Duke to persuade his colleagues. 'I have my fears,' observed Gladstone to Granville on 1 December, 'lest he should be the Rupert of debate in the Cabinet.'[35] From this prospect Gladstone was delivered by the serious illness of Argyll's Duchess, which isolated him in the Highlands. Foreseeing a prolonged absence the Duke wanted to resign, but said that his leaving office might be misinterpreted by the Opposition.[36] Gladstone, naturally, would not hear of resignation.[37] A little ahead of the news about his wife, Argyll had a letter which nicely displays Granville's knowledge of men. He was alarmed by the Duke's 'somewhat light' reference to the danger of the administration's breaking up, he appealed not only to his awareness of political duty, to his party loyalty and his sense of responsibility, but also to personal obligations and weaknesses – pardonable ones in a politician, but nevertheless weaknesses. Granville did not think there was a single member of the government 'not strongly perturbed with...Irish Land...and puzzled how to deal with it, so as to do enough without doing too much'. There had been 'much reticence and self-control in the language of nearly all'. Clarendon's loud and indiscreet talk was an exception; but so it always had been, and he was too old to change: while 'at our age it is worth our while to limit to one another any thing one thinks may be a mistake.' 'You are' he wrote 'one of the cleverest in the Cabinet, and...certainly not the least honest... You are a little impulsive and fizzing, and have already revelled, I have no doubt, in the prospect of an easy victory over our feeble Irish secretary and even a triumphant success in discussion over our great chief.' Their own feelings of obligation apart, he wished Argyll to reflect on the inevitable result of overthrowing Gladstone, or of gravely weakening him. An Irish land bill would be passed by the Conservatives or a coalition, and he inquired whether it would 'smell sweeter' for that and for the delay. He asked Argyll to 'act as a cement, and not as a dissolvent in a negotiation, for such it is in which everyone must yield something'.[38] The final sentence accurately described the situation in the cabinet – a negotiation. It may be wondered whether the letter was particularly effective. Argyll and the rest *had* conceded more than a little, and it was Gladstone's turn.

LORD KIMBERLEY'S SECOND MEMORANDUM

A memorandum by Lord Kimberley dated 8 November was printed on the 11th for the cabinet, which had already seen his comments on Lowe's plan. The effect Argyll had had is clear when Kimberley's paper is compared with his letter of 29 October to Gladstone. In that letter he wrote of the good results of Ulster custom, and now of the bad. The custom must be legalized – he did not see how they could avoid taking that step – but not extended. 'There seem to me to be insurmountable objections to the simple extension of this custom by law to the rest of Ireland. I agree generally with the arguments of the Duke of Argyll.'

He agreed with Argyll's memorandum also, in giving compensation for eviction and on its form and method. Thereby, Kimberley pointed out, a danger inherent in the plan introduced by Sullivan and Fortescue would not arise. Under their device of the hypothetical offer, the value of 'goodwill' might be freely enhanced, while it was intended that the landlord should be influenced in the fixing of rent.[39] On 22 November Gladstone said to Fortescue that the papers by other members of his government so far printed had not done much 'to advance our consideration of the Land Question'.[40] That is, they had not gone to the desired length. His remark covered Lord Chancellor Hatherley's memorandum which came after Kimberley's, and was equally firm against extending the custom.

THE LORD CHANCELLOR

The undated memorandum by the Lord Chancellor, Hatherley, was in circulation a few days after the cabinet of 10 November.[41] It is of great interest as showing by what reasoning a perfectly orthodox English lawyer adjusted himself to an unprecedented measure of interference with property-rights in the interests of the state. The document gladdened those who wanted a good alternative to the plan backed by Gladstone.

Hatherley began like the distinguished Chancery lawyer that he was. He held it to be 'of primary importance that Legislation in respect of the Tenure of land should be based on principles universally applicable to the subject, rather than on a custom which is only one form of the development of the principles'. There was no uniformity in the calculation of tenant-right payments, and there was the continuing perplexity how the tenant's purchase and sale of the occupancy and the landlord's right to enhance rent affected each other. These were the considerations that Hatherley adduced to show 'the inexpediency of resting the Bill upon an extension of the Ulster Custom to all Ireland', although it might be proper to make the usage lawful according to the practice on individual estates. By putting his legal weight into the scale against extending custom he reduced its weak prospects of being adopted by the cabinet.

His distinctive proposal was that, for small tenants only, with the line drawn at less than 10 acres, a court should have power to award them an unnamed sum, subject to an upper and lower limit, described as 'damages for eviction', and they should not be allowed to contract out of this special protection. This was more controversial than generous, because of the general principles on which he was positive that it must be justified. He invoked 'motives of common humanity' and 'the reasonable expectation of the disturbance of public order...were the tenants cast out penniless upon the world...[and] the burthen...in the shape of rates'. They were the arguments for the poor law and their application here to those who were not paupers is an early instance of the pragmatism out of which the 'welfare state' developed. They were as valid for British workmen as for Irish peasants, which was certainly one reason why Gladstone disliked Hatherley's proposed damages. 'Lowe is pleased,' wrote Argyll to Dufferin, 'with the Chancellor's paper, which in general principle is sounder than any before.'[42] Although the scheme was utterly opposed in its approach to his own of October, Lowe, and Cardwell too, had concurred with Hatherley's memorandum before it was submitted, Granville informed Gladstone after some days.[43] The Duke told the prime minister that Hatherley had furnished 'the rough materials for a good Irish Land Bill'.[44] The memorandum offered, replied Gladstone, 'much excellent matter but not a presentable plan'.[45] Of all the memoranda from Gladstone's colleagues and others, Hatherley's bestowed the least upon the Irish tenant. It was his argument that the most critical of the cabinet liked. The Lord Chancellor's presentation of 'damages for eviction' smoothed the path to the eventual adoption of compensation for disturbance. Invited to choose between the degree of state intervention frankly acknowledged, and justified, by Hatherley, and the extension of custom, which was intended to look like the transfer of a substantial joint property in the holding and to influence the fixing of rent, the cabinet inclined towards the dangers inherent in the first course.

LORD DE GREY

On 29 November Gladstone referred inquiringly in a letter to de Grey, the Lord President, to the possibility that he might give the cabinet his views on Irish land.[46] This may only have been politeness on the prime minister's part: but de Grey's memorandum, written before he got the letter, was very agreeable to Gladstone, even with its qualifications.[47] It supported turning to custom for an agrarian law. Its tone and arguments were sensible and conservative. It was a different statement, not an endorsement of the 30 October plan, especially in the treatment of overrented tenants. De Grey was so critical of custom, which he wished to adopt, that he undermined his own case.[48]

De Grey considered that the Cabinet must go beyond compensation for improvements: they should furnish 'something equivalent to those restraints upon unjust or capricious conduct which operate naturally but so forcibly in England'. This was a good argument – soothing to English feelings; and levelling up always sounds better than the reverse to those who are not radicals. Ministers should, however, try simultaneously to promote 'the adoption of real leases concluded by free contract between landlord and tenant...and...a gradual substitution of such leases for the less satisfactory system of regulated tenancies-at-will which would be established by...our measure'. Thirdly, and he made it seem the first criterion, there was 'the importance of selecting such limits for...action as will be most simple, and... have the least tendency to afford ground for future agitation under the pretence of merely extending a principle acknowledged in this Bill'. Like Gladstone, he perceived in custom the most prudent solution, politically.

A tenant-at-will's compensation should be reckoned from his improvements; claims under custom, as found locally; any money paid to his predecessor in occupation; and, lastly, 'the Court should also consider equitably any evidence proving that the outgoing tenant could have obtained a further sum, over and above the other heads, if the landlord had been willing to allow him to select his successor.' By the plan each occupier who held from year to year would be assured of a payment for occupancy-right: but subject to an important restriction. Having made every allowance for the influence of the pregnant word 'equitably', the tenant paying an exorbitant rent clearly would not benefit to the same extent as under the 30 October proposals because de Grey did not think that of the several elements in the total payment 'goodwill' ought to be the main one. With the check on extended custom went another, which had been integral to all the schemes since 30 October. The whole sum payable, taking the various heads together, should have a limit of so much per acre; and his explanation why he picked that specification instead of so many years' rent or the moneyv alue of a lengthened presumption of tenure, brings out his suspicion of provisions that might be remotely construed as leading to fixity of tenure. Of the two rejected alternatives, 'the first is open to the objection...What is the rent? and points, or may seem to point, to a fixing of the rent by the Court. The second suggests at once the idea of a lease, and...would give an apparent sanction to...all those who desire to convert...tenants-at-will in Ireland, without the consent of their landlords, into tenants under long leases at fixed rents.' To find such fears in someone as liberal for the time as de Grey was on social reform, puts into perspective those vehemently stated by Argyll and Clarendon. They did not misrepresent the apprehensiveness of the landed interest in Britain; they only expressed it more strongly.

Although Ulster custom's working proved, in de Grey's opinion, that 'in *Ireland* such a system is productive of good', he could not regard its permanence as desirable. Their bill would be hard to defend if it perpetuated what it was to extend. This statement, coupled with his view that the value of 'goodwill' should not be the main element in the tenants' compensation, which was, moreover, subject to a ceiling, left him awkwardly vulnerable to criticism. Why adopt a customary basis at all if it was so intrinsically objectionable and its central feature needed to be minimized to such an extent? De Grey answered that in a letter to Fortescue. 'I doubt much,' he wrote, 'about giving payment for "disturbance of occupation"; at all events *eo nomine*...if you...give the Tenant compensation for bare disturbance you will...rouse the susceptibilities of English Landlords and add not a little to the difficulty of carrying the Bill. One of the great recommendations of your proposals, as it has always seemed to me, is that they are founded on the special state of things in Ireland, and...are not applicable to England.'[49] Preoccupied with shielding the English landed class, he had overlooked the radical and popular interpretation of custom in Ireland which led her landlords to fight its spread and which would very probably inspire the tenants to agitate for the removal of his checks upon the extended version. The encouragement that Gladstone obtained

from this memorandum really had little justification and did not
make up for the trouble he met over Bright's.

BRIGHT'S LAST EFFORT

Bright's dogmatic moderation on agrarian issues, when he descended from anti-landlord rhetoric to practical suggestions, seemed
to have become less after the October and November cabinets.
He was almost sure that the parliamentary Liberal party would
not accept reforms such as they had been discussing unless
accompanied by those he mentioned, which had not been discussed. He would prepare a memorandum, 'to which I shall ask
you to give a little careful consideration'[50] – words doubtless
expressive of his annoyance at the rebuff he had received from
Gladstone in May. Bright was mistaken about feeling in the
parliamentary party, but the remark showed what he felt about
the opportunity, as it seemed to him, of carrying out the policies
everyone associated with his name. In his memorandum he placed
these policies above the matters that had absorbed the cabinet's
attention in trying to determine the land bill's scope. More
serious for Gladstone was the dislike of Ulster custom, and of
encroaching upon property-rights and freedom of contract otherwise than by 'free trade in land', which Bright indulged in his
paper, while saying that the prime minister and Irish secretary
had his backing.

Gladstone unsuccessfully attempted to discourage Bright from
composing a memorandum along the lines he indicated on the
29th.[51] Transmitting the document on 3 December, in the expectation, of course, that it would be circulated to the cabinet,
Bright accounted for his action which he knew must embarrass
the prime minister most inopportunely: 'Notwithstanding the
opinion...in your letter of yesterday, I venture to send it...for
it would be like treason to my own convictions to withhold it.'
If Gladstone thought the memorandum read more like an essay, a
leading article, or a speech than the contributions of other cabinet
ministers, 'it is...for good reason.' Few in Parliament – a polite
way, in the circumstances, of referring to the prime minister and
their colleagues – had gone into the land question, and Bright
had therefore had to supply the deficiency at some little length.
He repeated the warning of May that unless his advice was taken

the Irish would be demanding equal partition of the land among
the people: 'Every year's delay in doing what is right will make
it less possible to withstand what is wrong.'[52]

The memorandum began with an historical analysis of 'the
desperate malady of Irish discontent', which did credit to his
head as well as his heart.[53] It revealed with more lucidity than
his speeches the insight into the historical formation of Irish
grievances which an English Dissenting leader, though accustomed
to being moved by resentful memories of past sufferings, might
very well not have attained where a Catholic people was concerned.
The state 'found the Irish population semi-barbarous and hostile,
and...tended perpetually to degrade it...to embitter it to the
last degree against the strangers and intruders'. The core of his
argument was a truism: but one to which Englishmen had closed
their minds because appropriate steps were impracticable – or,
rather, adequate ones were, as the Encumbered Estates Act had
made a start on too restricted a scale. 'A monopoly of the soil,
this passage ran, 'is a great evil in any country, but where it is
settled and maintained in the hands of a class, strangers in race
and religion...whose original title is based on conquest and
confiscation...buttressed by cruelty and persecution thro' [sic]
many generations, it becomes a curse breeding a family of curses
...defying the wisdom and...courage of the highest statesmanship.' As he had acknowledged, this language sounded as though
he were addressing a public meeting. The style was second nature
to him, and it was not altogether misjudged in his memorandum.
The cabinet required a display of moral fervour, so Gladstone
found a little later, however unusual it might be in the privacy
of their meetings, if they were to understand that Irish claims
were better than the bombast of nationalist newspapers and
orators sometimes suggested.

Bright's description of the actual situation facing the government and the Irish landlords was not pitched in the same key,
but in a realistic one, strikingly so. He pointed to 'this most
strange picture', the superficial paradox of an Ireland where
tenants and labourers were enjoying a prosperity previously
unknown and yet continued their unending war against the landlords. Adverting to the other, highly relevant reasons for it
besides those in history, he thrust uncomfortable truths upon
the cabinet: 'There is more education among the people...more

self-respect...more self-assertion...greater power to combine, whilst at the same time the proprietary class and the Government are less able...less willing, by severity of punishment and military force to overawe and...suppress manifestations of violence or discontent.' Here Bright took note of the ultimate cause of the British government's vulnerability: its public opinion; and too many British politicians in both parties did not now have the stomach for repressing agrarianism without balancing legislation. Nor were Irish landlords themselves as tough-minded as they had been a generation earlier in standing up to a more primitive peasantry. There are things better left unsaid, and these observations fell into the category when a number of the cabinet were increasingly restive over the rural violence that was rising very steeply in November. Bright was safer when he referred to peasant methods of warfare, selective terrorism supported by passive resistance, and to the formidable temper of the class '...arrayed against the whole Proprietary...it looked on without rebuke, if not with satisfaction at the desperate acts of the most reckless, and vindictive...' He expatiated upon the wider consequences of agrarian unrest: 'Ireland is at once a humiliation and a weakness to the Empire.'

'What can Parliament offer as a remedy, if indeed now any remedy be possible?' With that he opened a critique of the land bill as it was shaping. He reaffirmed his faith in his own scheme of land purchase. It would take time to bear fruit but a start could be made next session. 'Free trade in land' was almost equally important for Ireland. He compared his proposals favourably with those which 'must be regarded as infractions, more or less extensive, of all...hitherto regarded as sound political economy'. Compensation for improvements and for eviction, altering the presumption of law as to improvements and tenure – 'All this we are asked to do,' he wrote, 'on the ground that discontent is widespread, and that some landowners have been harsh and unjust. It may be necessary...but let us not forget the nature and magnitude of the changes we are asked to make.' He passed on to tenant-right, 'not less startling to those who are afraid to infringe...sound principles and...freedom of contract,' and was doubtful of the wisdom of making it law even where it was accepted. 'To me,' he proceeded to argue, 'it is clear that all pretence for breaking down the bounds of sound principle fails until or unless we are willing first to do all that sound principle will sanction.' Or else, Bright asserted, as Argyll had done in his memorandum, the land bill would be roughly handled in Parliament.

Bright's detailed submissions comprised the full range of 'free trade in land' and his land purchase scheme, with the finance so arranged as to obviate any real cost to the taxpayer and with power to the administering commission to buy suitable wastelands for development and sale as additional farms for small owners. He urged with considerable emphasis that no individual rights of property would be affected in the slightest. He showed deep sympathy for Irish and British landlords: 'They are sensitive and in terror, because...ignorant of their true position and... interests.' The profession that he approved of compensation for improvements, legalizing custom in Ulster, some greater security of tenure and, 'if possible', deciding upon compensation for eviction in the form presented to the cabinet of 30 October – did not carry conviction in the light of everything in the nine foregoing pages.

Less persuasive, even, was his contention that the government should not be deterred by the natural alarm of British landlords at the introduction into the Irish bill of free trade in land, with the universal relevance of which radicals had familiarized them. He was aware that the land bill might not get through Parliament and not over worried by the prospect: 'Better to fail for a session with a complete scheme, effectual for its great purpose, than to succeed with one...feeble in its conception...insufficient to place the Irish question at rest for ever.' Courage, he finished sententiously, was needed in order to succeed 'where feebleness and timidity invite and...often atchieve[sic] only disappointment and disaster'. He was palpably reluctant to endorse what the cabinet had been considering – certainly after compensation for improvements – unless in conjunction with and at the price of his application of 'sound principles'. He, the reputedly fearsome radical, had provided the opposition to Gladstone in the cabinet with abundant ammunition for the approaching meetings. His memorandum and the intention to voice its arguments had to be stopped.

Gladstone wrote by return. He did not object to Bright's airing his own ideas, nor really to the resounding final sentence, except to say mildly: 'Men in a Cabinet do not like what may *seem* to imply that they are cowards.' He remonstrated with Bright for jeopardizing the progress made since October: 'You do not require to be told that the effect...is not counteracted by your adding "All this may be necessary".' With a directness all the more telling for being rare in his correspondence, Gladstone said: 'Had the Cabinet adopted at this moment a good and sufficient scheme for dealing with the Irish tenants as tenants I should care little how much you depreciated such a scheme.' He thought Bright's proposals would go a very short distance towards settling the Irish land question, but promised not to circulate a memorandum saying so. He compelled Bright to understand the damage he might do to the cause they both had at heart if his memorandum went out unchanged: 'The state of things is most critical. This is not a time at which those who in substance agree, can afford to throw away strength...It is most dangerous to discredit *propositions which you mean to adopt* in the face of any who (as yet) do not mean to adopt them and who may consistently and honourably use all your statement against them, nay, who would really be bound to do so.'[54]

'This very plain speech' succeeded. Bright's memorandum was not printed at all and he gave the prime minister the demanded co-operation. Thenceforth he was willingly yoked to the Gladstonian chariot for many years to come. He kicked a little about the omission of 'free trade in land' and received a *quid pro quo* not previously envisaged – something, that is, besides permissive land purchase, which Gladstone mentioned in his letter as certain to appear in the bill, and included in the September memorandum. At the cabinet of 7 December he asked for free trade in land to be embodied in the bill. 'The impolicy of this seemed patent to everyone except Bright', commented Kimberley drily, who joined him on a cabinet committee to prepare bills for the United Kingdom on that aspect of land law.[55] This looks suspiciously like a sop to Bright. The bills framed were brought in but quietly dropped during the session of 1870. There was never a serious danger that Bright would prove stubborn or try to bargain. On 21 November Granville had described him as wanting the legislation preferred in the memorandum he shortly produced but as readily agreeing that they must support Gladstone.[56] The prime minister, writing to Fortescue on 5 December, was amused by Bright's vanity and use of political economy to vindicate the state intervention he fancied, and did not anticipate trouble with him.[57] Bright was a great demagogue – in the best sense of the term – but he did not have a good political instinct nor the qualities for battles at close quarters, for intra-party warfare in the closed arena of the cabinet where policies and personalities conflicted in a way quite different from the public campaigning he knew. He admired his leader too much, and had hedged too much in his memorandum, to be a match for him. The famous radical could not resist an appeal for loyal aid against his erstwhile enemies, Robert Lowe and Whig nobles, instead of giving them the means of thwarting Gladstone. Making sure of Bright helped Gladstone, not, as he hoped, to get the extension of custom accepted, but to win the compromise that was the result of the crisis of which he spoke here.

Bright's memorandum bears out the verdict of a contemporary American statesman that 'there is a very large residuum of John Bull in him' – quoted by Granville to Gladstone some months before.[58] His sympathy for Ireland was unquestionable, but British interests – among them the integrity of private property in the United Kingdom – came first. Although he was quick to emotion in his humanitarianism and libertarianism, the weakness of his radicalism here would have surprised many of the unsophisticated. It needs to be stressed that he was less disposed to sacrifice landlord rights than was the Duke of Argyll, because he considered only a minority had abused these rights and the class ought to be bolstered by a wider diffusion of property, identifying the people with its defence through the creation of numerous smallholdings. The more intelligent and informed Irish landlords, like Bessborough and Dufferin, realized that he was not an enemy: to a great many he remained a bogy. His platform style tended to relegate to the background his Quaker respect for property and law and detestation of violence. In the memorandum suppressed by Gladstone, these beliefs were not obscured. He stood with Gladstone but was so obviously unenthusiastic about extending custom that his adherence did not brighten its prospects.

LORD CLARENDON

'The more I think of Fortescue's Bill, the less I like it,' Clarendon was writing to the prime minister before the end of the November cabinets.[59] In the foreign secretary's papers are scribbled notes on the plan, perhaps jotted down for those discussions.[60] He regarded the official assessment of rent as 'a groundwork for far more violent agitation': tenants on adjoining lands would compare assessments when the opportunity arose following use of the machinery for valuing compensation, and they would then call for reductions – 'to yield to such demands would be simply confiscation.' He complained of the absence of any encouragement to grant leases. The simmering anger he felt at having to consider the plan at all burst out and he called it 'an attempt to bribe the tenant into obedience to the laws by subsidizing [him] out of the pocket of the landlord'. His memorandum on Irish land of 11 December did not breathe this intemperate spirit; the accumulated experience of political life told him when to seek a distasteful accommodation which Gladstone and Granville helped to make easier for him – but Clarendon, too, would not have the extension of custom. He was concerned at some signs that English farmers were being moved to think of emulating the Irish, and he did not wish it to be concluded from the bill that a land agitation in England would handsomely reward them.

Gladstone's line with him, on 10 November, was to deploy the arguments that he tried on most of his critics in turn. Retrospective compensation for improvements was the '*strongest* thing we are likely to do'. If they took a further step, there was 'a great practical question...the best *form* in which to convey this boon'; Fortescue's scheme had been '*fired* into', and let different ones be produced for examination.[61] Clarendon did not oblige for over a month. In the interval he vented his angry fears to others. 'I hear a great deal' he wrote to Lord Spencer on the 26th 'about English tenants preparing...their claims to Tenant Right if it is given to the Irish.'[62] He enlarged on this menace to Granville a few days later. English farmers were watching and waiting with a deliberate intention: 'There is a general agreement to keep... quiet in order not to place difficulties in the way of the utmost possible concessions to Irish Tenants.' Quite apart from his alarm on the score of English property, Clarendon was more positive than ever that 'the extension of tenant right to the whole of Ireland is a measure no honest man could agree to.' He did not know what might be going on between Gladstone and Lady Waldegrave's 'feeble husband' and had communicated to her his foreboding that Irish land would destroy the government.[63] Granville's short paragraph in reply referred to the inevitability of a compromise:[64] but he thought it worth apprising Gladstone of Clarendon's frame of mind.[65]

The foreign secretary was imbued with all the old Whig distaste and distrust for Catholicism, especially the Irish variety. Remembering his viceroyalty in the troubles of the later 1840s and early 1850s he regarded the Catholic clergy as the principal instigators of movements against the landlords or the government – Palmerston's view. Fenianism and the upsurge in agrarian violence during the month, about which he corresponded with Spencer, naturally led him to urge a coercion bill and also to put out a feeler to the Vatican, policies with which he had been associated twenty years ago. He mentioned approaching the Pope in his letter of the 26th to Spencer: the British representative at the Papal Court was returning to Rome where the episcopate of the Catholic world was as gathered for the first Vatican council; 'he will find a host of these pleasant Gentlemen, the Irish R.C. Bishops, and I want him to get them lectured by the authorities there upon their conduct at home.'[66] 'I never expected an ounce of gratitude...on the part of the Irish R.C.s,' he told Granville 'as robbing of land and monopoly of education are their real objects.' The 'ministry of *Pacificators*' must overcome its reluctance to act firmly.[67] To Granville's response that they should keep the majority of the clergy opposed to Fenianism he countered that all the lower clergy were Fenians in the sense of 'treasonable haters of English rule'.[68] He was afraid that the Irish secretary was 'talking fixity of tenure and suchlike nonsense' and wanted to know whether Spencer was satisfied with Dublin Castle's cabinet minister who weakly registered Sullivan's views without being capable of defending their plan when got at by himself for an evening.[69]

'I hope but don't expect that we may discover a proper land bill.'[70] Clarendon's memorandum was printed on the 11th.[71] In it 'the limits of law and justice' had expanded since he defined them in September and October but 'they would be greatly overstepped by any attempt to introduce the Ulster tenant right throughout Ireland.' Custom should be accorded only limited recognition in the areas where it was established; specific restrictions maintained the control of the owner over the occupier. Where there was no custom a tenant-at-will or leaseholder for less than thirty years should be entitled to four or five years' notice to quit, with the option of going immediately and receiving half the rent payable during the statutory period of notice, together with the value of his improvements. The compensation was reduced for holders of leases of between thirty and thirty-five years and not valid after any term in excess of the latter figure. Retrospection in compensation for improvements was treated separately, with the landlord allowed the choice of a money payment or its equivalent by way of tenure. This, then, was the minimal interference with property-rights which the memorandum had as a postulate. The surest hope for the future consisted in disseminating leases by making them the joint interest of landlord and tenant, which his proposals were designed to do. The political tide had carried Clarendon a long way from the shore on which so lately he seemed determined to be stranded. Free with compensation for disturbance, his motive was to avoid the extension of custom from which would spring fresh and more extreme demands. He used the argument that evictions from 'caprice or vindictive causes' must be prevented, and it suited his purpose. As he had written in September, it was expedient to put a stop to those incidents which agitators exploited in order to damn a class. His letter to Gladstone with the memorandum was a wry expostulation: 'I enclose a few notions...probably...thought too careful of land-lord rights, but we must think of what we shall be able to carry thro' [sic] Parliament and not forget the manifestations...among English Tenant Farmers.'[72]

THE VICEROY OF IRELAND

When Spencer expressed the wish to send in a memorandum on Irish land, Gladstone told him on 6 November that there was no urgency.[73] 'I feel the very great difficulty of the subject,' the viceroy reflected, 'and first views are very likely to be modified.' He would postpone writing his paper for the moment, and meanwhile he let the prime minister have illustrations of the agrarian problem drawn from his correspondence and his travels about Ireland. Every day strengthened his opinion that the land bill must be '"thorough"'. If the bill did not command the acceptance of 'the sensible bulk' of the Irish people, the country would become hard to govern.[74] The apparent tendency of these remarks was all that Gladstone could desire from a person whose final judgment, when it came, might have an effect on the cabinet's: but Spencer's mind was made up on the essential point already. He had written frankly to Fortescue on the 2nd after receiving his account of the cabinet of 30 October with the plan put to it.

Spencer had close contacts with the ministry in England. He advised Fortescue that everybody would agree to the legalization of Ulster custom but predicted, and the cabinet of the 3rd proved him absolutely right, a 'strong disinclination' to extending it. The viceroy himself did not consider the latter course sound. By contrast, he did not think that the tenant who suffered from the exactions of a bad landlord was sufficiently protected under the plan.[75] He went into these objections in his memorandum of 7 December which was circulated to the cabinet and strove to combine his inbred regard for property with 'the immense necessity'[76] of a bill that would calm Ireland. He did not know the country well but, as an exemplary English landowner, one facet of the question impressed him forcibly. 'Nothing I can imagine,' he wrote to Gladstone in the middle of November when they were discussing collection of the facts relating to the different aspects of Irish land, 'has brought about the present state... more than the transfer of land from the old race of lax Proprietors to men who treat land as a purely commercial speculation.'[77]

His was in some ways the most radical of all the memoranda circulated to the cabinet[78] – excepting Lowe's and Gladstone's, which were based on quite other principles. The situation in the countryside induced him to go to such lengths. The law as it stood did not, and could not, work when neutralized by 'acts of ...terrorism and revenge...The full exercise of a Landlord's legal rights has been and is now in many places limited, if not altogether in abeyance.' He believed that nothing would have a greater impact for good than to invest inexpensive tribunals with jurisdiction upon rent; and that many landlords would not really complain at being thus delivered from 'their present... danger and suspense'. He was fully alive to the criticisms which this form of state intervention would provoke and admitted that they might be unanswerable. Whatever was done in this respect, a tenancy-at-will should be deemed to run for five or seven years at a fixed rent, from the date of notice to quit. Spencer did not commit himself to compensation for disturbance, to be paid if the tenant left quietly before the expiry of the above term. He argued that the alteration in the existing tenancies of the mass of Irish occupiers would constitute 'directly and as it were in kind...a reasonable concession' to the agitation for fixity of tenure; and that the occupier would henceforth enjoy a legal bargaining power, while not impairing the landlord's freedom to give a longer lease. What Spencer liked about his proposal was its 'elasticity'. The hesitancy over compensation for disturbance was explained in the letter to Gladstone that accompanied the memorandum. Spencer was opposed to giving the claim to large farmers, as unnecessary, and he wondered how they could be excluded. His lengthened presumption of tenure at a constant rent was applicable to all sizes of farms because stability was a prerequisite of modern agriculture.

On custom he was unyielding. Where sanctioned by prescription, it ought to be enforced by law. He was against imposing it on the rest of Ireland, ostensibly for purely economic reasons: but he remarked, in passing, that the custom 'amounts, in fact, to a share in the possession of the Farm'. He had earlier described Argyll's attack on extension as irrefutable, and in a letter of 9 December to Dufferin seemed distinctly pleased that Fortescue was giving up the idea.[79] To Spencer the success of the land bill would depend upon the peasantry's ease of access to, and confidence in, cheap, quick and clear verdicts upon disputes with their landlords. With Lowe, he anticipated this part of the case for the Land Commission set up under the Act of 1881, without at all relishing the breach of principle. One of the viceroy's themes was the hardships to which the very small Irish occupiers were liable. Their privations struck him forcibly, used as he was to the comfortable tenant-farmers of his English estates. He was apologetic to Dufferin about its most controversial feature when sending him a copy of the memorandum: 'I fear...you will not like rent arbitration. I wish I could see that the evil of rackrents would be overcome without.'[80]

Order, and humanity: they inspired Spencer, and distorted his political vision. He had set himself the aim of 'meeting to a certain extent the demands of the extreme party in Ireland without... incurring any overwhelming opposition in England'.[81] Seen from the Viceregal Lodge, the first posed the greater threat, but the two forces were more evenly balanced. The direct and general regulation of rent by the state transgressed Gladstone's axiom that government should be loaded with as few continuing responsibilities as possible under the land bill. Nor would the cabinet have tolerated the step for a moment. The memorandum's real significance for Gladstone lay in the fact that Spencer added his authority to Fortescue's withdrawal of support for taking custom as the way to legislate on Irish land, although the two differed on other points. The viceroy told Dufferin that he had been very careful in drafting his paper to avoid alluding to Fortescue's but he certainly had some tactful part in the retraction of its central idea by the minister who was touchy about his rôle in the bill's preparation. Halifax, whose advice on the custom the prime minister sought out, seemed to have a fairly open mind initially but came to very much the same conclusions about it as Spencer.

LORD HALIFAX'S ADVICE

In the last week of November Gladstone talked over Irish land with Halifax more than once, and encouraged him to draw up a memorandum, which was not printed for circulation like Spencer's but sent to selected individuals.[82] It was '*satisfactory* in the main, which is important', opined the prime minister when he got it, and wondered whether to try again to bring the writer into the cabinet.[83] Halifax's reaction to the scheme that was being matured was a test of its acceptability to the Liberal party, and particularly to the moderate Whigs whose co-operation could prevent or keep to safe proportions a rebellion on the government side in Parliament. He was afraid of overt rebellion in Ireland, and on 5 November had put it to Earl Grey that conciliation and coercion must go together. 'I don't think,' said Halifax '...John Bull, if it comes to that, will be very milk-and-waterish in his conduct.' Severe repression might for a time be vindicated, but only on conditions. These were a land bill that leant as far towards the tenants as a reasonable man would wish, one in which 'somehow or other' bad landlords should be compelled to act like the good: '...it would be a very sad state of things if the reign of force only enabled bad landlords to bully and evict their tenants.'[84] He had no love for Irish agitators, whom he considered impossible and professional troublemakers; he usually treated the popular sentiments they expressed as subversive – but the English landed interest, of which he and Spencer were admirable types, had never really been able to believe that the heavy hand of some few Irish landlords was justified. It did not happen here, so why in Ireland? – was their feeling, in spite of appreciating that the circumstances were different. Halifax had learnt from his years at the India Office to regard land agitations as specially catching and dangerous. This view could work both ways: and now persuaded him that the government must take action of a nature that it had repeatedly turned down. As to that action, Gladstone wanted him to acknowledge the potentialities of custom. Halifax was doubtful. Gladstone made an impression at first, but did not manage to convert him.

Before the memorandum which the prime minister sent to Granville, Fortescue and Argyll, Halifax had written another, a commentary upon a paper by Lord Monck, one more among those with whom Gladstone was consulting about Irish land. Monck proposed not perpetual tenure but rents fixed by the state, and that the price of 'goodwill' on a change of tenancy should be met by the new occupier or the owner. Halifax did not deny that the amount of the 'goodwill' might be cut by an increase of rent. Monck saw here an argument for interference with rent, Halifax a reason against compensation for 'goodwill'. 'The justice of such a payment by law is very *questionable* at best,' he observed, 'and the policy may be also.' He allowed, nevertheless, that in Ireland the custom of making this payment was '*generally*' found, with variations in the size, and legalization might be '*possible*'. He did not object to it as a transaction between outgoing and incoming occupiers, only as a legal claim upon the landlord. If it became law, the example of English courts in dealing with their tenant-right should be imitated and rulings made in accordance with the evidence as to the local practice.[85] This was the point of principle that separated him from Gladstone throughout – Halifax was not prepared to legalize custom where it, or the form in which it was adopted, did not deserve the name but was an artefact.

When he sent his second, longer and constructive memorandum to the prime minister, Halifax wrote that he had looked at the issues with two others and the conversation was reflected in the paper. They were the Honourable W. O. Stanley, M.P. for Beaumaris, a Whig, quite active though not articulate in the House, and Lord Penrhyn, a great Welsh landowner who was a Tory. They did not agree with everything in the memorandum but, he said, 'they both admitted the necessity of concession, and discussed it as you may expect English gentlemen to do.' He cautioned Gladstone that a bill which granted the right of tenants to the 'goodwill' would meet with considerable opposition from English landlords. To a great extent, the hostility would be diminished if a substantial number of Irish landlords declared for the measure: but Halifax added that he had no means of telling whether they were likely to. Definite information as to 'goodwill' payments outside the North of Ireland ought to be available, and he thought that the Parliamentary inquiries bore out most of Campbell's statements. 'I am sadly sceptical' was the candid comment in this letter on Gladstone's economic expectations if the custom passed into law.[86]

The accompanying memorandum[87] cited key quotations from Campbell and referred to a very long-winded paper for the cabinet by Dufferin; Halifax had previously read up the Blue Books on Irish land. The poles of his discussion were the convenience of 'goodwill' payments for the legislator, and the bluntly stated opinion that the peaceful extinction of the custom was desirable. The custom should become law in the manner suggested in his first paper, enforced as and where it existed. When a tenant was evicted, and not for non-payment of rent, or breach of covenant, Halifax now conceded that a claim for the 'goodwill' should lie against the landlord, subject to a bar on excessive amounts. Thus far there was agreement with the plan of 30 October. He departed from it on the determination of the sum payable in these circumstances. The figure should be reached by taking the average value for the district of payments between occupiers with the knowledge of, or without objection from, the owners for about the last five years. If under his scheme 'goodwill' was not fully protected from landlords who raised the rent and imposed stricter covenants, to Halifax the flaw was a virtue: by such means custom might slowly and quietly die out. Legislation must not affect those estates where the custom had not been permitted to operate, although the onus of proof might fairly be placed on the landlords.

Halifax's refusal even to contemplate extending custom was the main topic of his subsequent correspondence with Gladstone, who explained what does not appear to have emerged during their conversations, the device of the hypothetical offer. The device might supplement the procedure in Halifax's memorandum. The obstacle to be overcome in relation to custom was this: 'Though it seems to me that the idea is really universal or nearly so...the facts of it, and especially the facts of it as recognized by the landlord, are not so, though...very widely spread.'[88] Halifax was immovable. In reply, he agreed that the weakness of his memorandum was the absence of general recognition of 'goodwill' by the landlords, but pointed to the dangers that surrounded the ministry in Britain: 'You must be prepared to ...brave...the landlord interest, English, Scotch, and Irish... The question between us is not as to the payment, but as to the mode...and I do not think your plan is so practicable and so likely to disarm opposition as mine.' The hypothetical offer was a fertile source of confusion and prone to abuse. A good conservative Whig, Halifax preferred to keep his feet on the ground, in an almost literal sense here. He could not but think that 'merely turning custom into law, continuing...payments...made in practice – is a course which is not only more just...in Ireland, but is more consistent with English ideas and views, and will commend itself more to the minds of English landlords than payment based on the opinion of probably discordant witnesses.'[89] Gladstone rejoined that he assumed the offer to be decided, not by 'speculative evidence', but by what another tenant would actually be prepared to pay to enter upon the holding.[90]

On the politics of the question in Britain, Halifax's advice was as good as it was friendly. He hoped that the prime minister might find in Irish landlords many willing adherents, so advanced were Monck and others in their views. A lease as the alternative to 'goodwill' might please some landlords but not the tenants.[91] When Gladstone reasserted the material benefits of spreading the custom over Ireland,[92] he maintained: 'I do not believe in it *to any extent.*' Small Irish farmers did not improve in such a way as to push up their money profit. 'If I am wrong so much the better,' he said.[93]

THE CABINET DEBATE

When fighting a rearguard action against the land bill as settled at the December cabinets, Robert Lowe was to observe disgustedly that 'Irish landlords...in their present state of panic...are ready to yield almost to anything.'[94] It was very largely true. The previous amenability of Irish landowners to agrarian reform, compared with their brethren in Great Britain, was succeeded by a phenomenon resembling Charlemagne's conversion of the Saxons. Of the Irish proprietors consulted by the prime minister, all but one were satisfyingly co-operative or suggested a stronger measure than Gladstone liked. The odd man out was Dufferin whose surrender on the main issue in dispute was too long delayed to help. Yet he, too, began by extensively reinterpreting the principles on which property rested, although he did not hide his unhappiness.

Two of Dufferin's three papers for Gladstone were printed for cabinet ministers, whose meetings he could not attend, although compelled to accept and speak for their decisions if he stayed in office. With his speciality dominating the scene, he was unenviably situated. Argyll conveyed this to the prime minister, asking for Dufferin's admission to their confidence on Irish land as far as possible. The Duke described his friend as 'a far superior animal to Ch:[ichester] Fortescue'.[95] Approached by Gladstone, the man noted for his appeal to rational and scientific arguments on behalf of Irish landlords undertook a short but in the event prolix memorandum in which he made explicit his deep resentment of the unfairness of the landlords' opponents in Ireland and the cynical expediency of British statesmen, indulging in a luxury which he sensibly eschewed in public. Gladstone wished that these pages had been omitted.[96] They succeeded a useful consideration of how to formulate a claim for tenants' compensation additional to that for improvements. If rhetorical, the part of the memorandum which Gladstone thought dispensable was clear-sighted and a justifiable bid to exploit the guilt and alarm among members of the cabinet.[97]

Let them remember their responsibility not only for Ireland's prosperity but for 'the permanence, on an unshaken basis, of our whole social system'. While there was, in his opinion, probably no parallel to the efforts many of them had made, and were making, for the development of their country, the unpopularity of Irish landlords was manifest: they had been vilified without scruple; they were 'feared and hated' by the Catholic priesthood, on whose authority they were a curb. 'What body of men, subject to such attacks, would fail to become in the end anathema?' The bitterness of the loyal Anglo-Irish spilled over when he wrote that the great majority of the British would be likely to abandon the landlords of Ireland if they could thus obtain the acquiescence of her people in their rule. It was a temptation to be resisted out of pure self-interest, he reminded his fellow-ministers. As the foes of Anglicanism had fallen upon it in Ireland with the English church as their objective, so a powerful element saw in the overthrow of her landlords a success from which to launch an assault upon property in England. It was probable that the Tories would put party gain above obligations to the sacrificial victims. Dufferin denounced the abuse of Ireland's problems by British politicians looking for handy issues, and begged the cabinet to exercise 'a laborious and scrupulous nicety' in adjusting the interests of owners and occupiers. 'I have heard eminent persons suggest a rough and ready mode of settling the Irish Land Question...such expressions have filled my mind with indignation.' He was concerned for all elements in the agrarian structure threatened by Parliamentary meddling with 'functions which belong rather to the domain of Divine Government than of Civil Administration'. Tampering with economic forces might have consequences that no one wanted. Why the state had to interfere with the beneficent work of an invisible hand, why he himself had been studying how to do so, was plain from his final paragraph. Ireland was witnessing 'the decomposition of society', as the ability to protect life and property slipped out of government's hands.

If they must have exceptional legislation for the tenants, it should be substantial, otherwise it would not be worth the trouble. In order to find a principle proof against British radicals and the Irish, he invoked natural justice, arguing that, when properly analysed, it entitled the tenant to compensation for loss of '"anticipated profits"'. Of the reasoning behind the claim for 'anticipated profits', he remarked, 'This...though somewhat subtle, is undoubtedly plausible.' Good farming needed several years to produce its rewards: the tenant-at-will should be presumed to hold for a reasonable period, and compensated if it were cut short, the period to date from the moment when the prospect of eviction was directly or indirectly raised – as by a demand for higher rent. At any time during twenty-one years thereafter the tenant should be assured, if that prospect were realized, of compensation at the rate of five per cent of the capital value of however many years remained to him – with a sum added for his improvements. The recommendations of '"anticipated profits"' were that the power to dispossess a tenant was legally intact; that he was not the recipient of 'a co-proprietary right...a partnership in the soil'; and that the landlord whose rents were excessive would be forced to pay out proportionately when evicting. To make up in part for the 'injury and injustice' thus inflicted, the state ought to lend landlords money on easy terms to meet compensation for improvements and 'anticipated profits'. Dufferin would not allow the second claim on larger farms of 50 acres and upwards, where the tenant could not pretend 'to be in that abject condition which necessitates the legislature to treat him as an infant'. Turning to custom, he restated his former criticisms of it, but would make it legally binding in Ulster. By contrast, Bright's plan received the praise which he had publicly bestowed on its carefulness of property-rights. Dufferin wanted to supplement it with a bolder scheme: the purchase by the state of grazing, not wasteland, on which to settle people from wretched areas in Munster and Connaught. These small farmers would be tenants of the state, not peasant proprietors. The compelling reason for the experiment was to mitigate the risk and indeed certainty of a second Famine, for he was sure the calamity would return: only a landlord could prevent bad farming and especially the fragmentation of holdings, but in so far as this salutary power was operative it was bound to be weakened by the liability for 'anticipated profits'. He was indeed almost convinced that the action he proposed under duress, as that least insulting to the conscience and intelligence of his class, would leave the tenants worse off and excite 'social war'.

From the mélange of pessimism, reproach, and constructive thought, Gladstone selected 'anticipated profits' for discussion. His marginal note on the resettlement of near destitute peasants showed that the proposition was uncongenial. Complaining of its outlook on custom, Fortescue was apprehensive lest Dufferin's memorandum should harden the attitudes of some of the cabinet.[98] Not so the prime minister: he and most of those with whom he had conferred had a great deal in common with Dufferin. He wrote to him on the 3rd, inviting comment on Fortescue's memorandum. Though the Irish secretary had drawn up 'in form... an *extension* of Tenant Right', Gladstone did not feel that Dufferin and Fortescue would continue to disagree over their outstanding differences.[99] Dufferin replied with a second memorandum on the superiority of his plan; he was wholly against spreading the custom and the mechanism by which it was to be done.[100] There was neither logic nor equity in the hypothetical offer by a solvent tenant, in the disparity between 'fair' rent and the assessment of goodwill by competition: 'the tendency of the arrangement would be to convert the interest of the landlord into a rent-charge... and that of the tenant into a copyhold.' This was wrong, morally and as a matter of fact, because the custom involved 'not a tenant's but a co-proprietary right', the claim to which could be made out in Ulster but not beyond. He contended that the payments to outgoing tenants by landlords outside Ulster were nothing like the genuine if deplorable custom of the North. These sums were given to get vacant possession without delay, or as 'simply charity'. Or they were something else again which the state should not dream of imposing by law. In the memorandum's last words, 'to establish...rights out of the blood money occasionally paid under terror of assassination would be monstrous.'[101]

The attack on Fortescue's paper was lucid and forceful. He had indeed advised Gladstone not to let Dufferin see it for the time being.[102] When Dufferin's criticisms had been circulated, Fortescue revealed, in writing to him, the discomfort they had caused. They differed, according to the Irish secretary, because he thought it was not possible any longer to tolerate tenancy-at-will 'which Ulster, to the great honour of the Province, as I think, has transformed by its Custom...not free from faults and abuses, but comparatively excellent'. Then he minimized the proposed extension of custom: Dufferin and some cabinet ministers were unnecessarily alarmed by compensation dressed up as goodwill and the reference to fair rent. There was a limit on the amount of the first – which Fortescue now specified as about five years' rent – and as to the second: 'I do not intend any valuation. I only mean that the Court in its own breast sh[ould] fix the payment on the principle of a "fair rent" i.e. (mainly) a rent which would not confiscate the tenant's improvements and goodwill.' After so muddled and improbable an explanation, it was not surprising when he admitted that he did not regard the hypothetical offer as essential, had very nearly preferred to suggest compensation for disturbance under its own name fixed at so many years' rent, and still saw it as an alternative.[103] This admission, on 14 November, is the first indication in his letters of Fortescue's reluctance to go on with the plan drafted at the prime minister's instigation. Agreeing that he might have read more into Fortescue's memorandum than would be warranted if its statements were elucidated, Dufferin reiterated his aversion to the device on which it turned and to acknowledging that 'a Tenant whom I inducted yesterday into my Farm has, *ipso facto*, acquired a Proprietary right.'[10] Fortescue could not develop or explain away his paper in the sense Dufferin desired. By 3 December, when he answered, he was disengaging from the commitment to extend custom and wrote that he would never recognize 'any proprietary right in the soil as residing in the tenant, in Ulster or elsewhere.'[105] It was all he told Dufferin: but the significance was unmistakable.

Dufferin's tone to Fortescue was not the same as that he used to Gladstone, but his message was no different. He could not honourably stay in the government if fair rent, and goodwill determined by competition outside Ulster, appeared in the bill. His past protests against amending the law on these lines were too well known for him not to take that course. Yet he would continue to support ministerial policy on the land question, although from the back benches, such was 'the danger of any other set of men than yourself and the members of your Government being allowed to meddle with it'. Dufferin was not a very dangerous adversary: he offered to resign whenever the prime minister, on his side, felt that an apologist of the landlords was an embarrassment in the administration.[106] Gladstone ignored the threatened and the proffered resignation. He gave Dufferin another opportunity to review his thinking before being 'put into the scales against the other jockey'[107] – one of those incongruous metaphors that he occasionally lit upon. He had no time for '"anticipated profits"'. Opposite the argument in the second paper that the plan favoured low rents, Gladstone placed the comment: 'And *insecure tenures* with *frequent evictions*'. There is also a trace of asperity in his observation on 7 December that the cabinet had had the chancellor of the Duchy's views more fully than those of other ministers.[108] Gladstone had nevertheless asked him for a third memorandum, and a month after the request got a draft bill.[109] With compensation for improvements, and '"expectancy of occupation"', formerly '"anticipated profits"', the tenant-at-will obtained the right to exact a lease instead; to claim under custom wherever it was proved and, where it was not, to bequeath or sell the goodwill, subject to the approval of the chairman of quarter sessions and to an upper limit on the value, notwithstanding the landlord's objections. The chairman's discretion was wide. Had it come sooner, Dufferin's bill might have impressed the cabinet.

Dufferin took himself very seriously in the part of the Irish landlords' representative. Though sympathy for him was deep, other Irish landlord advisers were more helpful, to Gladstone, anyway. One of these was Lord Monck. His politics were Liberal; he had achieved distinction as a proconsul in the unification of British North America, which he had seen through difficult and long drawn out negotiations. He was the a-political person whose station, experience and temperament makes him a natural choice for membership of commissions. In November 1869 he was advocating statutory tenant-right to comprise two of the three Fs, withholding the absolute right to continue in occupation while the rent was duly paid. From an Irish landlord this seemed remarkably generous to Gladstone, who intimated that it exceeded his own notions.[110] As he correctly understood it, tenant-right, the custom, did not prevent increases of rent, consequent upon a price rise or for any other reason. When Monck did not modify his plan, Gladstone stated the limitations he thought should rule tenant-right: the money paid for goodwill ought to be uncontrolled and 'especially...rent should never be touched or adjudicated upon by a public authority'. He qualified the second condition at once. Rent 'would without doubt be contemplated and assumed at the particular period of the change of tenancy in the mind of the Court'.[111]

These verbal convolutions demonstrated the awkwardness of establishing custom. Monck's government rents were the way to cope with one of the two major problems raised, if the debate were proceeding on an abstract plane or related exclusively to

Irish politics. If the latter, he was arguably steering between extremes. He forgot, or mistook, the reactions of those who would decide. Cabinet ministers were rejecting Fortescue's hypothetical offer because it appeared conducive to what Monck was advocating. It may be that Monck did not know this, and tended to discount all the public signs that Britain would not join the Irish landlords who were capitulating to the tenants on such a right of property as a man's freedom to take the best rent he could get. Some check on that freedom might be tolerated, but it must be oblique.

Monck wished for a marked reinforcement of the custom when legalized and extended. Hartington, his father, the Duke of Devonshire and Bessborough seem to have had no important reservations about endorsing Gladstone's plan as it evolved. Nothing is recorded of Portsmouth except the claim under his entry in the *Complete Peerage* that he gave some detailed help, involving reference to the practice on his Wexford estate, to the prime minister when the Irish land bill was worked out. Hartington, Granville related on 21 November, was saying that since discussion had taken the cabinet past compensation for improvements, he concurred with the reasoning which led to the adoption of Ulster custom.[112] It was exactly what Gladstone wanted to hear. He talked to the Duke of Devonshire and Bessborough on 8 December: 'two interesting and satisfactory conversations'.[113] The Duke went away to write in his diary: 'I am in hopes he will not be in favor [sic] of a very extreme measure.'[114] The impression is of diluted pessimism. Gladstone examined his ideas in detail with Hartington and Bessborough. Bessborough surprised the prime minister by urging him not to exclude, as some cabinet members desired and he had proposed, the larger farmers – the leaders of the peasantry – from any major benefit under the bill. Earlier, Bessborough had written to Spencer that, on the analogy of the compensation paid by railways to sitting tenants when acquiring land, he saw no objection in principle to creating an occupancy-right similar to Ulster's, but not identical, because its value should be limited. He was also anxious to safeguard the landlord's power of veto on a tenant's successor under any such extension of custom.[115]

There was a feeling abroad in the Irish landlord class that they must submit to the fate from which they had been secure under Palmerston. A radical revision of the agrarian order had been carried out at the expense of Continental aristocracies in Austria, Germany and Russia in the last twenty years. It was unreasonable to suppose that Ireland could be exempt from a historical process that had been developing inexorably since the late eighteenth century. When even Dufferin's principles collapsed around him, Lowe's contemptuous remark quoted above was forgivable. The landed interest in Britain, conscious of the sympathy of a propertied and deferential middle class, was not prepared at this time to allow Irish landlords to submit to the historically inevitable. The helpfulness of Irish proprietors whom Gladstone consulted was not such an asset as Halifax had speculated that it might be.

GLADSTONE AND FORTESCUE

John Morley and J. L. Hammond thought that Gladstone took a narrower view than Fortescue of the reach which the land bill ought to have.[116] Morley and Hammond were wrong, and they were misled by their interpretation of what passed in November and December 1869. Soon after the November cabinets, Clarendon ascertained that the Irish secretary, on his own, could not, or would not, stand up for 'his' plan. Unhappy with the Ulster tenant-right solution which had been pressed upon him, Fortescue ceased to co-operate in the attempt to impose it. His change of attitude took the best part of a month to crystallize: a sign was the slant he tried to give the official review of custom and agrarian conflict started by Gladstone to build up the case for expanding their joint proposals. They were also divided over coercion. Gladstone did not want to think that it must accompany their land bill. The suggestion was repugnant to him. Here, too, he was going to be overborne, although able to temporize while he strove to get agreement to his cure, as he sanguinely regarded it, for the commonest causes of Irish violence. Fortescue, so unequal to Gladstone in force of character and intellect, escaped from his domination. It was from the landlord side that this Anglo-Irishman had always approached the land question. He had much enlarged the amendment to the law which he supported in 1866–8: but he could not believe that it was justifiable to concede 'any proprietary right in the soil as residing in the tenant'.[117] When he used these words to Dufferin on 3 December, he stated the real reason for dissociating himself from 'Universal Tenant Right'. With the prime minister, Fortescue tried to exploit his susceptibility to another kind of argument altogether. He began on 22 November to express doubt whether by following custom they would afford tenants adequate protection. He came to the point when he intimated his inability to accept the legitimacy of establishing custom as law throughout Ireland. This was his answer to two substantial memoranda in which Gladstone widened the application of the idea and dwelt on the fitness of it. At the last moment the prime minister realized the futility and the peril of trying to thrust his views on the cabinet. The desertion of his reluctant collaborator was the outcome of all the papers from ministers rejecting the extension of custom. Fortescue's compensation for disturbance became the centrepiece of a compromise scheme.

Clarification of the debatable facts of custom would, it was Gladstone's hope, break down the resistance to his wishes. It was not a task that he liked to entrust to the obvious person. In July he had called for a précis of land bills since the Devon Commission, and it had not materialized. 'I am almost afraid,' he said to Fortescue on 3 November, 'of asking...for information about Irish Land after the months since...my request.' He asked, instead, to whom inquiries about a number of very important detailed matters might be sent.[118] Seemingly forgetful of Fortescue's reply, he addressed them to Spencer. Fortescue told Gladstone of his surprise that they had not been sent to him.[119] In the interval, the prime minister at last received the purported summary of past bills. Its length exasperated him: 'I do not know how to commence the study of it. This is really...serious...'[120] It was indeed when he would not knowingly leave anything unread that might be useful, and one remembers how much business besides Irish land there was to absorb even his energies. The questions sent to Ireland were numerous and thorough, a compact whole and directed to proving a thesis. To oversee the compilation of the answers by Dublin Castle and its agencies, Gladstone picked his man and set aside Fortescue's choice. John Lambert was seconded from London. 'I wish I could come myself,' added Gladstone, 'but this I fear would be highly imprudent...'[121] He wanted proofs marshalled that would satisfy English minds of the accuracy of the picture he had formed of Irish land.

Before Lambert arrived in Ireland Fortescue issued a circular to poor law inspectors, dated 30 November.[122] In its scope it resembled the questionnaire which Spencer and Lambert had from Gladstone: but its emphasis was differently placed. The inspectors were instructed to survey 'the ordinary existing relations between Landlord and Tenant in respect of...Improvements', and discover how far expenditure in the various categories was attributable to the owners or to the occupiers. This was 'the main object in view'. What security the tenants had for their improvements, whether custom or an understanding gave them fair compensation in money or by continued occupation; whether there were many instances of their losing the entire value of improvements as the result of eviction or disproportionate increases of rent; whether notices to quit were frequent and, if so, usually executed; and whether improvements generally were growing, or declining – the aim of these questions was to investigate the allegations against landlords, not to demonstrate that just below the surface of the present alien system of tenure lay an indigenous one. The circular separated the custom of tenant-right from the preceding inquiries and implied that it was localized though not exclusive to a single province. 'It would further be desirable...to report,' said the instructions, on the occurrence in a poor law district of Ulster tenant-right, being payment, with or without the landlord's consent, for 'disturbance or goodwill'.

In his questionnaire,[123] the prime minister took Ulster tenant-right to be the most developed form of a universal phenomenon. 'Beyond the limits of the region in which Tenant-right, properly so called, prevails...are there not...indications of the idea, at least, as dwelling in the popular mind; such as dowers, legacies and the like charged upon temporary occupation...[and] permission to sell the right of occupancy?' He listed here the propensity of Irish leaseholders to bequeath their interest beyond the time for which their contract ran. The next step was to ask: 'Is there any part of Ireland in which [the] idea (if not the practice) of Tenant-right, more or less corresponding with Ulster custom, is wholly foreign to the mind and notions of the people?' In Fortescue's circular, the inspectors were told to record whether Ulster tenant-right extended to tenants under leases as well as to those holding at will; whether it was spreading; and whether tenancies-at-will were charged with the obligations to which Gladstone referred. There was no suggestion that Ulster custom was the healthiest embodiment of something discoverable, if one looked closely, everywhere in Ireland. As for the rest of his questionnaire, Gladstone was concerned to substantiate the claims of tenant-right's friends that it made for peace, prosperity and greater agricultural productivity. This query stands out: 'Has agrarian outrage ever been committed by a man who had obtained or who knew that he could obtain, the usual Tenant-right allowance, or who held lands where Tenant-right customs prevail, and where they were not interfered with?' Gladstone's anxiety to authenticate the functioning of, or belief in, occupancy-right all over the country was met by the definite evidence which his questionnaire elicited from good witnesses. Bessborough wrote to the viceroy: 'There is no doubt that a tenant-right exists in the minds of the peasantry, and is acted upon to a certain extent. Sale of goodwill [is] frequently allowed or winked at.'[124] And a few days later, from County Carlow, where he owned 10,000 acres besides 24,000 in County Kilkenny, he commented: 'Here I find the same answers will apply...The implied tenant-right does not perhaps exist to quite so great an extent as in Kilkenny, but...although...it is not recognized and has been totally disregarded by Landlords in many cases, yet it exists in the minds of the peasantry and marriages are made upon the supposition.'[125] A witness widely and intimately acquainted with the Irish countryside, C. P. Brassington, a Dublin surveyor, described how custom was spreading and intensifying its hold outside Ulster. Until recently landlords and agents had reserved the right to disallow family charges upon a tenancy, to choose which of the occupier's relations should succeed him, or even to bring in a stranger if the whole family were objectionable. 'Such a power, if now exercised would in all probability lead to agrarian outrage.' As the tenants' sense of property grew, so did the tendency to regard their interest as a marketable commodity.[126]

Such liking as Fortescue had for the extension of custom was dwindling, whatever the supporting testimony, of which his own was not the least valuable. Putting down interim replies to Gladstone's questionnaire on 17 November,[127] he confirmed that the idea of tenant-right, equivalent to Ulster's, was present throughout the country, and often the practice of it 'upon a smaller scale, and...less settled and...respected'. He had never heard of agrarian crime where the peasant had secured his due under tenant-right and there had been no interference with custom: 'Violations of the customs have produced outrage.' He gave details of Ulster's superiority with her characteristic tenure to other provinces. On the 22nd, however, he raised the alternative he had all along preferred to utilizing custom 'in which I still see great advantages'. The best plan he could think of was to compensate larger tenants, tentatively defined as those of above 50 acres, for improvements, with discretion to the courts to award, on top of that sum, a percentage of it for disturbance. Smaller tenants would have a minimum of so many years' rent, which might be increased on proof of substantial improvements. As Fortescue reminded him, this way of giving compensation for disturbance harked back to Gladstone's proposals of early October. Fortescue felt that his alternative should succeed 'provided the Cabinet will go in boldly for the *disturbance* element'.[128] The desired boldness would mask a withdrawal, and Gladstone tried to check him: they must not settle for anything else unless it was plainly much better. Sullivan had committed himself whole-heartedly to the memorandum of 2 November and nothing had emerged that could really be called 'a rival *plan*'. 'The question of Tenant Right,' said Gladstone, 'has not yet been half argued out.' He knew Fortescue's true motive, and rejected it: 'It is very desirable to have an easy and speedy agreement in the Cabinet on the question; but ulterior considerations are still more weighty...'[129] 'I quite understand', responded the Irish secretary; 'I feel the force of what you say as to the evil of proposing any alternative for the sake of agreement inferior to the plan already...before the Cabinet.' He had not stopped working on the main provision in his memorandum, although he was now comparing it with possible substitutes.[130]

Gladstone's next letter of 26 November, and Fortescue's of the 30th,[131] were about the Irish administration's wish for a coercion bill. 'I hope we have not descended quite so low as that,' was the prime minister's reaction to the thought of suspending Habeas Corpus. He propounded an apologia for Irish violence which was, in his phrase, 'very curious and instructive'. He invited Fortescue to judge his arguments for insisting that the land bill – such a one as he envisaged – should take priority over coercion. The unrest was a century old: and had grown worse with the accumulation of measures to undo the wrongs perpetrated by the Ascendancy. All the well-intentioned legislation had not touched the 'vital point'. Disaffection had become steadily more of a threat, culminating in 'the monster we call Fenianism', but Gladstone found it encouraging that in their use of force the Irish had got progressively less sanguinary: 'Personal torture and wanton cruelties are not heard of – victims are despatched in the most summary manner by agrarian crime, while Fenianism aims at giving to resistance the noble form of public war.' Since the Irish were now more civilized, he seemed to say, there was reason to suppose that the essential reform, of 'grossly unjust' land laws, might conciliate them. In any event, Gladstone was not ready to admit 'the deplorable and disgraceful necessity which God forbid' of new repression until the effect of his land bill was seen. His ardour led him, as sometimes happened, into a dangerously absurd contention. Violence in Ireland had not lost the element of primitive savagery, but even if it had, few people would have sympathized with a plea to be encouraged by the relative humanity with which contemporary victims were 'despatched in the most summary manner'. Fortescue tactfully praised the defence of his fellow-countrymen: but keeping down Fenians and Ribbonmen was extremely hard under the rules of a constitution 'framed for Yorkshire and the Lothians', as he complained in a nice tribute to the solid inhabitants of those parts. Gladstone was adamant that the land bill must come first.

Fortescue would perceive that in expanding the plan discussed by the cabinet he, Gladstone, was working 'substantially on your basis'. This was his comment when sending the Irish secretary letters from Monck, and a copy of his reply to one of them.[132] He followed these letters with de Grey's memorandum, Halifax's of 1 December, and news of the impending completion of 'my idea of applying your principle'.[133] When the last was finished, Gladstone made two general points about it in relation to the memorandum of 2 November: it offered certain concessions, which seemed more appreciable to him than they really were; and it was cast 'in what may be (as matters now stand) a more favourable form...for attracting assent...The sky is at present very far from clear: but we "must bate no jot of heart, or hope"'.[134] In advance of his paper, dated 3 December, he noted[135] very briefly where it diverged from that of 2 November. On resorting to the hypothetical offer, the court should never assume a lower rent than the tenant had been paying. The offending procedure, thus modified, might be bypassed in a way that had attracted the cabinet in their debates. The claim against the landlord for 'goodwill' could be barred by a long lease, unless custom had previously existed on the holding under such a lease. On holdings above a certain value, the law would absolutely decline to admit tenant-right, either the natural growth or the artefact. *All* arrears of rent were to be deducted from money due to the tenant. These concessions by Gladstone to the landlords and his critics in the government were designed to promote the acceptance of custom as the framework of landlord–tenant relations. Except on the larger farms where tenant-right was not to obtain, proceedings should not be 'divided as under custom, or under Act, but will in all cases be *prima facie* under custom'. The imitation of tenant-right had been attacked by ministers, while the equity of recognizing the genuine practice had been reluctantly acknowledged. Dropping the distinction which Gladstone had hitherto maintained between custom in Ulster and beyond would tend, although superficially, to disguise its relative weakness in the South. Accordingly, in his revised plan he spoke of 'Ulster custom' only once and as synonymous with 'the customary interest known by the name of tenant-right' or 'the custom of the country'. Under these descriptions the full custom of tenant-right was extended by enacting a universal presumption of law in its favour. It was as near as he could go to the extension recommended in Campbell's second pamphlet, which in turn was as near as any Englishman not out of touch with political realities could go to the extension demanded by Sir John Gray.

Gladstone's memorandum of 3 December must be read with a little paper he had written on 26 November,[136] in which he contended that the extension of custom would revolutionize agricultural productivity in Ireland. When he put this to Halifax and Argyll, they were incredulous. He made the assumption that much of Irish land was only 'half-cultivated' and based his calculations on doubling its average gross yield by furnishing tenants with the incentive, namely 'security for outlay and improvements, and for the goodwill of occupation'. The landlords, he held, should gain too. Their proportionate share of the produce would fall after allowance for the cost to the tenant of acquiring the goodwill: but in absolute terms they should draw more rent – a third more. The tenants did far better on this projection with a rise of 150 per cent in their absolute net profits. If a doubled gross yield were 'probably...above the average truth', a smaller increase might yet verify the proposition that a legal 'goodwill of occupation' would be profitable to the landlords, immensely so to the tenants, and the key to unlocking the wealth of the country. Gladstone's estimate of goodwill payments at ten years' purchase in normal circumstances was reasonable. The basic assumption of the document was not reasonable. It was true that the land of Ireland had often been described as underdeveloped both by those who took the tenants' part and those on the opposite side. Gladstone annexed the most optimistic assertions of the first, though, wisely, he cited no authorities. The exposé of the economics of tenant-right naturally damaged the cause he was pleading, and his motivation was suspect. He had over-persuaded himself in order to confound objectors by showing that everyone affected would enjoy a substantially higher income, safe from the apprehensions that had blighted efforts to improve Irish agriculture.

In the memorandum of 3 December[137] the onus of proof that 'the customary interest known by the name of tenant-right' had been extinguished by purchase was laid squarely upon the landlords. Otherwise that interest must be paid for, when the tenant's occupation was interrupted by notice to quit either arbitrarily or because he was unwilling to submit to an increase of rent or other alteration of his conditions of tenancy. If the landlords refrained from using their powers, it must augment the force of custom. Where 'the goodwill or occupation-value including... improvements...by the tenant' was in dispute, the court should always commence by gathering evidence of the sums that had changed hands 'in the place, district or neighbourhood upon the same or like holdings'. Only when the possibilities of this procedure had been exhausted might the hypothetical offer be brought into play. Gladstone had gone ahead and strengthened the essence of a plan that had not prospered in cabinet. The landlord who tried to fight custom would have the clear presumption of law against him. Peasant law was unambiguously given precedence over landlord law. Gladstone conceded quite a lot on other points with the fate of this in mind. Although tenants would now lose their claim for goodwill against the landlord if evicted for non-payment of rent, the landlord had the strongest incentive to allow them to sell their interest, because all arrears were recoverable from the proceeds. The controversial device of the hypothetical offer was modified to remove a main cause of complaint: that it put the public valuation of rent virtually within the tenants' grasp. Actual was substituted for fair rent in calculating what their interest was worth. A judge might not rule on rent except where it helped the landlord. An owner of land claiming that his property was let at less than its full value was entitled to have his liability for compensation settled by reference to the price the goodwill would fetch if the rent had been one 'fairly and adequately representing the average for similar farms in the locality'. Both the recognition and the extension of custom did not apply to holdings valued at over £80 or £100 per annum. The exclusion of a small minority of tenants would not be resented in Ireland, he thought, while making his proposals defensible by the argument of which so much had been heard – that most Irish farmers needed the aid of some positive discrimination by the law.

Gladstone realized there must be these concessions and more. Afraid that they would discredit the bill with the tenants and erode its customary basis, he went far towards neutralizing the bulk of them in the act of drafting. Earlier, he had replied to attacks on extended tenant-right by reminding critics of its unstated limit on awards for goodwill. An upper and a lower limit were now specified, the former being the high figure of seven or eight times the annual rent. This ceiling was mandatory whenever landlord and tenant went to court about the payment, and was not applicable only to extended tenant-right. Yet a bigger amount might be sanctioned if proved to have been usual for the occupancy of the holding concerned. There was nothing to stop the tenant from selling his interest, with the landlord's consent, for whatever it would fetch. The imposition for the first time of the lower limit – not less than three times the rent – ensured that the benefit to the occupier should not be illusory in financial terms, and held over the landlord the threat of a fine that became sharper in proportion as his rent approached, or exceeded, a commercial level. The landlord could reduce the award to the tenant by claiming, as above, that the land had been underlet: but in that case the tenant was presented with the right to counter-claim, to be compensated for all his improvements separately and on top of the sum for goodwill. The landlord also had the choice of avoiding liability for goodwill by granting a lease for not less than thirty-one years. The tender of such a lease was enough to exempt the landlord for that period, although refused by the tenant, if offered at the present rent or at one '*fixed...by indifferent* persons'. Gladstone was doubtful whether landlords should be permitted this way of shutting out tenant-right. 'Will the option of giving leases, as...proposed by me, repel the farmers? I hope not: but this point is very grave,' he wondered to Fortescue.[138] It was frankly conceived as a sweetener for tenant-right, 'softening the proposal with the attraction of a lease, which the cabinet appeared to relish a good deal'.[139] Almost all the cabinet wanted there to be a prospect of gradually and painlessly extinguishing custom, which had successfully defied common law and contract. Gladstone, however, inserted a proviso that a lease should not affect tenant-right where the two were shown to have hitherto co-existed,[140] and should never do more than suspend it. The landlord would obtain little advantage from the creation or tender of a leasehold. If he nevertheless created or tendered it, he might, at the end of the thirty-one years or longer initial term, offer a further lease of the same minimum length at the best rent it commanded from the sitting tenant or another: but where tenant-right had hitherto survived under leasehold, the tenant would be entitled to depart with the value of his interest, and custom would still apply on the holding. Where custom had been suspended, it would be enforced for the future, if the land were not kept under lease for a further term of the prescribed length. 'I see,' wrote Gladstone to Lord Monck, 'I must...add...this condition that after any lease of 31 years...the land shall come under tenant-right unless I grant another lease.'[141] Gladstone was endeavouring to whittle away in the same set of proposals the alternative freshly devised to conciliate colleagues about whose intelligence he must temporarily have deluded himself.

Improvements – all of which were normally to be included in the valuation of 'goodwill' – notice to quit lengthened to a year, some limited financial assistance for the purchase of farms by occupiers and for wasteland reclamation – these and several lesser items were included in his paper. Like his memoranda of September and October it was so explicit that it would have gone straight through a compliant cabinet to the parliamentary draughtsman. It did not reach the cabinet's agenda. The proposition that landlord and tenant should come, *prima facie*, under custom flew in the face of nearly every one of the opinions which ministers had circulated by request. Fortescue returned again to compensation for disturbance, before Gladstone's latest memorandum was sent to him. Gladstone entreated him to remember 'one thing is of pressing urgency, and that is...clear mutual comprehension and commerce among...a *nucleus* around which the deliberations of the Cabinet may group themselves in practical forms.'[142] It was a propitious moment for obduracy, and Fortescue dug his heels in.

He argued that 'the *Tenant Right* plan', in his memorandum of 2 November, or Gladstone's of 3 December, did not do enough for occupiers struggling with oppressive rents. He first asserted this on 4 December,[143] prior to his sight of Gladstone's newly completed paper. He suggested on the 4th that tenants considering themselves ill-treated should have the right to ask the courts for the exercise of a discretionary power compelling the landlord to buy out their interest or let them stay at a fair rent. The prefatory sentence read strangely: 'I have thought from the first, and I am still convinced, that we must not attempt to deal directly with rent.' Gladstone reacted immediately, 'staggered at ...any interference with present rents'.[144] His several memoranda had studiously avoided direct intervention to lower them. Fortescue discarded the idea,[145] but not compensation for disturbance, mentioned in this letter of the 4th, without elaboration, as very important and complementary to the options described.

When he had seen the memorandum of the 3rd, there was greater force in his renewed criticism of Gladstone's concentration upon custom, since the prime minister had taken fair rent out of the hypothetical offer. Fortescue fastened on this weakening of the occupier's security compared with the memorandum of 2 November, to which, nevertheless, he did not want to keep. He filled his long letter of the 6th with advocacy of compensation for disturbance. He contemplated a fixed payment of five years' rent to tenants of below 15 acres, diminishing as farms grew in size above that level. The right to this payment should be understood in a strictly limited sense, 'always meaning not indefeasible', he wrote. A tenant served with notice to quit for non-payment of rent had no claim for disturbance, except when his position was the consequence of an enhancement he considered unacceptable, or of an already oppressive rent. Outside Ulster the custom of tenant-right was to be mainly supplementary. A tenant could claim for the goodwill, where it had the landlord's express or tacit approval, in addition to compensation for disturbance. If the court was satisfied that it was a fair equivalent, the landlord might relieve himself of both claims by offering a tenant permission to sell the goodwill. Conversely, when the landlord refused permission, the court might increase his liability for disturbance. In amount, there was not much to choose between Fortescue's compensation and Gladstone's: for a plurality of occupiers Gladstone's maximum was higher, and his minimum lower, than Fortescue's fixed sum. The important disagreement between the two men was not over the Irish secretary's insistence on providing for the overrented tenant – such cases were not numerous. Fortescue sought to minimize the principal change he had made: 'It is a departure from the method of my former suggestions, but would, I think, reach the same end by a way less open to objection.'[146] He well knew how great was the significance of *not* extending custom.

Gladstone now, on the 7th,[147] reminded Fortescue that the fate of Irish land in cabinet depended on the existence of a group with concerted aims working to influence the rest of their colleagues. He asked him to note on an enclosed summary 'what you approve, or, where you differ from the developments or conditions which I have made to your original basis, what you would substitute'. This, Gladstone remarked on the following day,[148] was 'an effort to bring the matter to a head'. In other words to avert Fortescue's desertion. Opposite the prime minister's statement of his main purpose – 'To confirm the custom of Tenant Right generally' – Fortescue wrote defiantly: 'In my belief, there is no such general custom…throughout Ireland as would admit of being "confirmed" by statute.' The statement was not wholly inconsistent with his answers to Gladstone's questionnaire, but it was a misleading interpretation of the circumstances which they corroborated. If custom were extended, he felt it was essential to employ the hypothetical offer at an assumed fair rent. That, as he knew, would be unacceptable to the cabinet. His position was clear, and he repeated in a few lines the alternative scheme he put forward on the 6th.[149] Gladstone still clung to the illusion that he could reconvert him, saying in his next letter that on 'the custom of the country as the basis for compensation for eviction and the like – I cannot make out from your papers whether you wholly dissent from this...I hoped you had agreed in it – I have acquired a strong conviction upon it; of which I have written out the grounds; but I shall not circulate the paper until I understand your views more fully.'[150] He was here referring to a memorandum he had been preparing for some days and completed on 11 December. He was writing on the 9th, by the morning of which day, he had informed Fortescue, he proposed to form 'my conclusive opinion'.[151] The memorandum of the 11th was drawn up in accordance with that resolution. As he had been telling Fortescue, the cabinet was about to resume its consideration of Irish land and 'so far as preparation for discussion is concerned we are behind the point where we stood six weeks ago'.[152] He nevertheless proceeded on the assumption they were going to be at one again.

To that end, he devised an amendment on the 10th, after consulting Granville and Bessborough and finding them inclined to it. He went further towards satisfying Fortescue's wish to ensure special treatment for the overrented tenant than the Irish secretary now wanted, having given up the interference with existing rents envisaged in his letter of 4 December. A tenant who thought his rent was excessive could seek the landlord's consent to arbitration upon or judicial settlement of its level. If the landlord declined to go to arbitration or into court, or if, having gone, he refused to implement the award of a reduced rent, the tenant would be entitled to the full value of his occupancy. Together with this, Gladstone drafted a similar provision, which Hartington was anxious to see inserted, for landlords who felt that their rents were too low – the tenant held to be underrented and refusing to pay more would lose his claim to the goodwill, though not to improvements.[153] To win Fortescue back, Gladstone was prepared in the first of these two amendments to disregard his own earnest warning that the cabinet would not 'on any terms'[154] tolerate a proposal like the one he was suggesting. However, neither amendment figured in the memorandum of

11 December. Gladstone realized that, despite the approving noises elicited from Granville and Bessborough, he must heed his own advice when presenting the extension of custom for a final decision. Adjudication upon rent, even to help the landlord, was provocative, as the cabinet memoranda had amply shown.

The real interest of Gladstone's latest memorandum[155] consisted in the arguments supporting and illuminating its principle. Although the document was never circulated, its arguments were used, with one probable exception. Some he had been using repeatedly. Others had been allusions in his correspondence. The most absorbing were historical. These will be left until the end of the chapter.

The argument that Gladstone probably did not use except in his memorandum of the 11th was one to which he gave such prominence that it furnished the conclusion. The first of four changes in the provisions of this date compared with those of the 3rd removed the minimum on goodwill payments. It enabled him to argue that his plan was superior to any alternative – Hatherley's 'damages for eviction', or the unqualified custom – because self-extinguishing if and when the demand for land in Ireland fell off and did away with 'the true economical grounds' on which tenant-right rested. In the absence of a minimum on compensation for loss of occupancy, declining demand for land would be reflected in the sum fixed by reference, not to past payments which were no longer 'fair facts' but to the hypothetical offer. That procedure would accurately register the unwillingness of tenants to pay more than a nominal price for the occupancy of a holding when they lost little or nothing by being deprived of it. In his last paragraph Gladstone called the custom 'so far as it exceeds the value of improvements...the sign and concomitant of an imperfect state of things'. He added: 'The occupier ought not to want special and purchased security against either the landlord or the assassin.' These observations cannot be reconciled with earlier passages in his paper where he contended for a wider view of tenant-right. In the light of those passages, and of so much else that he wrote and said – to Argyll, for instance – he neither expected nor desired to see the purely commercial attitude to land which he was predicting in the peasantry. It was absurd for him to suggest that after its legal status had been enhanced

250

tenant-right might yet, to quote his closing words, 'if it will...
die a natural and easy death'. 'If it will' was a characteristic
indication of his reservations about the possibility. The cabinet
could not have taken him seriously.

Better calculated, of course, to impress the cabinet was the
thought which Gladstone had kept before himself and them, that
'tenant-right...local and peculiar to the country, or not represented by any correlative custom in either portion of Great
Britain...will best serve the purpose of handling the question of
Irish Land Tenures on its own proper ground, and will be more
likely on that account than other modes of proceeding to prevent
Irish legislation in this matter from being drawn into a precedent
for England or for Scotland, and to obviate the jealousies which
the anticipation of such a result could bring into action.' He
described tenant-right as 'generally recognized and acted upon
in a considerable part of Ireland...more or less observed in
practice, and familiar in idea to...the people in a great portion
of the remainder of the country...nowhere wholly foreign or
novel.' Since he believed custom to have this hold, it was sensible
not to exclude tenants over the £80 or £100 line from its operation
when law. That was the second of the four changes made by the
memorandum.

The third restored the distinction between custom in Ulster
and elsewhere. The former was recognized unconditionally. There
was here an implicit admission, not prompted by anything Fortescue
had written, that legislation should not be disadvantageous to
the tenants, as it must be if their acknowledged customary rights
were cut down on receiving statutory protection. Fourthly, goodwill payments outside Ulster were subjected to an absolute
maximum, replacing one effective only when landlord and tenant
took their dispute to court. This Gladstone put in to dispose of
the 'inconvenience' that the 'preposterous excess' sometimes
found in the price of tenant-right in Ulster might spread to the
South with legal sanction.

'The custom called tenant-right generally...must be the best,
and (so to speak) the cheapest medium in which to liquidate...
just claims.' Gladstone's attempt to prove it was thrown away
on Fortescue, who on the 9th had elaborated his counter-proposals
and sent them for printing.[156] The prime minister's memorandum
did not go out to the cabinet, but perished before they met on

14 December to resume consideration of Irish land. Gladstone saw Fortescue and Granville that day in advance of the meeting,[157] and drafted the brief propositions submitted at it. He relinquished the extension of custom and its mechanism, the hypothetical offer. In the North, custom was to be legalized as it stood. In the South it was recognized 'as far as...ascertained', and subject to limitations not applicable to Ulster. Where factual evidence of tenant-right was 'deficient', compensation for disturbance or damages for eviction should be awarded on a scale varying inversely to the value of the holding.[158] Thus amended, Gladstone's plan incorporated the most notable feature of Fortescue's. In the knowledge that the prime minister did not have the cabinet behind him, the Irish secretary had successfully held out. Gladstone had still brought him to proposals that struck some of those present on 14 December as wrong and dangerous.

'THE IDEA OF RESTITUTION'

Gladstone believed that the Irish people ought to be able to feel that they had been compensated, in a way they could appreciate for the ancestral wrongs inflicted by the confiscations and un-forgiven after many generations. Security for improvements and against the hardship caused by eviction had become secondary to his purpose as he delved into the land question. Besides all its other recommendations, the acceptance of custom was justice in a long historical perspective. This was the dominant consideration in his memorandum of 11 December,[159] and it continued to govern his attitude towards the bill when a customary basis was set aside.

His researches into 'the ancient rights of the Irish tenantry' were as thorough as the pressure of business allowed. He made note of the opinions of modern authorities; he read up and cited Sir John Davies's contemporary evidence. As happens to students of Celtic Ireland he groped about in 'the mists which overhang ...the details of...tenures'. He emerged with the firm impression that 'some recognition of tenant-right is not only the most convenient of all...expedients...but...the most agreeable to these historical and traditional rights, a contempt or disregard of which is in the worst sense an innovating and revolutionary principle whether the offence be committed by those who do not seek to disguise its true character or whether it be inadvertently perpetuated under the name and notion of a strict regard to the principles of property.' It could not be claimed, in his view, for the interests created by English law since the sixteenth and seventeenth centuries that their prolonged monopoly of legality had effaced, by lapse of time, the interests existing under and surviving from the Celtic land system. 'Prescription does not run against the Crown which is supposed to represent the public interest. It is harder far to make it run against the people.' This was scrupulous conservatism, and he had an astonishing threat from a British minister for any who objected that it was not: 'To urge too strongly the indefeasible character of [the landlords'] proprietary rights...may...provoke a discussion...how far the rights, undeniably attaching to the occupiers (in block as to each sept, though not perhaps individually) under the old native tenures have ever undergone a legal extinction: how far the forfeitures were acts affecting the rebel chieftains only: how far it was ever intended (nay, possibly ever competent) on the part of the State to destroy what may fairly be called the property of the old native occupier in the occupation and use of the soil ...these questions should not be drawn into the vortex of the present controversy.' As he said in the later passage quoted below, Celtic society could not be restored but the morality of its conquest was a live issue.

Gladstone had sifted the rhetoric of the peasant and national grievance about land until he was left with the source of its staying power. He understood, and declared himself: 'What the Irishman may think with great semblance and perhaps with the full reality of historic truth is this that, without at all questioning the landlord's title, he too had by the old customs of the country his share in a tribal property which however rude in adjustment gave a right to him and his race to remain upon the soil...That right, in its original shape, can hardly be defined and cannot possibly be re-established. But the moral of it was a just, beneficial and humane idea to the substantial aim of which, if in altered form, it seems...time to give some measure of effect.' The disclaimer of any intent to query the landlord's title was a diplomatic insertion, true only on the narrowest interpretation, that formal ownership would be unaffected by tenant-right.

Not for years afterwards did Gladstone let the world know

how far he shared the conviction of the Irish peasantry and people that they had a literal right to remain on the land. To have done so in 1869–70 would have been explosive. There would have been no restraining the agitation in Ireland, and the dismay and indignation in England may be imagined. His language was as much a vindication of fixity of tenure, of the 3 Fs, to which he came in the 1881 Land Act, as it was of his own scheme. At the climax of an arduous struggle – for that is what it was – within a small circle in conditions of secrecy, he revealed his whole mind to his colleagues. The original intention was to impart his belief in the memorandum's proposals and to show how committed he was to them. When Fortescue withdrew his co-operation, the probability that the cabinet would reject them became a certainty, and prevented the document being circulated. He did not put aside the lesson in Irish history. The cabinet heard it in conjunction with the modified scheme agreed between Fortescue and himself, to which it was not particularly relevant. Historical grounds were an unsuitable defence of compensation for disturbance when it was not intended to imply that the occupier possessed an interest comparable to the goodwill under tenant-right. Gladstone persisted in talking historically and, in the widest sense, he was justified. 'He is possessed by this idea of restitution,' wrote Robert Lowe after the cabinet meetings in December.[160]

7

OUTSIDE THE CABINET,
OCTOBER TO DECEMBER

SPECULATION AND SILENCE

What the press said now mattered rather less than in the preceding months. It had really done its part by helping to get the consideration of Irish land on to a plane where the rights of landlords were quite suddenly viewed as liable to thorough revision in the public interest and under popular pressure. That *The Times* and most British journals went on protesting against plain fixity of tenure, as understood by the Irish, made no difference: for they had given the status of practical politics to everything which did not bear too close a resemblance to it. Since he had abandoned the plan for compulsory long leases weeks ago, Gladstone was not inhibited by the press. Neither were the cabinet. When ministers reacted adversely to the extension of custom, *The Times* swung away from it. Other journals, possibly less well informed, did not. Others again suggested measures that were too strong for the cabinet without affording the endorsement of custom wanted by Gladstone. *The Times* was urgent in its advocacy of another scheme that was too drastic and made little or no impact on the government. Changeableness and doubt in the press increased the importance of the best of the pamphlet literature that was building up. The next section begins with these pamphlets.

In Britain Liberal backbenchers and the Conservatives elected to be remarkably silent. It must be asked why. The government clearly benefited – as it did from the handful of friends and opponents who brought Irish land into their speeches. In Ireland a spectacular jump in agrarian crime and a mood symbolized by the success of the Fenian convict, Jeremiah O'Donovan Rossa, in heading the poll at the County Tipperary by-election in November, frightened some more landlords into an extremely conciliatory posture. The effect on British opinion was mixed.

'The country is full of M.P.s and lawyers, studying the land question,' Spencer had written to Gladstone at the end of September. 'We counted twelve, besides newspaper correspondents, of whose movements we knew something.' The viceroy was then dispensing or had dispensed hospitality to George Campbell; to Brodrick of *The Times*, who was not in Ireland for his newspaper; to Peter Maclagan, a Scottish farmer and Liberal M.P.; to John Lambert; and H. S. Thompson, a wealthy North Country Liberal and chairman of the North-Eastern Railway.[1] By November the opinions of these returned travellers were pouring forth from the publishers, and Gladstone dutifully struggled to read them. 'The literature of the subject is large, and will be larger: much of it is trashy,' he had told Bright on 1 September, '...larger than I can master', he complained three months on.[2] Campbell, James Caird (an authority on agriculture) and Maclagan were the three authors who elicited the most extensive comment.

Caird and Maclagan did not take native custom for their guide. Campbell, of course, did. It became known that his ideas had been noticed in a very high quarter in the ministry.[3] The added attention now paid to Indian example is traceable to that. His pamphlet published in the summer was reissued bound with another, the sequel to his second Irish visit in September. Thus the development of his thought might be followed. He said in the preface to the slim volume which appeared at the end of October: 'After all, the subject is a difficult one, for which people in England and Scotland have not been long prepared. Perhaps ...those who may...read these pages will not be willing to make, with me, two steps of so wide a space as that which separates Britain from Ireland.'[4] He considered the suggestions in his first pamphlet were defective because beyond Ulster the custom was too weak, imprecise and irregularly distributed for its enforcement to function as intended. The commission he had proposed should apply the custom universally in the shape of the full Ulster tenant-right: with the alternative of compulsory leases, incorporating valuation of rent. Campbell preferred full Ulster tenant-right to the alternative. He did not seek a general settlement of Irish rents. Under custom fair rent should only be fixed by the state when unavoidable if the tenant was not to suffer. Such interference should be one of the reserve powers invoked only to deal with proven bad landlords on 'the principle of the Habitual Criminals Bill'. As the preface indicated, this language and these changes were a consciously hopeful reaction to the education of the British in Irish agrarian problems over the short period since his first pamphlet was privately printed. Campbell might stress that 'it would be the greatest possible object to let good landlords alone', and exempt tenancies 'really ...purely contract...let as in Britain'. It would be an impossibility not to affect proprietors of undisputed benevolence gravely if the Ulster custom were fully enforced where, he had just been compelled to admit, they had often not experienced the thing in such strength. As for the exemption for contractual tenures, it had been the aim of both his pamphlets to show that the conditions proper to free contract did not flourish and were not understood in Ireland. Campbell was more politically sophisticated than many Indian administrators – their typical naïveté in home affairs is quite absent from his writings – but he had let himself be carried away by the speed of the public shift in British thinking and by his enthusiasm for ruling in a manner that marked him as one of the vigorous 'Punjab school' of officials in India – John Lawrence's men. To Campbell the morality of empire was straightforward. He had no sympathy with Fenianism, but the strong had a duty to the weak, and 'Irish ryots' must be treated with even-handed justice.[5]

Caird and Maclagan had complete faith in the efficacy of commercial principles for Irish land. Politics obliged them to think of ways to encourage these principles while the present generation of tenants received some security of tenure during the transition to the full exploitation of free contract. Maclagan refused to search for enlightenment in Russian, Prussian, Indian or Celtic landholding. The abrogation of the last must not be queried: 'In endeavouring to settle the land question in Ireland I see no reason for importing into it as an element the Tribal tenure.' Yet Maclagan was forced to recognize the vigour of Irish custom everywhere: the Landed Estates Court might confer Parliamentary titles, but he had found that the purchasers of property in Ireland could rarely acquire complete control until they bought out the tenants. Landlords anxious to improve were thwarted by occupiers who 'usurping a proprietary right...decline to pay the fair value of their farms'. He wanted the Board of Works to advance owners the money to buy up the occupancy-right thus arrogated. Maclagan and Campbell disagreed utterly over the social and economic worth of custom but to both men its ubiquity was a fact impossible to ignore.[6] Argyll closed his mind to this notable admission in Maclagan's pamphlet. When examining the history and prospects of free contract in Ireland, Caird's arguments were better judged and more circumstantial. From the reports of the commissioners of income tax he computed that Irish rentals had risen less than English and Scottish since the early 1860s. The figures showed, he held, that competition for land did not force rents up to an oppressive level compared with Britain. To Caird the underlying evil resided in the low productivity of Irish agriculture, which he did not think had grown appreciably since the Famine.[7] For both men the aim was to create the prosperity of Lowland Scottish farming in Ireland by inducing landlords and tenants to undertake the commitments normal to each in that part of Scotland. His recommendations and Maclagan's went as far as a court or commission to hand down binding decisions on disputes concerning improvements or tenant-right. Their main hope was to encourage leases that would make this jurisdiction superfluous. These two pamphlets confirmed the doubts which were felt about the extension of custom. The authors absolved the landlords, save of lack of enterprise. But their soundness made Caird and Maclagan all the more persuasive when they counselled 'some slight sacrifice'[8] of principle.

On 2 November *The Times* bestowed high praise upon Caird's pamphlet: it was the work of an expert who could draw on his knowledge of what Ireland had been like at the end of the Famine. The paper gave particular attention to his preference for contract over custom, described as his most valuable contribution. Any attempt to reproduce Ulster tenant-right must fail, and its propagation was not desirable. The next day O'Connor Morris wrote in with the outline of a scheme closely resembling, as he remarked, that of Caird. Custom should be protected but not extended. 'Nothing could be more absurd,' he emphasized on the 6th when he had arrived in Ulster, 'than to apply it to a country (like the South where there is little confidence between landlord and tenant) in a wholesale way. It would be *ridiculous and criminal*.'

In privately scouting the idea of extension he put his finger on the inconvenient facts, as they were to some: 'The agitators are logical. Tenant Right *without fixed rents is humbug*; and as fixed rent is Robbery let us have no general tenant right.'[9] It looks as if O'Connor Morris veered sharply in response to the signal in the leading article of the 2nd. Preaching the need to avoid delay in ensuring justice – and inexplicably 'without infringing the laws of Political Economy or equity in the slightest'[10] – *The Times* carried first or second leaders on Irish land on 5, 8, 10, 11, 13, 17, 20 and 22 November – a veritable barrage. From the 17th, the paper urged the adoption of a frankly extraordinary measure, resembling that propounded in Lowe's cabinet memorandum. In place of a customary basis for legislation the *Times*'s previously suggested local courts should uphold the right to evict a tenant who did not pay his rent, whose farming injured the land, or who subdivided: but should otherwise enforce 'not merely security... but fixity of tenure'. This, it was argued, gave the sanction of law, instead of surveillance by the blunderbuss, to the current practice. The landlord's claim to a periodical adjustment of rent should be admitted.[11] The paper called these restrictions on the exercise of property-rights 'nominal', contending that easily the greater number of landlords would be unaffected while all tenants might have confidence in their safety from a Scully,[12] from 'felonious' behaviour. On the 5th the leading article had been sure that the government would refuse to consider fixity of tenure, and on the 13th that there would be no concessions to violence. There was no suggestion, as in Lowe, that the land courts should have a distinctive legal status in order not to set a dangerous precedent. *The Times* took it for granted that the conditions of Britain and Ireland were so different as to preclude an unwelcome analogy between them, and did not mention the possibility of one being drawn.

Delane was prompted to publish a leader on this aspect of his plan by a debate in the Staffordshire chamber of agriculture, which attracted a lot of attention. A Liberal peer, Lord Lichfield, well-known for his interest in social reform, delivered the speech that alarmed *The Times*. As a 'more just and efficient' policy, Lichfield wished the Irish land bill to apply to Britain, too, enforcing compensation for improvements and eviction. To the latter claim, he observed, there was a strong objection – 'if...

given by law, the right of the tenant to property in the soil would be recognized. Compensation under this head would have to be given, but in such a way that the rights of property...be not interfered with.' If Lichfield went further than the speaker who introduced the debate, the remarks of others supplied evidence that Clarendon's were not empty fears. It was said that English farmers would want to know why if a land bill was passed for Ireland and they were neglected. The character of chambers of agriculture – they were not strongholds of radicalism – made the discussion, although inconclusive, all the more significant. *The Times* had a full report on 6 December, and Delane asked one of his most reliable men to write on 'the Tenant Right meeting in Staffordshire and...denounce the establishment or recognition of such an abomination in this country'.[13] The leader printed two days later did what was expected, with Lichfield's speech as its text. The *Times*'s picture was too simple, and it ignored the undercurrent of anti-landlord sentiment in Britain and even among her capitalist farmers.

The *Times*'s leaders on Irish land between 22 November and the December cabinets on the bill were mingled with the expression of concern about the government's handling of violence and of Fenian or clerical incitement to its commission. The call was for firmness in proceeding to a good, complete land bill and in asserting the criminal law. O'Connor Morris's letters continued to appear, but they were beginning to seem an encumbrance to the management. John Walter demanded to know when they were likely to end, complaining that by the addition of much padding their special correspondent was aiming at a two-decker volume on publication of the letters in book form. The proprietor and editor were made uneasy by his discussion of fixity of tenure – even if the conclusion was still that it should be rejected.[14] He played down the menace of agrarianism when his employers were acutely worried by it. He did not react well to their criticisms and cuts. 'The truth must be told,' he answered Delane, 'and I wish *particularly* to indicate to the British Public how the peculiar state of...Ireland makes more economic ideas inapplicable.'[15] Offering the editor more thoughts on the *Times*'s land plan, he strongly favoured empowering the courts 'to *commute into leases of varying duration, the equities in the soil* of the *tenants*'. It was 'only *justice*'. Replying to the charge of bias against Irish landlords brought against him by one of them, he said heatedly: 'If they have resort to the base means of baffled faction, I can't help it. I have *enormously* understated the case that might be made against them.'[16] O'Connor Morris could not say what he had to Delane while working to his brief for *The Times*. The leader-writers were much under John Walter's eye, and not only Delane's, when they fashioned the opinions which the special correspondent was enjoined to keep to a minimum in his reports. Those who composed the leading articles of the *Daily News* were freer.

Their journal was presented with a chance and a challenge. Free trade in land had not been a real test of radical abstractions about the nature of landowners' property. The domestic political situation which confined Gladstone was plainly described by the first leader of 16 November: 'prejudices of the landlord class... prejudices of the manufacturing class...The Radicalism of the Manchester School has not yet advanced to the point of recognizing ...the difference between landed and other forms of property.' The paper continued to prefer the adoption of a customary basis after *The Times* had given it up. The *Daily News* regarded the alarming state of Ireland by December with more equanimity than did *The Times*. It was natural that the old structure of agrarian relations should perish violently: 'An euthanasia could not have been looked for.' The mooted suspension of Habeas Corpus received no countenance: security of tenure would restore social peace,[17] the Gladstonian argument. The *Manchester Guardian* was more independent on land and coercion. On 1 November, after a critical look at the *Times's* recent editorials on the land bill and Ulster tenant-right, it declared in a carefully matter-of-fact way that Irish tenants should have guaranteed possession of their holdings for thirty years, although this would probably do little except remove a sense of wrong. When *The Times* switched to its new and drastic approach after the 17th, the *Guardian* concurred but analysed the inherent problems. The initial task of the new jurisdiction might be compared to Chancery's beginnings: the formulation of a body of rules, although Parliament would afford guidance. The two papers had a common motive – to make sure the land bill worked; it was better that it should be thorough. The Tipperary by-election added to the *Guardian's* belief in that aim as overriding scruples about landlords and about the land bill's impact on Britain, which were relegated to a parenthesis.[18]

The *Spectator*'s predilection for the Indian model[19] might still be very much that of a minority, but it was a topical one as Campbell's book stimulated discussion of 'The Use and Abuse of Indian Precedents', the title of an article in the *Saturday Review*.[20] The *Saturday* saw their agrarian legislation as the outstanding achievement of the great Anglo-Indian figures, one not usually conceived as such, and wrote: 'The deductions which have to be made from the usefulness of their experience arise from the simple fact that Ireland is close to England, and India many thousand miles away.' There was also that 'radical difference' between Ireland and India: the contrasting positions of government in relation to the land of the two countries. On 4 December the *Saturday* decided that assuring a tenant, on eviction, of the value of his goodwill would cause less upset than other notions being canvassed. Thus the plan submitted to the cabinet on 30 October was endorsed at the moment when its authors set it aside. The continuous adjustment to the pressures that bore painfully on the Conservatives disclosed how unwilling the more reflective were to fight on the question.

India and Custom were allotted more space in the *Pall Mall Gazette*. On 1 November, the extension of Ulster custom was 'almost too foolish to be seriously discussed' – a retort to the *Times*'s hints, with which the article started. The *Pall Mall* tried out its aggressive conservatism again to impress a single point on the public: the trouble in Ireland was that one set of people wanted what belonged to another – in a word, confiscation – and the swift escalation of the agitators' demands proved that this had been their purpose all along. The first leader of the 8th dealt with absenteeism and used the unwise argument that the popular landlords were those who neglected their functions. Then the *Pall Mall* talked in its alternative vein, more liberal than *The Times* and more practical than the *Daily News*. The law should step in to prevent 'felonious' actions – 'to use Lord Clarendon's somewhat dangerous adjective', said the *Pall Mall*. How to intervene was the question for subsequent leading articles. 'Contract and Tenure in Ireland' was the heading of the first leader on the 15th. Irish peasants, as yearly tenants, did not really enter into contracts and for the law to assume that they did was 'violent and false'. Even so a tenant-at-will had six months' legal security, and to lengthen that would not be like varying the terms of a specific contract. Should the tenant be free to divest himself of such increased security? The *Pall Mall* did not minimize the consequent risk of 'a violent shock to the stability of property' if free contract were modified as seemed necessary.[21] Meanwhile, off the leader pages there were several articles on Campbell's little book. It was described – the anonymous author being Fitzjames Stephen, Law Member-designate of the Viceroy of India's Council – as having 'supplied an intelligible theoretical basis for the strongest demands...made by, or on behalf of, the occupiers'.[22] Stephen contributed two articles summarizing, rather than discussing, Campbell.[23] An assessment was envisaged but did not appear. If written, it was irrelevant by mid-December when the press knew that whatever the cabinet had done, it had not been as bold as Campbell.

The *Economist's* leading articles did not advise an imaginative policy. The Ulster tenant-right solution was a very natural model to propose: but introduced outside the North it would only cause landlord and tenant to battle over 'an undetermined sort of property'.[24] The first leader of 20 November believed ministers to entertain as a general idea the plan which *The Times* was putting forward, and recommended caution. What would the reported tribunals achieve in a deeply divided country? In many areas the owners did not have a 'tyrannical' monopoly of the land market justifying such intervention by the state. Nor should any legislation constitute a disincentive to emigration. In December the journal adverted to the Staffordshire chamber of agriculture's debate with pained disapproval: 'the bare notion that the Legislature should try to settle business matters between English tenants and landlords is surprising enough, in whatever shape.' It was a wild idea that threatened the Irish land bill's chances with English landlords, who would throw their whole influence against it if it was going to be taken as a precedent for England. English arrangements in this sphere were those ideally suited to a highly advanced society. The limited English customs of tenant-right were becoming intolerable to both landlords and tenants, alleged *The Economist* unjustifiably.[25]

The press, having helped to produce the climate of opinion in which the government could embark on its enterprise, was too variable to be of greater use. The pamphleteers were not agreed either, but they were more influential because of their admitted expertise, as regards those selected here. Whether or not *The Times* was in the know, its advice to the cabinet was impracticable: for much the same reasons that ruled out Lowe's scheme. The remaining journals that have been looked at here likewise expected a less moderate bill than the cabinet sanctioned. The journalists realized that the British people were not stirred as they had been by Irish disestablishment. The politicians had tacitly conspired to prevent it. The press discovered that it had been busily engaged in a controversy which the parties in Britain declined to conduct publicly. Professional frustration was noticeable. As the *Manchester Guardian* reflected on 15 December: 'One of the most remarkable features of the recess has been the persistent reticence of the political leaders on either side.' There was a 'grave question in suspense, but it cannot be said to be before the country in the sense in which the Church...was presented for discussion at the last general election'.

THE UTTERANCES OF LIBERAL M.P.S

In its last number for 1869 the *Spectator* discussed the strange abstention of Liberal M.P.s from commenting on Irish land. 'The Tenure Bill will be, more than any great bill we ever heard of, the Cabinet's Bill. Irish opinion...they have obtained, but how about English?' The journalists had had the field to themselves: 'About thirty individuals have...engaged as full and...attentive an audience and rather more substantive power than if they were all Peers.' The ultimate responsibility for the legislation would lie with the representatives of English constituencies, and who knew what they thought? The *Spectator* believed that Liberal members had received 'some faint but intelligible' hint to keep quiet. The advanced radical weekly reflected that they might have left ministers too much latitude. For it had 'an impression rather than an opinion' that the extraordinary reserve of the independent county members, and of the provincial press, concealed a burgeoning impatience with half-measures. This was inherently improbable. 'For aught we know the cry of property in danger may be speedily heard,' the article confessed. It asserted that no minister or M.P. had delivered a noteworthy speech about Irish land, or anything else, since the start of the recess.[26] It forgot Hartington and Clarendon and passed over some half-dozen speeches from backbenchers and a junior minister in November and December which were not negligible indications of the party's thinking.

Most of the speakers were associated with the wing that was critical of the landed interest but careful of property and free contract. E. A. Leatham told his constituents of Huddersfield that 'he had never been and was not in favour of...any remedy which would be unfair and unjust, he did not say inexpedient, if applied on this side of the Channel.' He was for encouraging leases in every way, not compelling their adoption, and similarly discouraging tenancy-at-will, not prohibiting it. The confiscations centuries ago were not a reason for 'counter-confiscation'.[27] Richard Shaw, M.P. for Burnley, said there that compensation for improvements would give the Irish tenant 'all the fixity of tenure he was entitled to and would...respect the rights of the owner'. Fixity of tenure would be economically harmful, and to the whole agricultural community.[28] At an agricultural society meeting in the county, Edward Brydges Willyams, member for East Cornwall, wanted the privileges which the land bill would confer to be granted to Englishmen: 'His belief was that if fixity of tenure meant...compensation for unexhausted improvements ...they would have it, but not otherwise.' He hoped for the prompt suspension of Habeas Corpus in Ireland.[29] Another county member, S. S. Marling, of West Gloucestershire, speaking at a Liberal rally in Bristol, was fully prepared to support the government's bill 'but, at the same time...thoroughly convinced that the rights of the landlord should be considered equally with those of the tenants while the wrongs of the latter were being redressed'.[30]

Two middle-class admirers of Gladstone, William Rathbone and Samuel Morley, insisted on the legitimate power of the state to revise the conditions of landholding. Speaking at Liverpool, his seat, Rathbone vigorously defended the principle of state intervention and its far-reaching application. 'Those – now comparatively few – who protested violently against the right of Government to interfere with this matter, only showed their ignorance of the first principles of English law...while Government could and ought to respect the pecuniary estate of the Irish landlord in his land, it was surely justified in putting limits on arbitrary and summary...eviction...in giving legal sanction to those rights of tenants which in the most prosperous parts of the country were enforced by custom and in others by the dread of violence.'[31] Samuel Morley, M.P. for Bristol, was more circumspect at the rally in the city. One of the political leaders of English Dissent and a chief proprietor of the *Daily News*, he was more important than Rathbone. Clearly concerned that the theory he enunciated should not upset people, he appealed to them not to mistake the views of men like himself, supposed extreme because they wanted a land bill for England as well as Ireland. The land question in either country seemed very difficult to him. The changes to affect English tenure mentioned in his speech were peripheral – such as reform of the game laws. All he said of the Irish bill was that he anticipated it would 'meet the necessity of the case'.[32]

The third Liberal M.P. to speak on Irish land at the Bristol rally was James Stansfeld, now financial secretary to the Treasury. Political economy might lay down that property in land was qualified, but, he admitted, 'what shall be the nature of... interference and the degree of...restriction is a problem of very considerable complication and difficulty.' He denied suggestions that Gladstone was hesitating over the land bill: it would be informed by the spirit in which the Irish Church Act was framed and passed.[33] In an editorial on the Bristol speeches the *Daily News* extracted their underlying meaning: 'The English nation and... the Liberal party look to Mr Gladstone to lead them out of a labyrinth which they could not thread themselves...The land system has to be brought into harmony with the needs and feelings of Ireland, without breaking wholly with the ideas and tendencies of England.'[34] This was how Gladstone saw the broad limits within which he had to work, although he deluded himself about the relationship it was possible to achieve between Irish and English requirements. The silence broken by so few Liberal M.P.s was of more help to him than the speeches which in one way or another betrayed the party's internal tensions.

The fragile unity of the Liberals was being strained behind the screen they had erected. M.P.s, like cabinet ministers, complained bitterly in private. 'It is clear,' wrote one observer to Earl Grey in November, 'that the government are in a fix, and not agreed even as to first principles...I hear...a great many English Liberal members are in open rebellion...Irish land...won't keep the party together. It is a hoop which does not fit the tub.'[35] George Odger, of Reform League notoriety, predicted 'a good and genuine Bill, but it was unfortunate for Mr Gladstone that he had a Whig drag-chain upon his wheel of progress'. It was a common misconception. Radical businessmen were as critical as the Whigs. Odger said 'a very great deal of the land of England – not to speak of Ireland – had been obtained under very doubtful conditions...that certainly invited investigation and consideration.'[36] This was a restrained reference to the time-honoured contention of popular agrarian reformers that the people had been robbed of the land in the feudal epoch. He was addressing voters in the Southwark by-election which he contested as an independent working man's candidate. As president of the International Working Men's Association, he participated in the formation in October of the Land and Labour League, designed to exploit the public preoccupation with land and advocate its nationalization, a policy unanimously approved by the Basle Congress of the International. The activities[37] of these bodies were to attract a lot of attention next year, but in the autumn of 1869 they were less disturbing to sensible men of property than the mutterings of English farmers and the Welsh agitation arising out of the political evictions that had marked the general election. In November the *Daily News* reproached Welsh landlords for being 'too prone...to stand by their order, right or wrong',[38] and before the turn of the year it was calling on Liberalism to act against them. There was, it alleged, a 'half political, half social war...raging in Wales'.[39] The considerable exaggeration reflected the persuasive disquiet which convinced some that the landed interest ought not to be weakened by incautious concessions, and some that it must placate its enemies. Gladstone gained and lost by this perplexity as he laboured to advance the Irish bill.

THE BEHAVIOUR OF THE TORIES

The equally politic silence of the Conservative leaders incurred very hostile criticism. Their outward failure to rethink Irish land policy looked in the eyes of many like an invitation to Liberals to combine against Gladstone with the Opposition, while reserving the Conservatives' freedom of action in the event of his fall bringing them into office. It is equally possible, indeed more likely, that the Conservative leaders did not know what to say about Irish land when the question had evolved so rapidly, the initiative lay with the government, and the inadvisability of raising the temperature of public debate was strongly felt.

Near the end of the month's interval during the cabinet discussions, on 4 December, *The Times* carried a scathing editorial on the suspected Conservative tactics: 'It is well to remember the contrast between their stubbornness when in and their suppleness when out.' An analysis of the principles of Conservatism concluded that they did not exist. It was not safe to suppose that because 'questions of deep principle – the respect for property, the security of law' were concerned, and not 'a matter of pure expediency', the lowering of the franchise, the Conservatives would refrain from outbidding the Liberals after turning them out on the same issue. The government might be compelled to make Irish land a test of Parliament's confidence in them. If the Conservatives thereby got into office, shrugging off their policy in opposition would present no problems. 'The excuses that might be advanced are so readily forthcoming,' said *The Times*: '"The experience of Ireland is exceptional." "The question was not one to be fought over between parties." "Every one was agreed that it must be settled."' *The Times* had recently welcomed this language on the lips of Conservative county members but its suspicions of the leadership were not more intense than those of Salisbury in his *Quarterly Review* article. Whatever Disraeli may secretly have thought, he had to reckon with his party, as Gladstone had to with his. The Conservatives did feel that lowering the franchise and encroaching upon the rights of property were not comparable. They would not follow blindly – '270 voting with the will of one', in the *Times*'s picture of their apprehended Parliamentary triumph.

This editorial appeared with the report of a speech by the Conservative chief whip, the Hon. G. J. Noel. He said in his constituency of Rutland that English politicians were prepared to grant full compensation for improvements but the Conservatives could not consent to fixity of tenure. He gave a warning reminiscent of Hartington's Sheffield speech: 'If we once broke through the rights of property we should find ourselves on the verge of revolution...The same law...applied to Ireland must be applied to England, and to every sort of property.' Noel did not indicate what the party would accept in the range between the two formulae mentioned. Disraeli did not know, although in November the *Standard*, his newspaper, had published an editorial on the topical Indian analogy, denying that peace and prosperity would flow from the enforcement of 'rights of occupancy of any kind' in Ireland.[40] One of the last cabinet, Lord John Manners, told him a fortnight afterwards that 'I do not see my way' beyond compensation for improvements made with the landlord's express or implied sanction and the substitution of written agreements for parole tenure.[41] Disraeli had sounded J. T. Ball, the attorney-general for Ireland in his administration and a man with a reputation earned as one of the main Conservative speakers in the Commons debates on the Irish Church bill. Ball was willing to add a lengthened notice to quit (twelve months) to 'liberal' compensation for improvements. But he pointed out unarguably 'the present agitation would regard such amendments as mere trifling. No system will approach to contenting the people which does not make them independent of the landlord, so far that he cannot dispossess them.' He did not believe that extending Ulster custom could work: it would produce 'constant struggles by each class to mould it for their own advantage'.[42] The sparse evidence shows, as one would expect, that the Conservative leaders were wondering how best to change the narrowly restrictive policy they owed to party pressure in 1867–8. Of course, they strove to glean news of the cabinets on Irish land. On 23 November Lord Derby (as he had become) reported to Disraeli 'from certain authority' what was substantially true, that ministers had not settled anything and had adjourned for more information.[43]

An element of opportunism is inseparable from politics but the few Conservatives who spoke out did not give the impression of being eager to exploit the government's delicate situation. Noel's remarks came after *The Times* had talked of 'not merely security but fixity of tenure'. He referred to the 'wild schemes' of unspecified members of the government but hoped better of the 'united wisdom' of ministers. That hope was apparent in the speeches of Conservative country gentlemen who echoed the M.P.s for Essex commended by *The Times* in October. H. F. Meynell-Ingram, the heir to Temple Newsam, who sat for West Staffordshire, told a party demonstration there: 'It was impossible that what was called fixity of tenure or compulsory leases could be the basis of a satisfactory measure...yet the whole of Ireland seemed bent on that...He hoped that a Bill falling far short of these two revolutionary enactments would be introduced by Government with the view of bringing justice to everybody and making it impossible for landlords to abuse their rights.'[44] Major R. S. Allen, who represented East Somerset, said at Bristol on 13 November that 'he earnestly sympathized with the Premier in his difficulties, and promised him his support and sympathy with any measure he proposed that was right. He hoped...when the Liberals got again into opposition...they would exercise the same amount of forbearance.'[45] So far as their public statements went, the Conservatives were taking Salisbury's advice not to undermine a Liberal ministry when the great political and social interests bound up with land were at risk.

In December the *Saturday Review* glanced apprehensively at the 'obvious and inevitable' danger that the coming Irish bill was encouraging attacks on landed property in Britain. It rebuked Lord Lichfield for lending his authority to the unwarrantable suggestion that English farmers should have statutory compensation for improvements, 'the first step to perpetuity of tenure'. In recent weeks 'revolutionary changes' had been demanded for Britain. Henry Richard, the Welsh radical M.P., was cheered by a meeting at Aberystwyth on political evictions in the principality when he claimed that a tenant who lived on his farm for twenty years acquired a right to its joint ownership. 'Demagogues', commented the *Saturday*, 'who tell any class...that its members are entitled to the property of their neighbours are not likely to want hearers...From the well meaning...Staffordshire Chamber ...and the strong language of the Aberystwyth agitators, systems of spoliation rise by successive degrees to the sweeping negation of all right of property in land, which finds enthusiastic supporters among the Continental Socialists and their disciples in England.' In this context, the 'mischievous nonsense' of the Land and Labour League could not be overlooked. The *Saturday* was resentful because 'English landowners who venture to criticize any of the numerous projects for dealing with Irish tenures are constantly reminded...if they make themselves troublesome, they will find that in England also there is a land question.'[46] On the journal's own showing, it was an argument that Conservatives and Liberals were wise not to disregard.

Behind the prudence of the Conservatives lay a rancour which had its chief outlet in the more partisan of their newspapers.

It was a cause of morbid satisfaction that disestablishment should have signally failed to pacify Ireland. It was naturally a cause of alarm as well. After the shock of O'Donovan Rossa's election, there was an outcry for firmness towards agrarianism and sedition. The same lack of principle which *The Times* saw among Conservative leaders was alleged of the government. The *Standard* discerned in recent developments 'the old plan – Fenians stimulating treason, the Radicals coquetting with it, and making its violence an excuse for subversive legislation'.[47]

The *Freeman's Journal* had a ready explanation of the defeat of its allies and policy in the Tipperary contest. The event proved that the Fenians could only be checked by depriving tenants of the incentive to revolt.[48] This was the paper's repeated message. One after another the county meetings were organized to call for fixity of tenure – four of them within two days.[49] A conference at the Mansion House in Dublin – attended mainly by civic worthies and representatives of the Catholic middle class – listened to Sir Dominic Corrigan, a rich Liberal in the city, arguing that fixity of tenure was not enough, that Bright's scheme should be lavishly financed and made compulsory. Parliament had given twenty millions to emancipate the West Indian slaves, and he asked whether they had a better claim on the British Exchequer than the Irish. 'There was not equality,' he said, 'when the landlord could take the tenant's property on paying...for it, while the tenant could not take the landlord's property.' Unless occupiers were converted into owners, Ireland would be more disturbed after a few years than she was at that moment. Sir John Gray, who had played his usual part in the conference, congratulated those substantial citizens on their progress. He remarked pleasantly of Corrigan and other lately mild reformers that 'the pupils had outstripped the master'.[50] He and the *Freeman* kept on pressing for fixity of tenure. In vain: the news from Tipperary intensified the anti-Irish reaction which the demonstrable inefficacy of disestablishment – such a great step in British history – had stimulated. Lord Kimberley was sensible of the feeling against his class in Britain which the Irish question was bringing out: but he was infuriated by O'Donovan Rossa's election – 'just what might be expected from the ruffians who inhabit that county...fitly represented by the rowdy felon they have chosen. What a descent from Grattan and O'Connell, or even Wolfe Tone and Emmet!'[51] His instinct was right. The English (and Scottish) sense of legality and propriety was outraged as it had not been since Gladstone steered the Liberal party on to its new Irish course.

John Platt, the Liberal M.P. for Oldham, said in his constituency on the announcement of O'Donovan Rossa's return: 'It was dreadful to think that in this the nineteenth century such a thing could come to pass in this realm.'[52] Platt was sufficient of a radical to have declared in September, during a speech which covered Irish land, that Whiggery was dead.[53] On that occasion and on this, he talked with fervour of compensating the tenant, although not of providing him with security or fixity of tenure, but now he insisted that the party must at the same time enforce obedience to law. The clamour in Britain for coercion was such that the *Spectator* realistically advocated the suspension of Habeas Corpus and a more centralized and authoritarian administration for Ireland on the French pattern. The issue of 4 December attributed the abstention among the voters in Tipperary to fear. Less liberal but less independent journals were not as prompt because they clearly did not like to embarrass the ministry. The assistance of this section of the press could not shield Gladstone from party and public impatience with the Irish. Before the election result burst, Gladstone would not hear of repression until a land bill that satisfied him as just should have disappointed his hopes of it. A week afterwards, remaining opposed to added powers for the Irish government, he told Fortescue that since the subject drew so much attention, the cabinet would give it a high priority in the December sessions about to start and the Irish executive should be ready with information and advice. In his letter to the Queen after the first of these meetings on 7 December, the prime minister reported a decision to despatch military and naval reinforcements to Ireland but said, quite misleadingly, that her Irish ministers did not consider extraordinary legislation necessary for the maintenance of order.[54] Naturally suspicious, and annoyed, Victoria asked to see regularly the Irish reports to Gladstone, complaining that the viceroys used to write to her, not to the prime minister.[55] She had excellent grounds for being distrustful.

The commander-in-chief in Ireland thought the position there appalling and was telling his correspondents in England so.

Strathnairn thought the Fenians must be well content with matters as they were by November. 'What,' he asked, 'can the enemies of the Public Peace wish for *more* than the present state of Ireland?' Agrarian conspiracy paralysed all but a few counties. The land market, 'the thermometer of...confidence', as the money market was in England and France, had fallen right down. Landlords dared not dismiss tenants and workers on their estates.[56] In his letters to the Duke of Cambridge he spoke with helpless indignation of 'intimidation, the historical, and invincible weapon of Irish agitators'.[57] The tally of agrarian offences kept by the constabulary soared from 59 in October to 144 in November and 337 in December. The total number of crimes of every kind rose from 226 to 548 over the three months.[58] Fortescue took comfort from the reported and sometimes real division between Fenianism and the land agitation.[59] Strathnairn accepted that this view had something to be said for it, but found the line distinguishing the two movements so blurred that he believed advanced land reformers and Fenians would eventually merge. Their fusion would be helped if, as he of course wanted, the hope of fixity of tenure were disappointed. Indeed, by-election slogans indicated that they had already joined forces: fixity and an amnesty for political prisoners were being demanded together.[60] This was not the sure sign of collaboration that he assumed, but a warning. When the tenants' traditional leaders felt that they must espouse what was notoriously a Fenian policy, that is, amnesty, they might not be capable of staving off a takeover of the land agitation. After Tipperary their displacement appeared imminent. Considerably over two-thirds of the voters abstained, although the defeated, clerically-backed candidate tried to recommend himself by using both the cries that Strathnairn mentioned.

Strathnairn did not ascribe the result of the contest to intimidation: it was greeted with deplorable enthusiasm, he said. He saw in it, and in the rampant agrarianism, the hand of the younger priests who had counteracted the exertions against O'Donovan Rossa of 'all the better class of the R.C. clergy'. The loyal element of the population, too generally, and the prosperous Catholics with no desire for revolution, were isolated and impotent.[61] For this Strathnairn blamed his own party in particular. 'The Conservatives,' he lamented to the Duchess of Abercorn, '...have brought things to their present state by a timid and undecided Policy with that certain guarantee of failure – toadying to their Enemies and alienating their friends.'[62] There is abundant evidence from the landlords that Strathnairn did not overstate their weakness and frustration. They had lived through the violence and threats before, when those had assumed graver proportions. Their fortitude was being sapped by the knowledge that the government would not come forward with unconditional succour as in the past.

The letters to Clarendon of an old friend expressed this creeping defeatism. The Countess of Dartrey's husband owned 30,000 acres in Ireland, and she knew Clarendon so well that he sent her Kimberley's and Hatherley's memoranda. She mixed her sensible comments on the documents with acerbic ones on the Liberals' mistaken policy on Irish land and unrest. She was herself a Whig of the older generation, and imbued with the implacable anti-Catholicism often found in it. She wrote after the Tipperary election that the priests were bent on driving Protestants out of the country. Clerical sponsorship of fixity of tenure was aimed at stripping the landlords of their power and making them leave Ireland, when most of their co-religionists would follow. 'This would appear to be a bold assertion,' she explained, 'but when you remember the large majority of R.C.s and the way...*all* act in obedience to priestly orders, it becomes clear...the priests are making a bold push to get complete possession of Ireland, with a view to the future coercion of England in obedience to the aims of Rome.' Lady Dartrey attributed to the Catholic clergy a Machiavellian design that did not exist: but she did not mis-understand the temper of the people, displayed in a manner shocking to her – 'going along the roads not a R.C. *child* ever now touches his cap or curtsies to one.' She related how her acquaintances were constantly talking of departing from a country that was being made intolerable for them; and she wanted the government to reflect on the security of Ireland without the Protestant garrison in the event of war with France or America.[63] She complained that the suspense over the land question was doing great harm. Tenants were refusing to accept leases because they believed they would get the land at half its value.[64] However, she understood perfectly the futility of confining herself to protests.

Her letters to Clarendon were accompanied by papers she had written discussing the prospective land bill in an empirical fashion. She thought her suggestions combined 'equity to landlord and liberality to tenant'.[65] She considered that Kimberley was over-generous in the size of his contemplated payment to the evicted tenant.[66] She was better pleased with Hatherley's memorandum – 'I think every line of it admirable'[67] – but her own suggestions far outstripped his. Custom should be legalized where it had the landlord's sanction. Elsewhere her preferred evil was a compulsory four or five years' notice in the event of dispossession, with an option to the tenant of claiming instead half the rent for that period, plus whatever his improvements might be worth, and an option to the landlord of barring all claims by a lease in excess of thirty-five years.[68] The rights of property would only be 'as it were, placed in temporary abeyance, redeemable at a fixed rate...not an unjust concession...I feel sure it is one...landlords would willingly make, for the sake of promoting peace.'[69]

In one of her letters Lady Dartrey recounted a conversation with Chichester Fortescue's brother. Lord Clermont agreed with her that had Gladstone taken a recent opportunity, at the Mansion House on 9 November, to speak out against the political and physical attacks on landed property in Ireland, it would have had a good effect. Clermont's neighbourhood was as discontented as her own. He advised Chichester Fortescue on 9 November that the likelihood of a general refusal to pay rents was exaggerated, but that there was some risk of their being withheld and of agents and bailiffs being slain in the attempt to collect them. He re-membered the bloody incidents of the Tithe War, and hoped the Parliamentary session would take much of the heat out of the land question: 'I think Landlords ought to accept almost any measure with that object which keeps clear of Fixity of Tenure.'[70] Lord de Ros, writing to Dufferin, was near despair because 'with these agitators who are convulsing the frame of Irish society, argument is so hopeless, and with the English legislature so unavailing.'[71] These landlord accounts were borne out by a more detached witness, C. S. Roundell, formerly secretary to the Royal Commission on the causes of the Jamaica rebellion of 1865 and now private secretary to Spencer. Arguing in favour of stepping firmly between the owner and occupier of land, he told his cousin Sir Roundell Palmer: 'The landlords must concede something of their rights in an English point of view. It is better for them to recognize existing facts, and...by law what they now practically concede by fear...future improvement...at present is almost denied to them....No one can look forward without fear or even terror to the autumn and winter which would follow upon either the rejection of the Land Bill, or still more the failure of the Government to propound an adequate measure.' Englishmen who were ignorant of what agrarian outrage meant could not really understand, he said, the urgency of a settlement.[72]

It was reasonable for the tenants, their leaders and newspapers to believe that they had the landlords on the run. Fighting a by-election for Waterford city, Ralph Bernal Osborne was compelled to pledge himself from the outset to 'full security of tenure and an equitable arrangement of rents'. His opponent, another old Whig, Sir Henry Barron, had to do the same.[73] To the *Freeman's Journal* it seemed that the government was 'prepared, if supported by public opinion, to do anything...Ireland wants'.[74] This was more nearly true than the *Freeman* and its proprietor perhaps assumed: but the public opinion to which Gladstone and his colleagues were answerable was that of Great Britain and its educated and propertied classes. The government was under no illusion as to the strain its Irish policies were putting on peers, M.P.s and the interests they represented. Gladstone had to assure Sir John Gray that he personally was undaunted. He took the chance to tell Gray that the Irish were endangering the bill in preparation. 'That we could not propose to convert the landlords into stipendiaries has...been reasonably assumed,' he wrote. 'From my own mouth I am confident...nothing has been gathered beyond...that the land question...cannot now be settled by...compensation for improvements...although I know that unless great efforts be made...to moderate expectations and desires no less than...idle fears, we shall certainly fail.'[75]

8

THE LAST STAGES IN THE CABINET AND THE MOOD OF TWO COUNTRIES

THE BILL'S PROVISIONS

The bill presented to Parliament in February grew from the propositions put to the cabinet on 14 December, accepted by a majority of its members and amplified on the 17th. It needed a month to bring the minority round. Meanwhile the work of drafting went ahead. Seven cabinets followed between 22 January and 2 February, and thereafter a committee of ministers put the finishing touches to the bill. The pressure of individual ministers is discoverable at various places in the full text, which contains numerous qualifying and secondary provisions.[1] The Parliamentary draughtsman's translation of ministerial intentions into legal phraseology was, after an early misunderstanding, closely supervised by Gladstone; the two conferred alone in a series of meetings.[2] Clause 1 legalized Ulster custom in that province, as practised. Clause 2 recognized custom where it was found in the South, but only when the tenant's occupation was disturbed by the landlord. There was no ceiling on the sum then payable. Where the tenant was unable to claim, or had not been successful, under the first two clauses, clause 3 entitled him to compensation for disturbance according to a scale ranging from a maximum of seven years' rent for holdings rated at £10 and below, to a maximum of two years' rent for those rated at above £100. 'Disturbance' had its previous meaning. Under the first and second clauses the tenant was not entitled to separate compensation for improvements. Under the third, he might claim separately for expenditure on permanent buildings, the reclamation of land and unexhausted processes of cultivation; with something for improvements added to compensation for disturbance, he could expect to receive, by law, a sum closer to what the countryside would consider as the fair value of his occupancy. The bill was built round these three clauses.

The first clause applied to all Ulster holdings subject to custom, whatever their tenure; the landlord had no alternative but to buy up the tenant-right. The second clause applied to all holdings outside the North that were subject to custom, with the exception of those that might be covered by the offer of a lease for not less than thirty-one years, after which the limited tenant-right would revive if not again suspended in the same way. It was not possible to extinguish the tenant-right except by purchase. Where tenant-right was extinct by purchase, the occupier could have recourse to the third clause. The clause applied to existing and future tenancies-at-will, but not to land that was either under a current lease, or might be covered by a future lease for not less than thirty-one years. At the end of that period the landlord's liability to compensate for disturbance in respect of the new tenure was inescapable unless the holding was again put under lease for the minimum period of thirty-one years. The liability, unlike that under custom, North and South, was not extinguishable as long as the land was let to a tenant: it could only be perpetually suspended by an indefinite series of leases of the statutory length. The leasehold alternative open to the landlord had been revised since Gladstone worried over its inclusion in his memorandum of 3 December. The changes were made with the tenants' anticipated dislike of the option in mind. By clause 16 the offer of a lease for the period specified in clauses 2 and 3 was subject to the courts' approval of the rent and other conditions in the proffered agreement, unless and until the offer was the second or subsequent tender in a continuing series. If the tenant refused the initial lease, the landlord would notwithstanding have exempted himself, for not more than thirty-one years, from claims under clauses 2 and 3. On the other hand, the landlord had to find a taker for his offer when, as the second or subsequent tender in a series, it would not be subject to judicial approval. The compulsory reference of rent to the courts that formed a controversial part of this clause reappeared in the next. Clause 8 stated that eviction for non-payment of an agreed rent did not constitute disturbance except on 'special grounds' in the case of existing tenancies-at-will or leaseholds. The obscure wording held over an evicting landlord the threat of adjudication upon the fairness of rents actually levied. Clause 6 took the case of the tenant who could not get, or had not obtained, anything under the first three clauses but who on coming into the holding had made a payment, with the landlord's express or implied consent, to the previous occupier. The courts were to award him such compensation as they thought was 'just'; or they were to approve the terms on which he might be permitted to dispose of his interest. There could be no question of stipulating that the tenant must be reimbursed in full by his successor or the landlord: it would have been too much like the universal recognition of tenant-right. By clause 4 a tenant might claim, with certain limitations, for all improvements, if unable to get compensation under the first three clauses; a lease for thirty-one years or longer granted before or after the passing of the bill entailed some further restriction of this claim. Clause 5 reversed the presumption of law as to the property in improvements. Both the fourth and the fifth clauses were retrospective.

Clauses 2, 3 and 4 declared null and void any agreement by which the tenant might be induced to surrender his right to claim under them, other than one for the purchase by the landlord of the tenant-right recognized in clause 2. Nor under clause 4, could the landlord prohibit any improvement suited to the holding. They were grave incursions upon freedom of contract. As a palliative, there was clause 10 – called the Argyll clause by the prime minister. By the first part, all compensation, except for unexhausted processes of cultivation, was withheld from the tenant of a holding rated at £50 or more and occupied on a future lease of not less than *twenty-one* years, when it was shown that the British practice had been followed regarding improvements. The remaining part of clause 10 allowed occupiers of holdings rated at £100 and over, and not subject to custom in or out of Ulster, to contract themselves out of the bill.

Subdivision without the landlord's consent forfeited the right to claim under clauses 2 and 3; and the estate rules inseparable from Ulster custom legalized as practised had a similar effect. By clauses 2, 3 and 4, and by Ulster custom, all arrears of rent were deductible from money that his successor or the landlord paid to an outgoing tenant. On his side the tenant got certain additional benefits. There was the stipulation that the landlord might not forbid any improvement suited to the holding. It was said in the cabinet that this would seriously erode a proprietor's control over his estate. No tenant could be forced to quit until the compensation owed to him was met. The period of notice to quit a tenancy-at-will was lengthened to a year, and a duty of half a crown imposed on every notice served. It was at the landlord's expense that the burden of local government taxation on the tenant was reduced. The owner of the soil became liable for the county cess on holdings rated at £4 and below, and for half the amount on holdings above that level. Lands used wholly or mainly for pasture were covered by the clauses relating to security of tenure, and especially clause 3, although they had been excluded from the ambit of legislation in Gladstone's memorandum of 3 December, having previously been *in*cluded. The principal beneficiaries of the change back were the prosperous graziers. They did sometimes occupy their extensive farms under tenant-right, but they exemplified commercial and competitive qualities, hiring and relinquishing land as the market dictated. While they had often made themselves unpopular with the peasantry, and stood in no need of legislative help, they were an influential element among the Catholic population, and it was wise not to omit them from the bill.

Permissive land purchase had to appear in order to retain Bright in the government. The Irish Board of Works was empowered to lend a tenant up to three-quarters of the price of his holding at $6\frac{1}{2}$ per cent repayable over twenty-two years. The terms compared unfavourably with those on which the lands of the disestablished Anglican church were to be sold. Tenants buying under the Irish Church Act could secure a loan of three-quarters of the price at 4 per cent over thirty-two years. The sale of ecclesiastical property was an administrative convenience and a financial necessity.[3] Bright's scheme was quite another thing. In Gladstone's memoranda of September and December the rate of interest had been $3\frac{1}{2}$ per cent on three-quarters of the price over an undecided number of years. His scepticism and resolve not to commit the taxpayer too deeply had hardened and been reinforced by objections from Fortescue to encouraging the break-up of estates. The sum available to the Board of Works was limited to a million in the first instance. Further sums of a million at a time might be issued to the Board in the event of a greater demand to purchase than was anticipated.

For the purposes of the bill only, the restrictions of family settlements were relaxed to enable every limited owner to pay out compensation, grant leases and sell land to tenants. In his speech on the first reading next month, Gladstone referred to this alteration in the law as a step in the general direction of removing the 'fetters' on owners.[4] The remark was no more than a gloss meant to appeal to the British radicals who would not care for the bill's considerable departures from commercial freedom. The separate bills for the promotion of free trade in land in the United Kingdom were expendable. Advice to ministers like that from Sir Arthur Helps, clerk of the Privy Council and a warm admirer of Palmerston, was hardly necessary. Calling him 'an advanced liberal', Helps counselled de Grey to 'take care you do not advance yourselves or at any rate your sons, out of all your estates'.[5]

To sum up, the bill had a twofold aim. The more obvious intention was to increase *legal* security of tenure by the financial penalty on the landlord if he evicted without being protected by the statute. Less straightforward was the encouragement to custom. It was confirmed, not extended, and beyond Ulster restricted by clause 2. Clause 6, however, fostered it by the carefully unspecific protection given to the payments for occupancy-right that were unwillingly tolerated by so many Southern landlords. The bill thus drew nearer to Gladstone's conception of what it ought to do than appeared possible when he and Fortescue agreed on their submission to the cabinet of 14 December. At almost every turn the landlord was hemmed in by barriers, or hurdles, constructed to prevent him from undermining the security, independence *and* property in the holding which the tenant was intended to enjoy. The tenant was clearly vulnerable to eviction for non-payment of rent; but even here the 'special grounds' clause was some defence.

The machinery of enforcement mattered, and not only because of the bill's complexity and obscurity. Spencer had advised the institution of land tribunals, cheap and simple in their working, in which the peasantry would have confidence. Gladstone's view, faithfully reflected in the bill, was that in the allocation of new judicial functions government should strive to avoid incurring expense. Land cases were entrusted to the civil bill court, that is, to the chairman of quarter sessions for each county, who in Ireland was salaried and sat alone to handle the civil side of sessional business. From him an appeal lay to the judges of assize and thence to the Court for Land Cases Reserved drawn from the judges of the superior courts in Dublin. The only new appointment to be created was the part-time 'valuator and assessor' to the chairman of quarter sessions. A decade later the Bessborough Commission on the 1870 Land Act heard landlord and tenant witnesses complain that the civil bill court (renamed the county court in 1872) had proved unsatisfactory in agrarian disputes. Rather unexpectedly, Gladstone's old preoccupation with economy blinded him to the probability that this would happen.

For the cabinet, the second and third clauses were the contentious ones. Fortescue was emboldened by success to criticize the equation of custom outside Ulster with compensation for disturbance. Of much greater moment was the resistance to compensation for disturbance of Lowe, Cardwell and Argyll. The principles inherent in that form of compensation did not destroy the cabinet, as the extension of custom would have done. Gladstone had chiefly his own resolution to thank for that. The government would not have survived the loss of the three ministers.

He was assisted by the predicament of Irish landlords. He appealed on their behalf. Ireland was roused against them. They would be the sufferers if the objectors in the cabinet thwarted the decision of the majority. Nevertheless, Gladstone still was not ready to sanction the resort to coercion. The land bill was not what he had wanted to capture the imagination and loyalty of the Irish people. His determination remained to wait and see how the bill would impress them. There were few grounds for his persistent, though diminished, optimism. Kimberley was representative of those members of the cabinet, the moderates in the context of Ireland, who having helped to kill the extension of custom now supported the prime minister. He put down an assessment of the likely political returns: 'Our bill may satisfy English feeling as a measure of justice to Ireland; it may perhaps lay the foundations of better relations between landlords and tenants. But it would be idle to expect that it will work a miracle and suddenly convert a wrong-headed, turbulent people to sober and contented industry.'6 It was implicit that everything depended on the British reaction. The Irish reaction was not, unfortunately, problematical. How would the bill be interpreted in Britain? The signs were there as a rough idea of its scope got abroad, through guesswork and a seepage of information. The *Daily News* stated that ministers were about to launch 'the era...of creative Radical-ism'.[7] It was too true to be comfortable in the prevailing atmo-sphere. 'Other subjects,' said *The Times*, '...even Education...are trifles with the one topic engrossing the attention of the nation.'[8]

PERSISTENT OBJECTORS AND THEIR SUBMISSION:
FORTESCUE, LOWE, CARDWELL AND ARGYLL

The aggravation of Gladstone's trouble with Fortescue was, in the former's words, 'a subaltern controversy'.[9] There was a vital connexion between it and his trial of strength with Lowe, Cardwell and Argyll. These three and Gladstone did not disagree over custom outside Ulster, but over compensation for disturbance. The common ground would have been lost had the prime minister yielded to Fortescue's importunity. For that reason alone, the Irish secretary was told he could not have his way. Compensation for disturbance, as clearly foreseen, was exposed to the criticisms that Gladstone most feared. Anything that might help to disarm its opponents should be kept in the bill. Tactical necessity aside, he continued to think, and speak, of such compensation as supply-ing a local deficiency of custom.

Fortescue moved further away from this view. He tried, and failed, to persuade the cabinet to make compensation for dis-turbance the rule in what he proceeded to call 'the non-customary regions of Ireland' beyond Ulster, with landlord and tenant permitted to substitute the sale of the latter's interest wherever it seemed equitable to the courts. He claimed that the use of custom outside the North as the equivalent of compensation for disturbance would be unfair to the tenant. The illustration he gave of unfairness was the same one that he had employed against the *extension* of custom: a high rent would prevent the tenant from getting an adequate price for his interest.[10] It was surely the tenant, Gladstone responded, who would be keen to produce evidence of custom and if doubtful of the advantage to himself would choose the alternative method of securing compensation.[11] The answer disposed of Fortescue's specific objection. He would not accept that the whole issue was closed after the 17th, when authority was given for the draughtsman to begin work from the prime minister's memorandum of what had been decided on the first five clauses, as they became, and on other parts of the bill.[12]

In two letters of January, Gladstone declined to continue the argument 'after so many hours and pages of it'. The bill would be 'greatly endangered' if their dispute did not stop. The cabinet had heard Fortescue press his view, repeatedly, and had not adopted it. They had taken a '*decision*', which the draft must incorporate. On compensation for eviction without reference to custom, he asked Fortescue to appreciate why 'my object has been...to minimize this point of danger' and emphasized the personal responsibility that he bore and felt. He did not think that his colleague allowed sufficiently for the delicacy of the situation. He ended his second letter of remonstrance wearily: 'I have not...time or strength to prosecute it further.' The Irish secretary was shaken into a more co-operative frame of mind, though still refusing to admit that he was wrong.[13]

Indeed, 'the whole substance of the measure' was his, Chichester Fortescue told Clermont, but circumstances required Gladstone to carry it through the cabinet and introduce it in Parliament. 'It is something', he consoled himself, 'to have had so much influence upon so great a work, although behind the scenes.' Gladstone was by nature 'not a man ready or anxious to give credit to others'.[14] In fact, having adopted and made the best of compensation for disturbance, Gladstone gave him the credit for its inclusion. Fortescue knew – none better – how far the bill was founded on a different idea. Not unnaturally, he put the most flattering interpretation upon the part that he had played.

Compensation for disturbance was embodied in one of the clauses drafted after the cabinet of the 17th, leaving two contested points open. They were whether it ought to apply, as proposed, to existing tenancies-at-will and to holdings above a certain size or value.[15] Lowe and Cardwell were isolated at the discussion in maintaining stubbornly that it ought not. Argyll, who was absent, concurred with them on the second point. All three regarded the bill as impolitic and retrogressive. The two commoners were the more determined. Their objection to compensating existing tenants-at-will for disturbance promised to undermine the bill fatally. Too many disappointed occupiers, of holdings of every size, would have an added grievance when they saw how those under custom were treated.

Lowe said in cabinet 'that he would rather give up everything than consent to put his hand in one man's pocket and rob him for the benefit of another'.[16] It was a dramatic way of expressing a truth. A landlord might, in theory, avoid being caught by a change in the law affecting future tenancies; there was no obligation to let his land. To make customary arrangements legally binding was defensible as confirmation of a prior understanding. Whereas a statutory direction to construe current tenancies-at-will as implying compensation for disturbance did mean taking something from one man, if he acted consistently with an agreement concluded before the law was changed, and bestowing it on another. 'To those who think as I do,' wrote Lowe in an appeal to Granville, 'this would involve a direct attack on property...a precedent under which any amount of spoliation might as far as principle goes be justified...[and] forcing new and arbitrary terms into existing contracts.' He would have liked to press for the elimination of compensation for disturbance. He denounced it comprehensively. It was discriminatory on the basis of class, yet would not conciliate the tenants. Its principle was extensible 'with the utmost facility' to Britain. It showed that 'all our reverence for custom was a mere pretence in order to effect a foregone conclusion which must be attained at all events.' The sacrifice to 'conspirators and assassins' would profoundly alienate M.P.s: 'The House of Commons as a body hates and despises the Irish and will look with the greatest aversion on any attempt to break down established rules of property for their sake.'[17]

When Hatherley put forward his suggestion of 'damages for eviction' in November, Lowe and Cardwell had looked on it with favour. Their scruples about its application to current tenancies developed after Gladstone and Fortescue adopted it next month without excluding, like the Lord Chancellor, over half the tenants in Ireland. Argyll led in pressing for this compensation to be withheld from occupiers of holdings above Hatherley's line or one drawn with a similar purpose. Fortescue had originally intended to restrict compensation for disturbance to smaller occupiers. By not doing so now, he and Gladstone were embarrassed for a plausible explanation of the payment. It was depicted as an exercise of the state's protective function, an aid to tenants who through circumstances beyond their control were in a condition of dependence. Gladstone argued that Irish farmers were getting a remedy not for pauperism, which no one pretended was the lot of all evicted tenants, but for the handicap, common to all, of an 'abnormal' demand for land. If all the tenants were therefore eligible for this type of help, so were those in Britain, should the demand for farms in that country be more intense than he imagined. Argyll quoted what McCombie, one of the Scottish farmer M.P.s, had lately said to Lowe. According to McCombie, even such prosperous men as himself needed to be legally secured against some requirements in leases to which they were obliged to submit because 'there's sich competeetion for land that you can just make us agree to anything ye like.' 'I think we shall be in a Fool's Paradise,' the Duke admonished the prime minister, 'if we suppose that the main argument on which you rely...helps us to confine our Legislation to the Irish side of the Channel. If we are to legislate for the...protection of all...who in the "Struggle for Existence" are placed at comparative disadvantage in bargaining for the means of subsistence, I fear...the principle will carry us a long way. Even in manufacturing...the poor cannot deal "on equal terms" with the capitalist.'[18]

Argyll was afraid of the consequences of allowing compensation for disturbance to all. Gladstone was afraid of the consequences of limiting it to some. Pauperism was not the prerogative of Ireland: it was worse in England and Scotland, and compensation based on preventing it ought logically to be extended to them. Its relevance to Britain contravened one 'among the first of the prudential rules that should govern the construction of our measure'. Believing that the argument of abnormal demand was also relevant to Britain, the Duke put more emphasis on the prevention of pauperism because it would cover fewer people in Ireland and at home. He had to take some account of the other argument to justify 20 or 25 acres as the limit within which the occupier might claim for disturbance, instead of Hatherley's 'under ten acres' or the £10 valuation advocated by Lowe and Cardwell. Argyll wrote to Cardwell that the line, wherever it came, should include enough of the small tenants to satisfy them as a class. It would have been reassuring had he told Gladstone this at the same time.[19]

The prime minister received the impression that Argyll was being thoroughly intractable, as feared. The Duke composed a memorandum dissecting, point by point, the arguments in a letter, a copy of which went to him, written by Gladstone to Granville and designed to be shown to Lowe. The memorandum bristled with remarks like 'we ought not to...purchase peace at the sacrifice of Justice and Economic principles', and 'an Irishman is not tethered to Ireland any more than a Hebridean is...to the Hebrides'. The letter for Lowe did not dwell on the Irish past. That would not have been conciliatory; he had complained to Granville: 'Gladstone argues or rather declaims the case historically – he thinks that a great debt is due from England to Ireland and talks of the violence of two hundred years ago as if it were a thing of yesterday.' In their letters, the prime minister and Argyll did go over this ground again. The Duke hoped Gladstone would reflect very carefully before adverting publicly to 'ancient Celtic usages...those misty traditions...to unsettle all...as to what constitutes Property'. The lapse of a couple of centuries since it was overthrown must be held to have effaced 'Tribal Right'. The prime minister rejoined that he drew on 'Irish history not the polemical but the normal'. It would be an affront, returned Argyll, to defend the penalty on disturbance by the citation of rights which occupiers had not possessed for two or three hundred years. Gladstone insisted on the continuous existence of tenant-right through preceding generations. The Duke would realize it if he swallowed the 'large dose' of history prescribed. While he did not take the medicine, Argyll's reply indicated it was unnecessary. He said in a helpful spirit that both Gladstone's arguments and his own were contrived.[20]

Irish land was '*in a mess*' and the interests of landlords and tenants ought to be redefined. Argyll had already suggested that this might be the rationale of their bill. It was how he liked to put what Gladstone and Granville were telling the dissentients. 'My desire', wrote Gladstone, 'is to make a strenuous effort for "stability" of tenure, and the deliverance of the whole status of the landlord from present paralysis, and future chaos.' Granville warned Lowe that they must act to ward off the threat that the Irish agitation would grow into a rent strike. Gladstone said they could not bring 'peace and security to Ireland, and through Ireland to the Empire', unless compensation for disturbance embraced all tenancies-at-will not under custom without distinction between present and future occupation. He stated, as a certainty, that either their bill or a Conservative one outstripping it would be enacted. These political arguments prevailed with Lowe and Cardwell as with Argyll. The cabinet were by no means unsympathetic to the ministers who made a stand. Fortescue's account of the five-hour discussion on the 17th mentioned criticism from almost half of those there. Lowe was quite sure the majority were acting, and equally sure they would continue to act, against their real opinions. He told Cardwell not to expect any support. For a day or two, Lowe hoped that Hatherley might come over. The Lord Chancellor seemed to think the prime minister would accept the limitation to smaller tenants of a payment for disturbance. Gladstone quickly dispelled the illusion.[21]

The arguments used by ministers, Argyll observed, were perhaps more important than the bill's provisions. When Lowe withdrew his opposition, he would not swallow Gladstone's claim that after agreeing to the forcible transfer of ownership in compensation for past improvements, nobody ought to strain at anything in accompanying proposals. Or, as Granville remarked, 'it is said that no woman ever commits only one fault...and the minority have lost their immaculate reputations by consenting to retrospective compensation.' Argyll's robust common sense, too, rejected the argument as unconvincing beyond the realm of logic. Gladstone quoted Lowe's memorandum of October to the author. The unsuitability of free contract to Irish conditions had there been the reason advanced for interfering drastically with property. Lowe had made 'a temporary appeal to the principles of equity'. It was a short step, under duress, to arguing thus in the context of a permanent addition to statute law. He informed Cardwell: 'Gladstone's *argumentum ad hominem* has rather shaken me... the ground of property is gone.' It was acknowledged by all in the cabinet that the right and duty of the state to intervene positively must acquire new dimensions. Gladstone combined this broad theme with a second. He ascribed compensation for disturbance to economic pressure, and related the payment to the universality with which, through history, the Irish peasantry believed they had a proprietary interest in their land. With the extension of custom ruled out, the balance between the two arguments was a matter of nice judgment, which, in Parliament, he exercised. He could not be more explicit about what influenced him most. Still less could his colleagues refer frankly or at all in their speeches to such considerations as those put by Granville to Lowe.[22]

The cabinets at which the draft of the bill was filled out went quite smoothly. Gladstone was prepared for a recrudescence of trouble with clauses 2 and 3. It did not arise, to his profound relief. On the day clause 3 was reviewed, his diary read: 'Cabinet. The great difficulties of the Irish Land Bill *there* are now over. Thank God!'[23] Clause 6, apparently, was not resisted. Clause 10 – the Argyll clause – applied to fewer tenants than the Duke wanted. He grumbled ineffectually. The land purchase clauses were founded on propositions which Bright was invited to draw up. The lateness of the invitation, issued on 28 January, was an indication of the low priority assigned to this part of the measure. Bright's propositions were discussed on 1 and 2 February. The resulting clauses were Gladstone's rather than his in their detail. Fortescue excepted, the cabinet thought them innocuous. Kimberley, however, considered their omission would have seriously weakened the bill. He believed their psychological effect would be good, not that they would be widely used.[24]

A public impression of another sort was the object of Gladstone's request that the Queen should open Parliament in person. The departure from her semi-retirement of late years would mark the high importance of the session's Irish business. For the land was the main part of the Irish question, he wrote, and Ireland transcended all other questions. The state of that country presented 'the only real danger of the noble Empire of the Queen'. He wrongly supposed that the royal sympathies were with the government. The attitude of the Court was publicly correct and privately unfriendly. In Gladstone's memorandum to the sovereign on the bill, it was axiomatic that the tenantry were the injured party. 'The very reverse is, in a majority of cases, the fact,' asserted the Queen's private secretary. He noted, however, that the bill was 'very much what public expectation has looked for'.[25]

BRITISH EXPECTATIONS

'I can't wonder, considering his immense powers, his popularity and his influence that a majority of his colleagues is ready to go with him *quand même*,' wrote Lowe of the prime minister at this juncture, forgetting the cabinet's refusal to sanction the extension of custom.[26] Gladstone was not inclined to overestimate his own strength. Premature disclosure of the bill, giving opponents a head start, was something to guard against with unusual vigilance. He asked Bright 'to maintain the most absolute secrecy, and not to light the path, or track *towards* our intentions' when speaking to his constituents in January.[27] 'I shall avoid dangerous questions', promised Bright, 'and I know nothing more dangerous than the Irish land question.' Yet, as he pointed out, the newspaper debate had inevitably brought people close to the cabinet's position without the help of inside information. Ministers, Bright felt, were too much aware of everything at stake to permit themselves indiscretions, calculated or otherwise.[28] What they were saying, outside the circle of those who had been drawn into their deliberations, was that the bill would relieve the fears being entertained. These obligatory assurances were not taken at face value.

The *Daily News* of 10 January understood that the government had substantially adopted Campbell's plan. It would be doing them a disservice, the paper said, to enlarge on this before the bill's appearance. *The Economist* had cause to think that Campbell's was definitely the best plan published, but could not tell how it had impressed ministers.[29] The *Manchester Guardian* also proceeded to endorse Campbell, with reservations and without indicating where it thought the government stood.[30] The *Pall Mall* said it knew no cabinet secrets, and hardly erred in predicting what would be in the bill.[31] The *Standard*, on behalf of Irish landlords, supported only compensation for improvements in the absence of a specific agreement to the contrary.[32] The *Quarterly Review* was sensible. Nearly every scheme demonstrably threatened 'vast mischief' to material prosperity, or at least harm, so it did not pass censures, 'however relevant and efficacious', on their infractions of proprietary right. The favoured exception, or exceptions, was not indicated. It could find no valid argument for the extension of tenant-right. It knew where to look for a fair solution. 'But we are not going to suggest any. The Government has the matter in hand, and we have no desire...to supersede them, or anticipate.'[33]

Gladstone was too old a political hand not to know that leaks must occur, and he connived at one, as a reassurance and a warning. He made cautious use of the Whig *Edinburgh Review*, whose editor, Henry Reeve, had approached him to ask 'if he might be guarded against anything contrary to the Government's scheme being proposed, or if he might be told what the Government *cannot* do'. Gladstone did not accede to either request directly.

He consented to read in draft an article on Irish land to be written for the *Review*'s January issue, but did not return his copy of the draft, with a few general words of approbation, until the issue, and the article, had been printed. It is extremely unlikely that Reeve did not have a very good idea of what was passing in the cabinet: he had been close to the leaders of the party for years and was intimate with Clarendon, who confided freely in him. On the strength of this limited contact with the prime minister, Reeve was able to put it about that the article had been revised by Gladstone, reassuring Liberals and Tories and promoting his *Review*. One of those he informed was Sir Joseph Napier, a former Lord Chancellor of Ireland and a Tory authority on Irish land.[34]

'It is a muddle', Napier complained of the article, when transmitting Reeve's information to Disraeli.[35] It was written to support the compromise that had recommended itself to a majority of the cabinet in December. Observing 'the vast number of... tenants whom competent witnesses agree in describing as now, by custom, fairly secure in their tenure', it argued for backing this security with a legal claim to compensation for ' "occupancy" ' and improvements, payable when the tenant was disturbed. Anything less would not appease an agitation to which the Irish landlords were bowing. Anything more 'would be so clearly dangerous to the as yet unquestioned rights of property in Great Britain, that it would infallibly arouse hostility among the land-owning interest in both Houses.' The final paragraph emphasized that the article had tried 'to show at least what...a measure should *not* propose to do'. It had cited a report in the *Law Times*, an austerely professional journal, that the English land market was being affected by the loss of confidence in the political prospects for landed property.[36]

The Times first prepared its readers for a greater change than the cabinet had in store for them. It bestowed the editorial blessing upon O'Connor Morris's final letter. He advocated what he had seemed to favour at times – the conversion of tenancy-at-will into an inchoate copyhold. The landlord's power to evict and raise rent should not be exercised without authority from a tribunal which would set his claims against those of the occupier based on 'Tenant Right as a social fact', and on his improvements. The landlord's application would not be sanctioned if, as was

assumed, the occupier's 'moral rights' outweighed his. When the
tribunal allowed somebody to be put out and there was no custom
to provide him with a capital sum, damages for eviction against
the applicant were to supply it. O'Connor Morris expected the
tenant's security to approach that of a copyholder. His proposals
were very like those in the *Times*'s leading article of 22 November,
to which they added a realistic appreciation of the force of custom.
He refrained from confirming that the effect was to extend
tenant-right, since no curbs were envisaged on the sale and
inheritance of these virtual copyholds. He summed up what he
was suggesting as 'practically almost a Right of occupancy'. It
was hard to be franker when his previous letter had declared that
the extension of tenant-right would result in 'a monstrous confusion of rights...and subvert and violate rights of property'.[37]

The Times started to retrace its steps in the last few days
before the bill was revealed. On 7 February it condemned as
'nothing short of naked confiscation' the resolutions in favour
of the 3 Fs passed by a national conference in Dublin. On the
morning of the first reading a leading article rediscovered some
of the old confidence that the Irish should and would conform
to English ways. The subject was the analogy between Indian
and Irish tenure. The article was a rejection, rather than a
refutation, of Campbell, although his name was not mentioned.
The creation of occupancy-right in Ireland might have been
appropriate in the days of Strongbow, or even of James I, when
her native institutions possessed the vitality of India's. Not now,
The Times insisted: 'We are no longer dealing with a people
deriving their notions...from Brehon law, but with a people
who for at least two centuries and a half have been living under
nearly the same law as ourselves. Custom, doubtless...important
...in the relations between Irish landlords and tenants...is not
the sole basis at present, and it would be madness to make it the
sole basis in future.' The Irish landlord was a very different
person from his Indian equivalent, and had a far more positive
function in the land system. The history of Indian legislation
had little but historical significance and furnished no precedent
for the Irish land bill.[38]

These views were expressed – that is, reaffirmed – when they
were certain to be safe ones. The belated upsurge of interest in
Campbell's plan, the speculation that it had been adopted, showed

how widely the initiative was felt to lie with the cabinet. The powerlessness of the Conservatives, and of any Liberal objectors, seemed clear to the *Saturday Review*.[39] *The Times* was less sure of the 'submissive unanimity' of Liberal members. It sought encouragement in the Conservative leadership's reticence, which it had assailed a month ago, and repeated at intervals that this was not an issue for party politics. It did not try to hide the question-mark hanging over the government: 'We shall soon see how far it possesses these elements of authority – unity in itself; the power to control followers, and to hold opponents in check – without which the most distinguished personal talents fail.'[40] Halifax was impelled to send the prime minister 'a simple hint'. Knowing of the cabinet's intention to invest tenants with some form of claim additional to their improvements, he confided in Lord Devon, a former Conservative minister and an Irish landowner, whose friendly reaction he passed on. Devon entirely agreed with the idea of the claim but deemed it essential for government to quote native custom as a reason, and not grounds that British landlords would apply to themselves.[41]

When the Irish land bill was imminent, Kimberley, who could not be called a frightened reactionary, saw his forebodings acquiring reality. He had protested ineffectually to Gladstone against clause 4 of the bill, where it stopped the landlord from preventing a tenant's improvements: even more than compensation for disturbance, it was 'obviously a principle which might easily cross the Channel'.[42] He wrote in his diary on 5 February: 'To me it seems...likely that the possession of land beyond what the owner can conveniently occupy himself will become every year less desirable. The tenant will probably by degrees oust the landlord just as the copyholder ousted the lord of the manor.'[43] Bright, still in the eyes of many the scourge of the landed class, recoiled at a particular manifestation of the new British radicalism: an article in the *Fortnightly Review* for January by the economist, J. E. Cairnes, vindicating the theory of state intervention to determine fair rent, and containing the statement that no reform of Irish land would succeed that did not directly control rent.[44] The heresies were Mill's: '...if he be absent', said the *Freeman's Journal* of the retirement in which he was living, 'his principles will be remembered'.[45]

At Birmingham on 11 January, although Bright gave no facts

away, he conveyed that he had been, and was, labouring under great anxiety of a nature to earn him the gratitude of the most unfavourable Whig or Tory. 'It is not a question for class or party contest,' he finished.[46] The contrast of these words to the rhetoric of his past speeches bespoke his discomfort. The *Spectator* shrewdly inferred that he was wondering how far he might conscientiously defend decisions incompatible with his canons of political economy.[47] Bright's speech was followed by one from W. E. Forster, a minister outside the cabinet, in his constituency of Bradford. He put the elementary education bill, for which he was principally responsible, second to Irish land, 'our chief business'. The Irish church and land bills were 'destructive' and 'constructive' respectively, closing and starting a legislative era. From Irish land they would proceed to new laws on criminal justice, education, pauperism and licensing. It was a lapidary statement of the land bill's significance.[48] The two speeches threw into relief the divergent tendencies in Parliamentary radicalism. The *Daily News* perceived that Bright's, 'cautious, hesitating and timid' in its language, was dated. Discovery of the insufficiency of commercial principles, of free trade in land, had left him at a loss. Few men of his ability, said the paper cruelly, were as unreceptive to new ideas. It recalled how taken aback he had been by Mill in the House of Commons. Forster displayed the 'creative Radicalism' which was arriving.[49]

It was all true, but the *Daily News* should have credited Bright with a tactical success. In his presentation of the land question he had, wrote Gladstone in a congratulatory note, 'succeeded admirably...and maintained all the dignity and interest of its position'.[50] The prime minister had cause to be well pleased. Clarendon had been afraid of what Bright might say because 'if the agitators in Ireland get an inkling of what is really intended they will move Heaven and earth and *the other place as well* to render it impossible.'[51] Bright had avoided the pitfall. Although the Irish were clamouring, louder than ever, for fixity of tenure the bill would fare better if the Commons supposed that its beneficiaries might be grateful when they had had time to digest it.

LAST STAGES IN THE CABINET

As 1869 went out, the *Freeman's Journal* displayed an understandable irritation with 'the oracular utterings of the Times':[52] it would be 'politic as well as merciful' to let the Irish people have an authoritative indication that government really meant to deal justly by them. Isaac Butt had told a meeting of the Tenant League that no land bill would pass in 1870, but that they should obtain their full demand in the session of 1871. The ministry were stronger than he supposed in their determination to carry the promised bill in 1870 and to prevent violence from getting such a hold on the country that the tenants' movement would be able to dictate terms to Parliament in about a year's time. Gladstone was willing to stand or fall by the land bill in the Houses, while the cabinet were not prepared to postpone action against outrage and intimidation failing a turn for the better in the first few weeks of the new year. In that short period, up to the unveiling of the bill, the violence kept on growing and the agitation disappointed British hopes that its leaders would begin to move away from their extreme position now that, as everybody inferred, the cabinet had gone some distance towards them. The mood of Ireland did not admit of public concessions by the popular leaders, whatever they felt.

It was plainer than ever that tenant-right and nationality were intertwined. The Mallow Farmers' Club in County Cork carried a resolution welcoming Tipperary's choice of O'Donovan Rossa, 'one of the truest representatives of an Irish constituency in an alien Parliament since...the great tribune O'Connell'. The club declared that the outcome of the Tipperary election would 'in no way damage or embarrass the great question now at issue – namely, the land...in...the Legislature'.[53] Sir John Gray greeted the National Land Conference in Dublin on 4 February as 'a substantial representative Parliament...he often prayed that he might live to address an Irish Parliament.' Gray had proposed it to bring together the politicians, clergy and delegates of tenants' associations who were working for the same end. The gathering was a demonstration rather than a conference, a show of strength to insist on the three Fs. He and Butt were pre-eminent in the assembly, supported by The O'Donoghue, J. F. Maguire and a dozen other M.P.s. Dean O'Brien was there. Lords

Portsmouth, Granard and Greville had put their names to the requisition for the conference; the Catholic Lord Bellew presided when it met. The majority of Irish Liberal members neither attended nor apologized for their absence. The *Freeman's Journal* blamed them for the shortcomings which the government bill might reveal.[54]

As landowners, most Irish Liberal members were exposed to the rising force of peasant expectations. His Mayo tenantry did not spare an old champion of tenant-right, G. H. Moore. A notice circulating among them, and headed 'Important. Caution.', warned everyone not to pay rents, henceforward, that exceeded the rating valuation of their holdings: any person who did so would 'at his peril mark the consequences'.[55] Moore responded angrily – through an intermediary, Father Lavelle – that his advocacy of the rights of occupiers did not imply that he would ever surrender his claims in the matter of rent: 'I am determined to vindicate my own rights without fear or flinching...if it be necessary to evict every tenant who refuses to pay...in full.' He tempered his resolute threat by putting the affair in the priest's hands. Lavelle induced the tenants to promise payment of what they owed, leaving future rents to be negotiated between their landlord and himself.[56] In the circumstances, few landowning Liberal M.P.s were not afraid to oppose the agitation: but they would not convert themselves to it unequivocally by attending the Land Conference.

'You can hardly conceive the state of this country at present ...this state of non-administration of law,' wrote Lord Clanricarde from Galway to Earl Grey.[57] Bad as things were in the West, they were more frightening elsewhere. The viceroy wondered whether he ought to resign if, as happened, ministers would not sanction the Irish administration's request for coercive legislation put by Fortescue at the cabinet of 2 February. Gladstone was adamant. Spencer decided against resignation, out of his regard for the authority of Gladstone and the cabinet, out of the conviction that the land bill was worth the political sacrifice he made by staying in office, and because 'I have a horror of making a splash or kick up.'[58] Hartington contemplated resigning if Spencer did. His letter of 3 February to his father gives the impression that he would readily have taken the step had the viceroy or a cabinet colleague resolved to go. Hartington wrote that Gladstone trusted much too much to the land bill: 'I think very strongly that the decision of the cabinet is wrong; and that a vigorous repressive measure would have a good effect in every way.' He was isolated in the discussion on the 2nd; none but he – not Fortescue – spoke so positively for immediate recourse to coercion. The Duke of Devonshire advised his son not to resign, for reasons similar to those which weighed with Spencer. Hartington was glad to reflect, mistakenly as it transpired, that in his post he would not be called upon to defend the ministry's Irish policy.[59]

The Queen's Speech at the opening of the session on 8 February promised that the government would ask Parliament for greater powers if they were 'required by the paramount interest of peace and order', but claimed to observe a partial improvement in agrarian 'crime'. The second was a strange statement when outrage in January had increased by sixteen per cent over December. Offences against property had gone up; so had threatening letters and notices. Offences against the person, other than threats, had gone down.[60] A reasonable explanation of the decline was that the threats were working. Gladstone maintained that, on the contrary, it was a hopeful sign. The cabinet's hesitation to agree with Hartington's view – that 'quite cause enough exists...without waiting for more murders'[61] – owed something to Papal condemnation of Fenianism in January, which they expected to quieten Ireland. Whether the condemnation was due to lobbying by the British government and its representative at the Vatican, Odo Russell, or rather to Cardinal Cullen's fear of revolutionary nationalism, is irrelevant here.[62] Spencer believed the Pope's action would be very damaging to the Fenians, although Clarendon doubted it. The decree was no more effective than previous ecclesiastical censures.[63] The Irish bishops gathered in Rome for the Oecumenical Council distinguished between Fenianism as such and the land agitation in which its adherents were busy. The bishops wished Russell to inform Gladstone that 'fixity of tenure would deal the strongest blow that Parliament could strike at Fenianism'. They repeated this message, through Manning, on 5 February.[64] Russell had asked the Pope to instruct the Irish Hierarchy to suspend priests whose language was an incitement to agrarian outrage. That impracticable petition was not granted.[65]

9

THE PASSING OF THE BILL

Gladstone introduced the land bill on 15 February.[1] He told the House that 'the stability of the Empire' depended upon it. The full significance of his remarks on the conflict between legal and customary ideas of tenure in Ireland escaped contemporaries and has eluded historians because they did not and do not know that he had tried to persuade the cabinet to enforce tenant-right all over Ireland. He was obliged to understate his view of the tenantry's traditional rights. Those rights were too strong an argument in relation to the bill that he had to explain. The attention of Parliament and the press was drawn to more suitable arguments which for him were secondary. He asserted unequivocally the right of the state to determine the conditions on which private property was enjoyed, and freedom of contract permitted. The precedents he adduced were necessarily weak. There could be no concealing the enormous development of state intervention in the bill. *The Times* signalized it as 'without doubt the most considerable proposal of constructive legislation...presented to Parliament since 1832...It enlarges the scope of law.'[2] A part of Gladstone was glad to challenge 'that Parliamentary spirit with which we have to deal, and which has had in this country a too unbridled sway'. He chafed at the circumspection without which the bill would never pass. Revealing his mind to a man of integrity and influence on the Liberal backbenches, someone whose doubts he feared, Gladstone admitted: 'We have *not* proved the cruelty and atrocity of evictions. We have *not* shown that the Irish occupier as such has any equitable claim to occupancy beyond his contract? No. And why?...I have advisedly remained almost, if not altogether, silent on each of these...chapters of argument...because I was fearful of...new dangers.' 'Timid as well as aggressive' was how he described the propertied mentality.[3] It was an apt summary, at any rate, of the reactions which, could the balance between them be preserved, would carry him and the bill to a great political, if not an imperial success.

The British Elementary Education Bill of that session, important and politically difficult, was of little moment to Gladstone compared with Irish land, of which he said 'until it is disposed of... it seems to engross and swallow up my whole personal existence.'[4] In Parliament, as in cabinet, a sustained personal effort was required of him, and was everything. A naturally cynical backbencher with whom his relations were not particularly good, wrote after his Parliamentary labours on the land bill: 'Gladstone is an Atlas with the globe on his shoulders or rather he is like a great beech tree which overshadowed all and under whose shade no blade grows...Gladstone seems to trust nothing to any of his colleagues in the...Commons, which leaves the future of the Liberal Party hanging by a single thread.'[5] Most other observers thought the prime minister's colleagues had failed to support him adequately. Fortescue visibly lacked the ability and stature.[6] John Bright was incapacitated for the session by a nervous breakdown to which his scruples about the bill must have contributed. Hartington, Lowe and Cardwell were the others well qualified to speak on Irish land, but the last two were compromised by past pronouncements. Cardwell maintained silence throughout; Lowe and Hartington each made a single speech of any length during the prolonged committee stage. The cabinet peers were compelled and inclined to make a better showing, no matter what they thought, for the sake of their House when the bill arrived there with large Commons majorities behind it. There is every reason to suppose that members of the cabinet, as a body, subscribed to Clarendon's pessimism with regard to the legislation and Ireland: 'You have a fervent imagination and a yearning for benevolent action towards your fellow-creatures,' he wrote to Gladstone, 'I am sorry to go between you and your dream, for a dream it will prove, that justice will make the Irish happy or contented.'[7]

The satisfaction in Ireland that a British government had so far exceeded the limits of previous land bills was very short-lived. Archbishop Manning forwarded a memorandum from the Irish bishops asking for amendment of the bill to confer the three Fs.[8] That was inconceivable, replied Gladstone, for reasons which he explained to a deputation of representatives from the Tenant

League and the National Association, accompanied by their Parliamentary supporters.[9] The cabinet had had to consider in framing the bill 'the opinion of England and Scotland – which would not permit any government to carry exceptional legislation in the case of Ireland to a point...calculated to produce a rupture of our [British] social relations'. The reception of the land bill in Britain was good, but it did not indicate that the government might have been bolder. 'Our own friends...are thoroughly pleased,' Gladstone reported to the viceroy of Ireland. 'I doubt whether they would well have taken a stronger bill.'[10] The Liberal party's feelings differed little from those among Tories. Relief and pleasure were the prevailing sentiments in both parties. Relief was uppermost. In the crowded Carlton Club on the 16th, Disraeli's private secretary found 'a babel of talk on the land bill which I...hear denounced by nearly all'.[11] The talk in the Carlton registered an instinctive reaction which it was natural to voice in those precincts. Gathorne Hardy set down in his diary the conclusion of the Tory leaders that they had to deal with 'a comparatively mild measure'.[12] To no one's surprise, they decided not to oppose the second reading.[13] As early as the 21st, however, Kimberley noted that the 'undiscriminating praise' bestowed on the bill was starting to change.[14] As the implications of compensation for disturbance sank in, as the disappointing attitude of Irish popular M.P.s, tenant societies and bishops was emphasized by agrarian outrage, Gladstone was forced, with extreme reluctance, to consent to a coercion bill. The decision was announced after the second reading when Gladstone awaited the disabling amendments to the land bill that would be attempted in committee.

THE COMMONS

The Liberal majority stood up well to the strains imposed upon it: but there were anxious moments. At one point Gladstone resorted to threatening resignation and a dissolution if he were defeated on amendments which he deemed critical. As already decided the Conservatives acquiesced in the second reading. The bill was carried by the enormous margin of 442 votes to 11. It was shown to be a deceptive triumph when the Opposition attacked at the committee stage. Their leaders were ineffective: it was too easy to imagine them in the government's shoes. The attack on the bill was 'led and officered', Gladstone complained, by several Liberals, the first among them being Sir Roundell Palmer.[15] These candid friends set out to minimize the damage to principle in the legislation and they had a lot of sympathy on their own side. 'The bite of R. Palmer and the gentlemen behind the Treasury Bench is much more formidable than the bark *below the Gangway,*' observed W. V. Harcourt, a prominent Liberal back-bencher, to Clarendon.[16] The bulk of the government's followers liked the bill less and less as the weeks went by and its rejection in Ireland became ever clearer. Few voted against but a number expressed their feelings by abstaining, so that the government's majority looked vulnerable for a time. The quietly unco-operative disposition shown by many Liberal Members was more worrying than the loud protests of a few. After seven nights in committee, the Commons had reached and stuck at the contentious third clause, on which they had spent nearly five of those nights when they adjourned for the Easter recess. Changing the metaphor, Harcourt believed there was 'some danger of the ship foundering in a profound calm like the *Royal George*' unless the House reassembled in a better frame of mind.[17] Gladstone encouraged the belief as the best way of disarming the persistently troublesome Liberals. He prevailed, and thereafter the bill had a comparatively smooth passage through the Commons.

The second reading lasted for four nights between 7 and 11 March. The debate produced no surprises. The advocates of tenant-right among the Irish members registered their conflicting opinions. J. F. Maguire, The O'Donoghue and G. H. Moore felt the government should have gone further and taken the bill to its 'natural conclusions'[18] but had certainly done enough to deserve their support. Sir John Gray declared against the measure 'in the most solemn and emphatic manner', because it withheld the 'right of continuous occupancy...security of tenure...fixity of tenure...He saw no difference between these terms.' He credited Gladstone with good intentions in this respect and thought the prime minister had been 'coerced or persuaded' by those around him. Ministers were playing into the hands of the revolutionary nationalists.[19] Four Irish Liberals with popular sympathies joined him in voting against the bill. So did five of the Irish Whigs. The point of view of this latter group was cogently explained by W. H. Gregory, although he, and others who agreed with him, went into the government lobby: 'All Ireland understands the principle of Ulster tenant-right, and all Ireland apparently cries aloud for its extension.' The alternative was 'to flounder about amid continued agitation, continued discontent...continued terrorism'.[20] Chichester Fortescue argued at length that the extension of Ulster custom would be unfair to landlords and bad for tenants.[21] Gladstone confirmed there could be no going back on the refusal to enforce the custom of tenant-right everywhere and commented: 'I must...wait to see in what manner any Gentleman...will be able to point out any closer mode of applying out of Ulster the same principle as we apply in Ulster.'[22]

In deciding not to oppose the second reading, the Conservatives hesitated over the implications of the third clause, Disraeli said. Disapproving entirely of compensation for disturbance he was nevertheless prepared to swallow it, so long as the clause was not construed to mean the recognition of 'property in occupation', of tenant-right. The bill was of 'vast importance', and there must be some sacrifice of principle to the exigencies of the situation. But he wanted the clauses relating to custom left out, as indefinable and unenforceable without wrong. Instead, in all disputes between landlord and tenant high court judges unaccompanied by a jury – not assistant barristers – should decide on the equity of the case with reference to the non-customary clauses that applied. Disraeli also took exception to the permanence of the restrictions on contracting out.[23] Those of his colleagues who spoke did not hide their dislike of the bill. 'I frankly admit it goes too far for me,' said Gathorne Hardy.[24] Their common theme was criticism of the recognition and encouragement of custom. They miscalculated if they reckoned that this was the issue which would divide the Liberals in committee as it had in cabinet. In a speech that established him as an authoritative spokesman for Irish landlords, A. M. Kavanagh, the Tory member for County Carlow, concurred in wanting the clauses on custom omitted. Otherwise he welcomed the bill, and its third clause, in a way that contrasted with the attitude of his party's English leaders.[25]

Hardly any British Liberals sitting on the backbenches took part in the debate. The best indication of what was passing in their minds came with the well received speech of Sir Roundell Palmer. He acquitted the government of having framed a measure that was 'in any degree whatever revolutionary': he would not have supported one that departed seriously from 'those great and necessary principles on which...the rights of property rest'. But compensation for disturbance did amount to 'giving something to the tenant which does not belong to him, and taking away from the landlord something which belongs to him'. Only the imperative necessity of a check on arbitrary eviction, in the interests of property itself, could justify that, and he was influenced by Kavanagh's acceptance of the third clause as a deterrent to a small number of landlords. Palmer gave notice that he intended to scrutinize the clause in committee for 'any possible injustice' to the landlord.[26] His moderation and grasp of political realities enhanced the danger from his express preoccupation with principle: he was not a doctrinaire such as Lowe had been and a backbench Liberal like Lord Elcho still was.[27] O'Connor Morris, for one, had foreseen the effect he had.[28] Gladstone described it after the government had experienced the worst of its difficulties in committee: 'We have had a most anxious time...The fear that our Land Bill may cross the water creates a sensitive state of mind among all Tories, many Whigs, and a few Radicals. Upon this state of things comes Palmer with his legal mind, legal point of view, and legal aptitude and inaptitude...and stirs these susceptibilities to such a point that he is always near bringing us to grief.'[29]

The government did not sweeten the temper of the House by several amendments designed to make the bill more attractive to the tenants. However, ministers easily defeated, by 296 votes to 220, Disraeli's attempt to exploit the feeling by his proposal that compensation for disturbance should be struck out. Much more serious were the amendments to the third clause put down by English Liberal members, and particularly that in the name of William Fowler, a Liberal with leanings to the older radicalism. It sought to deny compensation for disturbance to occupiers of holdings rated at over £50 – men occupying more than 100 acres. 'What was the difference between a substantial farmer in England and one in Ireland?' he inquired, backed by Palmer.[30] Though he tried, Gladstone knew he could not convincingly argue that some thirty thousand tenants above Fowler's line were in the same position as the half million below it. He told the Commons that to exclude 'the leaders of opinion among the tenantry' from compensation for disturbance would be fatal to the government's policy. If the amendment were carried, he announced, others must be responsible for endeavouring to settle the Irish land question.[31] Naturally, the threat worked. Palmer asked Fowler to withdraw his amendment, and when he refused left the House without voting, as did Sir George Grey, the Whig elder statesman, and a number of other Liberals. The government won, but their majority was cut to thirty-two in a division in which nearly five hundred voted.[32] Over a dozen Liberals went into the opposing lobby.[33] The amendment was only one among so many that it was doubtful whether the bill would reach the Lords, where it could not expect to have an easy passage, in time to become law that session. There was a grimmer prospect: 'If operations like that [sic] of last night are repeated,' wrote Gladstone next day, 'the House of Lords cannot have the self-denial to keep its hands off, and there will probably be a break down of the Bill between the two Houses, even should we carry it now.'[34] Moreover, the mood of the Commons had extracted concessions to balance those made to the tenants. Palmer held the key to the crisis. While he persisted in standing up to the government, the Liberal party would be difficult to control. Lesser men took heart from the example set by someone of his reputation and talents, who was doing nothing worse than obey convictions which Liberalism had so often and lately maintained.

Gladstone had been in negotiation with Palmer before Fowler's amendment and pressed him hard during the recess that followed soon afterwards. He enlisted the aid of cabinet ministers sympathetic to Palmer who had come to terms with their own equally sensitive consciences. Gladstone wished to hear from Cardwell whether Palmer, an old and close friend, had comprehended his warning to the House before the vote: 'Did he, or did he not know that if the Bill...Parliament and the Government succumbed, he...would be the person to whom the country would have a right to look as responsible for the government of Ireland?'[35] Gladstone reminded Palmer himself that 'in these great passages of political life' the opponents of the ministry had a constitutional and a patriotic duty. 'The tremendous task we have undertaken with respect to Ireland is one we can only pursue upon certain conditions. The risks overhanging the safety of the Empire... beyond the Atlantic have much added to the weight of the problem. It would be a breach of faith to the country to attempt to carry on the work except with that...freedom...we are convinced is necessary.' The prime minister would be severely judged who threw in his hand, replied Palmer, when Parliament did not want to displace him or defeat the bill. He could not see that it had been his duty to vote against an amendment which he approved and thought important, and which had not, in his judgment, been the equivalent to reversing their decision on the second reading. He sent Gladstone a long memorandum on the points in the bill which he had contested and meant to contest. The ministerial case did not, as he understood it, rest on recognizing the tenant's occupancy-right 'or co-proprietorship', but on the need to secure those who were unable to protect themselves against the abuse of property-rights. To intervene on behalf of those who manifestly could help themselves was 'confiscation or Communism'.[36]

The prime minister was utterly committed to getting the bill through without extensive changes and lit upon a strange simile in deadly earnest. 'I feel', he said to Clarendon, 'as a bee might feel if it knew that it would die upon its sting.'[37] Gladstone loosed off a letter of mingled expostulation and menace to Palmer,[38] and on the same day dropped a heavy hint to Argyll that he would welcome assistance in this 'arduous correspondence'. 'Palmer... has nearly been the death of the...Bill...The *next* Bill will be adequate and something more. The something more I should regret, and have striven to avert: but the return made has been grievous, and the excess, though grievous, would be the lesser evil.'[39] Disraeli, he told the Duke, would find plenty of room for manoeuvre in his recent speeches. Argyll believed him implicitly. 'I dread the loss of this Bill more than I can say,' he informed Palmer, and made much of a concession of Gladstone's by which freedom to contract out was allowed to occupiers not subject to custom and rated at £50 and over, instead of £100 and over. He produced the rather desperate argument that the bill disappointed the claimants of tenant-right more than it hurt landowners. The lengths to which some Irish landlords had been driven in their proposals for a settlement gave the Duke an oppressive sense that 'the anchors of opinion, on which all Rights of Property depend, are dragging.'[40]

Palmer submitted to the pressure upon him. When the committee stage resumed, an Irish Tory taunted him with having undergone 'some mysterious mesmeric process...persuaded...by arguments ...not exhibited for the consideration of the Committee'.[41] His behaviour, responded Palmer, had been determined by 'the simplest and most intelligible principle upon which a man could act', of trying to get all he could and accepting what he had been able to get.[42] It was true that ministers had eased his submission, and placated the House by deciding to exclude from compensation for disturbance existing but not future occupiers rated at over £100. Another pertinacious Liberal critic of the bill, T. E. Headlam, returned subdued by a 'jobation' – the word that a satisfied prime minister used – which his efforts had earned from radically minded constituents in Newcastle.[43] As for Fowler, he had repented of defying the government even as the machinery of the division on his amendment was in motion.[44] Resistance to clause 3 and the bill suddenly crumbled. 'Our futile divisions only showed the compactness of the majority,' commented Gathorne Hardy in his diary.[45]

The speeches of Lowe before the recess and Hartington after it stood out in their different ways. The Tories had enjoyed themselves during the second reading with Lowe's strictures of 1866 and 1868 on legislative intervention between landlord and tenant. In his one major contribution made in committee, to Parliament's discussion of the bill, Lowe refuted his well-known views, without acknowledging that he had ever held them: 'The principles of political economy! Why, we violate them every day.' It was a brazen performance. The bill, according to him, was a purely pragmatic measure, 'to save society from rushing down towards destruction; to give to property the security it is fast losing'. Irish landlords were wise to accept the bill, as he thought they did. For if the bill were lost, they would have to rely on Disraeli: 'In the claws of the right honourable Gentleman...they might indeed tremble!'[46] Hartington said, as he had when the cabinet argued over the bill, that once they left compensation for improvements behind legislation ought to promise 'effective results'; he regretted the denial of compensation for disturbance to tenants above the £100 line. He believed his fellow landlords of Ireland had most reason to be, and were, grateful for the bill. Reacting to Opposition mirth at the suggestion of landlord gratitude, he affirmed that 'Irish landlords have, as a body, done their duty to their tenants, while they have, perhaps, put up with more, sacrificed more, than any...landlords in either England or Scotland...'[47]

The attitude of the Tory party in the Commons; Gladstone's success in quelling the troublesome Liberals; the lack of fight shown by Irish landlord members, both Liberal and Tory, which exasperated Gathorne Hardy; Lowe's insistence that 'abstract principles' must be put aside in dealing with Ireland – it all presaged the surrender by the Lords which the leader of the Conservative peers informed them was inevitable on the opening day of the second reading in the Upper House. After they had passed the bill, Gladstone, the traditionalist, deplored their acquiescence with a bad grace and out of – he said privately – 'fear rather than any larger wisdom'.[48] In the interval the House had thrown off the the control of its leaders and indulged in a demonstration which did not unduly worry the Liberal ministry and press. 'The Upper Chamber, in proportion as it has lost real power, seems to plume itself upon its dignity and authority,' observed the *Daily News*. 'The Peers have taken out of the Bill what they will have to put back.'[49]

THE LORDS

Following the advice of the Duke of Richmond, the new Tory leader in the House, the Lords gave the Irish land bill an un-opposed second reading. If they rejected it, said Richmond with appalling frankness, the result was hardly in doubt: 'Next year we should have to discuss a measure probably worse, if anything could be worse, than the Bill now before us.' He did not attempt to mask his impotent resentment and alarm. The bill was tanta-mount to 'taking away my property and giving it to someone else', and he quoted the Liberal candidate in the current South Leicestershire by-election who advocated similar legislation to benefit the English farmer.[50] Granville's mastery of delicate phrasing merely served to emphasize certain truths in his intro-ductory speech. Admitting that Irish landlords had their grievances, too, he recalled the late Lord Derby's explanation that virtual fixity of tenure existed in Ireland, partly because it was the practice and partly, said Granville, 'from a cause...which un-luckily, it was only too easy for us to understand'. Then he rehearsed, much more briefly, the arguments used by Gladstone in his marathon address on the first reading in the Commons, and finished by pointing out that the landlords and members of landed families who comprised the great bulk of the lower House had endorsed the bill by large majorities.[51] Subsequent speakers, wittingly or unwittingly, underlined the constraint they felt. Yet the weakness of Richmond's leadership held a threat. Lord Salisbury, estranged from the heads of the party by his feud with Disraeli, was by far the most formidable Tory in the House. The suggestions, heard on every hand, that the Lords were of little account exasperated him. He did not propose to seek the rejection of the bill but was resolved to stand his ground upon amendments. 'I feel convinced', he told his friend and ally, Lord Carnarvon, 'that if we make any substantial retreat from the very moderate position we have taken up, our future...in the constitution will be purely decorative.'[52]

Lord Dufferin, painfully conscious of everything he had spoken and written against tenant-right and state intervention, elicited amused cheers from the Opposition by his defence of the bill's clauses on custom: 'It will be said...how can you be a party to its legalization? Well, for the same reason that I would sentence the murderer of an illegitimate infant to be hanged. I do not approve of adultery; but the creature is there, and being there, is entitled to the protection of the law.' He went out of his way to repudiate as 'altogether monstrous and intolerable, any claim... of the tenant...on the ground of ancient Irish habits, or tribal laws...or any other of the fantastic apologies...lately invented ...' Not unreasonably, he offered his resignation after his speech. It was not accepted, and he did not press it. When he vented his bitterness to the peers, he had yet entreated them to pass the bill 'without material alteration'.[53] The incident did the government no harm, laying bare the futility of such protests in the Lords. The Duke of Argyll, unlike his friend, made the best of custom in the bill. If it did not have the same force as in Ulster, there was ample evidence of tenant-right all over Ireland. The peasants' habit of bequeathing their holdings and charging them with family liabilities witnessed to that. Landlords and agents must be considered to have encouraged the tenants by permitting what British landlords would find 'astonishing and absurd' in tenants-at-will. Compensation for disturbance was frankly a substitute for custom. 'No one', he confessed, 'came to...the land question with greater prejudices against tenant-right than I did; nor did anyone see more clearly the economical objections... I maintain we have taken an eminently conservative course in resting our Bill upon the great principle of legalizing...custom.'[54] They were the arguments which Gladstone had patiently put to him during the weeks of discussion among the cabinet in the autumn. Lord Kimberley contended that since it was the practice of Irish landlords to pay off evicted tenants, the bill did no more than was done already.[55] Lord Chancellor Hatherley traced the need for legislation to the failure of the courts in Ireland to adapt English law to Irish custom and circumstances.[56]

Lord Cairns, the previous Chancellor, was emboldened by the government's difficulties at the committee stage in the Commons to tell Gathorne Hardy that the Lords should not yield on compensation for disturbance: 'The country will in the end see what is just...Disguise this as you will, it is giving the landlord's property to the tenant.'[57] That confidence had evaporated when he rose to address the peers in June. Irish landlords in the two Houses were willing to submit to clause 3, and so, therefore, was he.[58] As an Irish landlord, Lord Derby was ready to sacrifice 'undoubted rights' in order to convince British opinion, of all shades, that they had gone to the limit of concession and must meet the nascent Home Rule movement with immovable firmness.[59] Lord Salisbury was concerned for Britain rather than Ireland. The recent commercial recession had been the cause of much hardship in London. Why should not the British workman receive so many years' wages on being 'disturbed' in his employment? 'The difference...is this – that in England we put up with loss of bread, and in Ireland they shoot...a paternal Parliament, therefore, compensates the Irish to induce them not to shoot their landlords.' British labour would soon insist on being treated in the same fashion. Salisbury was consequently bent on narrowing the eligibility for compensation for disturbance.[60]

He carried the amendment by 119 votes to 101. Richmond voted with the government, protesting that Salisbury's action was 'not judicious'.[61] The Duke himself inserted a number of amendments in defiance of Granville's warning that it was not sensible to pare down the measure, as by cutting the lease to bar compensation under clause 3 from thirty-one years to twenty-one. These Opposition amendments, official and unofficial, were mostly reversed at the report stage or on the Commons' insistence. Richmond and Cairns negotiated the Lords' retreat privately with Granville. The Duke assured Granville that he now had his followers under control,[62] and Granville did what he could by small concessions to help restore the Duke's authority after the blow Salisbury had dealt it.[63] Gladstone was quite confident that the upper House would be manageable: 'Though the Lords have been unwise about the Land Bill, I fully expect the Commons will stand firm, and if so of course we win.'[64] He strove to prevent what everyone knew must end in the peers', and the government's, discomfiture. The prime minister was worried by the ill effects of the Lords' behaviour on Irish opinion, which he persisted in believing would come round when the whole bill, as nearly as possible, was passed. Irish M.P.s on the popular side did not miss the opportunity presented to attack the upper House. Gladstone disliked involving the bishops in 'mere politics', but he circulated an appeal to selected prelates to turn out and support the land bill in committee. 'It really appertains not so much to the well-being as to the being of civilized society...in Ireland.'[65]

The Lords were unexpectedly stubborn on several points, and the disputed amendments went back and forth between the Houses. One of these proved to have been more important than Gladstone imagined when the agricultural depression of the late 1870s struck the Irish farmer. The point in question was the courts' discretionary power to award compensation for disturbance on 'special grounds' to a tenant evicted for non-payment of rent. The Lords succeeded in having the 'special grounds' defined restrictively. Compensation might be awarded, at the courts' discretion, only to existing tenants paying an annual rent not over £15 which in the circumstances was deemed 'exorbitant'. Gladstone readily assented to the Lords' insistence on 'exorbitant' where the Commons put in 'excessive'. 'Excessive' was a word inserted without his knowing, and he told Granville: 'I decidedly disapprove of it.' He strenuously objected to £15 rental instead of rateable value – the rule throughout the bill – because it would take in many fewer occupiers.[66] Eventually, he gave way. As he informed Fortescue for the benefit of the peers' Irish landlords: 'I think they will see however they may protest that we *ought not to meet the obstinacy of the Lords with a counter obstinacy of our own on such a point.*'[67] Gladstone yielded because he personally envisaged the clause as protection for the victim of a demonstrably bad landlord, not for 'the tenant reduced by misfortune'. The upper House thus showed once again that it could prevail in small things, if not in great. So long as the House survived with powers legally unimpaired,¦ it was impossible to threaten a constitutional crisis over comparatively minor matters in a complex piece of legislation.

While the amendments in either House favoured the landlords, the bill had reached the statute book without extensive changes.[68] The first clause – custom in Ulster – was intact. By the revised second clause custom out of Ulster was put on the same footing as Ulster tenant-right where the two corresponded 'in all essential particulars'. This seemed only fair to the Commons where landlords had allowed custom to operate with their consent and co-operation as in the North. Clause 7, formerly 6, protecting tenant-right payments not covered by the first and second clauses, went through remarkably smoothly. The third clause, having been a battlefield in both Houses, passed into law with a more elaborate and, at the higher levels, less generous scale, ranging from the original maximum of seven years' rent for holdings rated at £10 and below to a new maximum of one year's rent for those rated at above £100. Occupiers rated at £10 and below were now permitted to claim separately for all improvements. Leaving aside anything awarded for improvements, or for permanent improvements only in the case of tenants above £10, compensation under the scale in clause 3 was limited in amount to £250. The government put in that limit when they were experiencing the worst of the committee stage in the Commons – immediately before the vote on Fowler's amendment. The change had no practical effect on the tenants of smaller holdings. The removal of existing occupiers above £100 from the scope of this clause was another such concession. The tenant's freedom to contract out of the clause was suspended for twenty years instead of being taken away without limit of time – a modification that brought some small comfort to M.P.s who ardently upheld free contract. They derived more from the reduction of the line – in clause 12, previously 10 – above which a tenant not under custom in or out of Ulster was at liberty to sign away rights under any of the bill's provisions. It came down from £100 to £50.

The leasehold alternative was taken out of the revised second clause to achieve conformity with the first in this respect. The option remained in clause 3: but the lease had now to be accepted to exempt the landlord. Clause 16 disappeared. A little surprisingly, Irish popular M.P.s objected that it would be unfairly exploited by landlords and lawyers. The import of the altered clause 8, renumbered 9 in the final version, has been described. The first part of clause 12 (10), the 'Argyll clause', was wiped out in the Commons; estates with the British practice as to improvements were deprived of special treatment. The Duke himself considered it superfluous when £50 tenants had freedom of contract. Clause 13, inserted by the Lords, contained safeguards for the landlord against having to compensate for disturbance someone to whom a tenancy was transferred without his consent and who was neither closely related to his predecessor nor likely to be a satisfactory tenant. Clause 15 excluded claims for any kind of compensation relating to lands used for pasture and rated at £50 or more.

The Bright clauses, as they were quickly labelled, drew mixed comments: but the character of the rest of the bill disposed conservatives in both British parties to look more kindly at this part of it. The Commons gave the operative clause a majority of 87 after the terms offered to the purchasing tenant were modified: he might borrow two-thirds of the price at 5 per cent over thirty-five years. Gladstone satisfied himself that the state's financial position would be more secure as a result.[69] In the Lords Salisbury commended this use of public money and implied that he would like to extend it, as he did at the head of Tory administrations from 1885. He realized what other statesmen, even Bright, did not or did not want to admit, that the Irish landlords were finished: 'they are not capable of holding their own in the open fight of politics.' The bill, he said, was the proof.[70]

RESULTS

The Irish land bill did not pacify Ireland. The accompanying Coercion Act brought the agrarian violence under control, when reinforced by the so called Westmeath Act of 1871, which went further and suspended Habeas Corpus in that unruly county and adjacent districts where Ribbonism was entrenched. Two Coercion Acts in successive years from the Gladstone ministry inevitably attracted bitter sarcasm. The Earl of Longford, a former Tory minister who had 15,000 acres in Westmeath wrote ungratefully:

'We are now passing through Parliament a...Bill for my County
...under which the Lord Lieutenant [of Ireland] may imprison
...anybody, whom anybody else may *suspect* of having been in
a district at a time when a Ribbon outrage was committed. Only
a very liberal Government could so improve the British Constitution.'[71] Gladstone was grievously disappointed at the popular
Irish reaction to the land bill. He addressed a long letter of
remonstrance to Cardinal Cullen: 'A perverse and vengeful spirit
seems to meet every pacific and just indication on the part of
Parliament, by...outrages and an extension of terrorism, which
create on this side of the Channel not apprehension, but disgust.'[72]
Clarendon's prophecy to Gladstone that the only effect of the land
bill would be to encourage agitation for repeal of the Union came
true even more rapidly than he expected. Isaac Butt began the
public organization of the 'Home Government', later the Home
Rule, movement, with the open participation of known Fenians,
while the bill was still going through the Commons. The movement
grew apace, and a majority of Irish M.P.s professed allegiance
to it after the next general election in 1874. In British politics
the bill was a notable achievement in more than one sense.
Looking back on the bill in August, *The Times* ascribed its passage
to the prime minister's singular insistence. 'Mr Gladstone is not
only the chosen leader of the Liberal majority, but through his
popularity out of doors he is its master.'[73] Never again did
Gladstone wield such authority over the Commons. The meaning
of the Land Act for British society, disapprovingly recalled by
Lecky in the nineties, was inescapable at the time and no amount
of special pleading could minimize it. It breached 'that great
monopoly which the age...steadfastly maintains, but which
helps...to hasten change, the right of private property itself'.
The words quoted do not come from Marx and Engels, who like
the contemporary Irish underrated the importance of the Act,[74]
but from the Cambridge historian, J. R. Seeley, remembered as
an imperialist, writing in 1870.[75]

For much of rural Ireland the bill was a monumental irrelevance. Those who did not benefit from the direct recognition
of tenant-right custom under the first clause, or the amended
second clause, were totally dissatisfied. Gray himself, well able to
appreciate how Gladstone was placed in terms of British politics,
was at first inclined to support the bill; and the *Freeman's Journal*

acknowledged that some of the Irish Members voting for the
second reading were patriots who sincerely thought they were
acting for the best.[76] The failure to recognize tenant-right universally compelled the paper to find, within a week of the bill's
introduction, that it was 'radically wrong in principle, and...
acceptance by the country...a simple impossibility'. The legislation was judged from the angle of 'the great question of
occupancy'. Why, asked the *Freeman's Journal*, should non-
payment of rent forfeit compensation for disturbance, which it
preferred to call 'compensation for loss of occupancy-right'?[77]
Some moderate nationalists were more outspoken than Gray and
his newspaper. Bishop Gillooly of Elphin – a diocese in Connaught
– condemned the bill in a letter published in the press, and deemed
'infamous' by Clarendon. The bishop referred to the tenants'
'natural right to occupy...and enjoy the soil of their country...
[so] that they are no longer slaves or aliens on the land of their
birth', and declared: 'No half-measure will save either the landlord...or public order...If the landlord class be not blind or
insensible to their social duty as well as their private interest,
they will unite with the representatives of the tenants...in
demanding the amendment of Mr Gladstone's bill so as to make
it a settlement...not for Ulster only, but for all Ireland.'[78]
Gladstone reproached Cullen with failing to understand his British
difficulties, with making 'impossible' demands which, if they
could be granted, would bring in their train 'a social revolution
throughout...three countries'. And this when the land bill, in
the prime minister's view, undeniably changed 'the balance of
right and wrong' between Great Britain and Ireland. The last
was a point that Gladstone often made – as in a letter of 16 April
to Manning and in one of 1874 to de Grey.[79] He was asking Cullen
to do what was beyond the Catholic Hierarchy. No one knew
better than Gladstone that universal tenant-right offered the sole
hope, if hope there was, of permanently appeasing the Irish
peasantry, since land purchase on an imaginative scale had been
ruled out. His second Land Act of 1881 certainly came too late.
Even then it was, perhaps, possible only because of the spread
of the attitude taken by Northcote in 1870 when giving Disraeli
his opinion about the land bill and the Irish: 'There is a good
deal to be said under existing circumstances for letting them go
to the devil in their own way.'[80]

314

RESULTS

In that article of August 1870 *The Times* enlarged upon the advantage that Gladstone derived from the effects of the 1867 Reform Act in weakening Members' independence by making them – or many of them – answerable to a democratized electorate. That was true as far as it went: but his 'peremptory suppression of independent criticism' – the *Times*'s description – owed more to the temporary belief for a couple of years after the 1868 election that British politics were ripe for radicalization, and that the dreaded change would come about through his agency. 'Strange to say,' remarked Gladstone to Spencer when the Tories were abetting the bill's Liberal critics at the Commons' committee stage, 'I begin to believe that it was our resolute resistance to fixity of tenure...which made the Opposition think they might safely assail the Bill as it stood, while they had before regarded it as a needful means of escape from greater evils.'[81] There was a sizeable element of truth in this surmise: the land bill showed that his will for reform had definite limits, and so had the cabinet's acquiescence in his domination.

In the Land Act of 1870 Parliament sacrificed on the altar of Anglo-Irish union the notion that the individual's rights of property were indefeasible, and with that cherished notion the concomitant freedom of contract. The conservatism of the British people deprived the precedent of revolutionary significance, as Seeley forecast in his essay entitled 'The English Revolution of the XIX Century'. It was no accident, however, that the trickle of collectivist legislation passed to cope with the pressures of a growing industrial and urban society started to broaden into a stream from the year 1870. Nor would that developing society indefinitely bear the strains of the Union with the comparative resoluteness displayed by Parliament when it answered to a far smaller and propertied electorate. The Home Rule bill of 1886 admitted the incompatibility of democracy, in its British version, with colonial or quasi-colonial rule over an unwilling people, though only, at that date, if the recalcitrants were Europeans.

NOTES

REFERENCES AND ABBREVIATIONS

In the notes on pp. 316–50 the conventions usual in a book of this kind are employed, with the following exceptions, designed to save space and expense.

1. Mr Gladstone is normally cited by his initials as W.E.G.

2. References to MSS. in the British Museum are shortened. In the case of the Gladstone Papers, which are used extensively, instead of Gladstone Papers (B.M. Add. MSS. 44536), Gladstone to Manning, 3 June 1869, the reference becomes G.P.(44536), W.E.G. to Manning, 3 June 1869. In the case of other collections in the Museum, instead of Rose Papers (B.M. Add. MSS. 42826), Strathnairn to the Duke of Cambridge, 3 December 1869, the reference becomes Rose Papers (42826), etc.

3. References to A. Ramm (ed.), *The Political Correspondence of Mr Gladstone and Lord Granville, 1868–1876* (2 vols, Camden, 3rd Series), LXXXI–LXXXII (1952) are simply to Ramm, I, followed by page, the writer and the recipient of the letter and the date. The 1st Earl of Kimberley's political diary, *A Journal of Events during the Gladstone Ministry 1868–74*, ed. E. Drus (Camden, 3rd Series, 1958), XC is cited as the *Kimberley Journal*, with the page and date of the entry.

4. The majority of newspapers and periodicals used appear so often that abbreviations are employed where sensible. D.N. for the *Daily News*; F.J. for the *Freeman's Journal*; M.G. for the *Manchester Guardian*; P.M.G. for the *Pall Mall Gazette*; Q.R. for the *Quarterly Review*; S.R. for the *Saturday Review*.

INTRODUCTION

1   W. E. H. Lecky, *Democracy and Liberty* (2 vols, 1896), I, p. 145.

2   E.g., R. D. Collison Black, *Economic Thought & the Irish Question, 1817–1870* (Cambridge, 1960), ch. II.

3   J. P. Mackintosh, *The British Cabinet* (1962), p. 281.

4   M. J. Cowling, *The Impact of Labour 1920–1924* (Cambridge, 1971), pp. 1–12. Mr Cowling is sometimes criticized for the opacity of his language, but the following seems clear enough: 'There was a well-understood...language in which "crisis", "principle" and "novelty" were conventional instruments for establishing positions in the monastic, or rotarian, world we are discussing.' Ibid. p. 10. These assumptions permeate Mr Cowling's earlier book, *1867: Disraeli,*

Gladstone and Revolution: The Passing of the Second Reform Bill (Cambridge, 1967).

5 A. B. Cooke & J. R. Vincent (eds.), *Lord Carlingford's Journal* (Oxford, 1971), Introduction, p. 7.

6 P. S. O'Hegarty, *A History of Ireland under the Union, 1801–1922* (1952), p. 462. The words quoted are taken from the title of ch. XXXIX.

7 Hansard (3rd ser.), CLXXXI, cols. 271–2 (8 February 1866).

8 P. N. S. Mansergh, *The Irish Question, 1840–1921* (1965), p. 119. See E. D. Steele, 'Gladstone and Ireland', *Irish Historical Studies* (1970).

1: TENANT-RIGHT AND NATIONALITY IN NINETEENTH-CENTURY IRELAND

1 P.P. 1876, LXXX, Summary of the Returns of Owners of Land in Ireland, p. 59.

2 Calculated from J. Bateman, *The Great Landowners of Great Britain and Ireland*, 4th edn (1883), reprinted by Leicester University Press (1971).

3 P.P. 1872, XLVII, Return for the year 1870 of the No. of Landed Proprietors in Ireland, classed according to Residence, p. 782.

4 P.P. 1839, XI, XII, Lords' Select Committee on the State of Ireland in respect of Crime; XI, p. 591, evidence of Matthew Barrington, crown solicitor for the Munster circuit, answers 7445–6.

5 Ribbonism awaits its historian. Meanwhile there is the evidence collected by three Parliamentary inquiries – that of 1839 cited in note 4 above, with the Commons' Select Committees on Outrages (Ireland), P.P. 1852, XIV, and on Westmeath, &c (Unlawful Combinations), P.P. 1871, XIII. G. Broeker, *Rural Disorder and Police Reform in Ireland 1812–36* (1970) is a study, not of Ribbonism, but of the governmental response to it.

6 *Transactions of the Royal Historical Society* (1949), pp. 17–28.

7 E. R. Norman, *A History of Modern Ireland* (1971), p. 18.

8 J. C. Beckett, *The Making of Modern Ireland 1603–1923*, paperback edn (1969), p. 359.

9 *The Irish Convention* (1970), p. 215.

10 O'Hegarty, op. cit., pp. 462–3.

11 O'Hegarty, op. cit. p. 799. Lyons (*Ireland since the Famine*, pp. 29–30) comes close to agreeing.

12 P.P. 1845, XXII, Appendix to Evidence before H.M. Commissioners, no. 95, p. 171.

13 Manchester (1957), p. 54, note *a*.

14 Figures for holdings in the 1840s as corrected by P. M. A. Bourke, 'The Agricultural Statistics of the 1841 Census of Ireland. A Critical Review', *Econ. H.R.* (1965).

15 P. Lynch & J. Vaizey, *Guinness's Brewery in the Irish Economy, 1759–1875* (Cambridge, 1960), p. 12.

16 G.P.(44758), W.E.G.'s memorandum on Irish land of 7 December 1869.

17 Hansard (3rd ser.), CCII, col. 886 (24 June 1870).

18 Lord Greville; ibid., col. 887.

19 G. A. Hayes-McCoy, 'Gaelic Society in Ireland in the late Sixteenth Century', in Hayes-McCoy (ed.), *Historical Studies IV* (1963). For the condemnation of Celtic customary tenure by the Court of King's Bench in Ireland see E. Curtis & R. B. McDowell, *Irish Historical Documents, 1172–1922* (1943), pp. 126–8.

20 P.P. 1825, IX, Foster's evidence before the Lords' Select Committee on the State of Ireland, pp. 53, 70, 81; quotation from p. 53.

21 C. S. Orwin & E. M. Whetham, *A History of British Agriculture, 1846–1914* (1964), pp. 153–7.

22 R. B. McDowell, *Public Opinon and Government Policy in Ireland, 1801–1846* (1952), p. 74; Hansard (3rd ser.), I, cols. 386–8 (11 November 1830).

23 Ibid., col. 387.

24 See the account of him in the British *Dictionary of National Biography*.

25 P.P. 1836, XXXIV, Royal Commission on the Condition of the Irish Poor, Appendix (H), Pt II. Remarks on the Evidence by One of the Commissioners; quotations from pp. 659, 690. P.P. 1870, XIV, Reports from Poor Law inspectors in Ireland as to existing Relations between Landlord and Tenant. A county by county summary of the evidence on 'Tenant Right or Goodwill' will be found under that heading in the index to the Devon Commission's inquiries, P.P. 1845, XXII, pp. 662–78.

26 The student of Irish land in the nineteenth century has no substitute for the evidence amassed by the contemporary Parliamentary and official investigations: the Royal Commission on the Condition of the Irish Poor, P.P. 1835, XXII; 1836, XXX to XXXIV; 1837, XXXVIII and LI; 1845, XLIII; the Devon Commission, P.P. 1845, XIX to XXII; the Commons' Select Committee in P.P. 1865, XI; the Poor Law Inspectors' Reports, P.P. 1870, XIV; and the Bessborough Commission, P.P. 1880, XVIII, XIX. Apart from Freeman's book, which deals with the law and custom of tenure only in passing, modern studies include Lynch & Vaizey, op. cit., chs. I and IX; E. R. R. Green, 'Agriculture', ch. II in R. D. Edwards & T. D. Williams, *The Great Famine: Studies in Irish History 1845–52* (Dublin, 1956); R. D. Crotty, *Irish Agricultural Production: Its Volume and Structure* (Cork, 1966), discussed by J. Lee in *Agricultural History Review* (1969), pp. 64–76; and L. M. Cullen, *An Economic History of*

Ireland since 1660 (1972), chs. V & VI. There are in addition two works by American scholars: J. E. Pomfret, *The Struggle for Land in Ireland, 1800–1923* (Princeton, 1930) and B. L. Solow, *The Land Question and the Irish Economy, 1870–1903* (Cambridge, Mass., 1971). None of these works is satisfactory in its treatment of tenant-right, e.g. Cullen, p. 83, 'two main features…made up the nineteenth-century concept of tenant-right…compensation for improvements and security of tenure.'

27   P.P. 1845, XXI, pp. 537–8, 541, 543–4, answers 61–3, 47–56, 28–31 relating to the Fitzwilliam estate; and XX, p. 504, answer 35, Le Poer Trench.

28   P.P. 1870, XIV, p. 79.

29   P.P. [H.L.] 1841 (28), Letter by Lord Oxmantown. Also Memorial from Justices of King's County, pp. 3–6.

30   Ibid., pp. 6–7.

31   W. O'Connor Morris, *Letters on the Land Question of Ireland* (1870), pp. 99–103; George Campbell, *The Irish Land* (1869), pp. 134–5.

32   P.P. 1839, XII, pp. 183–90, evidence of Viscount Lorton; R. D. King-Harman, *The Kings, Earls of Kingston* (Cambridge, 1959), pp. 94–5 and Appendix XI. Lord Lorton was a member of the King family.

33   Hansard (3rd ser.), CLXIV, cols. 248–51 (2 July 1861).

34   P.P. 1881, LXXVII, Return of Evictions, 1849 to 1880, p. 727; ibid., Return of Outrages, 1844 to 1880, pp. 891–2.

35   In the Famine year of 1847 the government accepted an Irish landlord amendment – the 'Gregory clause' – to the Poor Relief (Ireland) Bill, debarring occupiers of more than $\frac{1}{4}$ acre from relief unless and until they surrendered their land. The cabinet member in charge of the bill, Sir George Grey, 'had always understood that…small holdings were the bane of Ireland'. Hansard (3rd ser.), XCI, col. 587 (12 March 1847).

36   Hansard (3rd ser.), CIII, cols. 185–93 (5 March 1849), Peel; ibid., CIV, cols. 168–80 (2 April 1849), Bright; ibid., CV, cols. 617–22 (17 May 1849), Russell.

37   P.P. 1873, LXIX, Agricultural Statistics of Ireland for 1871, p. 387.

38   Bourke, art. cit.

39   Deducting Highland crofts, and the small holdings of Wales and North-Western England the true average size of British farms was much higher than 102 acres; Orwin & Whetham, op. cit., pp. 1–2. P.P. 1863, LXIX, Agricultural Statistics of Ireland for 1861, p. 558.

40   Clarendon Papers (MS. Clar. Dep. (Irish), box 26), Russell to Lord Clarendon, viceroy of Ireland, 19 October 1849.

41   Buyers of encumbered estates came in for criticism from the

poor law inspectors reporting on landlord–tenant relations in 1869, who referred rather disparagingly to the social origins of people 'purchasing merely as a mercantile speculation'. P.P. 1870, XIV, quotation from p. 132.

42 Hansard (3rd ser.), LXXXI, cols. 211–29 (9 June 1845); quotation from col. 221.

43 G. Locker-Lampson, *A Consideration of the State of Ireland in the Nineteenth Century* (1907), p. 334; Q.R., January 1870, 'The Irish Cauldron', p. 268.

44 Hansard (3rd ser.), CXCVI, cols. 718–24 (13 May 1869); quotations from cols. 723, 722.

45 Larcom Papers (National Library of Ireland, 7638). A cutting from the *Daily Express* (Dublin), reproducing an item from the *Clonmel Chronicle*.

46 P.P. 1881, LXXVII, pp. 727, 891–6.

47 Campbell, op. cit., p. 6.

48 P.P. 1845, XX, p. 40, answer 115.

49 K. H. Connell, *Irish Peasant Society* (Oxford, 1968), ch. IV.

50 P.P. 1870, XIV, Reports from Poor Law Inspectors on the Wages of Agricultural Labourers in Ireland; see esp. pp. 9, 13–14, 30, 32, 34.

51 P.P. 1865, XI, pp. 445, 459–60; quotations from answers 1805, 2094, 2106.

52 Sir C. Gavan Duffy, *The League of North and South* (1886), pp. 26–7.

53 F.J., 4 January 1868.

54 Hansard (3rd ser.), CXC, cols. 1617–18 (13 March 1868).

55 P.P. 1870, XIV, p. 156.

56 Ibid., p. 109.

57 Ibid., p. 65.

58 Ibid., p. 190.

59 Ibid., p. 79.

60 Ibid., p. 156.

61 Grey Papers (Durham University Library), Clanricarde to Earl Grey, 3 January 1870.

62 The Hon. C. W. W. Fitzwilliam, M.P., Hansard (3rd ser.), CCLXII, col. 708 (16 June 1881).

63 P.P. 1881, XIX, pp. 317–18, evidence of Thomas Dowling, answers 34512, 34549.

64 Ibid., p. 436, evidence of Lord Lansdowne, answer 37475.

65 Hansard (3rd ser.), CCLXII, col. 720 (16 June 1881).

66 P.P. 1881, XIX, p. 438, answer 37526.

67 Ibid., XVIII, pp. 9, 7.

68 *Special Commission Act, 1888. Reprint of the Shorthand Notes of the Speeches, Proceedings and Evidence...before the Commissioners under the above-named Act* (12 vols, 1890), III, p. 153, cited in

question 25496 put by Davitt; King James was James II, the last Catholic ruler of Ireland.

69 R. B. McDowell, *Public Opinion and Government Policy in Ireland, 1801–1846* (1952), p. 124.

70 P.P. 1852, XIV, pp. 319–24; quotation from p. 320. There is no study of this important churchman: but see J. H. Whyte, 'Political Problems, 1850–60' and P. J. Corish, 'Political Problems, 1860–1878', published together (Dublin, 1967) as vol. V, pts 2 & 3, of *A History, of Irish Catholicism*; also the sketch in E. R. Norman, *The Catholic Church and Ireland in the Age of Rebellion, 1859–1873* (1965), pp. 4–12.

71 O'Hegarty, op. cit., p. 463; Q.R., January 1870, pp. 256–9, gave examples, culled from Irish press reports, of the extreme language held by some Catholic clergy at rallies during the contemporary agitation. Similar instances can be found earlier in the century, and later.

72 F.J., 30 December 1864.

73 Hansard (3rd ser.), CXIV, col. 189 (7 February 1851).

74 P.P. 1835, XVI, Select Committee on Orange Lodges, pp. 126–7, evidence of Capt. David Duff, chief constable of Co. Tyrone. The sole academic monograph on the Orange Order does not go beyond its attempted suppression in the 1830s. H. Senior, *Orangeism in Ireland and Britain, 1795–1836* (1966).

75 *The Times*, 27 November 1860.

76 E. Strauss, *Irish Nationalism and British Democracy* (1951); the most notable piece of Marxist historical writing on Ireland.

77 See C. C. O'Brien, *Parnell and his Party*, new impression (Oxford, 1964).

78 P.P. 1852, XIV, p. 580, evidence of Fr M. Lennon, P.P., question 5628.

79 Ibid., question 5597 and answer 5604.

80 G.P. (44134), Clarendon to W.E.G., 11 September 1869.

81 Peace Preservation (Ireland) Act, 1870, ss. 30 to 34.

82 F.J., 30 December 1864.

83 *Despatches, Correspondence and Memoranda of Field Marshal the Duke of Wellington, 1818–1832*, edited by the 2nd Duke (8 vols, 1867–80), V, pp. 133–6, 252–4, Wellington to the King, 14 October, 16 November 1828; J. A. Reynolds, *The Catholic Emancipation Crisis in Ireland, 1823–1829* (New Haven, 1954), esp. ch. VIII.

84 McDowell, op. cit., pp. 237–9; P.P. 1845, XXI, pp. 939–48, evidence of O'Connell; see esp. answers 9–11, where he advocated virtually compulsory leases.

85 Curtis & McDowell, *Irish Historical Documents*, pp. 250–1.

86 Hansard (3rd ser.), LXXXV, cols. 493–527 (3 April 1846).

87 Ibid., cols. 526–7.

88 *James Fintan Lalor, Patriot and Political Essayist. Collected Writings*, ed. L. Fogarty, revised edn (Dublin, 1947); quotations from pp. 59, 77, 103–4, 96.

89 *Daily Express* (Dublin), 17 August 1863. T. W. Moody (ed.), *The Fenian Movement* (Cork, 1968) is a collection of very short essays.

90 O'Luing, 'A Contribution to the Study of Fenianism in Briefne', in *Breifne* (1967), p. 157, quoting Jeremiah O'Donovan Rossa. Donal McCartney, 'The Church and the Fenians', in M. Harmon (ed.), *Fenians and Fenianism* (Dublin, 1968). John O'Leary, *Recollections of Fenians and Fenianism* (2 vols, 1896), I, p. 181. Hughenden Papers (B/VII/116), observations on Fenianism from Lord Strathnairn, C.-in-C. Ireland, forwarded by the Duke of Cambridge, C.-in-C. at the Horse Guards, 7 June 1867, and printed for the cabinet.

91 O'Luing, art cit.. p. 172.

92 *The Times*, 9 March 1867.

93 Hughenden Papers (B/VII/116), Strathnairn's observations on Fenianism.

94 P.P. 1871, XIII, p. 600, evidence of W. Morris Reade, resident magistrate in Co. Westmeath, answers 1147, 1149.

95 Special Commission Act, 1888. Proceedings and Evidence, VII, p. 11, answers 58, 368–9; p. 245, answers 61,054–7, 61,066.

96 Hansard (3rd ser.), XV, cols. 1326–37 (28 February 1833).

97 Ibid., quotations from cols. 1331, 1332–3, 1335. W. J. Fitzpatrick, *The Life, Times, & Correspondence of the Rt. Rev. Dr Doyle, Bishop of Kildare & Leighlin*, new edn (2 vols, 1880), II, pp. 458–9, Doyle to Henry Lambert, M.P. for Co. Wexford, 1 March 1833.

98 *The Times*, 2 January 1852.

99 P.P. 1865, XI, p. 435, answer 1599.

100 Clarendon Papers (MS. Clar. Dep., letter book II), Clarendon to Lord John Russell, 19 February 1848 and (letter book I) 26 October 1847.

101 P.P. 1845, XIX, p. 253, answer 3.

102 P.P. 1846, II, p. 81.

103 P.P. 1847–8, IV, p. 557.

104 Hansard (3rd ser.) CXLIX, col. 1088 (14 April 1858).

105 Bright Papers (43383), Bright to Richard Cobden, 12 October 1850.

106 Hansard (3rd ser.), CXIX, col. 346 (10 February 1852).

107 *The Panmure Papers*, ed. Sir G. Douglas & Sir G. D. Ramsay (2 vols, 1908); II, pp. 436, 446, Palmerston to Lord Panmure, 28 September, 11 October 1857.

108 J. S. Mill, *Considerations on Representative Government* (Everyman's Library edn, 1954), pp. 364–5; *Principles of Political Economy*, 5th edn (1862), chs. IX and X.

109 Hansard (3rd ser.), CXLII, col. 1575 (17 June 1856).

110 Larcom Papers (7585), Larcom to Lord Carlisle, the Viceroy, 28 June 1863.
111 Hansard (3rd ser.), CLXXXI, cols. 271–2 (8 February 1866).
112 W.E.G., *The Irish Question* (1886), p. 22.
113 Hansard (3rd ser.), CCCIV, cols. 1038, 1039, 1041 (8 April 1886).
114 Ibid., cols. 1041, 1043.
115 Ibid., col. 1037.
116 Ibid., CCCVI, col. 1271 (10 June 1886).
117 Lord Dufferin to Sir J. F. Stephen, 28 July 1886, in Sir A. Lyall, *The Life of the Marquis of Dufferin & Ava* (2 vols, 1905), II, pp. 139–40.
118 Hansard (3rd ser.), CXCIX, cols. 340, 341 (15 February 1870).
119 Ibid., CCLXI, col. 601 (16 May 1881).
120 Ibid., CCIV, cols. 1787–8 (16 April 1886).
121 W. E. H. Lecky, *Democracy and Liberty*, I, p. 145.

2: IRISH LAND AND BRITISH POLITICS IN THE 1860s

1 Orwin & Whetham, op. cit., p. 306; the Scottish figure is calculated from J. Bateman, *The Great Landowners*.
2 H. J. Hanham, *Elections and Party Management: Politics in the Time of Disraeli and Gladstone*, new impression (1964), p. xvii.
3 *The Times*, 4 February 1864.
4 W. L. Burn, *The Age of Equipoise: a Study of the Mid-Victorian Generation* (1964).
5 Clarendon Papers (MS. Clar. Dep. box 82), Clarendon to the 7th Duke of Bedford, 25 February 1860.
6 Ibid., 17 July 1858.
7 Letter-Books of the 3rd Viscount Palmerston (48579), Palmerston to Henry Labouchere, 19 December 1855. The 'Tenant Right Under-Secretary' at the Colonial office was John Ball (1818–89), M.P. for Co. Carlow.
8 J. Morley, *The Life of William Ewart Gladstone*, new edn (2 vols, 1905), I, pp. 344–7.
9 See, for example, the speech to his largely working-class constituents of Greenwich on 28 October 1871, reported at length in *The Times* of 30 October.
10 Hansard (3rd ser.), CXC, col. 1746 (16 March 1868).
11 W.E.G., 'Notes and Queries on the Irish Demand', in *The Nineteenth Century*, February 1887, p. 81.
12 G.P.(44758), Gladstone's memorandum on Irish land of 11 December 1869.
13 A. Patchett Martin, *Life and Letters of the Rt. Hon. Robert Lowe, Viscount Sherbrooke* (2 vols, 1893), II, p. 298, Robert Lowe to his brother, 9 June 1866.

14 Morley, op. cit., I, p. 835, quoting W.E.G.'s description of Bright at that time.

15 For a warm expression of this feeling, see Cobden's letter of 7 April 1857 to W. S. Lindsay in John Morley, *The Life of Richard Cobden*, Jubilee edn (2 vols, 1896), II, p. 198.

16 Hansard (3rd ser.), CXC, col. 1645 (13 March 1868).

17 J. R. Vincent, *The Formation of the Liberal Party 1857–1868* (1966), p. 180.

18 J. E. Thorold Rogers (ed.), *Speeches by the Rt. Hon. John Bright M.P.*, popular edn (1878), pp. 176 ff.

19 *The Times*, 2 November 1866. Lowe's authorship is attested by a daily record of leader-writers in the Printing House Square Papers. His connexion with the newspaper lasted until 1868.

20 Rogers, op. cit., pp. 192 ff.

21 Hickleton Papers (folder A4/51), Stansfeld to Halifax, 11 November 1866.

22 P.M.G., 5 February 1868.

23 G.P.(44100), Argyll to W.E.G., 4 November 1866.

24 J. S. Mill, *Autobiography*, World's Classics edn (1955), p. 199.

25 J. S. Mill, *Principles of Political Economy*, p. 230 in the 2nd vol. of the variorum edn comprising vols II and III of the *Collected Works of John Stuart Mill* (Toronto, 1963–).

26 Hansard (3rd ser.), CLXXI, col. 1375 (23 June 1863).

27 Mill, *Works*, II, pp. 226–9.

28 Ibid., pp. 228, 224–6, 229.

29 H. S. R. Elliot (ed.), *The Letters of John Stuart Mill* (2 vols, 1910), II, Mill to Frederick Lucas, 28 March 1851; and Mill, *Autobiography*, p. 237.

30 For a detailed analysis of Mill on Irish land in successive editions of the *Principles*, see E. D. Steele, 'J. S. Mill and the Irish Question: the Principles of Political Economy, 1848–1865', *Historical Journal* (1970), pp. 220–33.

31 Ibid., pp. 225–8.

32 Ibid., pp. 228–9.

33 Ibid., pp. 229–33.

34 Ibid., p. 233.

35 Henry Fawcett, *Manual of Political Economy*, 1st edn (1863), p. 240.

36 Steele, art. cit., p. 236.

37 Ibid.

38 Ibid., p. 233.

39 Ibid., p. 234.

40 *Westminster Review*, July 1866, 'Tenant-right in Ireland', quotations from pp. 4, 6, 16.

41 *Spectator*, 9 June 1866.

42 P.M.G., 27 February 1866.

43 P.P. 1865, XI, p. 112, answers 2181–2.

44 See pp. 262, 275 of the pamphlet.

45 F.J., 27 April 1865.

46 There are some brilliant pages on Mill's influence in J. R. Vincent, op. cit., pp. 149–61.

47 The pamphlet and its impact are examined in E. D. Steele, 'J. S. Mill and the Irish Question: Reform, and the Integrity of the Empire, 1865–1870', *Historical Journal* (1970), pp. 419–50.

48 Mill, *England and Ireland*, p. 26.

49 The activities of the socialists in Britain during this period are detailed in H. Collins and C. Abramsky, *Karl Marx and the British Labour Movement: Years of the First International* (1965).

50 Ripon Papers (43548), Kimberley to de Grey, 25 November 1867.

51 Hansard (3rd ser.), CLXXVIII, cols. 588–9 (31 March 1865).

52 Orwin & Whetham, op. cit., p. 314.

53 C. Hope, *George Hope of Fenton Barns* (Edinburgh, 1881), p. 258; quoting an essay by this farmer's leader published in 1870.

54 Orwin & Whetham, op. cit., pp. 168–70.

55 K. O. Morgan, *Wales in British Politics, 1868–1922*, revised edn (Cardiff, 1970), chs. I & II.

56 Reprinted in book form as *Letters and Essays on Wales* (1884); quotation from p. 107.

57 Hansard (3rd ser.), CLXXXIII, col. 1067 (17 May 1866).

58 Ibid., CLXXXV, col. 544 (18 February 1867).

59 D.N., 30 April 1867.

60 Hansard (3rd ser.), CLXXXVI, col. 1728 (29 April 1867). The speaker was G. M. W. Sandford, M.P., a severe critic of Disraelian flexibility.

61 Selborne Papers (MS. 1862), Dufferin to Palmer, 3 January 1867.

62 Dufferin Papers (P.R.O. Northern Ireland, D.1071 H/B/F.150), Palmer to Dufferin, 4 January 1867.

63 Ibid.

64 Ibid., Palmer to Dufferin, 10 January 1867.

65 *The Times*, 20 and 23 December; P.M.G., 27 December 1867, for Hughes' defence.

66 *The Times*, 23 January 1868.

67 *The Economist*, 25 January 1868.

68 Delane Correspondence (vol. 24), Walter to Delane, 17 December 1867; Walter sat for Berkshire 1859–65, 1868–85.

69 *The Times*, 6 February 1868.

70 Hughenden Papers (B/XX/S/796), Stanley to Disraeli, 25 January 1868.

71 Mayo Papers (National Library of Ireland, 11,164), Disraeli to Lord Mayo (formerly Naas), 7 February 1868.

72 Hansard (3rd ser.), CXC, col. 1780 (16 March 1868).

73 Ibid., cols. 1669–70 (13 March 1868).
74 Ibid., cols. 1532–5 (12 March 1868).
75 P.M.G., 10 February 1868.
76 Carlingford Papers (H 324/CP1), Gladstone to Chichester Fortescue, 11 December 1867.
77 *The Times*, 20 December 1867.
78 Hansard (3rd ser.), CXC, cols. 1740 ff. (16 March 1868).
79 P.M.G., 14 March 1868.
80 *Daily Telegraph* (then a Liberal paper), 13 March; D.N., 16 March 1868.
81 Hansard (3rd ser.), CXCIV, cols. 2106 ff. (23 March 1869).
82 *The Times*, 6 August 1868.
83 Ibid., 15 October 1868.
84 Royal Archives, Windsor (D/24/61), General Grey to the Queen, 18 October 1868.
85 G.P.(44419), Bessborough to W.E.G., 28 October 1868.
86 Ibid. (44100), Argyll to W.E.G., 16, 20 and 23 October 1868.
87 Ibid. (44756), copy of Fortescue's election address.
88 Ibid. (44100), Argyll to W.E.G., 23 October 1868.
89 Granville Papers (P.R.O. 30/29/29A), Clarendon to Granville, 26 November 1868.
90 Delane Correspondence (vol. 24), John Walter to Delane, 24 December 1865.
91 Carlingford Papers (H324/CP1), Gladstone to Chichester Fortescue, 11 December 1867.
92 Hansard (3rd ser.), CLVIII, cols. 1346–7 (15 May 1860).
93 Ibid., CLIX, col. 2145 (19 July); CLVII, col. 1564 (29 March).
94 Ibid., CLVII, cols. 1569–71.
95 Hansard (3rd ser.), CLXXI, col. 1375 (23 June 1863).
96 F.J., 30 December 1864; E. R. Norman, *The Catholic Church and Ireland in the Age of Rebellion* (1965), ch. IV.
97 P.P. 1865, XI, p. 243.
98 F.J., 12 September 1865.
99 Larcom Papers (7585), Larcom to Sir Robert Peel, 3rd Bt (Irish secretary 1861–5), 6 May 1863.
100 F. W. Hirst, 'Mr Gladstone as Chancellor of the Exchequer', in Sir Wemyss Reid (ed.), *The Life of William Ewart Gladstone* (1899), p. 441; and see *The Times*, 15 October 1864, for W.E.G.'s speech at Manchester.
101 Chichester Fortescue, Irish secretary, Hansard (3rd ser.), CLXXXIII, cols. 214 ff. (30 April 1866).
102 F.J., 26 February 1867; *Nation*, 2 March 1867.
103 *The Times*, 23 January 1868; extracts from a report presented by Dean R. B. O'Brien and their committee to a meeting of the Declaration's signatories in Limerick on 20 January.

104   There is no biography of this fascinating figure, but he has an entry in the *D.N.B.* See the *Freeman's Journal* for the speech; ibid., 9, 13 January for citations of the support for it in the Irish provincial press.

105   Michael Davitt, *The Fall of Feudalism in Ireland* (1904), p. 77.

106   Davitt, p. 77 note 1; Mayo Papers (National Library of Ireland, 11,191), Larcom to Mayo (Irish secretary), 29 August 1868, reporting that 'there is no chance of anyone giving information'. Scully sold Ballycohey to a Liberal M.P. prepared to leave tenants in peace; Larcom Papers (7597), Sir Thomas Larcom to C. de Gernon, resident magistrate, 12 September 1868, saying that the Tory viceroy was 'very averse to affording him [Scully] protection'.

107   P.P. 1881, LXXVII, Return of Outrages reported to the Royal Irish Constabulary Office from 1844 to 1880, p. 900.

108   D. Thornley, *Isaac Butt and Home Rule* (1964), ch. II, 'The Disestablishment Election'.

109   *The Times*, 15 October 1868.

3: THE APPROACH TO LEGISLATING, JANUARY TO AUGUST 1869

1   George C. Brodrick, *Memories and Impressions, 1831–1900* (1900), p. 241.

2   Morley, *Life of Gladstone*, I, pp. 874–5.

3   Ibid., I, p. 902, W.E.G. to the Queen, 5 June 1869.

4   Sir A. Lyall, *The Life of the Marquis of Dufferin & Ava* (2 vols, 1905), I, p. 171, Dufferin to Argyll, 11 January 1869.

5   Ibid.

6   G.P. (44101), Argyll to W.E.G., 12 January 1869.

7   Ibid. (44536), W.E.G. to Argyll, 14 January 1869.

8   Lyall, op. cit., I, pp. 172–3, Dufferin to Argyll, 14 January 1869.

9   Ibid., I, pp. 173–4, Dufferin to Argyll, 21 January 1869.

10   Dufferin Papers, P.R.O., Northern Ireland (D.1071 H/B/F.149), Bessborough to Dufferin, 23 January 1869.

11   Ibid., Russell to Dufferin, 15 January 1869.

12   Russell Papers (P.R.O. 30/22/16), Dufferin to Russell, 19 January 1869.

13   Dufferin Papers (D.1071 H/B/F.149), Russell to Dufferin, 21 January 1869.

14   Carlingford Papers (H322/CP3), Monsell to Granville, 7 January 1869.

15   Monsell was a Catholic convert, but in other respects a member of the Ascendancy.

16   Hansard (3rd ser.), CXCIV, col. 83 (16 February 1869).

17 Ibid., cols. 353–4 (26 February 1869).

18 *The Times*, 28 January 1869.

19 Hansard (3rd ser.), CXCIV, col. 1625.

20 Ibid., col. 1637.

21 Ibid., cols. 1651–2.

22 Carlingford Papers (H 324/CP1), Spencer to W.E.G., 26 March 1869.

23 Ibid., W.E.G.'s minute to Granville, 30 March, written upon Spencer to W.E.G., 26 March 1869.

24 Ibid., Granville to W.E.G., 1 April 1869.

25 Ibid., W.E.G.'s minute to Fortescue, 2 April, written upon Spencer to W.E.G., 26 March 1869.

26 Ibid., Fortescue's minute to W.E.G., 2 April 1869; Spencer Papers, Althorp, W.E.G. to Spencer, 3 April 1869.

27 Carlingford Papers (H324/CP1), memorandum by Lord Kimberley, 4 April 1869.

28 Grey Papers (Durham University), Clanricarde to Grey, 28 March 1869.

29 Granville Papers (P.R.O. 30/29/29A), Spencer to Granville, 12 April 1869.

30 Ibid.

31 G.P.(44637), minutes of the cabinet of 17 April 1869.

32 Spencer Papers, W.E.G. to Spencer, 28 April 1869.

33 Dufferin Papers (D.1071 H/B/F.148), Spencer to Dufferin, 6 June 1869.

34 Hansard (3rd ser.), CXCV, col. 1163.

35 Ibid., cols. 1164–7.

36 Ibid., col. 1178; *The Times*, 21 April 1869.

37 Hansard (3rd ser.), CXCV, col. 1181.

38 Ibid., col. 1183; Salisbury, the future prime minister, had, as Lord Cranborne, resigned from the Tory cabinet over Parliamentary reform in 1867.

39 Ibid., cols. 1188–91.

40 Ibid., col. 1552.

41 *The Times*, 21, 23 April 1869.

42 Derby Papers, Christ Church, Oxford (Box 197/2), Derby to Sir J. H. Maxwell, Bt, 3 April 1869.

43 Hansard (3rd ser.), CXCV, cols. 1998–2002 (30 April 1869).

44 Ibid., cols. 2010, 2016.

45 *Irishman*, quoted in *The Times*, 17 May 1869; the *Irishman* was an extreme nationalist paper.

46 *The Times*, 25 May 1869.

47 Ramm, I, p. 22, W.E.G. to Granville, 24 May 1869.

48 Hansard (3rd ser.), CXCV, cols. 2020–8 (30 April 1869).

49 P.M.G., 3 May 1869.

50 Hansard (3rd ser.), CXCVI, cols. 360–1.
51 Ibid., cols. 707–15.
52 Ibid., cols. 718–24.
53 Ibid., cols. 724–7.
54 Ibid., CXCV, cols. 1735–9 (27 April 1869).
55 Ripon Papers (43534), de Grey to Bruce, 5 May 1869.
56 *Kimberley Journal*, p. 5; entry for 13 May 1869.
57 *The Times*, 14 May; Granville Papers (P.R.O. 30/29/79), Russell to Granville, 14 May 1869.
58 *Spectator*, 22 May 1869.
59 Ramm, I, p. 22, W.E.G. to Granville, 21 May 1869.
60 Granville Papers (P.R.O. 30/29/66), Lowe to Granville, 16 May 1869.
61 G.P.(44112), Bright to W.E.G., 21 May 1869.
62 Ramm, I, p. 23, Granville to W.E.G., 26 May 1869.
63 G.P.(44112), W.E.G. to Bright, 22 May 1869.
64 Ramm, I, p. 24, W.E.G. to Granville, 27 May 1869.
65 Ibid., p. 23, Granville to W.E.G., 26 May 1869.
66 *The Times*, 18 May 1869.
67 Delane Correspondence (vol. 24), Walter to Delane, 18 May 1869.
68 *The Times*, 21 May 1869; for Mozley see A. I. Dasent, *John Delane 1817–1879* (2 vols, 1908), II, p. 349.
69 Delane Correspondence (vol. 24), Walter to Delane, 19 May 1869.
70 Delane Correspondence (vol. 18), O'Connor Morris to Delane, 16 May 1869.
71 Ibid. (vol. 24), Walter to Delane, 19 May 1869.
72 Ibid. (vol. 24), Walter to Delane, 20 May; W. O'Connor Morris, *Memories & Thoughts of a Life* (1895), pp. 221–2.
73 O'Connor Morris, *Memories & Thoughts*, p. 222.
74 Walter Papers, Walter to Delane, 25 May 1869.
75 O'Connor Morris, *Memories & Thoughts*, p. 222.
76 Delane Correspondence (vol. 24), Walter to Delane, 8 August 1869.
77 Ibid. (add. vol. (i)), Walter to Delane, 7 November 1869.
78 Roundell Palmer, Earl of Selborne, *Memorials* (4 vols, 1896–8), Part II, Personal & Political, vol. I, p. 138.
79 *The Times*, 22 July 1869.
80 Hansard (3rd ser.), CXCVII, cols. 1981–2 (16 July 1869).
81 *The Times*, 13 August 1869.
82 Ibid.
83 Ibid.
84 Delane Correspondence (vol. 24), Walter to Delane, 8 August 1869.
85 G.P.(44536), W.E.G. to Manning, 3 June 1869.
86 Hansard (3rd ser.), CXCVI, col. 1055.
87 G.P.(44112), Bright to W.E.G., 21 May 1869.
88 Ibid. (44637), minutes of the cabinet of 31 July 1869.
89 P.P. 1870, LXVII, Reports from H.M. Representatives concerning

the Tenure of Land in Europe 1869; pp. 9–13, F.O. circular to H.M. Representatives abroad, 26 August 1869, and enclosed questionnaire.

90 Ramm, I, p. 59, Granville to W.E.G., 23 September 1869.
91 G.P.(44537), W.E.G. to Fortescue, 25 August 1869.
92 Ramm, I, pp. 42–3, W.E.G. to Granville, 7 August 1869.
93 *The Times*, 11 September 1869.
94 Ramm, I, p. 68, W.E.G. to Granville, 18 October 1869; *The Complete Peerage*, new edn (14 vols in 13, 1910–59), vol. X, p. 613.
95 G.P.(44537), W.E.G. to Trevelyan, 13 August 1869.
96 W. O'Connor Morris, *Letters on the Land Question of Ireland* (1870), p. xi.
97 George Campbell, *The Irish Land* (1869), quotations from pp. 91–3.
98 Ibid., p. 87.
99 George Campbell, *Memoirs of my Indian Career*, ed. Sir C. E. Bernard (2 vols, 1893), II, p. 186.
100 Campbell, *The Irish Land*, p. 6.
101 Ibid., p. 40; see E. D. Steele, *Historical Journal* (1968), pp. 64–83.
102 G.P.(44101), Argyll to W.E.G., 13 January 1870.
103 Ibid. (44758), memorandum on Irish land, 11 December 1869, by W.E.G.
104 Ampthill Papers, India Office Library (MSS., Eur.E. 233/13), Morley to Lord Ampthill, 9 January 1906.
105 G.P.(44537), W.E.G. to Trevelyan, 13 August 1869.
106 Ibid., W.E.G. to Lambert, 24 August 1869. Lambert, Secretary of the Poor Law Board, had assisted Gladstone with the Irish Church bill, and, earlier, the statistics of Parliamentary reform.
107 Ibid., W.E.G. to Denison, 12 August 1869.
108 D.N., 22 April 1869.
109 Ibid.
110 Ibid., 3 May 1869.
111 Ibid., 14 May 1869.
112 Ibid., 24 August 1869.
113 M.G., 31 August 1869.
114 *Spectator*, 24 April, 22 May, 31 July 1869.
115 *The Economist*, 31 July 1869.
116 S.R., 24 April, 8 May, 21 August 1869.
117 F.J., 23 August 1869.
118 P.M.G., 22 April, 3, 6, 18 May, 4 August 1869.
119 Ibid., 16, 18 August 1869.
120 Q.R., July 1869, 'The Truth about Ireland'; *Standard*, 22 April.
121 G.P.(44242), MacColl to W.E.G., 30 September 1869.
122 Sir B. Leighton, Bt (ed.), *Letters & Other Writings of the late Edward Denison, M.P. for Newark* (1872), pp. 153–4, Denison to an unnamed correspondent, 16 September 1869.

4: FIRST THOUGHTS AND REACTIONS IN THE CABINET, SEPTEMBER AND OCTOBER

1 Leighton, op. cit., pp. 153–4.
2 G.P.(44134), Clarendon to W.E.G., 4 September 1869.
3 Clarendon Papers (MS. Clar. Dep.c.498), W.E.G. to Clarendon, 7 September 1869.
4 The 7th Earl of Granard (1833–89) had become a Catholic that year.
5 G.P.(44134), Clarendon to W.E.G., 11 September 1869.
6 Clarendon Papers (MS. Clar. Dep.c.498), W.E.G. to Clarendon, 14 September 1869; Gerald Fitzgibbon, *The Land Difficulty of Ireland, with an Effort to Solve It* (1869).
7 Clarendon Papers (MS. Clar. Dep.c.498), W.E.G. to Clarendon, 15, 16 September 1869.
8 Ibid., W.E.G. to Clarendon, 22 September 1869.
9 G.P.(44134), Clarendon to W.E.G., 19, 21, 24 September 1869.
10 Ramm, I, p. 59, Granville to W.E.G., 23 September 1869.
11 G.P.(44347), Glyn to W.E.G., 22 September 1869.
12 Clarendon Papers (MS. Clar. Dep.c.498), W.E.G. to Clarendon, 24 September 1869.
13 Ibid. (MS. Clar. Dep.c.501), Clarendon to W.E.G., 12 September 1869; ibid. (MS. Clar. Dep.c.498), W.E.G. to Clarendon, 16 September 1869.
14 Ibid. (MS. Clar. Dep.c.498), W.E.G. to Clarendon, 25 September 1869.
15 Campbell, *The Irish Land*, p. 91.
16 Granville Papers (P.R.O. 30/29/55), Clarendon to Granville, 27 September 1869.
17 J. L. Hammond, *Gladstone and the Irish Nation*, new impression (1964), p. 94.
18 G.P.(44421), Gray to W.E.G., 31 August 1869.
19 Ibid. (44537), W.E.G. to Gray, 2 September 1869.
20 *The Times*, 11 September 1869; a fuller report of the speech than had appeared on the 9th.
21 G.P.(44537), W.E.G. to Gray, 24 September 1869.
22 *The Times*, 11 September 1869.
23 G.P.(44537), W.E.G. to Maguire, 13 September 1869.
24 Ibid. (44422), Maguire to W.E.G., 17 September 1869.
25 Ibid. (44422), W.E.G. to Maguire, 20 September 1869.
26 *The Times*, 4 September 1869.
27 Ibid., 6 September 1869.
28 P.M.G., 4 September 1869.
29 *Spectator*, 11 September 1869. Earl Grosvenor had been one of the leading Liberal rebels against their party's Reform bill of 1866.
30 D.N., 6 September 1869.
31 *The Times*, 27 September 1869.

32 D.N., 27 September 1869.

33 Ramm, I, p. 58, W.E.G. to Granville, 22 September 1869.

34 Cardwell Papers (P.R.O. 30/48/2/6), W.E.G. to Cardwell, 21 September 1869.

35 *The Times*, 29 September 1869.

36 Cardwell Papers (P.R.O. 30/48/2/6), Argyll to Cardwell, 15 October 1869.

37 Sir H. Maxwell, Bt, *The Life & Letters of George William Frederick Fourth Earl of Clarendon* (2 vols, 1913), II, p. 361, Clarendon to Lady Salisbury (widow of the 2nd Marquess), 1 October 1869.

38 *The Times*, 29 September 1869.

39 Clarendon Papers (MS. Clar. Dep.c.498), W.E.G. to Clarendon, 2 October 1869.

40 Ibid. (MS. Clar. Dep.c.500), Argyll to Clarendon, 2 October 1869.

41 Ibid. (MS. Clar. Dep.c.499), Kimberley to Clarendon, 1 October 1869.

42 G.P.(44134), Clarendon to W.E.G., 28 [29] September 1869.

43 Ramm, I, p. 61, Granville to W.E.G., 29 September 1869.

44 Ibid., W.E.G. to Granville, 4 October 1869.

45 Granville Papers (P.R.O. 30/29/55), Clarendon to Granville, 5 October 1869.

46 G.P.(44134), Clarendon to W.E.G., 5 October 1869.

47 Ramm, I, p. 59, Granville to W.E.G., 15 September 1869.

48 Clarendon Papers (MS. Clar. Dep.c.498), W.E.G. to Clarendon, 6 October 1869.

49 G.P.(44134), Clarendon to W.E.G., 8 October 1869.

50 Carlingford Papers (H324/CP1), W.E.G. to Fortescue, 29 September 1869.

51 Hughenden Papers (B/IX/A/1), Lambert's memorandum on the Irish question, 1 March 1868.

52 G.P.(44235), Lambert to W.E.G., 27 September 1869.

53 G.P.(44347), Glyn to W.E.G., 22 September 1869. There is a flattering description of Fortescue's wife and her place in contemporary Society by O. Wyndham Hewett, *Strawberry Fair: a Biography of Frances, Countess Waldegrave, 1821–1879* (1956).

54 G.P.(44347), Glyn to W.E.G., 22 September 1869.

55 Ibid. (44121), Fortescue's memorandum on Irish land, 13 September 1869. For the 'hotchpotch' of ratable valuation of agricultural land in Ireland, see the supplement 'Griffith's Valuation' to R. B. O'Brien, *The Irish Land Question and English Public Opinion* (Dublin, 1880), pp. 85–124, esp. p. 110.

56 G.P.(44661), W.E.G.'s memorandum on Irish land drafted on 9 September, with the second quotation added on the 17th. This document was misplaced when his papers were sorted and bound.

57 Ibid. (44121), W.E.G. to Fortescue, 15 September 1869.

58 Ibid. (44758), W.E.G.'s memorandum on Irish land, dated 15 & 17 September 1869.

59 Ibid. (44536), W.E.G. to Argyll, 14 January 1869.

60 Ibid. (44347), Glyn to W.E.G., 22 September 1869.

61 Ibid. (44537), W.E.G. to Glyn, 24 September 1869.

62 Ibid. (44121), W.E.G. to Fortescue, 27 September 1869.

63 Ibid., Fortescue to W.E.G., 28 September 1869; Mr Justice Keogh had been, briefly, a leader of the old Tenant League's Parliamentary group.

64 Carlingford Papers (G.255/WW27), Gregory to Frances, Countess Waldegrave, 17 September [1869].

65 Ramm, I, p. 61, Granville to W.E.G., 29 September 1869.

66 G.P.(44121), W.E.G. to Fortescue, 1 October 1869.

67 Ibid., W.E.G. to Fortescue, 1 October 1869.

68 Spencer Papers, W.E.G. to Spencer, 21 September 1869.

69 Ibid.

70 *Spectator*, 18 September 1869.

71 Delane Correspondence (vol. 24), Walter to Delane, 23 August 1869.

72 *The Times*, 13 August 1869.

73 W. O'Connor Morris, *Letters on the Land Question of Ireland* (1870), p. 9.

74 *The Times*, 6 September 1869.

75 *Spectator*, 18 September 1869.

76 Clarendon Papers (MS. Clar. Dep.c.498), W.E.G. to Clarendon, 22 September 1869.

77 *The Times*, 14 September 1869.

78 Ibid., 24 September 1869.

79 Ibid., 30 September 1869.

80 Hughenden Papers (B/XX/S/851), Stanley to Disraeli, 16 September 1869.

81 *The Times*, 1 September 1869.

82 G.P.(44347), Glyn to W.E.G., 1 September 1869.

83 *The Times*, 6 September 1869.

84 Ibid., 13 September 1869.

85 Ibid., 27 September 1869.

86 Delane Correspondence (vol. 18), Delane to Dasent, 29 September 1869.

87 *The Times*, 30 September 1869.

88 D.N., 25 September 1869.

89 Ibid., 29 September, 1 October 1869.

90 M.G., 4, 14 September 1869. Trench, agent to Lord Lansdowne, had published his vivid account of the difficulties and dangers of Irish estate management in 1868.

91 Ibid., 20 September 1869.

92 Ibid., 22 September 1869.

93 Ibid., 30 September 1869.

94 *Spectator*, 25 September 1869.

95 G.P.(44121), W.E.G. to Fortescue, 1 October 1869.

96 Hickleton Papers (A4/88, Pt I), W.E.G. to Halifax, 1 October 1869.

97 Grey Papers, Halifax to Grey, 30 September 1869.

98 Hickleton Papers (A4/88, Pt I), W.E.G. to Halifax, 1 October 1869.

99 Grey Papers, Halifax to Grey, 5 October 1869.

1 Ramm, I, pp. 53–4, W.E.G. to Granville, 8 September 1869 and two letters dated the 14th.

2 Ibid., p. 58, W.E.G. to Granville, 22 September 1869.

3 Ibid., p. 59, Granville to W.E.G., 25 September 1869.

4 Ibid., p. 60, W.E.G. to Granville, 27 September 1869.

5 Ibid., p. 64, W.E.G. to Granville, 5 October 1869.

6 Lady Burghclere (ed.), *A Great Lady's Friendships: Letters to Mary, Marchioness of Salisbury, Countess of Derby, 1862–1890* (1933), pp. 231–2, Lowe to Lady Salisbury, 27 September 1869.

7 G.P.(44301), Lowe to W.E.G., 11 October 1869.

8 Ibid., Irish Land Question. Mem[orandum] by the Chancellor of the Exchequer, 29 September 1869.

9 Ramm, I, p. 65, Granville to W.E.G., 6 October 1869; Cardwell Papers (P.R.O. 30/48/5/28), Granville to Cardwell, 9 October 1869; Lord Edmond Fitzmaurice, *The Life of Lord Granville 1815–1891*, 3rd edn (2 vols, 1905), II, p. 293, Granville to Spencer, 6 October 1869.

10 Ramm, I, p. 66, W.E.G. to Granville, 8 October 1869.

11 Cardwell Papers (P.R.O. 30/48/5/22), Lowe to Cardwell, 13 October 1869.

12 Ibid., Lowe to Cardwell, 18 October 1869.

13 G.P.(44301), W.E.G. to Lowe, 12 October 1869.

14 Ibid., Lowe to W.E.G., 18 October 1869.

15 Ramm, I, p. 61, Granville to W.E.G., 29 September 1869.

16 Ibid., p. 65, Granville to W.E.G., 7 October 1869.

17 A. I. Dasent, *John Delane 1817–1879* (2 vols, 1908), II, p. 244.

18 G.P.(44611), Kimberley to Lowe, 3 October 1869; printed with Lowe's memorandum of 29 September on the Irish Land Question for circulation to the cabinet.

19 Ibid. (44301), Lowe to W.E.G., 18 October 1869.

20 Ibid. (44224), Kimberley to W.E.G., 29 October 1869.

21 Ibid., Kimberley's memorandum, undated, on Irish land accompanying his letter of 29 October 1869.

22 Dufferin Papers (D.1071 H/B/F.148), O'Hagan to Dufferin, 19 October 1869.

23 Ibid., Blennerhassett to Dufferin, 18 October 1869.

24 Ibid., O'Hagan to Dufferin, 19 October 1869.

25 Granville Papers (P.R.O. 30/29/64), Halifax to Granville, 24 October 1869.

26 Q.R., October 1869; quotations from pp. 540, 550, 552, 556–7, 566.

27 M.G., 27 October 1869.

28 Hughenden Papers (B/XX/S/851), Stanley to Disraeli, 16 September 1869.

29 S.R., 30 October 1869.

30 Cairns Papers (P.R.O. 30/51/9), Gathorne Hardy to Cairns, 2 October 1869.

31 *Q.R.*, October 1869, p. 544.

32 Ramm, I, p. 62, W.E.G. to Granville, 1 October 1869; Col. John Wilson-Patten was briefly chief secretary for Ireland in 1868.

33 S.R., 30 October 1869.

34 *The Times*, 15 September 1869.

35 D.N., 25 September 1869.

36 *The Times*, 24 September 1869.

37 Ibid., 5 April 1869.

38 Ibid., 13 August 1869.

39 Grey Papers, Halifax to Grey, 30 September 1869.

40 D.N., 4 October 1869.

41 Ibid., 2 October 1869.

42 Ibid., 4 October 1869.

43 *The Times*, 28 October 1869.

44 Ibid., 29 October 1869.

45 *The Times*, 9 October 1869.

46 Delane Correspondence (vol. 18), W.E.G. to Delane, 6 October 1869.

47 Ibid., Walter to Delane, 7 October 1869.

48 *The Times*, 9 October 1869.

49 Ibid., 14 October 1869.

50 Ibid., 20 October 1869.

51 Delane Correspondence (vol. 18), Delane to G. W. Dasent, 21 October 1869.

52 *The Times*, 27 October 1869.

53 Ibid., 30 October 1869.

54 Ibid., 4 October 1869.

55 Ibid., 9 October 1869.

56 Ibid., 15, 23 October 1869.

57 D.N., 29 September 1869.

58 Ibid., 14 October 1869.

59 Ibid., 20 October 1869.

60 Ibid., 21 October 1869.

61 Ibid., 28 October 1869.

62 M.G., 19 October 1869.

63 Ibid., 4 October 1869.

64 Ibid., 11 October 1869.

65 Ibid., 19, 27 October 1869.

66 *The Economist*, 9 October 1869.

67 Ibid., 23 October 1869.

68 *Spectator*, 2 October 1869.

69 Ibid., 9 October 1869.

70 Ibid., 30 October 1869.

71 S.R., 2 October 1869.

72 Ibid., 23 October 1869.

73 Ibid., 30 October 1869.

74 F.J., 13 October 1869.

75 P.M.G., 11 October 1869.

76 Ibid., 14 October 1869.

77 Ibid., 20 October 1869.

78 G.P.(44758), Irish Land: Memorandum No. I, by W.E.G., 9 October 1869.

79 Ibid., W.E.G.'s memoranda of 6 October and No. II of 9 October 1869.

80 Ibid. (44422), W.E.G. to Sullivan, 9 October; Sullivan to W.E.G., 12 October 1869.

81 Ibid. (44121), Fortescue to W.E.G., 28 September 1869.

82 Ibid. (44422), Sullivan to W.E.G., 12 October 1869.

83 Ibid. (44121), Fortescue to W.E.G., 12 October 1869.

84 Ibid. (44422), Maguire to W.E.G., 7 October 1869.

85 Ibid. (44537), W.E.G. to Fortescue, 9 October 1869.

86 Ibid. (44122), Fortescue's comments, undated, on W.E.G.'s Memorandum No. I of 9 October 1869. This document was misplaced when the papers were arranged.

87 Ibid. (44537), W.E.G. to J. E. Denison, 18 October 1869.

88 Ibid., W.E.G. to Fortescue, 9 October 1869.

89 Ibid. (44121), W.E.G. to Fortescue, 18 October 1869.

90 Carlingford Papers (H324/CP1), W.E.G. to Fortescue, 16 October 1869.

91 G.P.(44118), Bright to W.E.G., 15 October 1869.

92 Ibid. (44121), Fortescue to W.E.G., 18 October 1869.

93 Ramm, I, p. 68, W.E.G. to Granville, 18 October 1869.

94 Ibid., p. 69, W.E.G. to Granville, 20 October 1869.

95 G.P.(44121), W.E.G. to Fortescue, 19 October 1869.

96 Ibid., W.E.G. to Fortescue, 20 October 1869.

97 Ibid. (44537), W.E.G. to Fortescue, 21 October 1869.

98 Ibid., W.E.G. to Fortescue, 24 October 1869.

99 Ibid., W.E.G. to Fortescue, 27 October 1869.

100 Carlingford Papers (H322/CP3), Sullivan to Fortescue, 28 October 1869.

101 Ibid. (H336/C1), Frances, Countess Waldegrave to Fortescue, 30 October 1869.

102 *Kimberley Journal*, p. 9; entry for 31 October, describing the cabinet which in fact took place on the 30th.

103 G.P.(44134), Clarendon to W.E.G., 12 October 1869.

104 Clarendon Papers (MS. Clar. Dep.c.498), W.E.G. to Clarendon, 23 October 1869.

105 Ibid. (MS. Clar. Dep.c.499), Bright to Clarendon, 14 October 1869.

106 Ramm, I, p. 72, Granville to Gladstone, 1 November 1869.

107 *Kimberley Journal*, p. 9.

108 G.P.(44611), Fortescue's Suggestions for Legislation on Tenant Right &c, 2 November 1869.

109 Carlingford Papers (H324/CP1), Maguire to W.E.G., 2 August 1869.

110 Spencer Papers, W.E.G. to Spencer, 26 September 1869.

111 G.P.(44422), Earl of Limerick to W.E.G., 27 October 1869.

112 *The Times*, 18 October 1869.

113 F.J., 30 October 1869.

114 *The Times*, 13 October 1869.

115 Ibid., 18 October 1869. The paper's regular correspondent in Dublin is not to be confused with O'Connor Morris, its special correspondent.

116 P.P. 1881, LXXVII Return of Outrages...reported to the Constabulary Office, 1844–80, p. 901.

117 *The Times*, 20 and 13 October 1869.

118 Dufferin Papers (D.1071 H/B/F.148), Bruce to Dufferin, 4 October 1869.

119 F.J., 27 October 1869.

120 Ibid., 28, 29 October 1869.

121 M.G., 2 September 1869.

122 Ibid., 19 October 1869.

123 G.P.(44422), Bazley's paper, dated September 1869.

124 Ibid. (44537), W.E.G. to Bessborough, 30 October 1869.

6: THE CABINET DEBATE, OCTOBER TO DECEMBER

1 The quotation is taken from one of W.E.G.'s inquiries in his questionnaire about Irish land, 3 December 1869, G.P.(44235).

2 Hughenden Papers (B/XX/Co/51), M. Corry to Disraeli, 22 December 1869.

3 Carlingford Papers (H324/CP1), Bruce to Fortescue, 31 October 1869.

4 Morley, *Life of Gladstone*, I, p. 923.

5 Spencer Papers, Fortescue to Spencer, 31 October 1869.

6 Carlingford Papers (H336/C1), Frances, Countess Waldegrave to Fortescue, 31 October 1869.

7 Morley, op. cit., I, p. 923.

8 Spencer Papers, Fortescue to Spencer, 3 November 1869.

9 G.P.(44637), minutes of the cabinet of 3 November.

10 Ibid. (44758), memorandum on Irish Land Tenures as far as regards Tenancies at Will, 3 November 1869.

11 Granville Papers (P.R.O. 30/29/66), Granville to Lowe, 23 December 1869.

12 G.P.(44758), W.E.G.'s memorandum on Irish land of 11 December 1869.

13 Granville Papers (P.R.O. 30/29/51), Granville to Argyll, 4 December 1869; Argyll to Granville, 12 November 1869.

14 G.P.(44637), minutes of the cabinet of 10 November.

15 G.P.(44611), memorandum on Irish land by the Duke of Argyll; printed on 6 November 1869.

16 James Caird, *The Irish Land Question* (1869); see below, Chapter 7, pp. 256–8.

17 G.P.(44611), memorandum on Irish land by Lord Dufferin; printed on 2 November 1869.

18 Granville Papers (P.R.O. 30/29/51), Argyll to Granville, 12 November 1869.

19 G.P.(44101), Argyll to W.E.G., 22 November 1869; ibid. (44537), W.E.G. to Argyll, 23 November 1869.

20 Ibid. (44101), Argyll to W.E.G., 26 November 1869.

21 Ibid., W.E.G. to Argyll, 27 November 1869.

22 Ibid., Argyll to W.E.G., 27 November 1869.

23 Ibid. (44538), W.E.G. to Argyll, 29 November 1869. For his reply to Sir John Gray, see below, Chapter 7, p. 276.

24 Granville Papers (P.R.O. 30/29/51), Argyll to Granville, 1 December 1869.

25 G.P.(44101), Argyll to Gladstone, 29, 30 November 1869.

26 Ibid. (44538), W.E.G. to Argyll, 9 December 1869.

27 Ibid. (44101), Argyll to W.E.G., 10 December 1869.

28 Ibid., Argyll to W.E.G., 2 December 1869.

29 Ibid., Argyll to W.E.G., 30 November, 6 December 1869.

30 Ibid., Argyll to W.E.G., 2 December 1869.

31 Ibid., W.E.G. to Argyll, 4 December 1869.

32 Peter Maclagan, M.P., *Land Culture and Land Tenure in Ireland* (Edinburgh & London, 1869).

33 G.P.(44101), Argyll to W.E.G., 6 December 1869.

34 Ibid., Argyll to W.E.G., 10 December 1869.

35 Ramm, I, p. 76, W.E.G. to Granville, 1 December 1869.

36 G.P.(44101), Argyll to W.E.G., 9 December 1869.

37 Ramm, I, p. 78, W.E.G. to Granville, 11 December 1869.

38 Granville Papers (P.R.O. 30/29/51), Granville to Argyll, 4 December 1869.

39 (44611), memorandum on Irish land by Lord Kimberley, 8 November 1869.

40 Ibid. (44122), W.E.G. to Fortescue, 22 November 1869.

41 Granville Papers (P.R.O. 30/29/25), memorandum on Tenure of Land in Ireland, by Lord Hatherley, n.d. but November 1869.

42 Dufferin Papers (D.1071 H/B/F.148), Argyll to Dufferin, 29 November 1869.

43 Ramm, I, p. 78, Granville to W.E.G., 7 December 1869.

44 G.P.(44101), Argyll to W.E.G., 22 November 1869.

45 Ibid. (44537), W.E.G. to Argyll, 23 November 1869.

46 Ripon Papers (43513), W.E.G. to de Grey, 29 November 1869. De Grey is better known as the first Marquess of Ripon, as he became in 1871; he was viceroy of India 1880–4 and sat in Liberal cabinets until 1908.

47 G.P.(44122), W.E.G. to Fortescue, 2 December 1869.

48 Ibid. (44611), memorandum on Irish land by Lord de Grey, 29 November 1869.

49 Carlingford Papers (H324/CP1), de Grey to Fortescue, 13 December 1869.

50 G.P.(44112), Bright to W.E.G., 29 November 1869.

51 Ibid., Bright to W.E.G., 3 December 1869.

52 Ibid.

53 Cobden Papers, West Sussex Record Office, memorandum on Irish Land Question by John Bright, 1 December 1869.

54 G.P.(44112), W.E.G. to Bright, 4 December 1869.

55 Ripon Papers (43522), Kimberley to de Grey, 7 December 1869.

56 Ramm, I, pp. 73–4, Granville to W.E.G. 21 November 1869.

57 Carlingford Papers (H324/CP1), W.E.G. to Fortescue, 5 December 1869.

58 Ramm, I, pp. 27–8, W.E.G. to Granville, 15 June 1869.

59 G.P.(44134), Clarendon to W.E.G., 8 November 1869.

60 Clarendon Papers (MS. Clar. Dep.c.555), memorandum on Irish land by the Duke of Argyll, printed on 6 November 1869, with attached sheet of MS. comments by Lord Clarendon.

61 G.P.(44134), W.E.G. to Clarendon, 10 November 1869.

62 Spencer Papers, Clarendon to Spencer, 26 November 1869.

63 Granville Papers (P.R.O. 30/29/55), Clarendon to Granville, 30 November 1869.

64 Ibid., Granville to Clarendon, 1 December 1869.

65 Ramm, I, p. 77, Granville to W.E.G., 1 December 1869.

66 Spencer Papers, Clarendon to Spencer, 26 November 1869.

67 Granville Papers (P.R.O. 30/29/55), Clarendon to Granville, 26 November 1869.

68 Ibid., Clarendon to Granville, 30 November 1869.
69 Ibid., Clarendon to Granville, 24 November 1869; Ramm, I, p. 73, Granville to W.E.G., 21 November 1869.
70 Granville Papers (P.R.O. 30/29/55), Clarendon to Granville, 3 December 1869.
71 G.P.(44612), memorandum on Irish land by Lord Clarendon; printed on 11 December 1869.
72 Ibid. (44134), Clarendon to W.E.G., 11 December 1869.
73 Spencer Papers, W.E.G. to Spencer, 6 November 1869.
74 G.P.(44306), Spencer to W.E.G., 5 November 1869.
75 Carlingford Papers (H324/CP1), Spencer to Fortescue, 2 November 1869.
76 G.P.(44306), Spencer to Gladstone, 5 November 1869.
77 Spencer Papers, Spencer to W.E.G., 18 November 1869.
78 G.P.(44612), memorandum on Irish land by Lord Spencer, 7 December 1869.
79 Ibid. (44101), Argyll to W.E.G., 27 November 1869; Dufferin Papers (D.1071 H/B/F.1) Spencer to Dufferin, 9 December 1869.
80 Ibid.
81 G.P.(44612), memorandum on Irish land by Lord Spencer, 7 December 1869.
82 Ramm, I, p. 77, W.E.G. to Granville, 2 December 1869.
83 Ibid.
84 Grey Papers, Halifax to Grey, 5 November 1869.
85 G.P.(44184), memorandum on Irish land by Lord Halifax, 27 November 1869.
86 Ibid., Halifax to W.E.G., 1 December 1869. In this correspondence the references to Campbell are to his new pamphlet of October – for which see below, Chapter 7, pp. 256–7 – as well as to the original publication.
87 Ibid., Halifax's memorandum with his letter of 1 December.
88 G.P.(44184), W.E.G. to Halifax, 2 December 1869.
89 Ibid., Halifax to W.E.G., 7 December 1869.
90 Ibid., W.E.G. to Halifax, 8 December 1869.
91 Ibid., Halifax to W.E.G., 7 December 1869.
92 Ibid., W.E.G. to Halifax, 2 December 1869.
93 Ibid., Halifax to W.E.G., 7 December 1869.
94 Granville Papers (P.R.O. 30/29/66), Lowe to Granville, 21 December 1869.
95 G.P.(44101), Argyll to W.E.G., 10 October 1869.
96 Ibid. (44151), Dufferin to W.E.G., 16 October 1869; Carlingford Papers (H324/CP1), W.E.G. to Fortescue, 3 November 1869.
97 G.P.(44611), memorandum on Irish land by Lord Dufferin; printed on 2 November 1869.
98 Ibid. (44122), Fortescue to W.E.G., 3 November 1869.

99   Ibid. (44537), W.E.G. to Dufferin, 3 November 1869.

100 Ibid. (44151), Dufferin to W.E.G., 12 November 1869.

101 Ibid. (44611), Dufferin's 'Memorandum on the "Expectancy" Claim of a Tenant-at-Will as distinguished from his Claim on account of "Improvements" or under "Custom"'. Printed on 11 November 1869.

102 Ibid. (44122), Fortescue to W.E.G., 3 November 1869.

103 Dufferin Papers (D.1071 H/B/F.149), Fortescue to Dufferin, 14 November 1869.

104 Carlingford Papers (H324/CP1), Dufferin to Fortescue, 22 November 1869.

105 Dufferin Papers (D.1071 H/B/F.149), Fortescue to Dufferin, 3 December 1869.

106 G.P.(44151), Dufferin to W.E.G., 12 November 1869.

107 Ibid. (44537), W.E.G. to Dufferin, 13 November 1869.

108 Dufferin Papers (D.1071 H/B/F.149), W.E.G. to Dufferin, 7 December 1869.

109 G.P.(44151), printed 'Draft Sketch of a new Landlord and Tenant Act'; enclosure with Dufferin to Gladstone, 13 December 1869.

110 G.P.(44423), W.E.G. to Monck, 24 November 1869.

111 Ibid., W.E.G. to Monck, 30 November 1869.

112 Ramm, I, p. 73, Granville to W.E.G., 21 November 1869.

113 G.P.(44538), W.E.G. to Argyll, 9 December 1869.

114 MSS. of the Duke of Devonshire, diary of the 7th Duke of Devonshire, entry for 8 December 1869.

115 G.P.(44758), W.E.G.'s parenthetic comment in his memorandum on Irish land of 7 December 1869; ibid. (44612), extracts from Bessborough to Spencer, 9, 25 November 1869.

116 Morley, op. cit., I, pp. 917–18; J. L. Hammond, *Gladstone & the Irish Nation*, new impression (London, 1964), pp. 97–8.

117 Dufferin Papers (D.1071 H/B/F.149), Fortescue to Dufferin, 3 December 1869.

118 Carlingford Papers (H324/CP1), W.E.G. to Fortescue, 3 November 1869.

119 G.P.(44122), Fortescue to W.E.G., 22 November 1869.

120 Ibid., W.E.G. to Fortescue, 22 November 1869.

121 Ibid., W.E.G. to Fortescue, 30 November 1869.

122 P.P. 1870, XIV, Reports from Poor Law Inspectors in Ireland as to the existing Relations between Landlord & Tenant; pp. 39–41.

123 G.P.(44235), questionnaire about Irish land, 3 December 1869. These inquiries, or a version that was largely the same, had first gone out in the middle of November to Lord Spencer.

124 Ibid. (44612), extract from Bessborough to Spencer, 25 November 1869.

125 Ibid., extract from Bessborough to Spencer, 3 December 1869.
126 Ibid., Brassington's answers, 6 December 1869, to W.E.G.'s questionnaire about Irish land.
127 Ibid. (44122), Fortescue's answers, 17 November 1869, to W.E.G.'s questionnaire.
128 Ibid., Fortescue to W.E.G., 22 November 1869.
129 Ibid., W.E.G. to Fortescue, 24 November 1869.
130 Ibid., Fortescue to W.E.G., 25 November 1869.
131 Ibid., W.E.G. to Fortescue, 26 November; Fortescue to W.E.G., 30 November 1869.
132 Ibid., W.E.G. to Fortescue, 30 November 1869.
133 Ibid., W.E.G. to Fortescue, 2 December 1869.
134 Ibid., W.E.G. to Fortescue, 3 December 1869.
135 Ibid., W.E.G.'s first memorandum of 3 December on Irish land.
136 Ibid. (44758), W.E.G.'s memorandum on Irish land, 26 November 1869.
137 Ibid., W.E.G.'s second memorandum of 3 December on Irish land.
138 Ibid. (44122), W.E.G. to Fortescue, 3 December 1869.
139 Ibid., W.E.G. to Fortescue, 30 November 1869.
140 Ibid. (44122 and 44758), W.E.G.'s first and second memoranda of 3 December 1869.
141 Ibid. (44423), W.E.G. to Monck, 30 November 1869.
142 Ibid. (44122), W.E.G. to Fortescue, 7 December 1869.
143 Ibid., Fortescue to W.E.G., 4 December 1869.
144 Carlingford Papers (H324/CP1), W.E.G. to Fortescue, 5 December 1869.
145 Gladstone warned him, gratuitously, against reviving it: 'I do not think the cabinet will on any terms...meddle with rents now paid', ibid., W.E.G. to Fortescue, 8 December 1869.
146 G.P.(44122), Fortescue to W.E.G., 6 December 1869.
147 Ibid., W.E.G. to Fortescue, 7 December 1869.
148 Carlingford Papers (H324/CP1), W.E.G. to Fortescue, 8 December 1869.
149 G.P.(44122), Fortescue's comments, 8 December, on W.E.G.'s memorandum of 7 December.
150 Carlingford Papers (H324/CP1), W.E.G. to Fortescue, 9 December 1869.
151 Ibid., W.E.G. to Fortescue, 8 December 1869.
152 Ibid.
153 G.P.(44758), memorandum, 10 December, of amendments to the plan of 3 December 1869.
154 Carlingford Papers (H324/CP1), W.E.G. to Fortescue, 8 December 1869.
155 G.P.(44758), W.E.G.'s memorandum on Irish land of 11 December 1869.

156 Ibid. (44122), Fortescue's memorandum of 9 December; MS. and printed versions vary slightly. It was probably not circulated to the cabinet and another followed on 13 December, which was printed and circulated, filling out the proposals with argument tactfully and rather obscurely expressed; ibid. (44612).

157 Ramm, I, p. 78, W.E.G. to Granville, 13 December 1869. Sullivan also came over, as the prime minister wished.

158 G.P.(44758), W.E.G.'s memorandum of 'Propositions submitted Dec. 14 1869'.

159 G.P.(44758), W.E.G.'s memorandum on Irish land of 11 December 1869.

160 Granville Papers (P.R.O. 30/29/66), Lowe to Granville, 21 December 1869.

7: OUTSIDE THE CABINET, OCTOBER TO DECEMBER

1 G.P.(44306), Spencer to W.E.G., 29 September 1869.

2 Ibid. (44537), W.E.G. to Bright, 1 September 1869; ibid. (44538), W.E.G. to Argyll, 29 November 1869.

3 Campbell, *Memoirs of my Indian Career*, II, p. 191.

4 George Campbell, *The Irish Land*, p. iv.

5 Ibid., quotations from pp. 184–5, 167, 153. For 'the Punjab school' – John Lawrence's men – see R. B. Smith, *The Life of Lord Lawrence* (2 vols, 1883), I, chs. XI to XIII, and II, p. 282.

6 Peter Maclagan, M.P., *Land Culture & Land Tenure in Ireland* (Edinburgh and London, 1869), quotations from pp. 52, 31.

7 James Caird, *The Irish Land Question* (1869); the comparison of Irish and British rentals is on p. 15.

8 Maclagan, op. cit., p. 77.

9 Delane Correspondence (vol. 18), O'Connor Morris to Delane, 3, 6 November 1869.

10 *The Times*, 5 November 1869.

11 Ibid., 22 November 1869.

12 Ibid., 17 November 1869.

13 Delane Correspondence (vol. 18), Delane to G. W. Dasent, 6 December 1869.

14 Ibid. (add. vol. (i)), Walter to Delane, 7 November 1869.

15 Ibid. (vol. 18), O'Connor Morris to Delane, 11 November 1869.

16 Ibid., O'Connor Morris to Delane, 23 November 1869 [2 letters].

17 D.N., 9, 4 December 1869.

18 M.G., 24, 30 November 1869.

19 *Spectator*, 6 November 1869.

20 S.R., 27 November 1869.

21 P.M.G., 18 November 1869.

22 Ibid., 6 December 1869.

23 Stephen Papers, Cambridge University Library (Add. MS. 7439/ Box 2), Stephen to his wife, 13 November 1869.

24 *The Economist*, 6 November 1869.

25 Ibid., 11 December 1869.

26 *Spectator*, 25 December 1869.

27 *The Times*, 20 November 1869.

28 M.G., 20 November 1869.

29 *The Times*, 7 December 1869.

30 Ibid., 15 November 1869.

31 Ibid., 12 November 1869.

32 Ibid., 15 November 1869.

33 Ibid.

34 D.N., 16 November 1869.

35 Grey Papers, William Tighe Hamilton (an Irish Whig lawyer) to Grey, 12 November 1869.

36 *The Times*, 6 December 1869.

37 See R. Harrison, *Before the Socialists* (1965), ch. V; H. Collins & C. Abramsky, *Karl Marx and the British Labour Movement* (1965), pp. 161–70.

38 D.N., 18 November 1869.

39 Ibid., 28 December 1869.

40 *Standard*, 16 November 1869.

41 Hughenden Papers (B/XX/M/158), Manners to Disraeli, 17 December 1869.

42 Ibid. (B/XX/B/35), Ball to Disraeli, 5 December 1869.

43 Ibid. (B/XX/S/853), Derby to Disraeli, 23 November 1869.

44 *The Times*, 29 November 1869.

45 Ibid., 15 November 1869.

46 S.R., 18 November 1869.

47 *Standard*, 6 December 1869.

48 F.J., 29 November 1869.

49 Ibid., 2 November 1869.

50 *The Times*, 26 November 1869.

51 *Kimberley Journal*, p. 10; entry for 14 December 1869.

52 M.G., 29 November 1869.

53 Ibid., 27 September 1869.

54 G.P. (B.M. Reserved MSS. 25/6), W.E.G. to the Queen, 7 December 1869.

55 Ibid., the Queen to W.E.G., 13 December 1869.

56 Rose Papers (42826), Strathnairn to the Duke of Wellington, 12 November 1869.

57 Ibid., Strathnairn to Cambridge, 3 December 1869.

58 P.P. 1881, LXXVII, p. 901.

59 G.P.(44122), Fortescue to W.E.G., 30 November 1869.

60 Rose Papers (42826), Strathnairn to Cambridge, 3 December 1869.

61 Ibid., Strathnairn to Cambridge, 29 November 1869.
62 Ibid. (42828), Strathnairn to the Duchess of Abercorn, 29 November 1869.
63 Clarendon Papers (MS. Clar. Dep.c.558), the Countess of Dartrey to Clarendon, 27 November 1869.
64 Ibid., Lady Dartrey to Clarendon, 13 November 1869.
65 Ibid., Lady Dartrey to Clarendon, 14 November 1869.
66 Ibid., Lady Dartrey to Clarendon, 13 November 1869.
67 Ibid., Lady Dartrey to Clarendon, 27 November 1869.
68 Ibid., first memorandum on Irish land by Lady Dartrey, n.d. but November 1869.
69 Ibid., second memorandum on Irish land by Lady Dartrey, n.d. but November 1869.
70 Carlingford Papers (H338/C3), Clermont to Fortescue, 9 November 1869.
71 Dufferin Papers (D.1071 H/B/F.149), de Ros to Dufferin, 27 November 1869.
72 Selborne Papers, Lambeth Palace Library (MS. 1863), C. S. Roundell to Sir R. Palmer, 21 November 1869.
73 *The Times*, 2, 20 November 1869; Bernal Osborne was an Englishman, of Jewish origin, whose wife brought him a large estate in Tipperary and Waterford.
74 F.J., 15 November 1869.
75 G.P.(44423), W.E.G. to Sir John Gray, 28 November 1869.

8: THE LAST STAGES IN THE CABINET
AND THE MOOD OF TWO COUNTRIES

1 The bill as introduced is printed in P.P. 1870, II, pp. 259–94.
2 Lord Thring (Henry Thring), *Practical Legislation* (1902), p. 5.
3 H. Shearman, 'State-aided Land Purchase under the Disestablishment Act of 1869', *Irish Historical Studies* (1944–5), p. 61.
4 Hansard (3rd ser.), CXCIX, col. 361 (15 February 1870).
5 Ripon Papers (43539), Helps to Ripon, 24 December 1869.
6 *Kimberley Journal*, p. 10; entry for 14 December 1869.
7 D.N., 19 January 1870.
8 *The Times*, 12 January 1870.
9 G.P.(44122), W.E.G. to Fortescue, 12 January 1870.
10 Ibid., Fortescue to W.E.G., 16 December 1869.
11 Carlingford Papers (H324/CP1), W.E.G. to Fortescue, 17 December 1869.
12 G.P.(44637), minutes of the cabinet of 17 December; ibid. (44612), printed memorandum of 18 December for Henry Thring, the parliamentary draughtsman, incorporating W.E.G.'s short memorandum

headed 'General Propositions adopted 14 Dec. 69', which with the manuscript of the rest of the printed memorandum is in B.M. Add. MSS. 44758. An error in the printed version gives 1 December as the date on which the 'General Propositions' were adopted.

13 Ibid. (44122), W.E.G. to Fortescue, 10 and 12 January; Fortescue to W.E.G., 13 January 1870.

14 Carlingford Papers (H338/C3), Fortescue to Lord Clermont, 18 February 1870.

15 G.P.(44538), W.E.G. to Argyll, 20 December 1869.

16 Ibid. (44122), Fortescue to W.E.G., 7 January 1870, quoting Lowe's words.

17 Granville Papers (P.R.O. 30/29/66), Lowe to Granville, 21 December 1869.

18 Ramm, I, pp. 81-4, W.E.G. to Granville, 27 December 1869. This long letter was written for communication to Lowe, at Granville's suggestion; ibid., p. 80, Granville to W.E.G., 23 December. Argyll received a copy from the prime minister; G.P.(44538), W.E.G. to Argyll, 31 December. The Duke's remarks come from his reply on 4 January; ibid. (44101).

19 Ramm, I, pp. 81-4, W.E.G. to Granville, 27 December 1869; G.P.(44101), Argyll to W.E.G., 29 December, enclosing his detailed comments on the memorandum of 18 December from which Thring was working; Cardwell Papers (P.R.O. 30/48/6/34), Argyll to Cardwell, 29 December.

20 Granville Papers (P.R.O. 30/29/29A), memorandum by the Duke of Argyll, 7 January 1870, W.E.G. for (P.R.O. 30/29/66); ibid. Lowe to Granville, 21 December 1869; G.P.(44101), Argyll to W.E.G., 4 January 1870; ibid. (44538), W.E.G. to Argyll, 5 January; ibid. (44101), Argyll to W.E.G., 7 January; ibid., W.E.G. to Argyll, 8 January; Argyll to W.E.G., 13 January.

21 Ibid., Argyll to W.E.G., 7 January 1870; G.P.(44538), W.E.G. to Argyll, 5 January; Granville Papers (P.R.O. 30/29/66), Granville to Lowe, 23 December 1869; Ramm, I, pp. 81-4, W.E.G. to Granville, 27 December; Spencer Papers, Fortescue to Spencer, 17 December; Cardwell Papers (P.R.O. 30/48/5/22), Lowe to Cardwell, 24, 29 December.

22 G.P.(44101), Argyll to W.E.G., 4 January 1870; Granville Papers (P.R.O. 30/29/66), Granville to Lowe, 23 December 1869; Cardwell Papers (P.R.O. 30/48/6/34), Argyll to Cardwell, 29 December; Ramm, I, pp. 81-4, W.E.G. to Granville, 27 December; Cardwell Papers (P.R.O. 30/48/5/22), Lowe to Cardwell, 5 January 1870.

23 Morley, op. cit., I, p. 927; quoting the entry for 25 January 1870.

24 *Kimberley Journal*, p. 11; entry for 15 February 1870.

25 Ramm, I, p. 87, W.E.G. to Granville, 16 January 1870; Royal Archives (D/27/7), General Grey to the Queen, January 1870.

26 Granville Papers (P.R.O. 30/29/66), Lowe to Granville, 21 December 1869.

27 G.P.(44538), W.E.G. to Bright, 29 December 1869.

28 Ibid. (44112), Bright to W.E.G., 1 January 1870.

29 *The Economist*, 22 January 1870.

30 M.G., 1 January 1870.

31 P.M.G., 28 January 1870.

32 *Standard*, 31 January 1870.

33 Q.R., January 1870, 'The Irish Cauldron'; quotations from pp. 282, 299.

34 G.P.(44341), Algernon West, the prime minister's private secretary, to W.E.G., 17 November 1869; ibid. (44424), Reeve to W.E.G., 8 January 1870; Hughenden Papers (B/XXI/N/5), Napier to Disraeli, 15 February 1870.

35 Ibid.

36 *Edinburgh Review*, January 1870; quotations from pp. 299–301, 303.

37 O'Connor Morris, *Letters on the Land Question*, quotations from pp. 336–7, 340, 326–7.

38 *The Times*, 15 February 1870.

39 S.R., 1 January 1870.

40 *The Times*, 7 February 1870.

41 G.P.(44185), Halifax to W.E.G., 11 February 1870.

42 Ibid. (44224), Kimberley to W.E.G., 17 December 1869.

43 *Kimberley Journal*, pp. 10–11; entry for 5 February 1870.

44 G.P.(44112) Bright to W.E.G., 1 January 1870.

45 F.J., 2 February 1870.

46 *The Times*, 12 January 1870.

47 *Spectator*, 15 January 1870.

48 D.N., 18 January 1870.

49 Ibid., 19 January 1870.

50 G.P.(44538), W.E.G. to Bright, 13 January 1870.

51 Ibid. (44134), Clarendon to W.E.G., 27 December 1869.

52 F.J., 31 December 1869.

53 *The Times*, 6 January 1870.

54 *The Times*, 5 February; F.J., 7 February 1870.

55 Moore Papers (National Library of Ireland, 895).

56 Ibid., Moore to Fr Lavelle, 4 February; Fr Lavelle to Moore, 20 February 1870. Fr Lavelle was a local parish priest well known as a Fenian sympathizer. The dispute had not been resolved when Moore died in April.

57 Grey Papers, Clanricarde to Grey, 3 January 1870.

58 Devonshire Papers (340/434), Spencer to Hartington, 3 February 1870.

59 Ibid. (340/433/436), Hartington to his father, 3, 8 February 1870.

60 Hansard (3rd ser.), CXCIX, cols. 5–6. P.P. 1881, LXXVII, p. 901.
61 Devonshire Papers (340/433), Hartington to his father, 3 February 1870.
62 Corish, *Irish Catholicism*, pp. 41–4.
63 Clarendon Papers (MS. Clar. Dep.c.500), Spencer to Clarendon, 31 January; Spencer Papers, Clarendon to Spencer, 14 January 1870.
64 Royal Archives (D27/4), Odo Russell to Lord Clarendon, 24 January [copy]; G.P.(44249), Manning to W.E.G., 5 February 1870.
65 N. Blakiston (ed.), *The Roman Question : Extracts from the Despatches of Odo Russell 1858–1870* (1962), p. 381, Odo Russell to Lord Clarendon, 13 January 1870.

9: THE PASSING OF THE BILL

1 Hansard (3rd ser.), CXCIX, cols. 333–87.
2 *The Times*, 17 February 1870.
3 Selborne Papers (MS. 1864), W.E.G. to Sir R. Palmer, 21 April 1870.
4 G.P.(44249), W.E.G. to Archbishop Manning, 16 April 1870.
5 Clarendon Papers (MS. Clar. Dep.c.510), W. V. Harcourt, M.P. to Lord Clarendon, 18 April 1870.
6 *Kimberley Journal*, p. 13; entry for 1 April 1870.
7 G.P.(44134), Clarendon to W.E.G., 21 April 1870.
8 Ibid. (44249), Manning to W.E.G., 1 March 1870 with enclosure.
9 D.N., 7 March 1870.
10 G.P.(44538), W.E.G. to Spencer, 16 February 1870.
11 Hughenden Papers (B/XX/Co/56), Montague Corry to Disraeli, 16 February 1870.
12 Cranbrook Papers, diary of Gathorne Hardy, later 1st Earl of Cranbrook; entry for 16 February 1870.
13 Ibid., entry for 20 February.
14 *Kimberley Journal*, p. 11; entry for 21 February 1870.
15 Selborne Papers (MS. 1864), W.E.G. to Palmer, 21 April 1870.
16 Clarendon Papers (MS. Clar. Dep.c.510), Harcourt to Clarendon, 18 April 1870.
17 Ibid.
18 Quotation from Moore's speech, Hansard (3rd ser.), CXCIX, col. 1523 (8 March 1870).
19 Ibid., quotations from cols. 1681, 1683, 1701 (10 March 1870).
20 Ibid., cols. 1757–8 (11 March 1870).
21 Ibid., cols. 1440–3 (7 March 1870).
22 Ibid., col. 1838 (11 March 1870).
23 Ibid., quotations from cols. 1816, 1813.
24 Ibid., col. 1724 (10 March 1870).
25 Ibid., cols. 1406–13 (7 March 1870).

26 Ibid., quotations from cols. 1664–5, 1668 (10 March 1870).
27 Ibid., cols. 1760 ff. (11 March 1870), for Elcho's speech on the second reading of the Irish land bill.
28 Selborne Papers (MS. 1863), W. O'Connor Morris to Palmer, 3 February 1870.
29 Morley, *Life of Gladstone*, I, p. 929, W.E.G. to Earl Russell, 12 April 1870.
30 Hansard (3rd ser.), CC, quotation from col. 1460 (7 April 1870).
31 Ibid., quotation from col. 1480.
32 Cranbrook Papers, diary; entry for 8 April, describing the events of the previous night.
33 D.N., 9 April 1870, listed thirteen Liberals who voted for the amendment, all but one of them British Members; Fowler acted as teller.
34 Cardwell Papers (P.R.O. 30/48/2/6), W.E.G. to Cardwell, 8 April 1870.
35 G.P.(44538), W.E.G. to Cardwell, 8 April 1870 (another letter of the same date).
36 Ibid. (44296), W.E.G. to Palmer, 9 April; Palmer to W.E.G., 11 and 17 April, with memorandum of 16 April 1870.
37 Ibid. (44538), W.E.G. to Clarendon, 18 April 1870.
38 Selborne Papers (MS. 1864), W.E.G. to Palmer, 21 April 1870.
39 G.P.(44538), W.E.G. to Argyll, 21 April 1870.
40 Selborne Papers (MS. 1877), Argyll to Palmer, 23 April 1870.
41 The Hon. D. R. Plunket, Hansard (3rd ser.), CCI, col. 383 (6 May 1870).
42 Ibid.
43 G.P.(44538), W.E.G. to Spencer, 27 April 1870.
44 Cardwell Papers (P.R.O. 30/48/2/6), W.E.G. to Cardwell, 8 April 1870.
45 Cranbrook Papers, diary; entry for 10 May 1870.
46 Hansard (3rd ser.), CC, quotations from cols. 1200, 1202 (4 April 1870).
47 Ibid., CCI, quotations from cols. 19, 23 (2 May 1870).
48 G.P.(44538), W.E.G. to The O'Donoghue, M.P., 29 July 1870.
49 D.N., 27 June 1870.
50 Hansard (3rd ser.), CCII, quotations from cols. 35, 34 (14 June 1870).
51 Ibid., quotation from col. 5.
52 Salisbury Papers, Salisbury to Carnarvon, 20 June 1870.
53 Hansard (3rd ser.), CCII, quotations from cols. 64e, 66–7, 61 (14 June 1870); for the proffered resignation and the reply to it, see Lyall, *Marquis of Dufferin and Ava*, I, pp. 178–9.
54 Hansard (3rd ser.), CCII, quotations from cols. 246–8 (16 June 1870).

55 Ibid., cols. 83–90, esp. 87 (14 June 1870).

56 Ibid., cols. 369–80, esp. 374–5 (17 June 1870).

57 Cranbrook Papers (P501/262), Cairns to Gathorne Hardy, 6 April 1870.

58 Hansard (3rd ser.), CCII, cols. 183–213, esp. 206 (16 June 1870).

59 Ibid., quotation from col. 243.

60 Ibid., quotations from cols. 80–1 (14 June 1870).

61 Ibid., col. 888 (24 June 1870).

62 Ramm, I, p. 104, Granville to W.E.G., 2 July 1870.

63 Ibid., p. 110, Granville to W.E.G., 13 July 1870.

64 G.P.(44538), W.E.G. to Sir John Young, Governor-General of Canada, 28 June 1870.

65 Ibid., W.E.G. to the Bishops of Winchester, Salisbury, Bath and Wells, Exeter, Carlisle, Oxford, Chichester, Manchester and Chester, 20 June 1870.

66 Ramm, I, pp. 113–15, W.E.G. to Granville, 22 July, 24 July 1870.

67 Carlingford Papers (H324/CP1), W.E.G. to Fortescue, 24 July 1870.

68 Acts Public and General, 33 and 34 Victoria, ch. 46. The statute is there designated The Landlord and Tenant (Ireland) Act – a title rarely used outside legal proceedings.

69 Hansard (3rd ser.), CCI, col. 759 (16 May 1870).

70 Ibid., CCII, cols. 75–6 (14 June 1870).

71 Mayo Papers (Cambridge University Library, Aaa/7490/43), Longford to Lord Mayo, 9 May 1871.

72 G.P.(44425), W.E.G. to Cullen, 6 March 1870.

73 *The Times*, 10 August 1870.

74 *Marx and Engels on Ireland* (Moscow, 1971), p. 287; '...thus the mountain Gladstone has successfully given birth to his Irish mouse', Marx to Engels, 17 February 1870.

75 *Macmillan's Magazine*, October 1870.

76 F.J., 14 March 1870.

77 Ibid., 16, 21 February 1870.

78 Ibid., 25 March 1870.

79 G.P.(44249); Lucien Wolf, *Life of the First Marquess of Ripon* (2 vols, 1921), W.E.G. to Ripon, 4 October 1874.

80 Iddesleigh Papers (50016), Northcote to Disraeli, 5 March 1870.

81 G.P.(44306), W.E.G. to Spencer, 15 April 1870.

BIBLIOGRAPHY

MANUSCRIPT SOURCES

British Museum

Bright Papers
Gladstone Papers
Iddesleigh Papers
Palmerston Letter-Books
Ripon Papers
Rose Papers

Public Record Office

Cairns Papers
Cardwell Papers
Granville Papers
Russell Papers

National Library of Ireland

Larcom Papers
Mayo Papers
Moore Papers

Elsewhere

Royal Archives, Windsor
Carlingford Papers (Somerset R.O.)
Clarendon Papers (Bodleian Library)
Cobden Papers (W. Sussex R.O.)
Cranbrook Papers (E. Suffolk R.O.)
Derby Papers (Christ Church, Oxford)
Devonshire Papers (Chatsworth House)
Dufferin Papers (Public Record Office, Northern Ireland)
Grey Papers (Durham University Library)
Hickleton Papers (Earl of Halifax)
Hughenden Papers (National Trust)
Mayo Papers (Cambridge University Library)
Printing House Square Papers, Delane Correspondence and Walter
    Papers (*The Times*)
Salisbury Papers (Christ Church, Oxford)
Selborne Papers (Lambeth Palace Library)
Spencer Papers (Earl Spencer)
Stephen Papers (Cambridge University Library)

BIBLIOGRAPHY

NEWSPAPERS AND PERIODICALS

British

Edinburgh Review
Quarterly Review
Westminster Review
Macmillan's Magazine
The Economist
Saturday Review
Spectator
Daily News
Manchester Guardian
Pall Mall Gazette
Standard
The Times

Irish

Volumes 7585, 7706 to 7717 in the Larcom Papers with cuttings from the Dublin and provincial press.

OFFICIAL PUBLICATIONS

Hansard's Parliamentary Debates (2nd & 3rd series)
P.P. 1825, IX, Lords' Select Committee on the State of Ireland.
P.P. 1835, XVI, Commons' Select Committee on Orange Lodges.
P.P. 1835, XXII; 1836, XXX to XXXIV; 1837, XXXVII and LI;|1845, XLIII, Royal Commission on the Condition of the Irish Poor.
P.P. 1839, XI, XII, Lords' Select Committee on the State of Ireland in respect of Crime.
P.P. [H.L.] 1841, Letter by Lord Oxmantown. Also Memorial from Justices of King's County.
P.P. 1845, XIX to XXII, Royal Commission on the State of the Law and Practice in respect to the Occupation of Land in Ireland [The Devon Commission].
P.P. 1852, XIV, Commons' Select Committee on Outrages (Ireland).
P.P. 1863, LXIX, Agricultural Statistics of Ireland for 1861.
P.P. 1865, XI, Commons' Select Committee on the Tenure and Improvement of Land (Ireland) Act of 1860.
P.P. 1870, XIV, Reports from Poor Law Inspectors on the Wages of Agricultural Labourers in Ireland. Reports from Poor Law Inspectors in Ireland as to existing Relations between Landlord and Tenant.
P.P. 1870, LXVII, Reports from H.M. Representatives concerning the Tenure of Land in Europe.
P.P. 1871, XIII, Commons' Select Committee on Westmeath, &c (Unlawful Combinations).

BIBLIOGRAPHY

P.P. 1872, XLVII, Return for the year 1870 of the No. of Landed Proprietors in Ireland, classed according to Residence.

P.P. 1873, LXIX, Agricultural Statistics of Ireland for 1871.

P.P. 1876, LXXX, Summary of the Returns of Owners of Land in Ireland.

P.P. 1880, XVIII, XIX, Royal Commission on the Working of the Irish Land Act of 1870 [The Bessborough Commission].

P.P. 1881, LXXVII, Return of Evictions 1849 to 1880. Return of Outrages 1844 to 1880.

Special Commission Act (1888), Report of the Shorthand Notes of the Speeches, Proceedings and Evidence before the Commissioners under the above-named Act (12 vols, 1890).

OTHER SOURCES CITED IN THE TEXT AND NOTES

The place of publication is given only when it is not London.

Bateman, J., *The Great Landowners of Great Britain and Ireland*, 4th edn (1883); reprinted by Leicester University Press (1971).

Beckett, J. C., *The Making of Modern Ireland, 1603–1923*, paperback edn (1969).

Black, R. D. C., *Economic Thought and the Irish Question, 1817–1870* (Cambridge, 1960).

Blakiston, N. (ed.), *The Roman Question: Extracts from the Despatches of Odo Russell, 1858–1870* (1962).

Bourke, P. M. A., 'The Agricultural Statistics of the 1841 Census of Ireland. A Critical Review', *Economic History Review* (1965).

Brodrick, G. C., *Memories and Impressions* (1900).

Broeker, G., *Rural Disorder and Police Reform in Ireland, 1812–36* (1970).

Burghclere, Lady (ed.), *A Great Lady's Friendships: Letters to Mary, Marchioness of Salisbury, Countess of Derby, 1862–1890* (1933).

Caird, J., *The Irish Land Question* (1869).

Campbell, G., *Memoirs of My Indian Career*, ed. Sir C. E. Bernard (2 vols, 1893).

The Irish Land (1869).

Collins, H. and Abramsky, C., *Karl Marx & the British Labour Movement: Years of the First International* (1965).

The Complete Peerage, new edn (14 vols in 13, 1910–59).

Connell, K. H., *Irish Peasant Society* (Oxford, 1968).

Cooke, A. B. and Vincent, J. R. (eds.), *Lord Carlingford's Journal* (Oxford, 1971).

Corish, P. J., 'Political Problems, 1860–1878', in J. H. Whyte and Corish, vol. V, pts 2 and 3, published together (Dublin, 1967) of *A History of Irish Catholicism*.

BIBLIOGRAPHY

Cowling, M. J., *1867: Disraeli, Gladstone and Revolution. The Passing of the Second Reform Bill* (Cambridge, 1967).

The Impact of Labour 1920–1924 (Cambridge, 1971).

Crotty, R. D., *Irish Agricultural Production: Its Volume and Structure* (Cork, 1966).

Cullen, L. M., *An Economic History of Ireland since 1660* (1972).

Curtis, E. and McDowell, R. B., *Irish Historical Documents, 1172–1922* (1943).

Dasent, A. I., *John Delane, 1817–1879* (2 vols, 1908).

Douglas, Sir G. and Ramsay, Sir G. D. (eds.), *The Panmure Papers* (2 vols, 1908).

Dufferin, Lord, *Irish Emigration and The Tenure of Land in Ireland* (1867).

Duffy, Sir C. Gavan, *The League of North and South* (1886).

Elliot, H. S. R. (ed.), *The Letters of John Stuart Mill* (2 vols, 1910).

Ensor, R. C. K., 'Some Political and Economic Interactions in later Victorian England', *Transactions of the Royal Historical Society* (1949).

Fawcett, H., *Manual of Political Economy*, 1st edn (1863).

Fitzgibbon, G., *The Land Difficulty of Ireland, with an Effort to Solve it* (1869).

Fitzmaurice, Lord Edmond, *The Life of Lord Granville 1815–1891*, 3rd edn (2 vols, 1905).

Fitzpatrick, W. J., *The Life, Times and Correspondence of the Rt. Rev. Dr Doyle, Bishop of Kildare and Leighlin*, new edn (2 vols, 1880).

Fogarty, L. (ed.), *James Fintan Lalor, Patriot and Political Essayist. Collected Writings*, revised edn (Dublin, 1947).

Freeman, T. W., *Pre-Famine Ireland* (Manchester, 1957).

Gladstone, W. E., 'Notes and Queries on the Irish Demand', in *The Nineteenth Century*, February 1887.

The Irish Question (1886).

Green, E. R. R., 'Agriculture', in R. D. Edwards & T. D. Williams (eds.), *The Great Famine: Studies in Irish History, 1845–52* (Dublin, 1956).

Hammond, J. L., *Gladstone and the Irish Nation*, new impression (1964).

Hanham, H. J., *Elections and Party Management: Politics in the Time of Disraeli and Gladstone*, new impression (1964).

Harrison, R., *Before the Socialists: Studies in Labour and Politics, 1861–81* (1965).

Hayes-McCoy, G. A., 'Gaelic Society in Ireland in the late Sixteenth Century' in Hayes-McCoy (ed.), *Historical Studies IV* (1963).

Hewitt, O. Wyndham, *Strawberry Fair: a Biography of Frances, Countess Waldegrave, 1821–1879* (1956).

Hirst, F. W., 'Mr Gladstone as Chancellor of the Exchequer', in Sir Wemyss Reid (ed.), *The Life of William Ewart Gladstone* (1899).

BIBLIOGRAPHY

Hope, C., *George Hope of Fenton Barns* (Edinburgh, 1881).

Kimberley, 1st Earl of, *A Journal of Events during the Gladstone Ministry, 1868–74*, ed. E. Drus, in Camden (3rd Series), XC (1958).

King-Harman, R. D., *The Kings, Earls of Kingston* (Cambridge, 1960).

Lecky, W. E. H., *Democracy and Liberty* (2 vols, 1896).

Lee, J., 'Irish Agriculture', *Agricultural History Review* (1969).

Leighton, Sir B. (ed.), *Letters and Other Writings of the late Edward Denison, M.P. for Newark* (1872).

Locker-Lampson, G., *A Consideration of the State of Ireland in the Nineteenth Century* (1907).

Lyall, Sir A., *The Life of the Marquis of Dufferin and Ava* (2 vols, 1905).

Lynch, P. and Vaizey, J. E., *Guinness's Brewery in the Irish Economy, 1759–1875* (Cambridge, 1960).

Lyons, F. S. L., *Ireland since the Famine* (1970).

McCartney, D., 'The Church & the Fenians', in M. Harmon (ed.), *Fenians and Fenianism* (Dublin, 1968).

McDowell, R. B., *Public Opinion and Government Policy in Ireland, 1801–1846* (1952).

The Irish Convention (1970).

Mackintosh, J. P., *The British Cabinet* (1962).

Maclagan, P., *Land Culture and Land Tenure in Ireland* (Edinburgh & London, 1869).

Mansergh, P. N. S., *The Irish Question, 1840–1921* (1965).

Martin, A. Patchett, *The Life and Letters of the Rt. Hon. Robert Lowe, Viscount Sherbrooke* (2 vols, 1893).

Marx and Engels on Ireland (Moscow, 1971).

Maxwell, Sir H., *The Life and Letters of George William Frederick, Fourth Earl of Clarendon* (2 vols, 1913).

Mill, J. S., *Autobiography*, World's Classics edn (1955).

Considerations on Representative Government, Everyman's Library edn (1954).

England and Ireland (1868).

Principles of Political Economy, variorum edn, comprising vols. II and III of the *Collected Works of John Stuart Mill* (Toronto, 1963–).

Moody, T. W. (ed.), *The Fenian Movement* (Cork, 1968).

Morgan, K. O., *Wales in British Politics, 1868–1922*, revised edn (Cardiff, 1970).

Morley, J., *The Life of Richard Cobden*, Jubilee edn (2 vols, 1896).

The Life of William Ewart Gladstone, new edn (2 vols, 1905).

Morris, W. O'Connor, *Letters on the Land Question of Ireland* (1870).

Memories and Thoughts of a Life (1895).

Norman, E. R., *A History of Modern Ireland* (1971).

The Catholic Church and Ireland in the Age of Rebellion, 1859–1873 (1965).

O'Brien, C. C., *Parnell and his Party*, new impression (Oxford, 1964).

BIBLIOGRAPHY

O'Brien, R. B., *The Irish Land Question and English Public Opinion* (Dublin, 1880).

O'Hegarty, P. S., *A History of Ireland under the Union, 1801–1922* (1952).

O'Leary, J., *Recollections of Fenians and Fenianism* (2 vols, 1896).

O'Luing, S. 'A Contribution to the Study of Fenianism in Breifne', *Breifne* (1967).

Orwin, C. S. and Whetham, E. M., *A History of British Agriculture, 1846–1914* (1964).

Pomfret, J. E., *The Struggle for Land in Ireland 1800–1923* (Princeton, 1930).

Ramm, A. (ed.), *The Political Correspondence of Mr Gladstone and Lord Granville, 1868–1876* (2 vols, Camden, 3rd Series), LXXXI–LXXXII (1952).

Reynolds, J. A., *The Catholic Emancipation Crisis in Ireland, 1823–1829* (New Haven, 1954).

Richard, H., *Letters and Essays on Wales* (1884).

Rogers, J. E. Thorold, *Speeches by the Rt. Hon. John Bright, M.P.*, popular edn (1878).

Selborne, 1st Earl of, *Memorials* (4 vols, 1896–8).

Senior, H., *Orangeism in Ireland and Britain, 1795–1836* (1966).

Shearman, H., 'State-aided Land Purchase under the Disestablishment Act of 1869', *Irish Historical Studies* (1944–5).

Smith, R. B., *The Life of Lord Lawrence* (2 vols, 1883).

Solow, B. L., *The Land Question and the Irish Economy, 1870–1903* (Cambridge, Mass., 1971).

Steele, E. D., 'Gladstone and Ireland', *Irish Historical Studies* (1970).

'Ireland and the Empire in the 1860s', *Historical Journal* (1968).

'J. S. Mill and the Irish Question: the Principles of Political Economy, 1848–65', *Historical Journal* (1970).

'J. S. Mill and the Irish Question: Reform, and the Integrity of the Empire, 1865–70', *Historical Journal* (1970).

Strauss, E., *Irish Nationalism and British Democracy* (1951).

Thornley, D., *Isaac Butt and Home Rule* (1964).

Thring, Lord, *Practical Legislation* (1902).

Trench, W. S., *Realities of Irish Life* (1868).

Vincent, J. R., *The Formation of the Liberal Party, 1857–1868* (1966).

Wellington, 2nd Duke of, *Despatches, Correspondence and Memoranda of Field Marshal the Duke of Wellington, 1818–32* (8 vols, 1867–80).

Whyte, J. H., 'Political Problems, 1850–60', in Whyte and P. J. Corish, vol. V, pts 2 and 3, published together (Dublin, 1967), of *A History of Irish Catholicism*.

Wolf, L., *Life of the First Marquess of Ripon* (2 vols, 1921).

INDEX

Note: Gladstone is mentioned too often for an index of references to be practicable. He is, however, noticed separately under a large number of the entries below.

Abercorn, Duchess of (1812–1905), 274

Acts of Parliament: Cardwell's Act (1860), 68–70; Deasy's Act (1860), 68, 106; Encumbered Estates Act (1849), 14, 48, 216; Irish Franchise Act (1850), 6; Irish Reform Act (1868), 72; Irish Church Act (1869), 67, 75–6, 99, 114, 280; Irish Land Act (1870), *see* land bill, Irish, of 1870; Irish Land Act (1881), 2, 21, 32, 41, 45, 225, 254, 314; Peace Preservation (Ireland) Act (1870), 26–7, 312; Sub-Letting Act (1826), 8, 27; Suppression of Disturbances (Ireland) Act (1833), 32–3; Westmeath Act (1871), 312; *See also under* coercion; Parliamentary reform

Adair, J. G., and Derryveagh evictions, Co. Donegal, 13

Adullamites, 46, 63, 128

agrarian outrage, see esp.: manifestation of nationality, 4–5, 36–40; effectiveness of, 15–19; incidence of, 17; common British misconception of reasons for, 36–7; increases from latter part of 1868, 15, 77, 195, 273, 297; repression of in 1870–1, 312–13; *see also under* coercion; Ribbonism

agriculture, Irish: before the Famine, 5–7; afterwards, 14–15, 18, 69; economic conditions during the Land War (1879–82), 31–2; W.E.G.'s estimate of agricultural potential in 1869–70, 207, 229, 243–4

Allen, Major R. S., 270

America, United States of, Irish in and British policy towards Ireland, 67–8, 198, 304

Argyll, 8th Duke of (1823–1900): and W.E.G. during the 1868 election, 65; cabinet memorandum on Irish land, 204–5; possibility of resignation, 205, 209; prolonged correspondence with W.E.G., 206–9, 285–8; and Sir R. Palmer on Irish land bill in the Commons, 305; speech in the Lords, 308–9; mentioned, 48, 78, 86, 107, 202, 210–12, 225, 243, 279, 282–4, 289, 312

Bagehot, Walter (1826–77), 43, 60

Baillie-Cochrane, Alexander (1816–90), 1st Baron Lamington (1880), 114

Ball, John (1818–89), 44–5, 323n7

Ball, J. T. (1815–98), consulted by Disraeli, 269

Ballinamuck, Co. Longford, evictions at, 12–13

Ballycohey, Co. Tipperary: armed clash at, 65, 71, 327n106; significance of, 72–3, 77, 81, 106, 149

Barron, Sir Henry, 1st Bart (1795–1872), 276

Bazley, Sir Thomas, 1st Bart (1787–1885), 177, 197–9

Beckett, J. C., 4

Bellew, 2nd Baron (1830–95), 296

Bessborough Commission, 1880–1, so called after its chairman, the 6th Earl of Bessborough (1815–95), 21, 22, 282

Bessborough, 5th Earl of (1809–80): on large tenant farmers' part in Irish unrest, 6, 236; and W.E.G. during 1868 general election, 65; consulted by W.E.G. in 1869–70, 201, 236, 249; mentioned, 40, 80, 176, 199

Bessborough estates, Cos. Carlow and

Bessborough estates (*cont.*)
Kilkenny, practice as to tenant-right on, 240
Bethell, *see* Westbury, 1st Baron
Bicheno, J. E. (1785–1851), on tenant-right, 8–9
Bishops, Irish Catholic, *see* Catholic Church
Black, R. D. C., 1, 316n2
Blanqui, Auguste (1805–81), 58
Blennerhassett, Sir Rowland, 4th Bart (1839–1909), 166, 194
Brassington, C. P., 240
Bright, John (1811–89): dislike for the Tenant League of the 1850s, 36; 'sheep in wolf's clothing' as critic of aristocracy, 46–8; advocate of 'free trade in land', 48; of state-aided permissive land purchase by Irish tenants, 47–8, 61, 87; his Dublin speeches (1866), 47–8; political position as minister in W. E. G.'s first cabinet, 94–5; Parliamentary indiscretions in April 1869 and the prime minister, 87–96, 115; apprehensive about Irish land legislation, 188–9; cabinet memorandum by, 215–20; suppressed by W. E. G., 219; speech at Birmingham, January 1870, 290, 293–4; 'Bright clauses' in 1870 land bill, 280, 289, 312; mentioned, 14, 44, 52, 71, 143, 202
Brodrick, G. C. (1831–1903), 74, 96–7, 256
Bruce, H. A. (1815–95), 1st Baron Aberdare (1873), 86, 90, 196, 202
Butt, Isaac (1813–79): on agrarian secret societies in Ireland, 38; spokesman for tenant-right, 54, 70; National Tenant League and National Land Conference, 295; organizes Home Rule movement, 313

cabinet, see esp.: Gladstone's style of cabinet government, 1; his position in, 74–7; preliminary moves towards legislating on Irish land, 102; first thoughts and reactions on possible shape of a measure, 117–48; the adoption of a plan, 156–66, 182–93; the cabinets of October and November 1869, 202–4; and

memoranda subsequently circulated by individual members, 204–23, 251–2, 343n156; reaching a compromise, 200, 247, 252; last stages of discussion in, 283–9
Caird, James (1816–92), knighted (1882), 205, 256–8
Cairnes, J. E. (1823–75), 293
Cairns, 1st Baron (1819–85), 1st Earl Cairns (1878), 86, 205, 309–10
Cambridge, H.R.H. 2nd Duke of (1819–1904), 273
Campbell, George (1824–92), knighted (1873): his achievement, 104–8; first and second visits to Ireland (1869), 104, 137, 256; public interest in his ideas, 256; mentioned, 17, 121–2, 228, 243, 263, 290, 292
Canada, 67, 152
Cardwell, Edward (1813–86), 1st Viscount (1874): his Irish land bill of 1860, 68–70; his Oxford speech, September 1869, and W. E. G., 129–30; and Lowe, 162, 282–8; mentioned, 161, 202–3, 212, 299, 304
Carlton Club, 300
Carlyle, Thomas (1795–1881), 177
Carnarvon, 4th Earl of (1831–90): speech in September 1869, 170; mentioned, 308
Catholic Association, 8, 27
Catholic Church: and Irish nationalist and agrarian feeling, 23–7; bishops, 23, 24, 27, 30, 34, 137, 149, 222, 297, 299, 300, 314; lower clergy, 23–4, 26, 54, 72, 195, 222, 273–4
Catholic Emancipation, 25, 27, 63
Cave of Adullam, *see* Adullamites
Clanricarde, 1st Marquess of (1802–74), 21, 83–7, 170, 296
Clanricarde estates, Co. Galway, practice as to tenant-right on, 21
Clarendon, 4th Earl of (1800–70): on political character of British people, 44; estimates of W. E. G., 44, 66; and exchanges with, September–October 1869, 118–23, 125–6, 132–6; his Watford speech, 130–2; mentions resignation, 121–2, 222; and Granville, 122, 133; cabinet memorandum by, 221–3; and pessimism about effect of Land Act, 299, 313; mentioned, 26, 34, 103, 148, 153, 159, 195, 237, 274–5, 294

Clermont, 1st Baron (1815–87), 65–6, 275, 284

Cleveland, 4th Duke of (1803–91), 154

Cobden, Richard (1804–65), 44, 46–7

coercion, policy of: continual resort to, 32–3, 38–40; Liberal admission of its failure (1886), 39; pressure for in 1869–70, 241–2, 272, 296–7, 300; mentioned, 31, 68, 312

Commons, House of, see esp.: social composition of, 43; outlook on Irish land in 1865, 57; in 1867–8, 59, 62–3; and W. E. G. in 1869–70, 101, 300, 315; *The Times* on, August 1870, 315; *see also under* land bill, Irish, of 1870

compensation for disturbance, or damages for eviction, see esp.: 140, 142, 146–7, 183–5, 188, 205, 208, 211–12, 214, 223, 225, 231, 235, 241, 247–8, 252, 254, 277–82, 283–9, 300, 302–12; *see also under* Fortescue

compensation for improvements, see esp.: synonymous with tenant-right in England but not in Ireland, 8; Sir J. Gray dismisses, 71; mentioned, 58, 62, 69, 74, 75, 93, 113, 203, 208; *see also under* land bills, Irish, before 1870; land bill, Irish, of 1870

Conservative party: and Irish land when in government (1866–8), 58–62, 72; attitude of its leadership (1869), 81–2, 86–7, 101, 154, 166–71, 267–71; of rank-and-file Members, 114, 171–2, 269–71; and the land bill of 1870 in the Commons, 300–3, 306–7; in the Lords, 307–12; mentioned, 111–12, 210, 231, 293, 314

Cork: Munster farmers' clubs meeting at, 124; landlord conference at, 194

Corrigan, Sir Dominic (1802–80), 271

Corry, Montague (1838–1903), 1st Baron Rowton (1880), 201, 300

Courtown, 5th Earl of (1823–1914), 175–6

Cowling, M. J., 1, 316n4

Cranborne, Lord, *see* Salisbury, 3rd Marquess of

Crawford, William Sharman (1781–1861), 34–6

Cullen, L. M., 318n26

Cullen, Paul (1803–78), Archbishop of Armagh (1849–52), of Dublin (1852–78), Cardinal (1866): attitude to Irish land reform, 24, 27; John Lambert's interview with, 137; Gladstone's remonstrance with, 313–14; mentioned, 23, 26, 30, 69, 71, 297

Daily News: a party newspaper, 110; on Irish land in 1869: 109–10, 128–9, 152, 170–1, 177–8, 261–2, 266

Dartrey, Countess of (1823–87), 274–5

Dasent, G. W. (1817–96), knighted (1876), 151, 173–4

Davies, Sir John (1569–1626), 252

Davitt, Michael (1846–1906), 23

Deasy, Rickard (1812–85), 68

De Grey, 3rd Earl (1827–1909), 1st Marquess of Ripon (1871): a very liberal Whig, 90, 214, 281; on the House of Lords and the Gladstone government (1869), 90–2; cabinet memorandum on Irish land by, 212–15; mentioned, 56, 242, 314, 339n46

Delane, J. T. (1817–79): and John Walter, 61, 96–8, 100–1, 148; opposed to any extension of Irish tenant-right to Britain, 259–60; mentioned, 150, 163, 172, 174

Denison, Edward (1840–70), 116–17

Denison, J. E. (1800–73), 1st Viscount Ossington (1872), 108, 188

Derby, 14th Earl of (1799–1869), styled Lord Stanley until 1851: and first government bill on Irish land (1845), 15–16; as an Irish landlord, 16, 90; on British political situation (1869), 87; mentioned, 58, 307

Derby, 15th Earl of (1826–93), styled Lord Stanley until October 1869: speech at Bristol, January 1868, 60; interest in Liberal divisions, 169; privately ready to accept far-reaching land reform in Ireland, 154; speeches outside Parliament in 1869, 100, 170–1; in the Lords (1870), 309; mentioned, 61, 87, 150

De Ros, 23rd Baron (1797–1874), 275

Devon Commission, 1843–5, so called after its chairman, the 10th Earl of

Devon Commission (*cont.*)
Devon (1777–1859), 9, 10, 17, 34–5, 97, 318n25
Devon, 11th Earl of (1807–88), 293
Devonshire, 7th Duke of (1808–91), 176, 201, 236, 297
Devonshire, 8th Duke of, *see* Hartington, Marquess of
Dillon, John Blake (1816–66): on the immediacy of the Irish past, 19; mentioned, 34, 54
disestablishment of the Anglican church in Ireland: significance for British and Irish politics, 62–9, 72, 76–7, 84, 99, 114; stimulus to agrarian unrest in Ireland, 72, 77, 84; mentioned, 39, 62, 93–5, 116, 280
Disraeli, Benjamin (1804–81), 1st Earl of Beaconsfield (1876): on Irish land (1868–9), 58, 161, 169, 268–9; fear of, and Gladstone, 157, 167; on Irish land bill (1870), 302–3; mentioned, 44, 111–12, 128, 150, 291, 306, 314
Doyle, James (1786–1834), Bishop of Kildare and Leighlin (1819–34), 33
Dublin Castle (the Irish administration), 11–12, 19, 38, 82, 195, 222, 238, 241, 272, 296
Dufferin, 5th Baron (1826–1902), 1st Earl of Dufferin (1871), Marquess of Dufferin and Ava (1888): publicist for Irish landlords, 52–3; fears for their future, 59–60, 77–81; consulted by W.E.G., 201, 230–5; his memoranda for the cabinet, 230–5; self-revelation in House of Lords (1870), 308; mentioned, 82, 84–5, 205, 225
Duffy, Charles Gavan (1816–1903), knighted (1873), 19
Dundalk Democrat, 26

Economist, The, 60–1, 111–12, 152, 179–80, 263, 290
Edinburgh Review, 290–1
Education Bill, British, of 1870: 74, 294, 299
Elcho, Lord (1818–94), 10th Earl of Wemyss (1883), 303
elections and electorate
Irish: nature of, 6, 34, 37; mis-
leading results for British opinion, 6, 37; general election of 1868, 72; mentioned, 40, 69–70, 77, 276; *see also* Tipperary by-election
British: landed interest and general election of 1868, 64–7, 75–6; mentioned, 39–40, 46, 56–8, 307, 315
emigration from Ireland, effects, 14, 18, 51–2, 67
Encumbered Estates Act, *see* Acts of Parliament
Encumbered Estates Court (later the Landed Estates Court), 25, 257, 319n41
Engels, Friedrich (1820–95), 313
Ensor, R. C. K., 4
Erne, 3rd Earl of (1802–85), 120, 171
evictions: Irish, 12–15, 17, 273; Welsh, 57–8, 67, 267, 270

Famine, the Great Irish (1845–9): and structure of landholding, 14; mentioned, 5, 10, 12–13, 15, 17–18, 33–4, 51–2
Fawcett, Henry (1833–84), 52
Fenians and Fenianism: beginnings, 30–1; and the land question, 4, 22; and Ribbonism, 22, 30–2; and Home Rule movement, 31–2, 313; mentioned, 37, 40, 62, 67, 69, 173, 176, 195, 207, 222, 255, 257, 271, 273, 297
Fitzgibbon, Gerald (1793–1882): his pamphlet on Irish land, 120; influence on W.E.G., 142–3; mentioned, 137–8, 146, 154, 170, 189
Fitzwilliam, 4th Earl (1815–1902), 21
Fitzwilliam estates, Co. Wicklow, practice as to tenant-right on, 10, 21
fixity of tenure: defined, 27–9; tenant-right interpreted as, 71, 121, 186–7
foreign and imperial example in land reform, 68, 101–9, 236–7 Foreign Office circular of 26 August 1869: questionnaire and replies, 102–4, 108; *see also under* Campbell; India
Forster, W. E. (1818–86): on universality of tenant-right with or without landlord's sanction, 21–2;

Forster (*cont.*)
on Irish land reform (1865), 56–7; his Bradford speech, January 1870, 294

Fortescue, Chichester (1823–98) 1st Baron Carlingford (1874): and Irish land reform prior to the decision to legislate in 1869, 65–6; and Countess Waldegrave, 138–40, 145, 190–1; and early outlines of land bill in September–October, 138–48, 156, 182–93; and its evolution, November–December, 200, 202–4, 237–52, 254, 280, 283–4; cabinet memoranda by, 191–3, 251, 343n156; ineffectual in Parliament, 299; mentioned, 82–5, 102–4, 108, 122, 137, 154, 158, 161, 163, 204, 210–11, 219, 221–2, 224–7, 230, 232–4, 235, 272–3, 275, 285, 286–7, 296, 302

Fortnightly Review, 293

Foster, J. L. (d. 1842), 7–8

Fowler, William (1828–1905), 303–4, 306

freedom of contract, 36, 42, 86, 100, 159, 279, 288, 298, 311–12

Freeman, T. W., 5, 318n26

Freeman's Journal: place in Irish life, 26; on land question in 1865, 70; in 1868–9, 71, 194–6, 271, 276; rejection of 1870 land bill by, 313–14; mentioned, 112–13, 151, 179, 181, 184, 295–6

'free trade in land', 48, 50, 109–10, 152, 215, 218–19, 281

Gillooly, Laurence (1819–95), Bishop of Elphin (1858–95), 314

Glyn, G. G. (1824–87), 2nd Baron Wolverton (1873), 118, 121, 139–40, 145, 151

goodwill, *see* tenant-right

Gore-Booth, Sir Robert, 4th Bart (1805–76), 194

Granard, 7th Earl of (1833–89), 119, 185–6, 296, 331n4

Granville, 2nd Earl (1815–91): his political style and relationship with W. E. G., 66, 83, 156–9; mediation between prime minister and their colleagues, 209–10, 221–2, 285–6; on the Irish land bill of 1870 in the Lords, 307–10; mentioned, 82–6,

88–90, 91, 92, 94–6, 104, 120–2, 133–4, 137–8, 142, 146–7, 161, 163, 183, 189–90, 202–6, 208, 212, 220, 227, 236, 249, 252

Gray, Sir John (1816–75), knighted (1863): and the *Freeman's Journal*, 26; and the agitation for statutory tenant-right, 19–20, 71; contacts with W. E. G., 119, 121–3, 206–7, 276; speeches, 19, 71, 121–4, 196–9, 271, 295; on the 1870 land bill in the Commons, 301; mentioned, 54, 83, 104, 124–6, 129, 178, 184–5, 200, 243

Gregory, W. H. (1817–92), knighted (1876), 97, 140–1, 146, 301–2, 319n35

Greville, 1st Baron (1821–83), 6, 296

Grey, General the Hon. Charles (1804–70), 65, 289

Grey, 3rd Earl (1802–94), 85, 154–5, 226–7, 266

Grey, Sir George, 2nd Bart (1799–1882), 304, 319n35

Griffith's valuation, 332n55

Grosvenor, Earl (1825–99), 3rd Marquess of Westminster (1869), 1st Duke of Westminster (1874), 128, 331n29

Halifax, 1st Viscount (1800–85), formerly Sir Charles Wood: thoughts on the Irish land question, 154–5, 167; consulted by W. E. G., 201, 226–9; his memoranda for the prime minister, 227–9; mentioned, 48, 242–3, 293

Hamilton, Lord George (1827–1904), 171, 177

Hamilton, William Tighe, 266, 344n35

Hammond, J. L., 1, 122, 237

Harcourt, W. V. (1827–1903), knighted (1873), 299, 301

Hardy, Gathorne (1814–1906), 1st Viscount Cranbrook (1878), Earl of Cranbrook (1892): on Irish land in 1868–9, 62, 169; on the land bill in the Commons (1870), 300, 302, 306

Hartington, Marquess of (1833–1908), 8th Duke of Devonshire: his speeches at Sheffield and Lismore, September 1869, 127–9; readiness to accept statutory tenant-right, 236; wish for a coercion bill, 296–7; his speech of May 1870 in the

Hartington (*cont.*)
  Commons, 306–7; mentioned, 151, 167, 180, 202, 249, 268, 299
Hatherley, 1st Baron (1801–81): his cabinet memorandum on Irish land and importance of its arguments, 211–12; on the Irish land bill of 1870 in the Lords, 309; mentioned, 206, 208, 250, 285, 288
Headlam, T. E. (1813–75), 306
Helps, Sir Arthur (1813–75), 281
holdings, size of, 5–6, 14
Home Rule movement, 2, 4–5, 31–2, 38–42, 313–15
Hughes, Thomas (1822–96), his Lambeth speech, December 1867, and *The Times's* reaction, 60
Hume, Joseph (1777–1855), 36, 53
hypothetical offer for tenant-right, proposed legislative device, 192–3, 211, 229, 233, 236, 243–52

India and Indian legislation: J. S. Mill on, 53, 55; value of Indian precedent, 55, 112–14, 268–9, 292; *see also under* foreign and imperial example; Campbell
International, the First (International Working Men's Association), 55–6, 174, 267
Irishman, 88, 328n45
Irish People, 30
Irish Poor, Royal Commission on (1833–6), 8–9
I.R.B. (Irish Republican Brotherhood), *see* Fenians and Fenianism
Irish Times, 120

Kavanagh, A. M. (1831–89), 302–3
Kennedy, J. P. (1796–1879), 5
Keogh, William (1817–78), 146
Kickham, Charles (1826–82), 30
Kilkenny, Sir John Gray's speech at, 19–20, 71
Kimberley, 1st Earl of (1826–1902): on British politics (1867), 56; on Irish land, April–May 1869, 82, 84–6, 90–2; and Lowe, 162, 164–5; and Clarendon, 132; and W.E.G., 156, 165–6; his cabinet memoranda, 164, 210–11; on future of the landed class in Britain (1870), 293; on Irish land bill in the Lords, 309; in 1886, 40; mentioned, 89, 136, 191, 219, 271–2, 275, 282, 289, 300
King's County, magistrates of, 11, 14

Lalor, James Fintan (d. 1849), 29
Lambert, John (1815–92), knighted (1879): memorandum on Irish question for Conservative government (1868), 138; entrusted with unofficial task by W.E.G. on visiting Ireland, September 1869, 108; his report, 137–8; given official responsibility for gathering information on tenant-right, 201, 238–9; mentioned, 256, 330n106
Land and Labour League, 267, 270
land bills, Irish, before 1870: Crawford's and Tenant League's proposals, 35–6; purpose of government bills, 34; mentioned, 15–16, 46, 58, 63, 65, 68–70, 74, 83–7, 97, 140
land bill, Irish, of 1870, 1–2, 6, 10, 15–16, 22, 31–2, 41–2, 45; Lecky's estimate of, 1; the history of its preparation, chs. 3–8 *passim*; provisions of, 277–82; passage through the Commons, 300–7; through the Lords, 307–12; as amended, 311–12; *The Times* on, 298
Land League (Irish National Land League, 1879–81), 22, 31–2
landlords and the landed interest, see esp.:
  Irish: aliens outside Protestant areas in North of Ireland, and origins in conquest and confiscation unforgiven, 3, 19–20, 22, 29; landlord–tenant relations, 5–22, 72; behaviour towards their tenantry in the Great Famine, 13–14; in better times, 15, 18; and tenant-right before 1870, 7–13, 19–22, 240; reaction to events in Ireland and Britain (1868–70), 77–81, 194, 230–7, 274–6; political weakness of, 80, 236–7, 274, 312; W.E.G.'s consultations with in 1869–70, 230–7; his final solution for, in 1886, 40–2
  British: in mid-Victorian politics and society, 43–8; W.E.G.'s conception of their responsibilities, 45; their feeling of insecurity in

Landlords, British (*cont.*)
the later 1860s, 47–8, 55–7, 67, 76, 92, 118–36, 159–60, 167–8, 172, 210, 214, 221, 223, 293; and reception of the Irish land bill, 1870, 300, 307, 315

land purchase by Irish tenants, state aid for, 32, 40–1, 47–8, 80, 87–90, 92–5, 110, 115, 143, 168, 183, 215–20, 232, 246–7, 271, 280–1, 289, 312

Land War in Ireland (1879–82), 12, 32

Lansdowne estates (Kerry, Queen's Co., Dublin, Meath): practice as to tenant-right on, 21; allegations of landlord oppression on, 198

Lansdowne, 5th Marquess of (1845–1927), 22

Larcom, Major-General Sir Thomas, 1st Bart (1801–79): on physical intimidation in Ireland, 38; on the combination of religion and newspapers, 70; mentioned, 327n106

Lavelle, Father Patrick (d. 1886), 296, 347n56

Lawrence, 1st Baron (1811–79), and the 'Punjab School', 257

Law Times, 291

Leahy, Patrick (1806–75), Archbishop of Cashel (1857–75), 24

Leatham, E. A. (1828–1900), 265

Lecky, W. E. H. (1838–1903), 1, 41–2, 313

Lee, J. J., 318n26

Leitrim, 3rd Earl of (1806–78): notoriety of, 72; the press on, 177–8, 180–2; mentioned, 83

Lewis, G. C. (1806–63), 2nd Bart (1855), 36–7

Liberal party: and Irish nationalism, 37–42; and Irish land question, in the later nineteenth century, 31–7, 40–2; in the Palmerston era, 44–5, 52, 68–70; in 1865–8, 45–9, 54–68, 70–3; and Irish Church bill, 74–6; and Irish land in 1869, 76–7, 80–1, 114–16, 136, 154–5, 196–9, 264–7; and the land bill of 1870 in the Commons, 300–7

Lichfield, 2nd Earl of (1825–92), 259–60, 270

Limerick Declaration, January 1868, 70

Limerick, 5th Earl of (1840–96), 194

Lismore, Hartington's speech at, September 1869, 128–9, 136

Liverpool, W. E. G.'s speech at, 14 October 1868, 65, 73–4

Longford, 4th Earl of (1819–87), 312–13

Lords, House of: in 1869, 76, 81–7, 89, 91; and Irish land bill in 1870, 307–12

Lorton, 1st Viscount (1773–1854), 12–13

Lowe, Robert (1811–92), 1st Viscount Sherbrooke (1880): on Irish land bill of 1866, 46; as *Times* leader-writer, 47–8, 60, 324n19; his political position and Irish land in 1868, 63, 65; speech at Gloucester, January 1869, 81; on Bright, 92–3; and his memorandum on Irish land, September, 159–65; at October and November cabinets, 202–3; views subsequently, 212, 230, 254, 282–9, 306; mentioned, 74, 145, 156–8, 168, 183, 220, 225, 259, 299

Lucas, Frederick (1812–55), 36

Lyons, F. S. L., 4, 317n11

Macaulay, T. B. (1800–59), 1st Baron (1857), 32–3

MacColl, Reverend Malcolm (1831–1907), 114

McCombie, William (1805–80), 286

McDowell, R. B., 4

MacHale, John (1791–1881), Archbishop of Tuam (1834–81), 30

Mackintosh, J. P., 1

Maclagan, Peter, pamphlet on Irish land, 209, 256–8

Maguire, J. F. (1815–72): consulted by W. E. G., 124–6, 186–7, 193–4; speech at Skibbereen, 124; mentioned, 62–3, 68–9, 83, 295, 301

Mallow Farmers' Club, 295

Manchester Guardian, character of the paper, 152; concern for property and lack of sympathy for Irish landlords, 111, 152–3, 168–9, 178–9, 261; mentioned, 197

Manchester, Sir John Gray's speech at, October 1869, 196–9

Manners, Lord John (1818–1906), 7th Duke of Rutland (1888), 269

Manning, H. E. (1808–92), Archbishop of Westminster (1865–92),

Manning (*cont.*)
  Cardinal (1875), and W.E.G., 101, 115, 299, 314
Mansergh, P. N. S., 2
Marling, S. S. (1810–83), 1st Bart (1882), 265
Marx, Karl (1818–83), 313, 350n74
Mauleverer, assassination of, 26
Mayo, 6th Earl of (1822–72), styled Lord Naas until 1867, his Irish land bill (1867), 58–60, 70, 85, 169
Meynell-Ingram, H. F., 269–70
Mill, J. S. (1806–73): influence and ambiguity of *The Principles of Political Economy* on Irish land, 48–55; his pamphlet of 1868, 55–6, 60–1, 63; mentioned, 37–8, 47, 80, 93, 105, 110, 293
Monck, 4th Viscount (1819–94), consulted by W.E.G., 201, 227, 229, 235–6, 242
Monsell, William (1812–94), 1st Baron Emly (1874), 81, 146, 327n15
Moore, G. H. (1811–70), 296, 301, 347n56
Moriarty, David (1814–77), Bishop of Kerry (1856–77), the landlords' only friend in the Catholic hierarchy, 137
Morley, John (1833–1923), 1st Viscount Morley (1908), 1, 75, 107, 202, 237
Morley, Samuel (1809–86), 265–6
Morris, William O'Connor (1824–1904): chosen as *Times* special correspondent, 97–101; his relations with the paper, 98, 173, 258–61; his reports, 148–50, 175–7, 260; their influence, 98–9; and conclusions, 291–2; mentioned, 303
Mozley, Tom (1806–93), 97

Naas, Lord, *see* Mayo, 6th Earl of
Napier, Sir Joseph (1804–82), 1st Bart (1867), 291
National Association, 69, 300
National Education, Irish Board of, 26
nationalism and nationality, Irish: and religion, 3–4, 23–30, 37–8, 69–70, 72, 195–6, 274, 314; and tenant-right, 3–5, 11–12, 19–20, 38, 195–6, 271–3, 295–6; social class and, 25–6; constitutional and revolutionary nationalism, 4–5, 29–32, 273, 313; *see also* Fenians and Fenianism; Home Rule movement
National Land Conference (1870), 295–6
National Reform Union, 196–9
Navan, Co. Meath, tenant-right meeting at (1865), 54
Newdegate, C. N. (1816–87), 170
Noel, Hon. G. J. (1823–1911), 268
Norman, E. R., 4, 321n70
Northcote, Sir Stafford, 8th Bart (1818–87), 1st Earl of Iddesleigh (1885): in Commons debate on Irish question, March 1868, 61–2; on land bill of 1870, 314; mentioned, 169

O'Brien, Dean R. B. (1809–85), 70, 295
O'Brien, William Smith (1803–64), 29
O'Connell, Daniel (1775–1847): and the land question, 27–9, 33; mentioned, 8, 23, 37, 295
occupancy-right, sale of, *see* tenant-right
Odger, George (1812–77), 266–7
O'Donoghue, The (1833–89), 20, 129, 295, 301
O'Donovan Rossa, Jeremiah (1831–1915), 255, 271–3, 295
O'Hagan, Thomas (1812–85), 1st Baron O'Hagan (1870), 136, 166–7, 194
O'Hegarty, P. S., 2, 5, 24
O'Loghlen, Sir Colman, 2nd Bart (1819–77), 97, 140–1
O'Luing, Sean, 30–1
Orangemen and the Orange Order, 23–5; grand lodge of Co. Tyrone, resolutions (1832), 25
Osborne, Ralph Bernal (1808–82), 276, 345n73
O'Sullivan, Daniel, 88
Oxford, Cardwell's speech at, September 1869, 129–30

Pall Mall Gazette: its political alignment, 54, 89; its changing views on Irish land, 54, 62–3, 89, 112–14, 128, 181–2, 262–3, 290
Palmer, Sir Roundell (1812–95), 1st Baron Selborne (1872), 1st Earl of Selborne (1882): on rights of pro-

Palmer (*cont.*)
perty, 59–60; and the *Times* special correspondent, 98–9; opposition to the Irish land bill of 1870 in the Commons, 301–7; and W. E. G., 298, 304–5; mentioned, 275–6

Palmerston, 3rd Viscount (1784–1865): on standing threat from nationalism in Ireland (1857), 37; on Irish land question, 13, 36–7, 52, 68–9, 236–7; mentioned, 44–5, 57, 222

pamphlet literature on Irish land (1869–70), 104–8, 120, 170, 256–8

Panmure, 2nd Baron (1801–74), 11th Earl of Dalhousie (1860), 37

Parliamentary reform (1832–85), 39, 40, 43, 46, 56

Parnell, Charles Stewart (1846–91), 31–2

Peel, Sir Robert, 2nd Bart (1788–1850), 14

Penrhyn, 1st Baron (1800–86), 228

Platt, John, 272

Plunket, Hon. D. R. (1838–1919), 1st Baron Rathmore (1895), 305–6

Plunket, 2nd Baron (1792–1866), Anglican Bishop of Tuam (1839–66), 25

Pollok, Allan (1815–81), and tenant-right on his Co. Galway property, 12

Poor Law Inspectors Reports (Ireland): on landlord–tenant relations, 9–10, 20–1, 239–40; on agricultural labourers, 18

Pope, *see* Vatican

Portsmouth, 5th Earl of (1825–91), 104, 150, 189, 201, 236, 296

Portsmouth estates, Co. Wexford, 104, 150, 209, 236

press, see esp.:
Irish: power of popular newspapers, 26–7, 38, 70; and tenant-right, 26–7, 68, 71, 118–19, 276; legislative curbs upon (1870), 27;
British: movement of opinion in regarding Irish land, 109–14, 148–53, 172–82, 255, 258–64, 290–4; and the politicians, 263–4

Prince Edward Island, Canada, land question in, 44–5

property, rights of, according to British law and convention, Sir R. Palmer's legal opinion on (1867), 59–60

Proudhon, P. J. (1809–65), 58

Quarterly Review, 114, 167–8, 179, 268, 290

radicalism in Britain, the old and the new, 46–9, 52–4, 293–4

Rathbone, William (1819–1902), 265–6

rents: level of, 9–10, 15; affected by tenant-right, 9–10; W. E. G. on, 94, 144, 193; and Fortescue, 193, 247–8

Reeve, Henry (1813–95), 290–1

Reform League, 56, 66

repeal movement, 27, 37

Ribbonism: organized, and in wider sense, 3–4; oaths, 4, 23; Catholic Church and, 23–4, 30–2; *see also* agrarian outrage; Fenians and Fenianism

Richard, Henry (1812–88), 58, 270

Richmond, 6th Duke of (1818–1903), and Irish land in the Lords (1870), 307–10

Ripon, Marquess of, *see* De Grey, 3rd Earl

Rockites, *see* Ribbonism

Rogers, J. E. Thorold (1823–90), 179

Round, James (1842–1916), 171–2

Roundell, C. S. (1827–1906), 275–6

Ruggles-Brise, Colonel S. B. (1825–99), knighted (1897), 171–2

Russell, Lord John (1792–1878), 1st Earl Russell (1861), 14, 24, 46, 69, 80, 89–90, 92–3, 169

Russell, Odo (1829–84), 1st Baron Ampthill (1881), 297

Salisbury, Marchioness of (1827–99), widow of 2nd Marquess, after 1870 wife of 15th Earl of Derby, 131, 159

Salisbury, 3rd Marquess of (1830–1903): in Irish land debates, April–May 1869, 86, 89; *Quarterly Review* article, October, 167–9, 179, 268, 270; leads opposition to the land bill in the Lords (1870), 308–10, 312; approval of state-aid

Salisbury, 3rd Marquess of (*cont.*)
for land purchase by tenants, 312;
mentioned, 56, 328n38

Sandford, G. M. W., 58, 325n60

Saturday Review, 112, 181, 262, 270

Scotland: statistics of landownership,
43; landlord–tenant relations in,
57, 67, 92, 286; game laws, 57, 90–1;
mentioned, 111, 152–3, 207, 258

Scully, William: and his Ballycohey,
Co. Tipperary, tenants, 71–2,
327n106; becomes a byword, 72;
W. E. G. cites, 72–3; mentioned,
83, 100, 115, 160, 195, 259

secret societies, *see* Fenianism; Ribbonism

Seeley, J. R. (1834–95), knighted
(1894), 313, 315

Select Committees, Commons: on
'outrage' in Ireland 1852 and
1871, 23, 31; on tenure of land,
1865, 54, 68–70

Shaw, Richard, 265

Sheffield, Hartington's speech at,
September 1869, 127–8

Skibbereen, Sir John Gray's and
J. F. Maguire's speeches at, September 1869, 121–4

Slievenamon, Co. Tipperary, Fenian
rally on, August 1863, 30

Southport, W. E. G.'s speech at,
December 1867, 63–4

Spectator, 53–4, 71, 92–3, 111–12, 128,
148–9, 153, 180, 262, 264, 272

Spencer, 5th Earl (1835–1910): pres-
ses for land legislation, March–
April 1869, 82–5; memorandum for
the cabinet, 223–6; desire for
coercion bill, 296–7; mentioned,
40, 148, 154, 161, 169, 194, 201,
206, 238–40, 256, 281, 300, 315

Standard, 114, 268–9, 271, 290

Stanley, Lord, *see* Derby, 14th Earl of

Stanley, Lord, *see* Derby, 15th Earl of

Stanley, Hon. W. O. (1802–84), 228

Stansfeld, James (1820–98), knighted
(1895), 48, 266

Stein–Hardenberg Laws, 68

Stephen, James Fitzjames (1829–94),
1st Bart (1891), 263

Strathnairn, 1st Baron (1801–85), 31,
273–4

subdivision of tenanted land by the
occupiers, 7–8, 11, 18, 232, 279

Sullivan, Edward (1822–85), 1st Bart
(1881), 142, 156, 183, 185–6, 189–91,
241

Tenant League (1850–9), 19, 22, 24,
29–30, 35–6, 62

tenant-right, Irish, *passim*, but see
esp.: meaning of, 5–15; moral
strength of, 19–22; contrast with
English tenant-right, 8; prevalence,
8–10, 20–2, 240–1; family obligations secured upon, and sale of,
9; landlords' attitude towards, 10;
status in Ulster, 8, 28; W. E. G. and,
104–8, 121, 124–7, 147–8, 189, 209,
244–5, 252–4; *see also* rents; fixity
of tenure

Tenant-Right Conference (1850), 28, 35

tenant-right rallies, 54, 72, 195–6, 271

tenant societies and farmers' clubs:
Irish, 21, 57, 124, 195–6, 295;
British chambers of agriculture,
57, 259–60, 263

Thompson, H. S. (1809–74), 1st Bart
(1874), 256

three Fs, *see* fixity of tenure

Thurles, Synod of (1850), 24

Times, The: its policy on Irish land,
96–101; its special correspondent
and the press, 148–53; the paper
and W. E. G., 118, 172; the con-
tradictions of its editorials, 150–1,
258–9, 291–2; mentioned, 25, 33–4,
43, 47–8, 60, 128, 171–2, 175, 195,
259–60, 283, 293, 298, 315

Tipperary by-election, November
1869, 255, 258–60, 271–4, 283, 295

Trench, Hon. William Le Poer
(1771–1846), 10

Trench, W. S. (1808–72), 152, 333n90

Trevelyan, Sir Charles (1807–86), 104,
107–8

Union between Britain and Ireland,
32, 36–42, 309, 315

Ulster (Cos. Antrim, Armagh, Cavan,
Donegal, Down, Fermanagh, Lon-
donderry, Monaghan, Tyrone): race
and religion, 23–5; landlord–tenant
relations, 22, 28–9, 72; *see also*
Orangemen and the Orange Order

Ulster tenant-right, *see* tenant-right

'upas tree' speech, W. E. G.'s at
Wigan, 23 October 1868, 66

Vatican, 222, 297

Vatican Council, the First, 222, 297

Victoria, Queen: complains of not being kept informed by W.E.G., 272; attitude of Court to government and the Irish land bill, 289

Vincent, J. R., 1, 325n46

Waldegrave, Countess (1821–79), wife of Chichester Fortescue: ambitious for her husband, 121, 138–40, 145, 190–1; disappointed, 156, 191; mentioned, 202, 222

Wales, landlord–tenant relations and politics in, 57–8, 67, 111, 267, 270

Walter, John (1818–94): on W.E.G., 66–7; and *The Times*, 96–101, 151, 173, 261; speech at Maidenhead, 172–4; mentioned, 61, 148, 260

wastelands, proposals for settlement, 51, 143, 218, 247

Watford, Clarendon's speech at, September 1869, 130

Wellington, 1st Duke of (1769–1852), 27

Wellington, 2nd Duke of (1807–84), Lord Strathnairn's letter to, 273

Westbury, 1st Baron (1800–73), 205

Westminster Review, 53

Whiteboys, *see* Ribbonism

Wiggins, Mr John, 17–18

Willyams, Edward Brydges (1834–1916), 265

Wilson, George (1808–70), 197

Wilson-Patten, Colonel John (1802–92), 1st Baron Winmarleigh (1874), 170

Works, Irish Board of, 258, 280

Young Ireland, 29–30, 37